W9-DJG-071

THE MacARTHUR
NEW TESTAMENT
COMMENTARY
LUKE 1-5

John MacArthur

MOODY PUBLISHERS/CHICAGO

© 2009 by
JOHN MACARTHUR

All rights reserved. No part of this book may be reproduced in any form without permission in writing from the publisher, except in the case of brief quotations embodied in critical articles or reviews.

All Scripture quotations, unless otherwise indicated, are taken from the *New American Standard Bible®*, Copyright © 1960, 1962, 1963, 1968, 1971, 1972, 1973, 1975, 1977, 1995 by The Lockman Foundation, Used by permission. (www.Lockman.org)

Scripture quotations marked ESV are taken from *The Holy Bible, English Standard Version.* Copyright © 2000, 2001 by Crossway Bibles, a division of Good News Publishers. Used by permission. All rights reserved.

Scripture quotations marked NKJV are taken from the *New King James Version.* Copyright © 1982 by Thomas Nelson, Inc. Used by permission. All rights reserved.

Scripture quotations marked KJV are taken from the King James Version.

Cover Design: Smartt Guys design

Library of Congress Cataloging-in-Publication Data

MacArthur, John
    Luke 1-5 / John MacArthur.
        p. cm. — (The MacArthur New Testament commentary)
    Includes bibliographical references and indexes.
    ISBN 978-0-8024-0871-6
    1. Bible. N.T. Luke I-V—Commentaries. I. Title. II. Title: Luke one-five.

    BS2595.53.M33 2009
    226.4'077—dc22

                                    2009021035

We hope you enjoy this book from Moody Publishers. Our goal is to provide high-quality, thought-provoking books and products that connect truth to your real needs and challenges. For more information on other books and products written and produced from a biblical perspective, go to www.moodypublishers.com or write to:

Moody Publishers
820 N. LaSalle Boulevard
Chicago, IL 60610

5 7 9 10 8 6

Printed in the United States of America

*To the memory of Mike Taylor,
who served Christ faithfully at Grace to You for 27 years.
Among other things, Mike coordinated the editorial work
on these commentaries. It was a rich privilege not only to be
his pastor but also to work alongside him for all those years.
The Lord took Mike to heaven unexpectedly just as this volume
was going to press. I will miss his devoted partnership
and the joy-filled way he constantly encouraged all of us.*

Contents

CHAPTER   PAGE

Preface   vii

Introduction to Luke   1

1. Luke's Prologue (Luke 1:1–4)   9
2. God's Revelation to Zacharias (Luke 1:5–14, 18–25)   19
3. The Greatness of John the Baptist (Luke 1:15–17)   33
4. The Divine Announcement to Mary (Luke 1:26–33)   41
5. The Virgin Birth: A Divine Miracle (Luke 1:34–38)   53
6. Mary and Elizabeth: Confirming Angelic Prophecy   63
   (Luke 1:39–45)
7. Mary's Praise (Luke 1:46–55)   73
8. The Revelation of God in the Birth of John the Baptist   85
   (Luke 1:56–66)
9. Zacharias's Song of Salvation—Part 1:   93
   The Davidic Covenant (Luke 1:67–71)
10. Zacharias's Song of Salvation—Part 2:   103
    The Abrahamic Covenant (Luke 1:72–75)
11. Zacharias's Song of Salvation—Part 3:   113
    The New Covenant (Luke 1:76–80)

Excursus: Why Every Self-respecting Calvinist   125
      Must Be a Premillennialist

12. Jesus' Birth in Bethlehem (Luke 2:1–7)   139
13. The Announcement of Jesus' Birth (Luke 2:8–20)   151
14. Testifying to Jesus—Part 1:   165
      Joseph and Mary (Luke 2:21–24)
15. Testifying to Jesus—Part 2:   173
      Simeon and Anna (Luke 2:25–38)
16. The Amazing Child Who Was God (Luke 2:39–52)   187
17. Setting the Stage for Jesus (Luke 3:1–6)   199
18. True Repentance: God's Highway to the Heart (Luke 3:7–17)   213
19. The Boldness of John the Baptist (Luke 3:18–20)   225
20. The Messiah's Divine Confirmation (Luke 3:21–22)   233
21. The Messiah's Royal Lineage (Luke 3:23–38)   243
22. The Temptation of the Messiah (Luke 4:1–13)   251
23. Jesus Returns to Nazareth (Luke 4:14–30)   263
24. Jesus' Authority over Demons (Luke 4:31–37)   279
25. Jesus: The Divine Deliverer (Luke 4:38–44)   289
26. Characteristics of Jesus' Divinity (Luke 5:1–11)   299
27. The Healing, Forgiving Savior (Luke 5:12–26)   311
28. Calling a Wretched Sinner; Confronting   327
      Self-righteous Hypocrites (Luke 5:27–32)
29. The Uniqueness of the Gospel (Luke 5:33–39)   335

Bibliography   343
Index of Greek Words   345
Index of Scripture   346
Index of Subjects   364

Preface

It continues to be a rewarding, divine communion for me to preach expositionally through the New Testament. My goal is always to have deep fellowship with the Lord in the understanding of His Word and out of that experience to explain to His people what a passage means. In the words of Nehemiah 8:8, I strive "to give the sense" of it so they may truly hear God speak and, in so doing, may respond to Him.

Obviously, God's people need to understand Him, which demands knowing His Word of Truth (2 Tim. 2:15) and allowing that Word to dwell in them richly (Col. 3:16). The dominant thrust of my ministry, therefore, is to help make God's living Word alive to His people. It is a refreshing adventure.

This New Testament commentary series reflects this objective of explaining and applying Scripture. Some commentaries are primarily linguistic, others are mostly theological, and some are mainly homiletical. This one is basically explanatory, or expository. It is not linguistically technical but deals with linguistics when that seems helpful to proper interpretation. It is not theologically expansive but focuses on the major doctrines in each text and how they relate to the whole of Scripture. It is not primarily homiletical, although each unit of thought is generally treated as one chapter, with a clear outline and logical flow of thought.

Most truths are illustrated and applied with other Scripture. After establishing the context of a passage, I have tried to follow closely the writer's development and reasoning.

My prayer is that each reader will fully understand what the Holy Spirit is saying through this part of His Word, so that His revelation may lodge in the mind of believers and bring greater obedience and faithfulness—to the glory of our great God.

Introduction to Luke

The gospel of Luke is the first of a two-volume history, along with the book of Acts (both were addressed to the same man, Theophilus, and the "first account" mentioned in Acts 1:1 refers to the gospel of Luke). It is the longest book in the New Testament and, combined with Acts, makes Luke the author of more than one fourth of the New Testament—more than any other writer. In those two books, Luke presents the most comprehensive New Testament account of the history of redemption. His gospel and the book of Acts span six and a half decades from the birth of John the Baptist to Paul's first Roman imprisonment. Luke also includes a significant amount of new material (more than 40 percent of his gospel is not found in the other gospels [Darrell L. Bock, *Luke 1:1–9:50*, Baker Exegetical Commentary on the New Testament (Grand Rapids: Baker, 1994), 12]), including seven of Christ's miracles and seventeen of His parables.

Yet despite the significance of his work, Luke himself remains largely unknown. His name appears only three times in the New Testament—none of them in his own writings (Col. 4:14; 2 Tim. 4:11; Philem. 24). Those passages reveal only a few details about him—that he was a physician who was beloved by Paul and was with the apostle during his first and second Roman imprisonments. He was also a Gentile (see the discussion of Col. 4:10–14 in chapter 1 of this volume and Acts 1:19, where Luke's use of the phrase "their language" distinguishes him from the Jewish people). That he accompanied Paul on some of his missionary journeys is evident from the so-called "we" passages in Acts (see the discussion under Author below). But as will be seen in chapter 1 of this volume, the prologue to Luke's gospel helps paint a more complete portrait of this remarkable man.

AUTHOR

The unanimous testimony of the early church is that Luke wrote the third gospel; no alternative author was ever proposed. In the middle of the second century the apologist Justin Martyr (c.A.D. 100–165) quoted from Luke 22:44 and 23:46 in his *Dialogue with Trypho*. Although Justin did not name Luke as the author (citing as his source "the memoirs which . . . were drawn up by His [Christ's] apostles and those who followed them" [Chapter 103]), those two verses are unique to Luke. They demonstrate the fact that Justin was familiar with Luke's gospel and recognized it as authoritative. Justin's pupil Tatian included Luke's gospel in his *Diatessaron*, the first known harmony of the Gospels. The Muratorian Canon, a second-century list of the books recognized as Scripture by some in the church, attributes the third gospel to Luke, as do such second and third century writers as Irenaeus, Tertullian, Origen, Clement of Alexandria, and the heretic Marcion. The Anti-Marcionite prologue to Luke, written to combat Marcion, also declared Luke to be its author. The oldest manuscript of Luke's gospel (Bodmer Papyrus XIV [p75]), dating from the late second or early third century, names Luke as the author.

Summarizing the significance of the early church's testimony to Luke's authorship of the third gospel, Robert H. Stein writes,

> Such unanimity in the tradition is impressive. . . . In general such uncontested and ancient tradition should be accepted unless there is good reason to the contrary. This is especially so when it names a minor figure in the early church and a non-apostle as the author of over one quarter of the entire NT. (*Luke*, The New American Commentary [Nashville: Broadman & Holman, 1992], 21)

Stein's last point is especially significant. The apocryphal gospels were attributed to well-known figures, such as Peter. Why would someone forging a work purporting to have come from one of Paul's companions have chosen the relatively obscure Luke instead of someone more prominent?

Further proof that Luke wrote Luke and Acts comes from the so-called "we" passages in Acts, where the writer's use of the first person pronoun indicates that he was traveling with Paul (16:10–17; 20:5–21:18; 27:1–28:16). Thus, the writer of Acts could not be any of Paul's coworkers mentioned by name in those sections (e.g., Silas, Timothy, Sopater, Aristarchus, Secundus, Gaius, Tychicus, and Trophimus). By process of elimination, that leaves Luke and Titus among Paul's coworkers as the possible authors of Luke and Acts. No one, however, has ever seriously argued for Titus as the author, which leaves Luke, as the unanimous testimony of the early church affirms (see the discussion above).

DATE, PLACE OF WRITING, ADDRESSEES

Luke was written before Acts, which is a sequel to it (Acts 1:1), so the question of when it was written is closely connected to the date of Acts. Some liberal scholars date Luke in the second century. They argue that its author drew some of his material from the Jewish historian Josephus, who wrote late in the first century. But the differences between the two accounts far outweigh the similarities (cf. Alfred Plummer, *A Critical and Exegetical Commentary on the Gospel According to St. Luke*, The International Critical Commentary [Edinburgh: T. & T. Clark, 1969], xxix; D. Edmond Hiebert, *An Introduction to the New Testament*, Volume One: The Gospels and Acts [Chicago: Moody, 1979], 137). In the middle of the second century the heretic Marcion included his revised version of Luke as the only gospel in his canon of Scripture. If Luke had been written only a short time earlier, it could not have become widely respected enough in the church for Marcion to have chosen it. Nor could a second-century author have consulted eyewitnesses to the life and ministry of Jesus (Luke 1:2–3); most, if not all of them, would have been dead.

Two dates for Luke and Acts have been proposed by conservative scholars: either between A.D. 70 and 80 (following the completion of Mark's gospel), or around A.D. 60 (near the end of Paul's first Roman imprisonment). The primary argument for the later date is Luke's alleged use of Mark's gospel as a source. Since Mark is usually dated after Peter's death during the persecution instigated by Nero, Luke would have to have been written still later. The priority of Mark, however, has never been established, and the absence of any evidence for it has led scholars to question Luke's dependence on Mark's gospel (e.g., Robert L. Thomas and Stanley N. Gundry, eds., *A Harmony of the Gospels* [Chicago: Moody, 1979], 274–79; Eta Linnemann, *Is There a Synoptic Problem?* [Grand Rapids: Baker, 1992]; Robert L. Thomas and F. David Farnell, eds., *The Jesus Crisis* [Grand Rapids: Kregel, 1998], especially chaps. 1, 3, 6). Since Luke's dependence on Mark cannot be established, the argument for the later date collapses.

A number of facts support the earlier date for the writing of Luke and Acts. That date best explains the abrupt ending of Acts; Luke did not mention Paul's release and subsequent travels because the apostle was still in prison when he wrote Acts. Further, there is no mention in Luke's writings of any event later than about A.D. 61, including such significant events as the death of James, the brother of Jesus and head of the Jerusalem church (around A.D. 62); Nero's persecution, during which Peter and Paul were martyred (in the mid-60s); and the destruction of Jerusalem by the Romans in A.D. 70. Finally, Luke does not refer to Paul's epistles, suggesting that he wrote Luke and Acts before the collection of those epistles was widely circulated in the church. The most natural explanation for those omissions is that Luke wrote his gospel and Acts before those events happened. The best date, therefore, for Luke's gospel is A.D. 60–61.

Where Luke wrote his gospel is not known for certain. Some in the early church speculated that he wrote from the Greek province of Achaia; others argued for Rome. Since Luke was with Paul during his imprisonment in Rome (cf. Col. 4:14; Philem. 24), the latter possibility is more likely.

As will be discussed in chapter 1 of this volume, Luke addressed his gospel to a man named Theophilus and, by extension, other Gentiles. He avoids using Aramaic terms that his Gentile readers would be unfamiliar with (e.g., Abba, Rabbi, hosanna, Golgotha), and explained Jewish customs (e.g., 22:1, 7) and Israel's geography (e.g., 1:26; 4:31; 23:51; 24:13) for them.

PURPOSE AND THEMES

Luke's purpose in writing his gospel was that his readers might "know the exact truth about the things [they had] been taught" (1:4; see the exposition of that verse in chapter 1 of this volume). To that end, he did careful research (see the discussion of his sources in chapter 1).

Many themes stand out in this marvelous gospel, foremost of which is God's love for sinners. That love caused Him to send His Son into the world "to seek and to save that which was lost" (Luke 19:10; cf. 15:1–32). Luke paid particular attention to the outcasts of Jewish society, including Gentiles, Samaritans, women, tax collectors, and lepers. God offers repentant sinners forgiveness (3:3; 5:20–25; 6:37; 7:41–50; 11:4; 12:10; 17:3–4; 18:13–14; 24:47), which results in another of Luke's emphases, joy (1:14, 44, 47, 58; 2:10; 6:23; 13:17; 15:5–10, 22–32; 24:52). He alone records the five great tributes of praise connected with Christ's birth, those of Elizabeth (1:41–45), Mary (1:46–55), Zacharias (1:67–79), the angels who announced Christ's birth (2:13–14), and Simeon (2:25–32). Luke also describes the fear people experience when in the presence of God or His works (1:12, 30, 65; 2:9–10; 5:10, 26; 7:16; 8:25, 37, 50; 9:34). He also stresses the Holy Spirit's ministry (1:15, 35, 41, 67; 2:25–27; 3:16, 22; 4:1, 14, 18; 10:21; 11:13; 12:10, 12), and the prayers of Jesus (3:21; 5:16; 6:12; 9:18, 28–29; 11:1; 22:32, 40–46). Chapter 1 lists more of the distinctive themes of Luke.

OUTLINE

  I. The Prelude to Christ's Ministry (1:1–4:13)
      A. The Prologue (1:1–4)
      B. The Birth of Jesus (1:5–2:38)
          1. The annunciation to Zacharias (1:5–25)
          2. The annunciation to Mary (1:26–38)
          3. The visit of Mary to Elizabeth (1:39–45)
          4. The Magnificat (1:46–56)
          5. The birth of the forerunner (1:57–80)
          6. The nativity (2:1–38)
      C. The Boyhood of Jesus (2:39–52)
          1. In Nazareth (2:39–40, 51–52)
          2. In the temple (2:41–50)
      D. The Presentation of Jesus (3:1–4:13)
          1. The preaching of John the Baptist (3:1–20)
          2. The baptism of Jesus (3:21–22)
          3. The genealogy of the Son of Man (3:23–38)
          4. The temptation of the Son of God (4:1–13)
  II. The Ministry in Galilee (4:14–9:50)
      A. The Commencement of Christ's Ministry (4:14–6:16)
          1. Nazareth (4:14–30)
          2. Capernaum (4:31–42)
              a. A demon cast out (4:31–37)
              b. Multitudes healed (4:38–42)
          3. The cities of Galilee (4:43–44)
          4. The Sea of Galilee (5:1–6:16)
              a. Calling four fishermen (5:1–11)
              b. Healing a leper (5:12–16)
              c. Forgiving a sinner (5:17–26)
              d. Receiving sinners, but rejecting the righteous (5:27–32)
              e. Proclaiming the uniqueness of the gospel (5:33–39)
              f. Declaring that He is Lord of the Sabbath (6:1–11)
              g. Choosing the twelve apostles (6:12–16)

B. The Continuation of His Work (6:17–9:50)
1. Preaching on the plateau (6:17–49)
   a. Beatitudes (6:17–23)
   b. Woes (6:24–26)
   c. Commandments (6:27–49)
2. Ministering in the cities (7:1–8:25)
   a. He heals a centurion's servant (7:1–10)
   b. He raises a widow's son (7:11–17)
   c. He encourages John the Baptist's disciples (7:18–35)
   d. He forgives a sinful woman (7:36–50)
   e. He proclaims the kingdom of God (8:1–3)
   f. He teaches the multitudes with parables (8:4–21)
   g. He stills the winds and waves (8:22–25)
3. Traveling in Galilee (8:26–9:50)
   a. He delivers a demoniac (8:26–39)
   b. He heals a woman (8:40–48)
   c. He raises a girl (8:49–56)
   d. He sends out the Twelve (9:1–6)
   e. He confounds Herod (9:7–9)
   f. He feeds the multitude (9:10–17)
   g. He predicts His crucifixion (9:18–26)
   h. He unveils His glory (9:27–36)
   i. He casts out an unclean spirit (9:37–42)
   j. He instructs His disciples (9:43–50)
III. The Journey to Jerusalem (9:51–19:27)
A. Samaria (9:51–10:37)
1. A village turns Him away (9:51–56)
2. He turns away the halfhearted (9:57–62)
3. He sends out the seventy (10:1–24)
4. He gives the parable of the Good Samaritan (10:25–37)
B. Bethany and Judea (10:38–13:35)
1. Mary and Martha (10:38–42)
2. The Lord's Prayer (11:1–4)
3. The importance of importunate prayer (11:5–13)
4. Increasing opposition (11:14–36)
5. Woes upon Pharisees and lawyers (11:37–54)
6. Teaching along the way (12:1–59)
   a. About hypocrisy (12:1–12)
   b. About worldly materialism (12:13–21)
   c. About worry (12:22–34)
   d. About unfaithfulness (12:35–48)
   e. About love of ease (12:49–53)
   f. About unpreparedness (12:54–56)

g. About division (12:57–59)
7. Answering questions (13:1–30)
   a. About the justice of God (13:1–9)
   b. About the Sabbath (13:10–17)
   c. About the kingdom (13:18–21)
   d. About salvation (13:22–30)
8. Lamenting over Jerusalem (13:31–35)
C. Perea (14:1–19:27)
  1. Dining with a Pharisee (14:1–24)
    a. He tests them about the Sabbath (14:1–6)
    b. He teaches them about humility (14:7–14)
    c. He tells them about the heavenly banquet (14:15–24)
  2. Teaching the multitudes (14:25–18:34)
    a. The cost of discipleship (14:25–35)
    b. The parable of the lost sheep (15:1–7)
    c. The parable of the lost coin (15:8–10)
    d. The parable of the two sons (15:11–32)
    e. The parable of the unjust steward (16:1–18)
    f. The rich man and Lazarus (16:19–31)
    g. A lesson about forgiveness (17:1–4)
    h. A lesson about faithfulness (17:5–10)
    i. A lesson about thankfulness (17:11–19)
    j. A lesson about readiness (17:20–37)
    k. The parable of the persistent widow (18:1–8)
    l. The parable of the Pharisee and the publican (18:9–14)
    m. A lesson about childlikeness (18:15–17)
    n. A lesson about commitment (18:18–30)
    o. A lesson about the necessity of the cross (18:31–34)
  3. Seeking sinners (18:35–19:10)
    a. He opens blind eyes (18:35–43)
    b. He seeks and saves the lost (19:1–10)
  4. Rewarding His followers (19:11–27)
IV. The Passion Week (19:28–23:56)
A. Monday (19:28–44)
  1. The triumphal entry (19:28–40)
  2. Christ weeps over Jerusalem (19:41–44)
B. Tuesday (19:45–48)
  1. He cleanses the temple (19:45–46)
  2. He teaches the Passover crowds (19:47–48)
C. Wednesday (20:1–22:6)
  1. He contends with the Jewish rulers (20:1–8)
  2. He again teaches the Passover crowds (20:9–21:38)
    a. The parable of the wicked vinedressers (20:9–19)

      b. An answer to the Pharisees about paying taxes (20:20–26)
      c. An answer to the Sadducees about the resurrection (20:27–40)
      d. A question for the scribes about messianic prophecy (20:41–47)
      e. The lesson of the widow's mites (21:1–4)
      f. Teaching about the end times (21:5–38)
   3. The plot against Jesus (22:1–2)
   4. Judas joins the conspiracy (22:3–6)
 D. Thursday (22:7–53)
   1. Preparation for Passover (22:7–13)
   2. The Lord's Supper (22:14–38)
      a. The New Covenant instituted (22:14–22)
      b. Disputes among the disciples (22:23–30)
      c. Peter's denial predicted (22:31–34)
      d. God's provision promised (22:35–38)
   3. The agony in the garden (22:39–46)
   4. Jesus' arrest (22:47–53)
 E. Friday (22:54–23:56)
   1. Peter's denial (22:54–62)
   2. Jesus mocked and beaten (22:63–65)
   3. The trial before the Sanhedrin (22:66–71)
   4. The trial before Pilate (23:1–25)
      a. The indictment (23:1–5)
      b. The hearing before Herod (23:6–12)
      c. Pilate's verdict (23:13–25)
   5. The crucifixion (23:26–49)
   6. The burial (23:50–56)
V. The Consummation of Christ's Ministry (24:1–53)
 A. The Resurrection (24:1–45)
 B. The Ascension (24:46–53)

Luke's Prologue (Luke 1:1–4)

Inasmuch as many have undertaken to compile an account of the things accomplished among us, just as they were handed down to us by those who from the beginning were eyewitnesses and servants of the word, it seemed fitting for me as well, having investigated everything carefully from the beginning, to write it out for you in consecutive order, most excellent Theophilus; so that you may know the exact truth about the things you have been taught. (1:1–4)

The world is full of stories. Some are compelling, others are moving, many are impactful, and a few are even capable of profoundly changing how people think and live. Many such stories have come and gone throughout history, from the legends of the ancient world, the myths of past civilizations, the fanciful stories surrounding the pantheon of Greek gods, to the classics of literature from Aesop's fables to Beowulf to Shakespeare to modern writers. But there is one enduring and true story that stands above all the rest: the life of Jesus Christ. It is, as the title of a mid-twentieth-century Hollywood retelling of His life proclaimed, "The Greatest Story Ever Told."

This is the compelling and glorious story of how God purposed in eternity past to save lost sinners from eternal hell. His gracious, loving plan was to send His Son to be the atoning sacrifice for the sins of all who put their faith in Him. Jesus, as Paul wrote to the Romans, was "delivered over because of our transgressions, and was raised because of our justification" (Rom. 4:25). John wrote concerning Him, "He Himself is the propitiation for our sins; and not for ours only, but also for those of the whole world" (1 John 2:2). It was only because "God displayed [Jesus] publicly as a propitiation in His blood through faith" that He could "demonstrate His righteousness" (Rom. 3:25) and both "be just and the justifier of the one who has faith in Jesus" (v. 26). Because "all have sinned and fall short of the glory of God" (Rom. 3:23), the gospel message of salvation from sin and judgment in Christ alone completely transcends the limitations of culture and time and definitively determines every person's eternal destiny (cf. John 3:36; 8:24; 14:6; Acts 4:12).

Accordingly, the central theme of both the Old and New Testaments is the Lord Jesus Christ (cf. Rev. 19:10). Just before His ascension He told the disciples, "These are My words which I spoke to you while I was still with you, that all things which are written about Me in the Law of Moses and the Prophets and the Psalms must be fulfilled" (Luke 24:44). It is the "Scriptures" (the Old Testament), Jesus declared to the hostile Jewish leaders, "that testify about Me" (John 5:39). The New Testament Epistles unpack all the theological riches of salvation in Christ, while the book of Revelation chronicles Christ's second coming in glory (cf. Matt. 24:30).

But of all the books of the Old and New Testaments, the Gospels most clearly focus on the life and ministry of Jesus Christ. The gospel of Luke is the longest, and most thorough and complete of the four (Luke covers approximately forty pages, Matthew thirty-seven, Mark twenty-three, and John twenty-nine). Including the book of Acts, Luke's accurate, inerrant, comprehensive narrative of the life of Jesus and its impact spans more than sixty years. It begins with the birth of His forerunner, John the Baptist, and concludes with the apostle Paul's first imprisonment and ministry of the gospel in Rome. Altogether, Luke's writings make up more than one fourth of the New Testament. (For a further discussion of Luke's writings, see the Introduction to Acts in *Acts 1–12*, MacArthur New Testament Commentary [Chicago: Moody, 1994], 1–6.)

But despite his major role in chronicling the history and spread of the good news of salvation, Luke remains virtually unknown. Nowhere in his inspired writings does he refer to himself by name—not even in Acts, where he was one of Paul's traveling companions. In keeping with Luke's humble anonymity, the rest of the New Testament mentions his name only three times (Col. 4:14; 2 Tim. 4:11; Philem. 24). He was content to remain in the background and allow the majesty of Christ, who pervades his writing, to be the focus. Luke's accurately recorded history and theology establish his readers' understanding of the Lord's life and ministry.

The four verses that constitute the prologue to Luke's gospel are one long sentence, crafted in the polished style of a Greek literary classic. (The remainder of the gospel was written in the *koinē* Greek used in common, everyday speech, as were the other New Testament books.) Such prologues, explaining the writer's sources, purpose, and approach, were common in the scholarly writings of the Greco-Roman world (including those by such noted historians as Herodotus, Thucydides, Polybius, and Josephus). Luke's prologue thus marks his gospel as a serious literary and historical work, commanding the respect of even the most sophisticated, well-educated Gentile readers.

Despite his anonymity four elements of the evangelist's identity appear implicitly and explicitly in the prologue. Luke is revealed as a physician and historian, and as a theologian and pastor.

LUKE THE PHYSICIAN AND HISTORIAN

Inasmuch as many have undertaken to compile an account of the things accomplished among us, just as they were handed down to us by those who from the beginning were eyewitnesses and servants of the word, it seemed fitting for me as well, having investigated everything carefully from the beginning, (1:1–3*a*)

The phrase **it seemed fitting for me as well** contains this gospel's only reference to its author. As noted in the introduction to this volume, the early church unanimously identified Luke as the author of the gospel that bears his name; there was never any other suggestion concerning its authorship.

All that is known about Luke's life before he became one of Paul's partners in spreading the gospel is that he was a physician. In Colossians 4:14 Paul referred to his dear friend as "Luke, the beloved physician." Since verses 10 and 11 of that chapter identify Aristarchus, Mark, and Jesus Justus as the only ones among this list of Paul's fellow workers who were "from the circumcision" (i.e., Jewish), it is reasonable to conclude that the people Paul refers to in verses 12–17, including Luke (v. 14), were Gentiles. (For further evidence that Luke was a Gentile, see the introduction to Luke in this volume.)

Being a physician in the ancient world did not carry the dignity that such a profession does today. Howard C. Kee gives a helpful historical perspective:

An obvious question is: did most of the Roman populace share the exalted view of the medical art propounded by its chief practitioners, and particularly by Galen [a second–century A.D. Roman doctor]? Galen is caustic in his denunciation of the money-seeking, routine-bound quacks who "enter the sickroom, bleed the patient, lay on a plaster, and give an enema." Both from the epigrams and from non-medical writers of the second century [A.D.] it is evident that the medical profession was regarded as being characteristically greedy and fond of public display. Plutarch, in *The Flatters*, mocks the smooth bedside manner of the day. Dio Chrysostom describes the efforts of physicians to drum up trade by public lecture-presentations, intended to dazzle hearers and attract patients:

> This sort of recitation ... is kind of a spectacle or parade ... like the exhibition of the so-called physicians, who seat themselves conspicuously before us and give us a detailed account of the union of joints, the combination and juxtaposition of bones, and other topics of that sort, such as pores and respirations, and excretions. And the crowd is all agape with admiration and more enchanted than a swarm of children.

In his fine survey, *Roman Medicine*, John Scarborough notes that there were two different classes of physicians serving two different groups of patients. The aristocrats had physicians as servants or as private employees in their own establishments, or had access to them despite their high fees and lofty reputations. There were also many illiterate doctors, quacks, charlatans; exploiters of a gullible and needy public. He remarks that, "The intellectuality of Galen fails to pierce the growing gloom of an age gradually turning from rational answers posed by the Greek heritage of questioning to the mystical, all-encompassing solutions of religion." By the second half of the second century, there were many wonder-workers and rhetoricians, of whom Lucian draws satirical sketches in *Alexander the False Prophet and The Passing of Peregrinus*. ... Although we cannot generalize from Lucian's satirical remarks about the healing profession—in both its medical and its mystical aspects—we can safely conclude that [it] was [not] beyond criticism or universally esteemed in the later second century.

In the New Testament there are only seven occurrences of the word *hiatros*, and in only one of these is there a positive estimate of the physician. In Mt. 9:12 (=Mk. 2:17; Lk. 5:31) there is a proverbial expression about the physician's role being to care for the ailing, rather than the well. This is offered in the synoptics as justification for Jesus' attention to the sick, the unclean and the outcasts. In Mk. 5:26 (=Lk. 8:43), ... the physicians have taken money from the woman with the menstrual flow but have not cured her ailment. Another proverbial expression in Lk. 4:23, "Physician, heal yourself!", is a challenge to the one who points out problems that he must cure them. In Col. 4:14, Luke is identified as "the beloved physician," with no indication of the nature of the medical role he may have performed. (*Medicine, Miracle and Magic in New Testament Times* [London: Cambridge, 1986], 63–65)

At the very outset of his gospel Luke acknowledged that **many** others had already **undertaken to compile an account of** the life of Jesus. He did not specifically identify any of these early sources, which have all been lost. The only ones still extant that Luke may have consulted are the inspired gospels of Matthew and Mark, which probably were written before he penned his gospel (although Luke's omission of the material in an important section of Mark [6:45–8:26] suggests that he may not have seen Mark's gospel before he wrote). Whether or not Luke saw their gospels, he had personal contact with both Mark and Matthew, since Mark and Luke both traveled with Paul (cf. Philem. 24), and Luke could have visited Matthew in Jerusalem during Paul's two-year imprisonment at Caesarea (Acts 24:27). During that same period, Luke could have interviewed those in the Jerusalem church who had known the Lord, including the apostles and His mother, Mary. In addition, Luke had access to many others who had followed Jesus during His lifetime (such as the seventy [Luke 10:1–12], the women who ministered to Him [cf. Matt. 27:55; Mark 15:40–41; Luke 8:1–3; 23:49, 55], the 120 believers who gathered in Jerusalem following Christ's ascension [Acts 1:15], and the 500 who gathered in Galilee [1 Cor. 15:6]). They would have vividly remembered the things that Jesus did and said, and Luke could have interviewed them, or possibly read their writings.

Luke's goal was not to produce just another biography of Jesus, though that would have been a noble end in itself. Far more than that, he understood that the gospel is the story of what God accomplishes through Jesus Christ in the lives of sinners. The verb translated **accomplished** (*peplērophorēmenōn*) is an intensive compound word that indicates the complete fulfillment of something, in this case the redemptive plan of God. Luke's gospel, like the other three canonical gospels, emphasizes the theme of divine accomplishment. It chronicles how God accomplished salvation for His people (cf. Matt. 1:21; Luke 19:10) through the redemptive work of His Son, the Lord Jesus Christ. The gospels do not relate the story of a misunderstood ethical teacher, a failed social revolutionary, a model of selfless humility, or even a heroic martyr; they reveal the Savior who is God incarnate, the "Lamb of God who takes away the sin of the world" (John 1:29).

It is important to note that Luke was not critical of those who had **undertaken** (a term often used in connection with literary endeavors) **to compile an account** (a phrase often used to refer to historical writing) of Jesus' life and ministry. He did not pen his gospel as a corrective to those accounts, but because God prompted him to write a comprehensive narrative of the life of Christ and the spread of His salvation gospel.

Luke's reason for referring to his sources was twofold. First, it establishes his history as a legitimate, reliable account. He was a careful historian who used credible methods of research and writing, and based his content on the firsthand accounts of eyewitnesses. Second, Luke's use of those sources places his gospel squarely in the orthodox tradition. His volume was not a bizarre, different, heretical gospel. Luke's account was consistent with the teaching of the apostles (cf. Acts 2:42) and with those of eyewitnesses and especially the other Spirit-inspired gospel writers (cf. John 20:30–31; 21:24–25).

In writing his gospel Luke utilized the source material **handed down to** him **by those who from the beginning were eyewitnesses.** These same men (one definite article in the Greek text modifies both groups) later became **servants** (cf. 1 Cor. 3:5–9; 4:1; 2 Cor. 3:6) **of the word** (a synonym for the gospel [cf. 5:1; 8:11–13, 15; Acts 6:4; 8:4, 14, 25; 10:36; 11:1, 19; 13:5, 7, 44; 14:25; 15:7; 16:6, 32; 17:11; 18:5; 19:10). They observed Jesus' ministry firsthand and used that knowledge to faithfully preach the gospel. God preserved and transmitted the truth through them until He inspired four specific writers to record it in the New Testament. **Eyewitnesses** were the most significant sources who **handed down** (a technical term denoting the passing on of authoritative truth) the true information upon which Luke's account was based. That Luke was not an eyewitness himself makes it evident that he was not an apostle, since one qualification of apostleship was to have witnessed the resurrected Christ (Acts 1:21–22; cf. Luke 24:45–48; John 20:19–29; 1 Cor. 9:1; 1 John 1:1–3). Like Mark, he was not himself one of their number, but was a companion of some of the apostles (most notably Paul).

Since Luke had access to this wealth of firsthand, eyewitness testimony, it was **fitting** ("good," "proper") for him to write his account. The phrase **having investigated everything carefully from the beginning** ("having had perfect understanding of all things from the very first" [NKJV]) further marks Luke as an accomplished and accurate historian. His careful and thorough research gave him a precise understanding of Jesus Christ's life and ministry. As a result, he was uniquely qualified to write this gospel narrative under the Spirit's inspiration.

Luke's acknowledgement of his use of source material must not be misconstrued as a disclaimer of divine inspiration for his gospel. The process of inspiration never bypassed or overrode the personalities, life experiences, vocabularies, or writing styles of the Bible's human authors; their unique traits are indelibly stamped on all the books of Scripture. The Spirit used Luke's knowledge, gave him additional information, guided his selection of material, and controlled every word so that he wrote exactly what God wanted written (cf. 1 Cor. 2:12–13; 2 Tim. 3:16; 2 Peter 1:20–21).Therefore, his original account is infallibly and inerrantly true.

LUKE THE THEOLOGIAN AND PASTOR

to write it out for you in consecutive order, most excellent Theophilus; so that you may know the exact truth about the things you have been taught. (1:3*b*–4)

A good theologian is analytical, logical, and systematic. His goal is to persuade people to understand and accept doctrinal truth by means of a thoughtful, logical, progressive, consistent, persuasive explanation. Luke revealed himself to be a master theologian by writing his account **in consecutive order.** The New American Standard's rendering implies that Luke's gospel will be strictly chronological from beginning to end. Certainly it is generally chronological, starting with the birth of Christ, His circumcision and boyhood, moving on to His baptism and public ministry, and culminating with the cross and resurrection. (See the outline of Luke in the introduction in this volume.) There were instances, however, in which Luke arranged his material thematically to illustrate or expound a particular theological point (e.g., Luke's record of John the Baptist's arrest, 3:15–20). So Luke's narrative exhibits a basic chronological flow, but not to the exclusion of thematic, doctrinal discussion, in which he uses material out of chronological sequence.

So the phrase **in consecutive order** is better understood as a reference to the logical, systematic nature of Luke's writing. The New King James Version's translation of this phrase, "an orderly account," captures the essence of Luke's purpose in writing. His goal was to persuade; to lead his readers to believe the gospel by means of his carefully researched, logical, systematic presentation of the truth concerning God's saving purpose in Christ.

The first vital theological truth Luke wanted his readers to understand is God's sovereignty in history. He viewed God's sovereign plan of redemption, which unfolded through the life and work of Jesus Christ (cf. Acts 2:22–24), as of supreme importance. It was to die as a substitute for the sins of His people that He came into the world (19:10; cf. 9:22–23; 17:25; 18:31–34; 24:25, 26, 44). Second, Luke saw the significance of the universal sweep of redemption. He understood that salvation was available to everyone, not just the Jews (cf. Acts 10:34–48; 14:24–27; 15:12–19). Luke wanted to make it clear that the wonderful reality of God's saving purpose included Gentiles (e.g., Luke 7:1–10; 14:15–23). He himself was a

Gentile and he wrote to Theophilus, also a Gentile (Acts 1:1). In fact, Luke viewed the gospel not only as being for all ethnic groups, including Jews, Samaritans, and Gentiles, but also for all categories of individuals within those groups, including women (even prostitutes), outcasts (including lepers), those possessed by demons, even tax collectors (cf. 7:36–50; 10:25–37; 15:11–32; 16:19–31; 17:11–19; 19:1–10). Luke's emphasis on the gospel's universal appeal can be seen in his genealogy of Jesus. Unlike Matthew, who began his genealogy with Abraham, the father of the Jewish people, Luke traces Christ's genealogy all the way back to Adam, the father of the entire human race.

Though the main doctrinal emphasis in his gospel is the person and work of Jesus Christ, Luke did not neglect other important realities. Luke not only revealed God's sovereign control over history, but also described His tender, compassionate concern for lost sinners (cf. the parables in chapter 15). The doctrine of salvation is critical in Luke's gospel (his is the gospel that refers most specifically to the doctrine of justification, 18:14; cf. 7:36–50; 15:11–32; 19:1–10). In fact, the cross is the focus of more than half of his gospel, from 9:53 to the end of chapter 23. Luke also focused more on the ministry of the Holy Spirit than the other gospel writers, and recorded the Lord's teaching on His second coming. In addition, Luke the theologian addressed several areas of practical theology, such as worship, forgiveness, mercy, thanksgiving, and prayer. Profiles of discipleship are presented.

Finally, Luke's prologue reveals his pastor's heart. He addressed this massive work to a single individual, a man whom he called **most excellent Theophilus.** No personal details are known about him, but the title **most excellent** suggests that he was likely from the upper level of society. (Luke uses the same phrase in the book of Acts to designate the governors Felix and Festus [23:26; 24:3; 26:25].)

Theophilus had already **been taught** certain **things** about Jesus. But some of that teaching had been unclear or incomplete and Luke wanted him to **know the exact truth.** The word translated **exact** means "reliable," "certain," or "accurate." Luke presented to Theophilus and all others who would read his account a precise, accurate, and complete understanding of the gospel and the life of Christ. Whether Theophilus was an interested unbeliever or a new believer is not known. In either case, Luke's intensive research and detailed writing reveals the immensity of his pastor's heart. He cared enough about Theophilus's soul that he made this Spirit-empowered effort to bring that one man to a more precise, accurate knowledge of the truth concerning the Lord Jesus Christ. (For other New Testament examples of that kind of concern, see Acts 18:26; 19:1–5.)

In the remarkable providence of God, the Holy Spirit ensured that the book Luke wrote initially to one man would be disseminated around the world. The beloved physician, historian, theologian, and pastor had the privilege of becoming the instrument God used for the salvation and edification of millions throughout history (cf. 24:44–53).

God's Revelation to Zacharias
(Luke 1:5–14, 18–25)

2

In the days of Herod, king of Judea, there was a priest named Zacharias, of the division of Abijah; and he had a wife from the daughters of Aaron, and her name was Elizabeth. They were both righteous in the sight of God, walking blamelessly in all the commandments and requirements of the Lord. But they had no child, because Elizabeth was barren, and they were both advanced in years. Now it happened that while he was performing his priestly service before God in the appointed order of his division, according to the custom of the priestly office, he was chosen by lot to enter the temple of the Lord and burn incense. And the whole multitude of the people were in prayer outside at the hour of the incense offering. And an angel of the Lord appeared to him, standing to the right of the altar of incense. Zacharias was troubled when he saw the angel, and fear gripped him. But the angel said to him, "Do not be afraid, Zacharias, for your petition has been heard, and your wife Elizabeth will bear you a son, and you will give him the name John. You will have joy and gladness, and many will rejoice at his birth." . . . Zacharias said to the angel, "How will I know this for certain? For I am an old man and my wife is advanced in years." The angel answered and said to him,

"I am Gabriel, who stands in the presence of God, and I have been sent to speak to you and to bring you this good news. And behold, you shall be silent and unable to speak until the day when these things take place, because you did not believe my words, which will be fulfilled in their proper time." The people were waiting for Zacharias, and were wondering at his delay in the temple. But when he came out, he was unable to speak to them; and they realized that he had seen a vision in the temple; and he kept making signs to them, and remained mute. When the days of his priestly service were ended, he went back home. After these days Elizabeth his wife became pregnant, and she kept herself in seclusion for five months, saying, "This is the way the Lord has dealt with me in the days when He looked with favor upon me, to take away my disgrace among men." (1:5–14, 18–25)

The opening of Luke's narrative finds Israel in the midst of a long night of spiritual darkness. The nation's history had been marked by blessing and cursing, faithfulness and apostasy, obedience and rebellion. But all through the centuries—from the call of Abraham, the father of the nation, to the 400 years of bondage in Egypt, the forty years of wandering in the wilderness, the conquest and occupation of Canaan, the chaotic days of the judges, the zenith of Israel's power and glory under David and Solomon, the captivity and dissolution of the northern kingdom, the seventy-year exile and subsequent return of the southern kingdom, and the period of Gentile domination culminating with the nation's subjugation to Rome—what sustained the faithful, believing remnant was the hope that one day light would break through the darkness. In Luke 1:78–79 Zacharias expressed the fervent desire of those who feared God that the "Sunrise from on high" (the Messiah) would come and dispel the spiritual darkness that had held the nation in its grip for so long.

Zacharias undoubtedly had in mind the promise God had made four centuries earlier through the prophet Malachi: "But for you who fear My name, the sun of righteousness will rise with healing in its wings; and you will go forth and skip about like calves from the stall" (4:2). The prophecy looks forward to the coming of the Messiah, the Lord Jesus Christ, who will deliver all who savingly believe in Him from the darkness of sin (cf. Isa. 9:2; Matt. 4:16; Luke 2:25–32; John 1:5; 8:12; 12:35–36, 46; Acts 26:18; Eph. 5:8; Col. 1:13; 1 Thess. 5:4–5; 1 Peter 2:9; 1 John 1:6–7). Further, the Savior and Deliverer who was to come would be God Himself; according to Malachi's prophecy it would be "the Lord, whom you seek, [who] will suddenly come to His temple" (3:1).

The Old Testament, then, ended with the most positive, hopeful promise. The sun of righteousness would arise, and His glorious light would dispel the spiritual darkness that engulfed the people. But just as the darkness is deepest just before dawn, so also the four centuries since Malachi's day had been the darkest time of all for Israel. The Jewish people had sunk deeper and deeper into apostasy. The nation had abandoned the Old Testament truth that salvation is by faith alone (Gen. 15:6; cf. Rom. 4:3, 9, 20–22; Gal. 3:6) in favor of salvation by legalism, self-righteousness, and meritorious works. Their religion consisted of empty, self-serving (cf. Matt. 23:5–7) ritual that could not save (Rom. 3:20) and drew the Lord's scathing rebuke (cf. Deut. 9:4; Isa. 29:13; 64:6; Jer. 12:2; Matt. 23:27–28; Mark 7:6–7; Luke 16:15). As the apostle Paul sorrowfully concluded, "For I testify about them [the unbelieving Jews] that they have a zeal for God, but not in accordance with knowledge. For not knowing about God's righteousness and seeking to establish their own, they did not subject themselves to the righteousness of God" (Rom. 10:2–3). In the face of such hypocrisy, God had remained silent; He had not communicated with His people through prophet, revelation, or miracle during the four hundred years since Malachi's day.

Malachi's prophecy had included God's pledge to send a "messenger" ("herald"; "forerunner") before the coming of the Messiah (3:1). The arrival of that messenger would signal the breaking of God's long silence toward His people. His preaching would be a beacon of light in Israel's spiritual darkness; he would proclaim the long-awaited news of "the true Light" (John 1:9), Messiah's imminent arrival (Matt. 3:3; Mark 1:2–3; Luke 3:4–6; John 1:23), and call the people to prepare their hearts to receive Him (Mark 1:4; Luke 1:16–17, 76–77; cf. Isa. 40:3; Mal. 3:1).

It was essential that Luke begin the saga of salvation with the story of that forerunner, John the Baptist, for several reasons. First, doing so connected the Old and New Testaments. They do not teach two different religions or propose two different ways of salvation. Rather, they are one unified revelation from God, offering the hope of redemption through faith in the true and living God and His Son, the Lord Jesus Christ.

Second, John the Baptist was the fulfillment of Old Testament prophecies. That fulfillment demonstrates the accuracy of those predictions, further linking the Old and New Testaments, and placing the New Testament as Scripture on a par with the Old.

Third, as noted above, it was through John the Baptist that God broke His centuries-long silence. Gabriel's appearance was the first supernatural communication and John was the first prophet in 400 years.

Fourth, John's birth was miraculous, in that his parents (like Abraham and Sarah) were beyond child-bearing age. That foreshadowed the even more miraculous virgin birth of the Lord Jesus Christ.

Finally, and most significantly, the story of John the Baptist establishes that he was the divinely prophesied forerunner of the Messiah. Therefore, his testimony concerning Jesus (cf. John 1:29) verifies that Jesus was the Messiah.

Like any competent historian, Luke knew the importance of placing his narrative in its proper context. Therefore, he began his account with a brief description of the historical setting before relating the amazing story of Gabriel's announcement to Zacharias regarding John.

HISTORICAL BACKGROUND

In the days of Herod, king of Judea, (1:5*a*)

Herod (Herod I or the Great) is the first and best known of the Herod family mentioned in the New Testament (the others are Antipas [Luke 3:1; cf. Matt. 14:1–12; Luke 23:7–12], Philip [Luke 3:1], Archelaus [Matt. 2:22], Agrippa I [Acts 12], and Agrippa II [Acts 25:13; 26:1ff.]). Though the gospels mention him only here and in Matthew 2:1–22, **Herod** played a major role in the events surrounding the birth of Christ.

Herod's father, Antipater, had supported Julius Caesar, even risking his life for him during the latter's war with Pompey. In gratitude, Caesar made Antipater procurator (governor) of Judea. Antipater in turn appointed Herod (then only twenty-five years old) governor of Galilee. Herod immediately gained favor with both the Galilean Jews and the Roman officials by killing a notorious bandit leader and many of his followers. After his father's death Herod, having fled to Rome to escape a Parthian invasion of Palestine, was declared **king of Judea** by Octavian and Antony (with the Senate's confirmation) in 40 B.C. With the aid of the Romans, Herod drove the Parthians out of Palestine and established his kingdom, becoming undisputed ruler in 37 B.C.

Herod was not a Jew, but an Idumean (Edomite). Since the Edomites (descendants of Esau) were traditional enemies of Israel (Num. 20:14–21; 1 Kings 11:14–22; 2 Kings 14:7; 2 Chron. 25:5–16; Ps. 137:7; cf. Jer. 49:7–22; Ezek. 25:12–14; 35:15; Amos 1:11–12; Obad. 1–21), Herod felt the need to ingratiate himself with the Jewish people. He married Mariamne, a member of the prestigious and wealthy Jewish Hasmonean family, which had ruled Israel during much of the intertestamental period. He also utilized all of his considerable diplomatic, oratorical, and administrative skills to increase his standing with the Jews. Herod conducted a vast public works program, highlighted by the rebuilding of the temple (still ongoing during Jesus' ministry), and the construction of the port city of Caesarea. He also revived the city of Samaria and built the remark-able and virtually impregnable fortress of Masada. He showed favor toward the people by twice lowering their taxes, and during the severe famine of 25 B.C. Herod even melted down gold objects from his palace to buy food for the poor. He was so popular with some Jews that they formed the pro-Herod party called the Herodians (Matt. 22:16; Mark 3:6; 12:13). Like the Pharisees and the Sadducees, the Herodians were ene-mies of Jesus (Mark 12:13).

But in spite of those positive achievements, there was a dark side to Herod. He could be ruthless, vicious, and merciless, and was incredi-bly jealous and paranoid, constantly afraid that someone would usurp his power. Herod's cruelty and bloodthirstiness manifested itself, among other things, in the murder of his wife, her brother, her mother, and several of his own sons. His barbaric savagery reached a horrifying low point in the slaughter of the innocents (Matt. 2:16–18), which was motivated by his fear that the one "born King of the Jews" (Matt. 2:2) would supplant him. As Luke's narrative opened, Herod's long reign was drawing to a close.

Having laid out the historical background, Luke turned his atten-tion to Zacharias. He portrayed his personal righteousness, his priestly responsibility, his faithless response to prophetic revelation, and the divine reproof for his unbelieving response.

ZACHARIAS'S PERSONAL RIGHTEOUSNESS

there was a priest named Zacharias, of the division of Abijah; and he had a wife from the daughters of Aaron, and her name was Elizabeth. They were both righteous in the sight of God, walking blamelessly in all the commandments and requirements of the Lord. But they had no child, because Elizabeth was barren, and they were both advanced in years. (1:5b–7)

Luke's cast of characters abruptly transitions from the proud king Herod to the humble **priest named Zacharias. Zacharias,** or Zechariah, ("Yahweh has remembered"), was a common name in Scripture, and this particular Zacharias was just one of thousands of priests in Israel, carry-ing out his duties in obscurity in a remote village in Judea.

To be a priest was to represent God to the people; it was a sacred and respected position (cf. Ex. 29:8–9, 44; Num. 18:7). The priests were the agents of God's rule in Israel's theocracy. They brought God to the people as they taught and interpreted Scripture and counseled and judged them (Num. 5:14–15; Deut. 17:8–13; 21:5; 33:8, 10; Mal. 2:7). It was also the priests' sacred duty to bring the people to God by offering sacrifices in the temple for their sins (Ex. 29:10–19; Lev. 4:13–20; 2 Chron. 29:34; 35:11). During the course of a year, each priest would leave his local duties to serve in the Jerusalem temple twice for one week. The beginning of Luke's narrative finds Zacharias in the temple for one of his semiannual weeks of service.

Luke's note that Zacharias was part **of the division of Abijah** does not necessarily indicate that he was a descendant of Abijah. David, Zadok, and Ahimelech had organized the priesthood into twenty-four divisions (cf. 1 Chron. 24:4–19), the eighth of which was that of Abijah (v. 10). But after the Babylonian captivity, only four of the twenty-four priestly divisions returned to Judah (Ezra 2:36–38). For the sake of tradition, however, the Jews wanted twenty-four divisions, so the leaders divided the remaining four divisions into twenty-four and restored the former names to them. So Zacharias, while probably not in the family line of Abijah (Abijah was not one of the divisions that returned after the exile), nevertheless served in the division that bore his name.

Priests were expected to marry an Israelite woman who was a virgin (cf. Lev. 21:7, 14; Ezek. 44:22). Zacharias went beyond that, however, and chose his **wife from the daughters of Aaron.** She was named **Elizabeth,** after Aaron's wife, a name that means "My God is an oath" and celebrates the faithfulness of God. Since all qualified male descendants of Aaron were priests (Ex. 29:9; 40:13–15; Lev. 21:17–23; Num. 3:3; 18:7), she was familiar with the priesthood; most of the men in her family would have been priests.

Zacharias and Elizabeth were a remarkable pair, well suited to be the parents of Messiah's forerunner. In a bleak period of hypocrisy, legalism, and defection from the true worship of God, **they were both righteous.** And unlike the self-righteous hypocrites whom Jesus excoriated (cf. Matt. 6:2, 5, 16; 23:13–29; John 5:44), Zacharias and Elizabeth were righteous not in the sight of men, but **in the sight of God.** God justified them the way He has always justified the redeemed: by faith. As Moses wrote of Abraham, "Then he believed in the Lord; and He reckoned it to him as righteousness" (Gen. 15:6). Zacharias and Elizabeth believed in the true and living God and the revelation of His Word in the Old Testament (cf. Acts 24:14). They also believed that God's law was right and true (cf. Ps. 19:7–8; Rom. 7:12) but knew that they could not keep it (cf. Acts 15:10; Rom. 3:20; 8:7; Gal. 2:16; 3:11, 24). Because Zacharias and Elizabeth realized that they fell short of the law's standards of righteousness, they also knew that they needed to turn in repentance and faith (cf. Hab. 2:4; Luke 18:13–14) to a merciful, gracious, and loving God. He would then grant them forgiveness (Ps. 130:3–4; Isa. 1:18; Dan. 9:9; Mic. 7:18–19; Acts 10:43) and not impute their sins to them (Ps. 32:1–2; Rom. 8:33–34; cf.

Rom. 3:25–26; 4:3, 9). The basis for that forgiveness was Messiah's sacrificial death on behalf of all who believe (Isa. 53:5–6, 10–12). Thus God covers the penitent sinner with His righteousness, as Isaiah wrote centuries earlier: "I will rejoice greatly in the Lord, my soul will exult in my God; for He has clothed me with garments of salvation, He has wrapped me with a robe of righteousness" (Isa. 61:10; cf. 53:4–6). Zacharias and Elizabeth were shining examples of the godly remnant of believing Jews in the midst of an apostate nation. They were declared righteous by grace through faith according to the new covenant promise to be ratified in the death of Christ.

Zacharias and Elizabeth were not merely justified, however; they were also being sanctified, **walking blamelessly in all the commandments and requirements of the Lord.** When God imputes righteousness to believers, He also sanctifies them (1 Cor. 1:30; 6:11). Justification and sanctification are inseparably linked, since "Christ … justifies no man without also sanctifying him" (John Calvin, *Institutes of the Christian Religion,* III, 16, 1). That Zacharias and Elizabeth lived blamelessly before the Lord does not mean they were sinless, but rather that their lives were characterized by obedience to God's law (cf. Deut. 30:8–10; Josh. 1:8). They were like Job, who "was blameless, upright, fearing God and turning away from evil" (Job 1:1).

Ironically, though God viewed Zacharias and Elizabeth as righteous many of those who knew them did not. The sad truth was that **they had no child, because Elizabeth was barren.** Many in that culture would have wondered whether sin in their lives had caused God to withhold children, which were recognized as His gift (cf. Gen. 33:5; Pss. 113:9; 127:3). Childlessness was an extremely difficult burden for women (and their husbands) to bear in Jewish society, as the Old Testament illustrates (see, for example, the stories of Rachel [Gen. 30:1–2, 23], and Hannah [1 Sam. 1:4–11]).

Humanly speaking, the situation for Zacharias and Elizabeth appeared hopeless, since **they were both advanced in years.** Despite being righteous in God's sight, they had lived all their married lives bearing the stigma of childlessness. But those who viewed Elizabeth's barrenness as God's punishment for her or her husband's sin (cf. John 9:1–3) were wrong; hence Luke's emphasis on the couple's righteousness. Their circumstances were sovereignly ordained by God, and they would be vindicated when God gave them a son—and not just any son, but the forerunner to the Messiah, John the Baptist, the first prophet in 400 years, the final prophet of the Old Testament era, and the greatest man who had ever lived up until that time (Matt. 11:11).

ZACHARIAS'S PRIESTLY RESPONSIBILITY

Now it happened that while he was performing his priestly service before God in the appointed order of his division, according to the custom of the priestly office, he was chosen by lot to enter the temple of the Lord and burn incense. And the whole multitude of the people were in prayer outside at the hour of the incense offering. (1:8–10)

This event marked the pinnacle of Zacharias's **priestly service before God.** He was on duty for one of his two weeks of service in the temple, **in the appointed order of his division, according to the custom of the priestly office.** Luke's understated, matter-of-fact wording does not convey to modern readers how thrilled and excited Zacharias would have been for this once-in-a-lifetime opportunity.

To be **chosen by lot to enter the temple of the Lord and burn incense** was the highest honor for a priest. Because of the large number of priests, many would never have the privilege of performing this sacred rite. The priests kept the incense in the temple burning perpetually (cf. Ex. 30:7–8; Lev. 16:12–13; 2 Chron. 29:11) in front of the veil that separated the holy place from the most holy place (the Holy of Holies; cf. Ex. 26:31–33). The incense altar, though located outside the most holy place, was closely associated with it (Heb. 9:1–5; cf. Ex. 30:1–10; 40:5, 22–27; Lev. 16:12–13). One priest offered incense each morning and evening while the other priests **and the whole multitude of the people were in prayer outside** the holy place. Luke's reference to a large **multitude** of **people** suggests that this incident took place during the evening offering, when there would have been a larger crowd.

The priest would normally perform his duties as quickly as possible because he feared ministering so near to the most Holy Place. He was afraid he might do something—even something seemingly trivial—that might be blasphemous or dishonoring to God. The High Priest on the Day of Atonement had bells on his robe so that those outside could hear him moving around inside the most Holy Place and know that he was still alive.

The ascending, aromatic cloud of incense smoke symbolized the people's prayers of repentance, of confession and thanksgiving, for the coming of Messiah, the peace of Jerusalem, the nation, the family, salvation, and for the coming kingdom. Thus the incense represented the people's dependence on God (cf. 1 Chron. 29:12), their submission to Him (cf. Deut. 27:10; 1 Sam. 15:22–23), and acknowledged His sovereignty over them (cf. Ps. 103:19).

ZACHARIAS'S RESPONSE TO PROPHETIC REVELATION

And an angel of the Lord appeared to him, standing to the right of the altar of incense. Zacharias was troubled when he saw the angel, and fear gripped him. But the angel said to him, "Do not be afraid, Zacharias, for your petition has been heard, and your wife Elizabeth will bear you a son, and you will give him the name John. You will have joy and gladness, and many will rejoice at his birth." (1:11–14)

At this crucial moment in redemptive history, God miraculously intervened once again in the affairs of His people. Simply, and without fanfare, Luke records the startling truth that **an angel of the Lord appeared to** Zacharias. This was something totally unexpected; the last appearance of an angel had been to the prophet Zechariah nearly five centuries earlier. But while that Zechariah saw the angel in a series of visions (Zech. 1:9; 2:3; 4:1; cf. Dan. 7:15–16), this Zacharias actually saw this angel with his own eyes. That the heavenly messenger was visible, **standing to the right of the altar of incense,** shows that he was really there; he was not some vague apparition or figment of Zacharias's imagination.

Zacharias's immediate response to this incredible sight was understandable: **[he] was troubled . . . and fear gripped him. Troubled** translates a form of the verb *tarassō,* which literally means, "shaken," or "stirred up" (John 5:7); figuratively, it means, "terrified" (Matt. 14:26), "troubled" (Matt. 2:3), or "agitated" (Acts 17:8). Zacharias's fearful reaction was typical of those visited by angels (cf. Judg. 6:22–23; 13:15–22; Dan. 8:15–18; Rev. 19:10; 22:8–9); the presence of such perfectly holy beings made people acutely aware of their sin and God's judgment of it (Gen. 2:17; 6:5–7; 19:24; Ex. 20:5; Num. 11:1; 32:23; Deut. 29:20; Ps. 98:9; Isa. 13:11; Jer. 32:19; Ezek. 18:4). In light of his obvious terror the angel replied comfortingly, **"Do not be afraid, Zacharias"** (cf. Dan. 10:12, 19; Luke 1:30; 2:10).

The angel had not come with a message of judgment, so Zacharias had nothing to fear. On the contrary, the angel delivered a message of blessing, informing him, **Your petition has been heard, and your wife Elizabeth will bear you a son.** The **petition** that God would grant them a child was undoubtedly one that Zacharias and Elizabeth had made through the years and maybe abandoned in the past. They might have lost hope that God would answer, in light of their advanced age. But now at last, when all hope, humanly speaking, was gone, God, in accord with His divine purpose, graciously granted their request. Zacharias's **wife** would **bear** him **a son,** and they would **give him the name John,** the Greek form of the Hebrew name "Johanan" ("God is gracious"). The choice of that name for the Messiah's forerunner symbolized the turning point in redemptive history. God was about to pour out His grace through the gift of His Son, the Lord Jesus Christ (cf. John 1:14, 17).

The news that they were to have a son naturally brought great **joy and gladness** to Zacharias and Elizabeth. But **many** others would share their joy and **rejoice at his birth,** because John would "turn many of the sons of Israel back to the Lord their God" (Luke 1:16) in preparation for Messiah's imminent arrival.

THE DIVINE REPROOF FOR
ZACHARIAS'S UNBELIEVING RESPONSE

Zacharias said to the angel, "How will I know this for certain? For I am an old man and my wife is advanced in years." The angel answered and said to him, "I am Gabriel, who stands in the presence of God, and I have been sent to speak to you and to bring you this good news. And behold, you shall be silent and unable to speak until the day when these things take place, because you did not believe my words, which will be fulfilled in their proper time." The people were waiting for Zacharias, and were wondering at his delay in the temple. But when he came out, he was unable to speak to them; and they realized that he had seen a vision in the temple; and he kept making signs to them, and remained mute. When the days of his priestly service were ended, he went back home. After these days Elizabeth his wife became pregnant, and she kept herself in seclusion for five months, saying, "This is the way the Lord has dealt with me in the days when He looked with favor upon me, to take away my disgrace among men." (1:18–25)

Incredibly, Zacharias's initial fear at seeing the angel soon turned to unbelief. Instead of being grateful, Zacharias reacted with skepticism. Expressing doubt and faithless distrust, he asked incredulously, **"How will I know this for certain? For I am an old man and my wife is advanced in years."** Much like those praying for Peter's release from prison (Acts 12:12–16), Zacharias refused to believe even when given the answer he had requested. So like all believers, he was righteous before God, but not sinless.

To doubt the certainty of the word of God and the reliability of His promises (cf. Josh. 23:14; 1 Kings 8:56; 2 Cor. 1:20; Titus 1:2; Heb. 10:23) is to deny His truthfulness. Thus Zacharias's unbelief drew the angel's stern rebuke. **"I am Gabriel,"** he declared, **"who stands in the presence of God."** The phrase translated **I am Gabriel** is emphatic, indicating that this was no ordinary angel. One of only two angels named in Scripture (the other is Michael [Dan. 10:13, 21; 12:1; Jude 9; Rev. 12:7]), Gabriel was God's primary messenger, sent to communicate some of the most monumental announcements in redemptive history (Dan. 8:16–26; 9:21–27; Luke 1:26–38).

Further, he had been **sent to speak to** Zacharias **and to bring** him **this good news** from God Himself. God is sovereign over the holy angels, and they always do His bidding (cf. Ex. 23:20, 23; 33:2; Num. 20:16; 1 Chron. 21:15; 2 Chron. 32:21; Ps. 103:21; Dan. 3:28; 6:22). **Good news** translates a form of the verb *euangelizō* ("to announce good news"). This word was familiar to Gentiles, since it was used to express joyous news, especially related to the accession of the Caesars to the throne, thus noting the inauguration of a new era. The word appears eleven times in the gospels, ten of them in Luke. It refers elsewhere to proclaiming the good news that God sent His Son to die for the sins of all who believe in Him.

As chastisement for his sinful unbelief, Gabriel declared that Zacharias would **be silent and unable to speak until the day** that **these things** took **place.** When John was circumcised eight days after his birth, Zacharias "asked for a tablet and wrote as follows, 'His name is John.'...And at once his mouth was opened and his tongue loosed, and he began to speak in praise of God" (1:63–64). But until then he would be unable to describe to others his supernatural experience in the temple, or relate the wonderful, unbelievable news that he and Elizabeth were to have a son. He also would be unable to perform his priestly duty to teach the people in his village. Zacharias would bear the shame of God's judgment **because** [he] **did not believe** [God's] **words, which** would **be fulfilled in their proper time.**

Gabriel's closing words highlight Zacharias's lack of faith, but they also emphasize God's sovereignty. God's plans and purposes, established in eternity past, will infallibly come to pass. However, the blessedness and reward saints enjoy from participating in those realities can be forfeited through unbelief, and replaced by chastening.

Meanwhile, as this conversation was going on, **the people were waiting** outside **for Zacharias, and were wondering at his delay in the temple.** The priest was only supposed to offer the incense and then exit to pronounce the familiar benediction (Num. 6:23–27). But Zacharias, delayed by his conversation with Gabriel, failed to come out on time. That led the people to wonder if he had done something wrong and been judged by God. Leviticus 10:1–7 describes the dire consequences that could ensue when priests were careless or disobedient:

> Now Nadab and Abihu, the sons of Aaron, took their respective firepans, and after putting fire in them, placed incense on it and offered strange fire before the Lord, which He had not commanded them. And

fire came out from the presence of the Lord and consumed them, and they died before the Lord. Then Moses said to Aaron, "It is what the Lord spoke, saying, 'By those who come near Me I will be treated as holy, and before all the people I will be honored.'" So Aaron, therefore, kept silent. Moses called also to Mishael and Elzaphan, the sons of Aaron's uncle Uzziel, and said to them, "Come forward, carry your relatives away from the front of the sanctuary to the outside of the camp." So they came forward and carried them still in their tunics to the outside of the camp, as Moses had said. Then Moses said to Aaron and to his sons Eleazar and Ithamar, "Do not uncover your heads nor tear your clothes, so that you will not die and that He will not become wrathful against all the congregation. But your kinsmen, the whole house of Israel, shall bewail the burning which the Lord has brought about. You shall not even go out from the doorway of the tent of meeting, or you will die; for the Lord's anointing oil is upon you." So they did according to the word of Moses. (cf. 2 Sam. 6:3–4, 6–7; 2 Chron. 26:16–21)

God, however, had not taken Zacharias's life, but rather temporarily eliminated his ability to speak. Exactly as Gabriel had said, when he finally **came out, he was unable to speak to them.** As a result, the people **realized that he had seen a vision in the temple.** Zacharias's facial expression and body language made it obvious to the onlookers that something traumatic and extraordinary had taken place. Trying to communicate what had just happened, **he kept making signs to them, and remained mute.** The text does not refer to a formal sign language—neither Zacharias nor the people would have known one. He just sought, in the best way that he could, to communicate with gestures what had occurred.

Giving a rather anticlimactic conclusion to what had been a phenomenal week for Zacharias, Luke noted that **when the days of his priestly service were ended, he went back home.** The narrative gives no details about his reception by his wife, nor her reaction to the incredible news he bore.

Again simply, and without fanfare, Luke related the fulfillment of God's promise to Zacharias: **After these days Elizabeth his wife became pregnant.** Luke wanted to make it clear that she did not become pregnant until after Zacharias returned home, lest false accusations of infidelity be made against her.

The New Testament story of redemption began with this miracle of an older couple having a child. It was the first of many miracles that would characterize the era of Jesus and the apostles. And as was typical of those miracles, it was not only a spectacular display of supernatural power, but also met a real human need.

After Elizabeth realized she was pregnant **she kept herself in seclusion for five months.** Because of her age and barrenness, no one would have believed she was pregnant until she was far enough along that it was obvious. When it was visible she finally did speak of her pregnancy, and it was to praise God, as her exclamation, **"This is the way the Lord has dealt with me in the days when He looked with favor upon me, to take away my disgrace among men,"** indicates. Like Hannah centuries earlier (1 Sam. 1:19–2:10), Elizabeth was profoundly grateful that the Lord had miraculously removed the stigma of her childlessness.

The portrait Luke paints of Zacharias and Elizabeth is one of flawed, but genuine, believers. They were humble, righteous, obedient, prayerful, and served the Lord; at the same time, they were doubting, fearful, and even chastened by Him. God is the God of humble beginnings and humble people, and He used Zacharias and Elizabeth because of their faithfulness and in spite of their shortcomings. He gave them a son who would have the highest privilege of all— to be the greatest prophet because he was the forerunner of the Messiah. Though today is no longer the age of miracles, God still uses common people to faithfully proclaim the good news of salvation in the Lord Jesus Christ (Matt. 28:19–20; 1 Peter 2:9; 3:15)—the story that began with God's miraculous intervention in the lives of two humble, righteous people.

The Greatness of John the Baptist (Luke 1:15–17)

3

"For he will be great in the sight of the Lord; and he will drink no wine or liquor, and he will be filled with the Holy Spirit while yet in his mother's womb. And he will turn many of the sons of Israel back to the Lord their God. It is he who will go as a forerunner before Him in the spirit and power of Elijah, to turn the hearts of the fathers back to the children, and the disobedient to the attitude of the righteous, so as to make ready a people prepared for the Lord." (1:15–17)

Nothing typifies the world's view of greatness better than the brash claim by former heavyweight boxing champion Muhammad Ali, "I am the greatest." Ali's repeated statement generated an enormous amount of public response, both pro and con, during the 1960s and 1970s. His boast, which Ali often backed up by dominating his opponents in the ring, helped open the floodgates of tolerance for the blatant, arrogant egotism that prevails in sports and throughout contemporary society.

History has chronicled many truly great and honorable men, but in recent times it has become increasingly difficult to distinguish greatness from mere fame. In today's culture, famous people are most often celebrated for their wealth, success in business, athletic skills, acting ability, or musical talent. Many are creations of the media; famous merely for being famous.

A more realistic, but less common, view of greatness measures it in terms of significant achievement. It singles out those who leave an indelible, positive mark on society, whether in war, education, science, medicine, the arts, or humanitarian causes.

But God's standard of greatness transcends all human measure, focusing on eternal heavenly realities, not ephemeral worldly ones. It can best be seen by examining the life of someone whom God calls great. Such a man was John the Baptist.

John's life had none of the trappings the world associates with greatness. He was born into a common family from the Judean hill country (Luke 1:39, 65), not an upper-class family in Jerusalem. There is no evidence that he had any formal education. Instead of hobnobbing with the rich and famous, "he lived in the deserts until the day of his public appearance to Israel" (Luke 1:80), far from the centers of commerce, culture, and power. John's camel's hair garment and leather belt did not exactly make a fashion statement, nor was his diet of locusts and wild honey (Matt. 3:4) likely to start a culinary trend. The fact that he disconnected from the styles of the culture of his people, in the will of God, put no limits on his message or impact. On the contrary, Matthew records that "Jerusalem was going out to him, and all Judea and all the district around the Jordan," being baptized and confessing their sins (Matt. 3:5–6).

John was not associated with any of the official institutions of his day. He started no social or political movements, formed no organization, founded no religious cult. In fact, he consciously downplayed his own importance in deference to Christ (Matt. 3:11; John 1:30), even directing his followers to Him (John 1:35–37). Though born into a priestly family, he was not part of the priesthood. The religious authorities were at first baffled by him (John 1:19–27), but soon grew to hate him for his blistering denunciations of their hypocrisy (Matt. 3:7–12). Nor did John fare any better with the political establishment. Herod the tetrarch (Herod Antipas), embarrassed by John's bold denunciation of his sinful relationship with his brother's wife (Matt. 14:3–4), imprisoned him and eventually had him executed. As far as the world was concerned, John ended his life as little more than an eccentric preacher, decapitated at the instigation of a seductive dancing girl and her vindictive mother (Matt. 14:1–12; Mark 6:14–29).

But the world's evaluation of John completely missed the mark. No less an authority than the Lord Jesus Christ, God incarnate, testified that "among those born of women there has not arisen anyone greater than John the Baptist!" (Matt. 11:11).

Three marks of John the Baptist's greatness flow from this passage: his personal character, his privileged calling, and his powerful contribution.

JOHN'S PERSONAL CHARACTER

"For he will be great in the sight of the Lord; and he will drink no wine or liquor, and he will be filled with the Holy Spirit while yet in his mother's womb. (1:15)

Great is a relative term, measured within a specific cultural and historical context. John the Baptist's greatness, however, transcends time and culture. As noted above, Jesus declared him to be the greatest man who had lived up to his time. That amazing commendation means that John was greater than all the notable men of the Old Testament, including Enoch, who walked with God and was translated to heaven without dying (Gen. 5:24; cf. Heb. 11:5); Noah, whom God spared from the flood (Gen. 7:1–7; cf. Heb. 11:7); Melchizedek, the king of Salem and priest of the Most High God, to whom Abraham paid tithes (Gen. 14:18–20; cf. Heb. 7:1–10); Abraham himself, the father of the nation of Israel (Gen. 12:1–7; cf. Heb. 11:8–10); the patriarchs Isaac (Gen. 17:19, 21; Ex. 3:15), Jacob (Gen. 28:10–15; Lev. 26:42), and Joseph (cf. Gen. 37:3; 39:2–4; 41:38–45); Moses, the lawgiver and leader of the exodus (Jer. 15:1; Matt. 23:2; Heb. 11:23–29); David and Solomon, Israel's greatest kings (1 Kings 3:10–13; 2 Sam. 7:1–17; 1 Chron. 29:25; Ps. 78:70–71; 89:35; Mark 11:10; Luke 1:32; Acts 13:22–23); the miracle-working prophets Elijah (1 Kings 17:17–24) and Elisha (2 Kings 2:14; 4:1–7, 18–37; 5:1–19); the major writing prophets Isaiah (Isa. 6:6–10), Jeremiah (Jer. 1:4–19), Ezekiel (Ezek. 2:1–3:9), and Daniel (Dan. 1:8–16; 2:46–49; 6:1–4; 9:1–23); or any of the other Old Testament heroes of the faith mentioned in Hebrews 11.

John was **great** in the only way that truly matters—**in the sight of the Lord** (or "God"; a common New Testament phrase signifying divine approval; cf. 1:6; Acts 4:19; 7:20; cf. 7:46; 2 Cor. 2:17; 4:2; 7:12; 8:21; 12:19; 1 Tim. 2:3; 5:4; James 1:27; 1 Peter 2:4; 3:4). (It should be noted that when Gabriel used the term **great** in 1:32 in reference to Jesus he did not qualify it by adding "in the sight of the Lord." Jesus Christ, as God in human flesh, was already great in the absolute, highest sense.)

Implicit in God's approval of John was the reality of his justification, since no one can be approved by God whose sins are not forgiven. In anticipation of His work on the cross, God imputed to John the righteousness of Jesus Christ (cf. Isa. 61:10; Rom. 3:22; 2 Cor. 5:21). The promise of salvation to one not yet conceived (cf. Jer. 1:5; Gal. 1:15–16) is of monumental significance in understanding the doctrine of election (cf. Eph. 1:4). God's choice of John is a profound illustration of how He has sovereignly chosen all who believe (John 1:12–13; 6:37, 44; 15:16; Rom. 8:29; 1 Thess. 1:4; 1 Peter 1:1–2) and written their names in the Lamb's Book of Life before the foundation of the world (2 Thess. 2:13–14; cf. Luke 10:20; Acts 13:48; Rom. 8:29; Rev. 13:8; 17:8).

Gabriel then gave two marks of John's greatness, one external and physical, the other internal and spiritual. First, John would **drink no wine or liquor.** His lifestyle would be one of temperance, moderation, and self-denial. John's choice of wardrobe (camel's hair coat and leather belt) and diet (locusts and wild honey) reflected his indifference toward worldly pleasures. Abstaining from wine and liquor took his disdain for and separation from the world a significant step further. John would be so preoccupied with the work that God commissioned him to do that he would distance himself from those things.

The Old Testament has much to say about **wine** and **liquor,** and those principles would influence John's decision to abstain. Two Hebrew words translated **wine** need to be considered. *Tirosh,* usually translated "new wine" (e.g., Gen. 27:28, 37; Deut. 7:13; 11:14; 12:17; 14:23; 18:4; 28:51; 33:28; 2 Kings 18:32; Ps. 4:7; Prov. 3:10), refers to grape juice as it came from the presses. It was then put in wineskins to age and ferment (Luke 5:37–38), and thus would eventually be capable of producing intoxication (Hos. 4:11). The Old Testament associates wine with God's blessing of His people (Gen. 27:28, 37; Deut. 7:13; 11:14; 18:4; 33:28; Jer. 31:12; Hos. 2:8; Joel 2:19, 24; Zech. 9:17). The second term, *yayin,* refers to fermented, intoxicating wine (e.g., Gen. 9:21, 24; 19:32–35; Lev. 10:9; Num. 6:3; 1 Sam. 1:14; 25:36–37; Est. 1:10; Ps. 78:65; Prov. 20:1; 23:29–35; Eccles. 2:3; Isa. 28:1, 7; Jer. 23:9; Zech. 9:15; 10:7). Without modern refrigeration, grape juice would ferment if stored for any length of time. The rabbis were concerned about the intoxicating capabilities of *yayin;* therefore, they required it to be diluted with a majority part being water (cf. Prov. 9:2, 5). That distinguished it from *shekar* (Gk., *sikera* [**liquor**]), which was not diluted. Mixing *yayin* with drinking water also helped disinfect the water by killing the harmful microorganisms that it might contain.

The Old Testament acknowledges that the Jews commonly drank wine, but it commands moderation and forbids drunkenness. Proverbs 20:1 warns, "Wine is a mocker, strong drink a brawler, and whoever is intoxicated by it is not wise" (cf. 21:17; 23:20, 29–35). The prophet Amos pronounced God's judgment on the abuse of wine (2:8; 6:6–7) but later revealed the blessings associated with its proper use (9:13–14).

The New Testament perspective on wine is similar to that of the Old Testament. Jesus, in His first miracle, changed water into wine at a wedding in Cana (John 2:11). Because it was created by the Son of God, it was the best wine the people had ever drunk (cf. vv. 6–10). That the wine was normally fermented and thus capable of causing drunkenness seems evident from the verb translated "drunk freely" in 2:10. This wine created by Jesus did not come from the normal process of fermentation and was the sweetest and freshest ever. (See the discussion of that verse in *John 1–11,* The MacArthur New Testament Commentary [Chicago: Moody, 2006], 82, and a full discussion of the issue of drinking wine in *Ephesians,* The MacArthur New Testament Commentary [Chicago: Moody, 1986], 229–44). Elsewhere the New Testament recognizes that fermented wine, when properly diluted, could be beneficial (just as the Old Testament had noted centuries earlier, [cf. Prov. 31:6]). The apostle Paul instructed Timothy, "No longer drink water exclusively, but use a little wine for the sake of your stomach and your frequent ailments" (1 Tim. 5:23). Paul's instruction would have helped protect Timothy from the harmful effects of drinking impure water, and was in keeping with the medicinal use of wine in the ancient world. However the New Testament, like the Old Testament, condemns drunkenness (Rom. 13:13; 1 Cor. 5:11; Eph. 5:18; 1 Peter 4:3). According to Proverbs 31:4, leaders were not to consume strong beverages. Similarly, New Testament elders and deacons were not to be fond of drinking (1 Tim. 3:3,8; Titus 1:7; cf. 2:3).

Abstention from wine and liquor was also a key element of the Nazirite vow (Num. 6:1–4), which may also explain why John refrained from them. The Nazirite vow was usually temporary, although Samson (Judg. 16:17) and Samuel (1 Sam. 1:11) were Nazirites all their lives. Whether John also was a lifelong Nazirite is not clear from the gospel accounts of his life.

John's outward consecration would flow from his inner spiritual empowerment in an unparalleled way. Gabriel promised that **he** [would] **be filled with the Holy Spirit while yet in his mother's womb.** From conception, John's entire life would be lived under the influence, control, and power of the **Holy Spirit,** dominated by His will. That will, of course, is specifically described and expressed in the Word of God (Ps. 119:105; 2 Tim. 3:16). The filling of the Spirit is essential for sanctification (1 Cor. 6:11; 2 Thess. 2:13; 1 Peter 1:2), and effective ministry (Acts 1:8). In the case of John the Baptist, the Spirit's work in his life began while he was **yet in his mother's womb.** Luke 1:41 illustrates that reality, noting that "when Elizabeth heard Mary's greeting, the baby [John] leaped in her womb; and Elizabeth was filled with the Holy Spirit." (The Spirit's filling of John in the womb clearly indicates that the fetus is a person and that life begins at conception. That argues strongly for the sanctity of life and against abortion [cf. Ex. 21:22–25; Ps. 139:13–16].)

John's being set apart by God while still in his mother's womb is reminiscent of Jeremiah, who wrote concerning his own calling, "The word of the Lord came to me saying,'Before I formed you in the womb I knew you, and before you were born I consecrated you; I have appointed you a prophet to the nations'" (Jer. 1:4–5).That was also true of Paul, who testified, "God, who had set me apart even from my mother's womb and called me through His grace, was pleased to reveal His Son in me so that I might preach Him among the Gentiles" (Gal. 1:15–16). Those verses underscore God's sovereign choice of His servants to salvation, sanctification, and service (cf.John 15:16).

JOHN'S PRIVILEGED CALLING

It is he who will go as a forerunner before Him in the spirit and power of Elijah, (1:17a)

This is the epitome of John's greatness. It came not because he was more holy than all others, but because he had a calling more noble than anyone else—to be the **forerunner** of the Messiah, the most privileged assignment any man could receive. John was a "man sent from God" (John 1:6), who "testified about [Jesus] and cried out, saying,'This was He of whom I said,"He who comes after me has a higher rank than I, for He existed before me"'" (1:15).John was "a voice of one crying in the wilderness,'Make straight the way of the Lord,' as Isaiah the prophet said" (1:23).When he "saw Jesus coming to him [John] said,'Behold, the Lamb of God who takes away the sin of the world!'" (1:29). It was his unequalled privilege to be the prophet who would at last identify the Messiah as having arrived.

In his role as forerunner, John would go **before** Jesus Christ **in the spirit and power of Elijah.** That statement is significant because the Jews believed that God would send a messenger before the Day of the Lord judgment and the Messiah's coming to set up His kingdom (Mal. 3:1).The closing promise of the Old Testament identified that messenger as Elijah:

> Behold, I am going to send you Elijah the prophet before the coming of the great and terrible day of the Lord. He will restore the hearts of the fathers to their children and the hearts of the children to their fathers, so that I will not come and smite the land with a curse. (Mal. 4:5–6)

Like Elijah (1 Kings 18:17–18), John faithfully, powerfully, boldly, uncompromisingly proclaimed divine truth (Matt. 3:7–11).That caused some to wonder if he might in fact be Elijah (John 1:21).But John squashed such speculation, replying to those who questioned him simply, "No" (v. 21). However, in Matthew 11:13–14, Jesus said, "For all the prophets and the Law prophesied until John. And if you are willing to accept it, John himself is Elijah who was to come." The obvious question that arises is, Was John Elijah? He was not literally Elijah, as his blunt denial in John 1:21 indicates. But if the Jews had been willing to accept Jesus as their Messiah, the Day of the Lord and the kingdom would have come then, and John would have been the fulfillment of Malachi's prophecy. Therefore, Gabriel's words are to be understood in a figurative sense; John was not actually Elijah or the final Elijah of Malachi's prophecy (cf. Matt. 17:10–13). Instead, he came **in the spirit and power of Elijah;** like the great Old Testament prophet, he would fearlessly and faithfully proclaim divine truth in the face of ruthless opposition (Matt. 4:12; 14:1–10; cf. 1 Kings 17:1; 21:17–29).

That the majority of the people of Israel rejected John the Baptist's message about Jesus means there must also be a future fulfillment of Malachi's prophecy, "before the coming of the great and terrible day of the Lord" (4:5). Before Christ returns to establish His earthly kingdom (Rev. 19:10–20:6), Elijah or another Elijah-like prophet will announce His arrival (perhaps one of the two witnesses described in Revelation 11).

JOHN'S POWERFUL CONTRIBUTION

**And he will turn many of the sons of Israel back to the Lord their God . . . to turn the hearts of the fathers back to the children, and the disobedient to the attitude of the righteous, so as to make ready a people prepared for the Lord." ** (1:16, 17b)

John's preaching was to have a powerful impact, turning the hearts of **many of the sons of Israel back to the Lord their God** (Matt. 3:1–6). The word rendered **turn . . . back** is a form of the verb *epistrephō,* used frequently in the New Testament in reference to conversion (cf. Matt. 13:15; Mark 4:12; Acts 3:19; 11:21; 14:15; 15:19; 28:27; 1 Thess. 1:9; James 5:19–20). John's preaching would call the children of Israel back from their disobedience, back from their apostasy, back from their rebellion, back from their sin, back from their self-righteousness to **the Lord their God.** Significantly, the phrase "the Lord their God" is the antecedent of "Him" (Jesus Christ) in verse 17, identifying Christ as God.

Later, at the time of John's circumcision, his father, Zacharias, prophesied of him, "And you, child, will be called the prophet of the Most High; for you will go on before the Lord to prepare His ways; to give to His people the knowledge of salvation" (1:76–77). He would proclaim the gospel, the good news of God's grace (Rom. 3:24; Eph. 2:5, 8), mercy (Isa. 55:7; Joel 2:13; Luke 1:50; Titus 3:5), and forgiveness of sins (Rom. 4:6–8; Eph. 1:7; Heb. 9:22) accomplished through the coming Messiah, the fullest expression of the "tender mercy of our God" (1:78).

Inseparably associated with his call for a return to righteousness, John would preach a message of repentance (Matt. 3:2; Mark 1:4), one result of which would be **to turn the hearts of the fathers back to the children** (cf. Mal. 4:6). His message would result in the repentance and conversion of entire families (cf. John 4:53; Acts 10:30–48; 16:34). Parents and children would repent of their sins, be converted, and return to God through faith in Messiah, resulting in family members being reconciled.

Describing conversion, Gabriel declared that John's preaching would turn **the disobedient to the attitude of the righteous.** The word translated **disobedient** (*apeithēs*) denotes someone who will not be persuaded, who stubbornly refuses to believe and obey the truth (John 3:36; Rom. 2:8; 11:30,31; 1 Peter 2:8; 3:1,20). John's preaching would confront obstinate, hard-hearted sinners and transform their **attitude** (*phronēsis*, ["mind-set," "understanding"]) into one of righteousness. The result of John's ministry would be to **make ready a people prepared for the Lord,** whose repentant and believing hearts were ready to receive the Messiah (cf. John 7:31; 10:40–42).

After extolling John as the greatest man who had lived up to that time, Jesus made the shocking statement that he "who is least in the kingdom of God is greater than he" (Matt. 11:11). True spiritual greatness comes not from the tasks we do, but from the life we possess as a gift from God. John's earthly greatness lay in the fact that he was assigned the greatest task that any man had ever been given—to identify the Messiah. But as great as John was in this calling, the least person in God's kingdom is greater, because the nature of spiritual greatness far exceeds the human efforts of ministry. Spiritual life is forever. Because he, too, belonged to the kingdom, John the Baptist shares that greatness with all other believers (cf. Matt. 20:16)—all the redeemed enjoy the same glorious honor of eternal life.

In Christ all possess the same divine life, capable of producing the same high quality of character and exhibiting the same high level of spiritual commitment. All have the same privilege of being filled with and empowered by the Holy Spirit to preach Christ. Like John, believers are commissioned to the same task, to proclaim repentance (Matt. 28:18–20), and be ambassadors of reconciliation (2 Cor. 5:19–20), urging people to turn to God through saving faith in the Lord Jesus Christ and His substitionary death (Mark 10:45; Rom. 5:8; 1 Peter 3:18). It is by doing so that they share John's greatness.

The Divine Announcement to Mary (Luke 1:26–33)

4

Now in the sixth month the angel Gabriel was sent from God to a city in Galilee called Nazareth, to a virgin engaged to a man whose name was Joseph, of the descendants of David; and the virgin's name was Mary. And coming in, he said to her, "Greetings, favored one! The Lord is with you." But she was very perplexed at this statement, and kept pondering what kind of salutation this was. The angel said to her, "Do not be afraid, Mary; for you have found favor with God. And behold, you will conceive in your womb and bear a son, and you shall name Him Jesus. He will be great and will be called the Son of the Most High; and the Lord God will give Him the throne of His father David; and He will reign over the house of Jacob forever, and His kingdom will have no end." (1:26–33)

Christmas is arguably the most widely celebrated of all the world's holidays, involving more people and nations than any other. But at the same time, it is perhaps the most misunderstood of all the major holidays. Other holidays honor famous people or commemorate significant historical events (as, for example, Presidents' Day, Independence Day, and Veterans' Day do in the United States). Christmas, however,

honors a divine person and remembers a divine event; it does not celebrate human achievement, but divine accomplishment. Santa Claus,
crowded shopping malls, office parties, alcohol consumption, gift giving,
holiday decorations, and family get-togethers do not reflect the true
meaning of Christmas. There is nothing man-made about the Christmas
story. It is the most miraculous, compelling narrative in history, as the Holy
Spirit relates the dramatic story of Jesus Christ's birth. Those who truly
celebrate Christmas do so by remembering the profound reality that
God sent His only begotten Son to die for the sins of all who put their
faith in Him.

Although the most complete accounts of Christ's birth appear in
the gospels of Matthew and Luke (Matt. 1:18–2:12; Luke 1:26–2:20), they
are not the first biblical references to the coming of God the Son. After
Adam and Eve's disobedience plunged the human race into sin, God
promised that one called the seed of the woman would come (Gen.
3:15) to "destroy the works of the devil" (1 John 3:8). In his prophecy concerning his sons, Jacob said about Judah, "The scepter shall not depart
from Judah, nor the ruler's staff from between his feet, until Shiloh (the
one to whom it belongs; i.e., the Messiah, the true King, the Lion of the
tribe of Judah [Rev. 5:5]) comes, and to him shall be the obedience of
the peoples" (Gen. 49:10). Moses had in mind the future coming of Messiah when he told the people of Israel,

> The Lord your God will raise up for you a prophet like me from among
> you, from your countrymen, you shall listen to him. This is according to
> all that you asked of the Lord your God in Horeb on the day of the
> assembly, saying, "Let me not hear again the voice of the Lord my God,
> let me not see this great fire anymore, or I will die." The Lord said to me,
> "They have spoken well. I will raise up a prophet from among their
> countrymen like you, and I will put My words in his mouth, and he shall
> speak to them all that I command him." (Deut. 18:15–18; cf. Acts 3:22)

Psalm 2:6–9 records God's promise that His Son, the Messiah, would
come to rule the world:

> "But as for Me, I have installed My King upon Zion, My holy mountain."
> "I will surely tell of the decree of the Lord: He said to Me, 'You are My
> Son, today I have begotten You. Ask of Me, and I will surely give the
> nations as Your inheritance, and the very ends of the earth as Your pos-
> session. You shall break them with a rod of iron, You shall shatter them
> like earthenware.'"

Isaiah predicted that "a virgin will be with child and bear a son, and she will call His name Immanuel" (Isa. 7:14). He further wrote concerning this amazing child,

> The government will rest on His shoulders; and His name will be called Wonderful Counselor, Mighty God, Eternal Father, Prince of Peace. There will be no end to the increase of His government or of peace, on the throne of David and over his kingdom, to establish it and to uphold it with justice and righteousness from then on and forevermore. (9:6–7)

Isaiah also predicted in detail Messiah's sacrificial death as a substitute for the sins of His people (52:13–53:12); Daniel predicted the time of His coming (Dan. 9:25–26); Micah the place of His birth (Mic. 5:2). The Old Testament is replete with other prophecies concerning His life and ministry (e.g., Pss. 40:7–8; 110:1, 4; 118:22, 26; Isa. 8:14; 11:2, 10; 28:16; 61:1–2; Jer. 23:5; Zech. 9:9; 12:10; 13:7), so much so that on the road to Emmaus the risen Christ chided His followers for failing to recognize their significance and applicability to Him:

> "O foolish men and slow of heart to believe in all that the prophets have spoken! Was it not necessary for the Christ to suffer these things and to enter into His glory?" Then beginning with Moses and with all the prophets, He explained to them the things concerning Himself in all the Scriptures. (Luke 24:25–27; cf. vv. 44–47)

The promise of a Savior, for centuries the hope of the faithful, believing remnant of Israel, continued its realization with Gabriel's second appearance, this time to a young woman. Luke's simple, unadorned, unembellished account of Gabriel's announcement to Mary emphasizes the divine character of Christ's birth. It reveals the divine messenger, the divine choice, the divine blessing, and the divine child.

THE DIVINE MESSENGER

Now in the sixth month the angel Gabriel was sent from God to a city in Galilee called Nazareth, (1:26)

As noted in the chapter 2 of this volume, Gabriel's appearance to Zacharias had broken four centuries of revelatory silence. Astonishingly, just a short while later **in the sixth month** (of Elizabeth's pregnancy) **the angel Gabriel was** once again **sent from God** with a revelation that would be the most significant birth announcement the world has ever known, heralding the most monumentally significant event in human history—the birth of the only Savior, the Lord Jesus Christ.

Gabriel delivered this crucial message from God not to Jerusalem as might be expected, but **to a city in Galilee called Nazareth.** To call **Nazareth** a **city** (as the NASB translation does) is somewhat misleading. Nazareth was by no stretch of the imagination a city in the modern sense of the word; it was actually a small village of only a few hundred people. (The Greek word translated **city** actually refers to a population center as opposed to a rural area, regardless of size.) For the benefit of his Gentile readers, who may not have been familiar with Palestinian geography, Luke noted that Nazareth was in **Galilee,** about seventy-five to one hundred miles north of Jerusalem.

So obscure and insignificant was this tiny hamlet that it is not even mentioned in the Old Testament, the Talmud, or the writings of Josephus. (Despite the claims of some skeptics, however, archaeological evidence proves that Nazareth did in fact exist in Jesus' day [cf. E. M. Blaiklock and R. K. Harrison, eds., *The New International Dictionary of Biblical Archaeology* (Grand Rapids, Zondervan, 1983) s.v., "Nazareth"; Lee Strobel, *The Case for Christ* (Grand Rapids: Zondervan, 1998), 102–103].) Nazareth was not on any of the major trade routes; all the important roads bypassed it. It was well off the beaten path, far from the important centers of Jewish culture and religion. Moreover, Galilee, where Nazareth was located, was known as "Galilee of the Gentiles" (Isa. 9:1; Matt. 4:15) because of its proximity to Gentile regions. God's choice of Nazareth to be Jesus' birthplace reveals that He is the Savior of the world, not of the powerful and elite of one nation only, but of all "those who are the called, both Jews and Greeks" (1 Cor. 1:24; cf. Isa. 11:10; 42:6; Luke 2:32; Acts 10:34–35; 13:48–49; Rom. 15:9–12).

THE DIVINE CHOICE

to a virgin engaged to a man whose name was Joseph, of the descendants of David; and the virgin's name was Mary. (1:27)

The angelic announcement of John the Baptist's birth came to an elderly priest in the temple at Jerusalem (1:11–13), but the announcement of Jesus' miraculous birth came to a young girl in a small, insignificant village.

She is described first of all as a **virgin.** *Parthenos* (**virgin**) refers to a person who has never had sexual relations, and would never be used to describe a married woman. In Jewish practice, girls were usually **engaged** at the age of twelve or thirteen and married at the end of a one-year betrothal period. The betrothal, arranged by the parents, was a more binding legal arrangement than a modern engagement. Only death or divorce could sever the contract, and the couple could be referred to as husband and wife. If her betrothed husband died, the girl would be considered a widow. The couple did not live together or have sexual relations during the betrothal period. During that year the girl was to prove her faithfulness and purity, and the boy was to prepare a home for his bride-to-be. When the year was up there was a seven-day wedding feast (cf. Matt. 25:1–13; John 2:1–11), after which the couple began their life together as husband and wife. Only then was the marriage consummated.

This particular virgin was betrothed **to a man whose name was Joseph.** Though just an ordinary carpenter, he was by lineage one **of the descendants of David,** Israel's greatest king, from whose loins the Messiah would come (2 Sam. 7:12, 16; Ps. 89:35–36; Jer. 23:5; Matt. 22:42; Mark 10:47; Acts 2:30; 13:23; Rom. 1:3). Matthew's genealogy of Christ traces His ancestry through Joseph (1:1–17), showing that He descended from David, thus Jesus is also "the son of David" (Matt. 1:1). Although Joseph was not Jesus' natural father, his adoption of Jesus made Him legally part of David's lineage. The genealogy in Matthew thus establishes Christ's claim to the throne of David as Joseph's legal heir.

Luke simply reports that the virgin's name was **Mary.** Unlike the commendation of Zacharias and Elizabeth that he recorded earlier (1:6), Luke ascribed nothing to Mary except her status as a virgin; he added nothing that would set her apart as a noteworthy young woman. Though she must have been righteous and obedient (as her testimony in vv. 46–55 proves), perhaps the Holy Spirit was avoiding anything that might make the Romish "Mary cult" any worse, if that were possible.

Like Joseph, Mary also traced her ancestry back to David; as noted in the exposition of 3:23–38 in chapter 21 of this volume, Luke's genealogy of Jesus records His ancestry through His mother. Thus Jesus inherited from His adoptive father, Joseph, the legal right to David's throne, while His physical descent from David came from His mother, Mary. In every legitimate sense—both legally and physically—Jesus Christ was the Son of David and born to be Israel's true King.

THE DIVINE BLESSING

And coming in, he said to her, "Greetings, favored one! The Lord is with you." But she was very perplexed at this statement, and kept pondering what kind of salutation this was. The angel said to her, "Do not be afraid, Mary; for you have found favor with God." (1:28–30)

The phrase **coming in** clearly implies that Mary was in her house, apparently alone, when Gabriel appeared. She was undoubtedly doing the normal domestic chores of a twelve- or thirteen-year-old Jewish girl. The angel's first word to her was the common, everyday salutation **"Greetings,"** or "Hello." Since Zacharias panicked when Gabriel appeared to him (cf. the discussion of Gabriel's appearance to Zacharias in chapter 2 of this volume), his low-key introduction and immediate statement of blessing was likely intended to calm and reassure Mary.

By addressing her as **favored one,** Gabriel indicated that Mary had nothing to fear, but was to become the recipient of God's grace. There was nothing intrinsically worthy about her that set her above other believers, as if she was perfectly holy; like all people, she was a sinner (cf. Job 25:4; Ps. 14:1–3; Eccles. 7:20; Isa. 53:6; Rom. 3:12, 23) in need of God's grace (Acts 15:11; 18:27; Rom. 3:24; 5:15, 17; Eph. 1:7; 2:5, 8; 2 Tim. 1:9; Titus 3:7). The salutation has been confiscated to form the basis of the familiar Roman Catholic prayer known as the Ave Maria ("Hail Mary"). The erroneous premise of that prayer, based on the Latin Vulgate's rendering of **favored one** as *gratia plena* ("full of grace"), is that Mary has been granted and possesses fullness of grace, which she then bestows on others. In his encyclical *Ad Diem Illum Laetissimum,* Pope Pius X, in a bizarre distortion of truth, has called Mary not the recipient of grace, but the "Dispensatrix [dispenser] of all the gifts that Our Savior purchased for us by His Death and by His Blood; the supreme Minister of the distribution of graces; the distributor . . . of the treasures of His merits." Pope Leo XIII agreed, declaring in his encyclical *Octobri Mense* that "Mary is the intermediary through whom is distributed unto us this immense treasure of mercies gathered by God." Pope Pius IX's encyclical *Ineffabilis Deus* cited the Catholic Church's belief that Mary is "the seat of all divine graces . . . adorned with all gifts of the Holy Spirit . . . an almost infinite treasury, an inexhaustible abyss of these gifts." Summing up the Catholic view that Mary is the mediator of all graces Ludwig Ott writes, "Since Mary's Assumption into Heaven no grace is conferred on man without her actual intercessory co-operation" (*Fundamentals of Catholic Dogma* [St. Louis: B. Herder, 1954], 209).

That false, unbiblical view of Mary is an integral part of the Roman Church's practice of Mariolatry (the veneration and worship of Mary), which blasphemes the Lord Jesus by worshiping another. In reality Mary was a humble, redeemed sinner. She was not sinless from her conception until her bodily assumption into heaven, as Catholic dogma maintains, since as Jesus Himself declared, "No one is good except God alone" (Luke 18:19; cf. Rom. 3:10). Nor is Mary the co-redeemer of the human race, since sinners are "justified as a gift by His grace through the redemption which is in Christ Jesus" (Rom. 3:24; cf. 1 Cor. 1:30; Eph. 1:7; Col.

1:13–14; Heb. 9:12). She does not hear and answer prayers or intercede for anyone, since there is "one mediator ... between God and men, the man Christ Jesus" (1 Tim. 2:5). The teaching of Roman Catholicism that "there is no surer or more direct road than by Mary for uniting all mankind in Christ and obtaining through Him the perfect adoption of sons, that we may be holy and immaculate in the sight of God" (Pope Pius X, *Ad Diem Illum Laetissimum*) is utterly false and blasphemous. The exalted, quasi-deified Mary of Roman Catholic dogma is far removed from the humble, unassuming "bondslave of the Lord" (Luke 1:38) revealed in Scripture. Gabriel's pronouncement to Mary, **"the Lord is with you,"** speaks of God's enabling of her (cf. Judg. 6:12). It reinforces the truth that Mary was a recipient of God's grace, not the dispenser of it to others. Only God gives grace to sinners, as Scripture indicates continually (cf. Rom. 3:24; 1 Cor. 1:4; Eph. 2:8, and the repeated use of the phrase "the grace of God").

Realizing that she was an unworthy sinner (in verse 47, she called God her Savior, and only sinners need a Savior), Mary **was very perplexed at** Gabriel's **statement, and kept pondering what kind of salutation this was.** It was not just his appearing to her that caused Mary's consternation, but what he said to her. **Very perplexed** translates a form of the verb *diatarassomai* ("greatly troubled, disturbed, or confused"), a more intense form of the verb translated "troubled" in verse 12, where it described Zacharias's reaction to Gabriel's appearance. Mary was perplexed because she knew that she was a sinner, and did not understand why God had favored her. But Mary's genuine humility manifested her true righteousness (cf. Pss. 34:2; 138:6; Prov. 3:34; Isa. 66:2; Matt. 18:4; 20:26–28; Luke 14:11; James 4:6). All genuinely righteous people are distressed and terrified in God's presence (or, as in this case, one of His holy angels), because they are acutely aware of their sin (cf. the reactions of Isaiah [Isa. 6:5] and Peter [Luke 5:8]). Gabriel's appearance and greeting unnerved Mary; nothing in her brief life could have prepared her for this astonishing event.

Seeking to calm her, Gabriel said to the frightened girl, **"Do not be afraid, Mary."** His explanation, **for you have found favor with God,** reassured Mary that she had nothing to fear; Gabriel had come to her with a message of blessing, not judgment. Like Noah, Mary had "found favor in the eyes of the Lord" (Gen. 6:8). God had sovereignly chosen to use her to help carry out His redemptive purposes. The issue was not her merit or worthiness, but God's sovereign grace which, like all His ways, is ultimately beyond human understanding (cf. Deut. 29:29; Ps. 36:6).

THE DIVINE CHILD

"And behold, you will conceive in your womb and bear a son, and you shall name Him Jesus. He will be great and will be called the Son of the Most High; and the Lord God will give Him the throne of His father David; and He will reign over the house of Jacob forever, and His kingdom will have no end." (1:31–33)

After Gabriel's greeting, Mary for the first time heard what the gracious work of God in her life was going to be. If his greeting had perplexed her, she must have been dumfounded at what he said next. Mary knew of only one way that she could **conceive** a **son**—through sexual relations with a man. She also knew that she had not had such relations, as her question in verse 34, "How can this be, since I am a virgin?" indicates. The concept of a pregnant virgin was utterly inconceivable to her; an impossibility, a contradiction in terms like a married bachelor, or a square circle.

Nevertheless Gabriel's stunning announcement, in words fulfilling Isaiah's prophecy of Messiah's virgin birth (Isa. 7:14; cf. Matt. 1:23), was that Mary without the seed from a man would **conceive in** [her] **womb and bear a son.** That staggering promise of a divine miracle was far beyond her understanding or any human comprehension.

Then, with breathtaking brevity, in one vast, glorious revelation Gabriel succinctly summarized the entire ministry of the Lord Jesus Christ: His saving work, righteous life, deity, resurrection, ascension, glorious return, and kingdom rule. He began with the command to **name Him Jesus,** the name that was the Greek form of the common Hebrew name *Yeshua* ("Yahweh saves"), which introduced the reality of Messiah's saving work. God is a saving God, and it was "to seek and to save that which was lost" (Luke 19:10; cf. 2:11, 30, 38; Matt. 1:21; 1 Tim. 1:15; cf. John 12:27; Rom. 8:3–4; 2 Cor. 8:9) that Jesus Christ came into the world. His saving work is the central theme of the New Testament (cf. Matt. 11:28–30; John 14:6; Acts 4:12; 5:31; 13:23, 38; Rom. 5:1–2; 2 Cor. 5:21; Heb. 7:25; Rev. 1:5). In obedience to the angel's command, Mary and Joseph named their newborn Son Jesus (Luke 2:21).

Gabriel then told Mary that her Son Jesus **will be great** (*megas*). Once again the understatement is striking. But all the synonyms that could be added, such as extraordinary, splendid, magnificent, noble, distinguished, powerful, or eminent, would be equally inadequate. It beggars human language to do justice to the majestic, glorious person of the Lord Jesus Christ. Adjectives and superlatives are not used because they are superfluous. His life will define **great.** And worshiping believers are always aware that language is inadequate to express the honor and glory of His person.

Unlike John the Baptist, whose greatness was qualified as being in God's sight (1:15), Jesus' greatness is unqualified. He is great in and of Himself; His greatness is intrinsic to His very nature as God, and is not derived from any source outside of Himself. Jesus Christ is "far above all rule and authority and power and dominion, and every name that is named, not only in this age but also in the one to come" (Eph. 1:21).

The true measure of Christ's greatness may be seen in His sharing of God's glory—of which God declared, "I will not give My glory to another" (Isa. 42:8). Referring to Isaiah's vision of God's majesty and glory (Isa. 6:1–10), the apostle John wrote, "These things Isaiah said because he saw His [Christ's] glory, and he spoke of Him" (John 12:41). John could say that when Isaiah viewed God's glory in the temple, he saw the glory of Christ, because He shares the Father's glory. That glory, though veiled in His human flesh, was nonetheless manifested during Christ's earthly life. John wrote, "The Word became flesh, and dwelt among us, and we saw His glory, glory as of the only begotten from the Father, full of grace and truth" (1:14). And for a brief moment on the Mount of Transfiguration, Jesus' majestic glory was unveiled to Peter, James, and John (Matt. 17:1–8).

Christ possesses the glory of God because as **the Son of the Most High** (cf. 1:35, 76; 6:35; Acts 7:48) He possesses the nature of God. **Most High** (*hupsistos*) is the Greek equivalent of the frequently used Old Testament title for God *El Elyon* (Gen. 14:18–20; Deut. 32:8; 2 Sam. 22:14; Pss. 7:17; 9:2; 21:7; 46:4; 47:2; Isa. 14:14; Lam. 3:35, 38; Dan. 4:17, 24; 5:18, 21). It is a title that refers to His position as the supreme sovereign ruler. To identify Jesus as **the Son of the Most High** is to affirm that He is of the same essence as God. In the words of the writer of Hebrews, "He [Jesus] is the radiance of His [God's] glory and the exact representation of His nature" (Heb. 1:3; cf. Matt. 1:23; John 10:30; Phil. 2:6–9; Col. 2:9).

This amazing Child would be God incarnate, perfectly righteous in everything He thought, said, and did. He would die as a sinless sacrifice, providing Himself as a substitute for sinners, offering His atoning death to save them from their sins. But that is not the end of the story. He would not remain dead, but would rise to reign. The culmination of Christ's work will come when **the Lord God** gives **Him the throne of His father David; and He will reign over the house of Jacob forever, and His kingdom will have no end.** As noted above, the Lord Jesus Christ was the rightful heir to **the throne of His father David** through His legal father, Joseph. Gabriel's words emphasize both the Jewish character of Christ's kingdom, since He will rule **over the house of Jacob** (Isa. 65:17–19; Zeph. 3:11–13; Zech. 14:16–21, as well as the rest of mankind; cf. Dan. 7:14, 27), and its eternality, since **His kingdom will have no end** (Rev. 11:15).

The promised kingdom is not limited to Christ's present spiritual reign, as amillennialists advocate. The Bible teaches that Satan will be bound during the millennium (Rev. 20:1–3); yet now, as Peter warned, he "prowls around like a roaring lion, seeking someone to devour" (1 Peter 5:8). Therefore, the present age cannot be the millennium. Nor does the church usher in the millennial kingdom, at the end of which Christ returns, as postmillennialists postulate. Jesus Himself posed the rhetorical question, "When the Son of Man comes, will He find faith on the earth?" (Luke 18:8). (For a further discussion of millennial views, see *Revelation 12–22*, The MacArthur New Testament Commentary [Chicago: Moody, 2000], 228–33).

The Lord Jesus Christ clearly did not establish His kingdom at His first coming. As John noted in the prologue to his gospel, "He came to His own [Israel], and those who were His own did not receive Him" (John 1:11; cf. 11:53; Matt. 9:34; 12:14; 21:37–43; Mark 6:3; 16:14; 1 Thess. 2:14–16). The Jewish people (particularly their leaders), "recognizing neither Him nor the utterances of the prophets which are read every Sabbath, fulfilled these by condemning Him. And though they found no ground for putting Him to death, they asked Pilate that He be executed" (Acts 13:27–28; cf. 2:23; 7:52; Matt. 27:22–23; Luke 23:13–24; John 19:12–16).

Jesus Christ rules spiritually in the heart of every believer (cf. Col. 1:13), and that spiritual rule will last forever because salvation is forever. But that does not preclude the future literal, earthly, millennial kingdom. During that blessed time, Jesus Christ, "the root and the descendant of David" (Rev. 22:16; cf. Isa. 11:1, 10; Matt. 1:1; Rom. 15:12), the Lion of the tribe of Judah (Rev. 5:5), will sit on His glorious throne, judging the nations with a rod of iron (Ps. 2:9; Rev. 12:5; 19:15) for a thousand years (Rev. 20:4–5). At the end of that time, God will uncreate the universe and create a new heaven and earth that will last for all eternity. The apostle Paul wrote,

> Then comes the end, when He hands over the kingdom to the God and Father, when He has abolished all rule and all authority and power. For He must reign until He has put all His enemies under His feet. The last enemy that will be abolished is death. For He has put all things in subjection under His feet. But when He says, "All things are put in subjection," it is evident that He is excepted who put all things in subjection to Him. When all things are subjected to Him, then the Son Himself also will be subjected to the One who subjected all things to Him, so that God may be all in all. (1 Cor. 15:24–28)

Gabriel's message to Mary introduces the pivotal point in redemptive history. How people respond to the Child of whom Gabriel spoke will determine their eternal destiny. As Simeon would later say to Mary, "Behold, this Child is appointed for the fall and rise of many in

Israel" (Luke 2:34), and the rest of the world as well. And as the Child Himself would warn, "Unless you believe that I am He, you will die in your sins" (John 8:24), since "there is salvation in no one else; for there is no other name under heaven that has been given among men by which we must be saved" (Acts 4:12).

The Virgin Birth: A Divine Miracle (Luke 1:34–38)

5

Mary said to the angel, "How can this be, since I am a virgin?" The angel answered and said to her, "The Holy Spirit will come upon you, and the power of the Most High will overshadow you; and for that reason the holy Child shall be called the Son of God. And behold, even your relative Elizabeth has also conceived a son in her old age; and she who was called barren is now in her sixth month. For nothing will be impossible with God." And Mary said, "Behold, the bondslave of the Lord; may it be done to me according to your word." And the angel departed from her. (1:34–38)

History has recorded some amazing births. Born near a small town in Ontario, Canada, on May 28, 1934, the Dionne sisters became the first known set of quintuplets to survive infancy. For the first decade of their lives they were Canada's biggest tourist attraction—bigger even than Niagara Falls—generating several hundred million dollars in tourist revenue. January 11, 1974, saw the birth of the Rosenkowitz sextuplets, the first recorded set of sextuplets to have survived to adulthood, in Cape Town, South Africa. The seven children born to Bobbi and Kenny McCaughey of Des Moines, Iowa, on November 19, 1997, are the first set of septuplets to survive infancy. Another notable birth involved only one child. On July 25, 1978, Louise Brown was born in Oldham, England. What was noteworthy about her, however, was not her birth, but the manner of her conception: she was the world's first "test-tube baby," conceived by means of in vitro fertilization. And in 2008 a single woman gave birth to octuplets by means of in vitro fertilization. All are currently alive.

The Bible also records some amazing births. Isaac's birth was nothing short of miraculous, since his father (Abraham) was one hundred years old and his mother (Sarah) was ninety years old and barren (Rom. 4:19). The Lord also miraculously opened the womb of Manoah's wife (Judg. 13:2), and she gave birth to Samson. Similarly, God allowed Hannah, who had also been barren (1 Sam. 1:2, 5) to become pregnant with Samuel. Only a few months before Gabriel's appearance to Mary, the Lord enabled an elderly, barren couple, Zacharias and Elizabeth, to conceive a child (Luke 1:7, 24). That child, John the Baptist, was called by God to be the forerunner of the Messiah, and was the greatest man who had ever lived up to his time (Matt. 11:11).

But the most remarkable birth of all was that of the Lord Jesus Christ. He was God the Son, the second person of the Trinity, incarnate; the eternal "Word [who] became flesh, and dwelt among us" (John 1:14); supernaturally conceived in a virgin without a human father. Jesus' virgin conception cannot be explained away as an example of parthenogenesis (lit., "virgin creation" or "generation"), which is found in some lower forms of life. Parthenogenesis in humans, even if it were biologically possible, could only result genetically in a female child, since women do not have the Y chromosome necessary to produce a male child.

The virgin birth of Jesus Christ is foundational to Christianity, since it is the only way to explain how He could be the God-man. To deny the virgin birth, then, is to deny the biblical truth that Jesus Christ is both God (cf. John 1:1; 10:30; 20:28; Rom. 9:5; Phil. 2:6; Col. 2:9; Titus 2:13; Heb. 1:8; 2 Peter 1:2; 1 John 5:20) and man (cf. John 1:14; Rom. 1:3; Gal. 4:4; Phil. 2:7–8; 1 Tim. 2:5; Heb. 2:14; 1 John 4:2; 2 John 7), and to affirm another, false Jesus (2 Cor. 11:4). For if Jesus had a human father, He was just a man. And if He was just a man, He could not be the Savior. And if Jesus is not the Savior, there is no gospel, no salvation, no resurrection, no hope beyond this life. As Paul notes, "If Christ has not been raised, your faith is worthless; you are still in your sins. . . . If we have hoped in Christ in this life only, we are of all men most to be pitied" (1 Cor. 15:17, 19). We may as well "eat and drink, for tomorrow we die" (v. 32). The serious implications of viewing Jesus as a mere man led Paul to pronounce a curse on those who propagate that satanic lie (Gal. 1:8–9).

Highlighting the crucial, indispensable role of the doctrine of the virgin birth John M. Frame writes,

The consistency of this doctrine with other Christian truth is important to its usefulness and, indeed, to its credibility. For Matthew and Luke the chief importance of the event seems to be that it calls to mind (as a "sign," Isa. 7:14) the great OT promises of salvation through supernaturally born deliverers, while going far beyond them, showing that God's *final* deliverance has come. But one can also go beyond the specific concerns of Matthew and Luke and see that the virgin birth is fully consistent with the whole range of biblical doctrine. For example, the virgin birth is important because of: (1) The doctrine of Scripture. If Scripture errs here, then why should we trust its claims about other supernatural events, such as the resurrection? (2) The deity of Christ. While we cannot say dogmatically that God could enter the world only through a virgin birth, surely the incarnation is a supernatural event if it is anything. To eliminate the supernatural from this event is inevitably to compromise the divine dimension of it. (3) The humanity of Christ. This was the important thing to Ignatius and the 2d-century fathers. Jesus was *really* born; he *really* became one of us. (4) The nature of grace. The birth of Christ, in which the initiative and power are all of God, is an apt picture of God's saving grace in general of which it is a part. It teaches us that salvation is by God's act, not our human effort. The birth of Jesus is like our new birth, which is also by the Holy Spirit; it is a new creation (2 Cor. 5:17). ("Virgin Birth of Jesus," in *The Concise Evangelical Dictionary of Theology,* ed. Walter A. Elwell, abridged by Peter Toon [Grand Rapids: Baker, 1991], 540, emphasis in original.) (For a further discussion of the virgin birth's crucial doctrinal importance, see John MacArthur, *Nothing But the Truth* [Wheaton, Ill.: Crossway, 1999], 101–13, and *God in the Manger* [Nashville: W Publishing, 2001], 1–12.)

Though fully revealed in the New Testament, the virgin birth is foreshadowed in the Old. In Genesis 3:15, God declared that the seed of the woman (Christ) would crush Satan's head. Psalm 2 predicts that at a specific time ("today"; v. 7) the eternal second person of the Trinity would be born into the world. The only way for that to happen, as previously noted, would be through a virgin birth. Isaiah 7:14 records the startling prediction that "a virgin will be with child and bear a son, and she will call His name Immanuel" ("God with us" [Matt. 1:23]). Some translations render the Hebrew word *alma* ("virgin") "young woman." But the common, everyday occurrence of a young woman becoming pregnant in the normal manner could hardly constitute the sign from the Lord promised earlier in verse 14. Further, "There is no instance where it can be proved that *alma* designates a young woman who is not a virgin" (R. Laird Harris, Gleason L. Archer Jr., and Bruce K. Waltke, eds., *The Theological Wordbook of the Old Testament* [Chicago: Moody, 1980] s.v., "alma"). Noted Old Testament scholar Edward J. Young agrees: "We may confidently assert that the word 'almah is never employed of a married woman" (*The Book of Isaiah* [Grand Rapids: Eerdmans, 1985], 1:287). Matthew's inspired translation of Isaiah's prophecy places the issue beyond doubt; it translates *alma* using the Greek word *parthenos,* which can only mean "virgin" (Matt. 1:23; cf. 1 Cor. 7:28, 34, 36–38; 2 Cor. 11:2). The Septuagint (an ancient translation of the Old Testament into Greek) also uses *parthenos* to translate *alma.*).

Despite the virgin birth's solid biblical foundation, there have always been false teachers, purveyors of "doctrines of demons" (1 Tim. 4:1) who, for the purpose of rejecting the deity of Jesus, deny it. In John 8:41, the Jewish leaders scornfully said to Jesus, "We were not born of fornication," thus implying that He was. Later Jewish writings propagated the blasphemous lie that Jesus' real father was a Roman soldier who slept with Mary. Others throughout history have maintained that Jesus was the natural son of Joseph and Mary, ignoring the Bible's explicit statement that Joseph "kept [Mary] a virgin until she gave birth to a Son" (Matt. 1:25). The biblical evidence clearly gives the lie to any teaching that denies the virgin birth.

This passage may be summarized under five points: Mary's supplication, God's strategy, God's sign, God's sovereignty, and Mary's submission.

MARY'S SUPPLICATION

Mary said to the angel, "How can this be, since I am a virgin?" (1:34)

The astonishing announcement from an angel of God that she was to be the mother of the long-awaited Messiah (1:30–33) left Mary shaken and confused (cf. v. 29). Overwhelmed by the implications of his announcement, and wondering how it would be practically implemented, she asked Gabriel, **"How can this be, since I am a virgin?"** The thought of having a child without the impregnation of a man was inconceivable. But Mary's question did not reflect doubt or incredulity (unlike Zacharias's [1:18–20]); she believed what the angel told her, but did not understand how it could happen.

It must be remembered that miracles were extremely rare in history, as the record of the Old Testament shows. By Mary's day there had been no divine revelation or miracles for four centuries. No one had seen an angel during that time either, until Gabriel's appearance to Zacharias (which Mary probably did not know about since the angel had to tell her about Elizabeth's pregnancy [v. 36]) a few months earlier. Mary realized that the angel did not mean that she would become pregnant naturally, after she consummated her marriage to Joseph. She understood that he was saying she would become pregnant while she was still a virgin; her question was not an expression of doubt, but a request for an explanation of the means for that impossibility.

GOD'S STRATEGY

The angel answered and said to her, "The Holy Spirit will come upon you, and the power of the Most High will overshadow you; and for that reason the holy Child shall be called the Son of God. (1:35)

In response to Mary's request for clarification, Gabriel told **her, "The Holy Spirit will come upon you."** The Spirit plays a prominent role in Luke's narrative of the Lord's birth (1:15, 41, 67; 2:25–27), and would also be the power source throughout His earthly life and ministry (cf. 3:21–22; Matt. 3:13–17; John 1:32–34). That the Holy Spirit would be involved in the creative miracle of the conception of the God-man is not surprising, since He is God and was involved in the creation of the world. When "the earth was formless and void, and darkness was over the surface of the deep,... the Spirit of God was moving over the surface of the waters" (Gen. 1:2). The Holy Spirit, the original agent of creation, would again become an agent of creation, this time in Mary's womb. There is not the slightest suggestion in this text or anywhere else in Scripture of human sexual activity involved in the conception of the Lord Jesus Christ.

Restating the profound reality of the Spirit's involvement to underscore its significance, Gabriel said to Mary, **The power of the Most High will overshadow you.** The familiar Old Testament title **Most High** (Heb. *El Elyon*) depicts God as the sovereign, omnipotent ruler of heaven and earth. (See the exposition of 1:31–33 in the previous chapter of this volume.) The God who made and upholds the universe (Ps. 104:30; Col. 1:16–17) through His Spirit (Job 33:4) would create life in Mary's womb.

The verb translated **will overshadow** (*episkiazō*) is also used in the accounts of the transfiguration (Matt. 17:5; Mark 9:7; Luke 9:34) when the glory cloud descended on Peter, James, and John. It means "to surround," "to encompass," or in a metaphorical sense, "to influence." The creative influence of the Spirit of God would **overshadow** Mary to produce a child in her womb.

That divine creative miracle guaranteed that two things would be true of Mary's Son. First, He would be a **holy Child,** unlike any other infant ever born. Everyone who has ever lived, with the sole exception of the Lord Jesus Christ, has been born a sinner (Job 15:14; 25:4; Eccles. 7:20; Isa. 53:6; Rom. 5:12; Gal. 3:22; cf. Gen. 3:6–13). David illustrated that truth when he wrote,"I was brought forth in iniquity, and in sin my mother conceived me" (Ps. 51:5). He was not saying that he was an illegitimate child, but that from the time of his conception he was a sinner. But Christ has always been the sinless Son of God (2 Cor. 5:21; Heb. 7:26; 1 Peter 1:19; 2:22; 1 John 3:5; cf. John 8:46).

Some have erroneously suggested the reason that Jesus was sinless was that He had no human father. But there is no biblical evidence that the sin nature is passed on genetically only through the father. All men and women are born sinners because "in Adam all die" (1 Cor. 15:22), since "through the one man's [Adam's] disobedience the many were made sinners" (Rom. 5:19). In a manner beyond human comprehension, Jesus was fully human, yet completely sinless from conception. The explanation of how that could be is shrouded in the unfathomable mystery of the incarnation.

Jesus had to be the perfectly holy **Son of God** because His nature is that of the Holy One Himself, God the Father. That rich title is uniquely appropriate for Him, and Jesus Himself (22:70; cf. 2:49; 10:22), God the Father (3:22; 9:35), Satan (4:3, 9), the demons (4:41; 8:28), and Paul (Acts 9:20; 13:33) all applied it to Him. The title has profound implications concerning the person and work of the Lord Jesus Christ (cf. John 1:49; 3:18; Rom. 1:4; 1 John 5:20, and the exposition of 2:49 in chap. 16 of this volume). Here, however, the term is used in a more restricted sense, signifying that Jesus is by nature the Son of God manifested in human flesh. In the words of the writer of Hebrews, Christ "is the radiance of [God's] glory and the exact representation of His nature" (1:3; John 1:14; Phil. 2:6).

GOD'S SIGN

And behold, even your relative Elizabeth has also conceived a son in her old age; and she who was called barren is now in her sixth month. (1:36)

Though Mary did not explicitly ask for a sign to remove doubt, God graciously gave her one to strengthen her faith. That divine sign involved her older **relative Elizabeth.** *Sungenis* (**relative**) is a nonspecific term for a kinswoman or female relative, and the exact relationship between Mary and Elizabeth is not spelled out. According to Luke's record of her genealogy (3:23–38), Mary was a descendant of David (v. 31) and through him of Judah (v. 33). Elizabeth, on the other hand, was a descendant of Aaron (Luke 1:5), and through him of Levi (Num. 26:59). Hence Mary must have been related to Elizabeth through her mother.

The shocking news (introduced by the exclamation, **behold**), which Mary was undoubtedly hearing for the first time, was that her kinswoman had **conceived a son in her old age.** Mary was well aware that Elizabeth was barren and past childbearing age. She must have been amazed and overjoyed to hear that **she who was** scornfully, derisively **called barren** (cf. 1:25; Gen. 30:22–23; 1 Sam. 1:6) was **now in her sixth month** of pregnancy.

The miracle that occurred for Elizabeth was one of conception in old age, not the virgin conception that Mary would experience. Nevertheless, Elizabeth's conception was a sign from God to Mary that He was still able to perform miracles, that He could do the humanly impossible (cf. Jer. 32:17, 27; Matt. 19:26). God gave the sign, not because Mary doubted the angel's words, but to provide an anchor (cf. Heb. 6:19) for her faith.

GOD'S SOVEREIGNTY

For nothing will be impossible with God. (1:37)

It is one thing to say something is going to happen, but quite another to make it happen. What Mary heard was, she realized, humanly impossible. Therefore, Gabriel reminded her that because of God's unlimited power, **nothing will be impossible with** Him. The proof Gabriel offered, as noted above, was Elizabeth's conception of John.

But there was another older couple that God miraculously allowed to conceive a child. Mary would have been familiar with the Old Testament account of Isaac's birth to Abraham and Sarah (Gen. 18:1–15). Like Zacharias and Elizabeth, Abraham and Sarah were well beyond their childbearing years. Genesis 18:12–14 is the key passage of that account:

> Sarah laughed to herself, saying, "After I have become old, shall I have pleasure, my lord being old also?" And the Lord said to Abraham, "Why did Sarah laugh, saying, 'Shall I indeed bear a child, when I am so old?' Is anything too difficult for the Lord? At the appointed time I will return to you, at this time next year, and Sarah will have a son."

Gabriel's emphatic declaration that nothing is impossible for God answered God's rhetorical question in verse 14. If nothing is too hard for God's omnipotence, then everything is possible with Him (Ps. 115:3; Dan. 4:35). God, whose power knows no limits (Deut. 3:24; Job 9:4;

Ps. 89:13), and who is not bound by the laws of nature that He created, can accomplish anything consistent with His holy nature and purposes. Gabriel's reminder of what God had done in the past reassured Mary of His power to keep His word to her.

And Mary said, "Behold, the bondslave of the Lord; may it be done to me according to your word." And the angel departed from her. (1:38)

In addition to the well-known story of Abraham and Sarah, Mary was familiar with another Old Testament account of a miraculous conception that must have come into her mind. First Samuel 1:1–2:10 records the story of Samuel's birth to Hannah. In 1:10–11 Hannah, who was barren (1:2,5), appealed to God for a son:

> She, greatly distressed, prayed to the Lord and wept bitterly. She made a vow and said, "O Lord of hosts, if You will indeed look on the affliction of Your maidservant and remember me, and not forget Your maidservant, but will give Your maidservant a son, then I will give him to the Lord all the days of his life, and a razor shall never come on his head."

Like Hannah, who called herself God's "maidservant," Mary also saw herself as **the bondslave of the Lord** (cf. v. 48). The Greek word rendered **bondslave** (*doulē*, which always should be accurately translated "slave") is the same one used in the Septuagint version of 1 Samuel 1:11, thus linking Mary's submissive attitude to Hannah's. Her humble response demonstrated Mary's willing submission to God's unfolding purpose. She saw herself as nothing more than His willing, humble slave, and responded by saying, **"May it be done to me according to your word."** She did not ask about Joseph, who obviously would know that the baby was not his. Mary would thus have to face the stigma of unwed motherhood and the appearance of having committed adultery—the punishment for which was death by stoning [Deut. 22:13–21; Lev. 20:10; cf. John 8:3–5].) But in humble, obedient faith Mary willingly trusted God to vindicate her (cf. Matt. 1:19–25).

One of the Roman Catholic Church's most egregious errors is its turning of this self-proclaimed humble slave of God into the exalted queen of heaven. Such worship of Mary, which would have appalled and horrified her, is nothing less than idolatry. There is no queen of heaven, only the true and eternal King (Pss. 29:10; 47:8; Dan. 4:37; cf. Matt. 11:25; Acts 17:24), the triune God.

Catholicism's elevation of Mary finds no support in Scripture; the concept of the "queen of heaven" does appear in the Old Testament in connection with ancient pagan religion. The idea derives from Assyrian and Babylonian beliefs and practices prevalent during Jeremiah's time in apostate Judah. Their idolatry caused God through the prophet to pronounce judgment on His people:

> "As for you [Jeremiah], do not pray for this people, and do not lift up cry or prayer for them, and do not intercede with Me; for I do not hear you. Do you not see what they are doing in the cities of Judah and in the streets of Jerusalem? The children gather wood, and the fathers kindle the fire, and the women knead dough to make cakes for the queen of heaven; and they pour out drink offerings to other gods in order to spite Me. Do they spite Me?" declares the Lord. "Is it not themselves they spite, to their own shame?" Therefore thus says the Lord God, "Behold, My anger and My wrath will be poured out on this place, on man and on beast and on the trees of the field and on the fruit of the ground; and it will burn and not be quenched." (7:16–20)

The "queen of heaven" (v. 18) was the pagan goddess Ishtar (also called Ashtoreth and Astarte), the wife of Baal or Molech. Because those false deities symbolized fertility, worship of them also involved prostitution.

Later, God once again used Jeremiah to confront His rebellious people over this issue. Defiantly, they replied,

> "As for the message that you have spoken to us in the name of the Lord, we are not going to listen to you! But rather we will certainly carry out every word that has proceeded from our mouths, by burning sacrifices to the queen of heaven and pouring out drink offerings to her, just as we ourselves, our forefathers, our kings and our princes did in the cities of Judah and in the streets of Jerusalem; for then we had plenty of food and were well off and saw no misfortune. But since we stopped burning sacrifices to the queen of heaven and pouring out drink offerings to her, we have lacked everything and have met our end by the sword and by famine." "And," said the women, "when we were burning sacrifices to the queen of heaven and were pouring out drink offerings to her, was it without our husbands that we made for her sacrificial cakes in her image and poured out drink offerings to her?" (44:16–19)

In response, the prophet solemnly warned them of God's impending judgment:

Then Jeremiah said to all the people, including all the women, "Hear the word of the Lord, all Judah who are in the land of Egypt, thus says the Lord of hosts, the God of Israel, as follows: 'As for you and your wives, you have spoken with your mouths and fulfilled it with your hands, saying, "We will certainly perform our vows that we have vowed, to burn sacrifices to the queen of heaven and pour out drink offerings to her." Go ahead and confirm your vows, and certainly perform your vows!' Nevertheless hear the word of the Lord, all Judah who are living in the land of Egypt, 'Behold, I have sworn by My great name,' says the Lord, 'never shall My name be invoked again by the mouth of any man of Judah in all the land of Egypt, saying, "As the Lord God lives." Behold, I am watching over them for harm and not for good, and all the men of Judah who are in the land of Egypt will meet their end by the sword and by famine until they are completely gone. Those who escape the sword will return out of the land of Egypt to the land of Judah few in number. Then all the remnant of Judah who have gone to the land of Egypt to reside there will know whose word will stand, Mine or theirs.'" (44:24–28)

To worship Mary as if she were the queen of heaven is to mix paganism with biblical truth and to blaspheme the true King of heaven. To proclaim that Mary is co-redemptrix and mediatrix of saving grace (cf. the discussion of Catholicism's unbiblical view of Mary in chapter 4 of this volume), only compounds its false, syncretistic view of her.

Mary's dramatic encounter with the angel Gabriel ended with this short, simple postscript: **And the angel departed from her.** His mission accomplished, Gabriel returned to the presence of God. The God-man was going to be born; the only begotten Son of God, Jesus, who would save His people from their sins, the divine Redeemer, the holy offspring, the divine King who will reign over a kingdom that will last forever.

This account demonstrates that God's promises will be fulfilled, as they were in Mary's life. It also reveals that the sovereign God accomplishes His purposes through His willing and obedient slaves, as He did through Mary. Without regard for the implications and potential risks, Mary faithfully rested in the sovereign purpose of her Savior and God. That is her true magnificence.

God is still doing His work today, if not through visible miracles, then spiritually through His people who trust Him (Isa. 26:3; cf. Prov. 29:25), obey His Word (Ps. 119:17, 67, 101; Matt. 7:24; Luke 11:28; James 1:25), and humbly submit as obedient slaves to His will (Josh. 24:24; Ps. 119:35; Eccles. 12:13; Phil. 2:12–13).

Mary and Elizabeth: Confirming Angelic Prophecy (Luke 1:39–45)

6

Now at this time Mary arose and went in a hurry to the hill country, to a city of Judah, and entered the house of Zacharias and greeted Elizabeth. When Elizabeth heard Mary's greeting, the baby leaped in her womb; and Elizabeth was filled with the Holy Spirit. And she cried out with a loud voice and said, "Blessed are you among women, and blessed is the fruit of your womb! And how has it happened to me, that the mother of my Lord would come to me? For behold, when the sound of your greeting reached my ears, the baby leaped in my womb for joy. And blessed is she who believed that there would be a fulfillment of what had been spoken to her by the Lord." (1:39–45)

Faith is the essence of the Christian life. At the outset, believers are "justified by faith apart from works of the Law" (Rom. 3:28; cf. 5:1; Gal. 2:16) and thus are "sons of God through faith in Christ Jesus" (Gal. 3:26). Paul wrote of living the Christian life, "the life which I now live in the flesh I live by faith in the Son of God" (Gal. 2:20). In John 20:29 Jesus said to Thomas, "Because you have seen Me, have you believed? Blessed are they who did not see, and yet believed" (cf. 1 Peter 1:8). "Faith," notes the writer of Hebrews, "is the assurance of things hoped for, the conviction of things not seen" (Heb. 11:1;cf. 2 Cor. 4:18; Rom. 8:25), apart from which it is impossible to please God (v. 6).

But as still fallen people, though "we walk by faith, not by sight" (2 Cor. 5:7), even those whose faith is strongest experience doubts and discouragement. The Bible makes it clear that all through redemptive history God has been the encourager of His people, confirming and strengthening their faith.

Tasked with the daunting responsibility of leading the exodus of the children of Israel from Egypt, "Moses said to God, 'Who am I, that I should go to Pharaoh, and that I should bring the sons of Israel out of Egypt?'" (Ex. 3:11). God encouraged him: "Certainly I will be with you, and this shall be the sign to you that it is I who have sent you: when you have brought the people out of Egypt, you shall worship God at this mountain" (v. 12). Despite God's reassurance, Moses's faith still wavered. "What if they [the Israelites] will not believe me or listen to what I say?" he demanded, "For they may say, 'The Lord has not appeared to you'" (Ex. 4:1). Again, God reassured His struggling servant:

> The Lord said to him, "What is that in your hand?" And he said, "A staff." Then He said, "Throw it on the ground." So he threw it on the ground, and it became a serpent; and Moses fled from it. But the Lord said to Moses, "Stretch out your hand and grasp it by its tail"—so he stretched out his hand and caught it, and it became a staff in his hand—"that they may believe that the Lord, the God of their fathers, the God of Abraham, the God of Isaac, and the God of Jacob, has appeared to you." The Lord furthermore said to him, "Now put your hand into your bosom." So he put his hand into his bosom, and when he took it out, behold, his hand was leprous like snow. Then He said, "Put your hand into your bosom again." So he put his hand into his bosom again, and when he took it out of his bosom, behold, it was restored like the rest of his flesh. "If they will not believe you or heed the witness of the first sign, they may believe the witness of the last sign. But if they will not believe even these two signs or heed what you say, then you shall take some water from the Nile and pour it on the dry ground; and the water which you take from the Nile will become blood on the dry ground." (vv. 2–9)

Gideon, the judge who delivered Israel from the oppression of the Midianites, also found his faith was not up to the task. Judges 6:16–23 relates Gideon's encounter with the Angel of the Lord (the pre-incarnate Christ), who charged him to deliver Israel:

> The Lord said to him, "Surely I will be with you, and you shall defeat Midian as one man." So Gideon said to Him, "If now I have found favor in Your sight, then show me a sign that it is You who speak with me.

Please do not depart from here, until I come back to You, and bring out my offering and lay it before You." And He said, "I will remain until you return." Then Gideon went in and prepared a young goat and unleavened bread from an ephah of flour; he put the meat in a basket and the broth in a pot, and brought them out to him under the oak and presented them. The angel of God said to him, "Take the meat and the unleavened bread and lay them on this rock, and pour out the broth." And he did so. Then the angel of the Lord put out the end of the staff that was in his hand and touched the meat and the unleavened bread; and fire sprang up from the rock and consumed the meat and the unleavened bread. Then the angel of the Lord vanished from his sight. When Gideon saw that he was the angel of the Lord, he said, "Alas, O Lord God! For now I have seen the angel of the Lord face to face." The Lord said to him, "Peace to you, do not fear; you shall not die."

As the Midianite army approached, Gideon sought further reassurance that God would do as He promised. Seeking to bolster his sagging faith, Gideon made the request for which he is most famous:

Then Gideon said to God, "If You will deliver Israel through me, as You have spoken, behold, I will put a fleece of wool on the threshing floor. If there is dew on the fleece only, and it is dry on all the ground, then I will know that You will deliver Israel through me, as You have spoken." And it was so. When he arose early the next morning and squeezed the fleece, he drained the dew from the fleece, a bowl full of water. Then Gideon said to God, "Do not let Your anger burn against me that I may speak once more; please let me make a test once more with the fleece, let it now be dry only on the fleece, and let there be dew on all the ground." God did so that night; for it was dry only on the fleece, and dew was on all the ground. (Judg. 6:36–40)

Afflicted with a terminal illness, the godly king Hezekiah "prayed to the Lord, saying, 'Remember now, O Lord, I beseech You, how I have walked before You in truth and with a whole heart and have done what is good in Your sight'" (2 Kings 20:2–3). In answer to Hezekiah's prayer, God sent Isaiah the prophet to him with the good news that his prayer had been answered (vv. 4–6). In disbelief despite God's swift answer to his prayer, "Hezekiah said to Isaiah, 'What will be the sign that the Lord will heal me, and that I shall go up to the house of the Lord the third day?'" (v. 8). As He had with Moses and Gideon, God granted Hezekiah a sign that what He had promised would come to pass:

Isaiah said, "This shall be the sign to you from the Lord, that the Lord will do the thing that He has spoken: shall the shadow go forward ten steps or go back ten steps?" So Hezekiah answered, "It is easy for the shadow to decline ten steps; no, but let the shadow turn backward ten steps." Isaiah the prophet cried to the Lord, and He brought the shadow on the stairway back ten steps by which it had gone down on the stairway of Ahaz. (vv. 9–11)

Even John the Baptist, the forerunner of the Messiah and the greatest man who had ever lived up to that time (Matt. 11:11), struggled with doubt:

> Now when John, while imprisoned, heard of the works of Christ, he sent word by his disciples and said to Him, "Are You the Expected One, or shall we look for someone else?" Jesus answered and said to them, "Go and report to John what you hear and see: the blind receive sight and the lame walk, the lepers are cleansed and the deaf hear, the dead are raised up, and the poor have the gospel preached to them. And blessed is he who does not take offense at Me." (Matt. 11:2–6)

As this passage opens, Mary had just received from the angel Gabriel the most astonishing, unimaginable, incomprehensible announcement any human has ever heard. Incredibly, his message to her was that she was to be the mother of the Messiah; the Son of God incarnate; the Lord Jesus Christ. Mary had responded in humble, obedient, submissive faith (1:38), trusting that God would do as He had said.

Although Mary did not ask for a sign, God, knowing how startling and unsetting His message to her was, gave her one anyway. The sign, communicated by Gabriel, was another conception miracle, this one involving her older relative Elizabeth. Luke's gospel record opens with the stories of these two miracles, one involving a barren, older woman past childbearing age, and the other a young, unmarried virgin in her early teens. The child of the first would be the forerunner of the Messiah, John the Baptist; the second would be the Messiah Himself, the Lord Jesus Christ.

Until this point, the two narratives had been separate. Elizabeth lived in the hill country of Judah, in the vicinity of Jerusalem, while Mary lived in the small Galilean village of Nazareth, approximately sixty miles to the north. But in this passage the two stories come together, as Mary visits Elizabeth. The two incidents, though separate in time and location, nonetheless contain many striking parallels.

For example, both accounts began by introducing the parents, or in Mary's case, parent (1:5–6, 26–27). Second, both accounts stated the obstacles to childbearing (Elizabeth's barrenness [1:7]; Mary's virginity [1:34]). Third, Gabriel arrived (1:11, 26), and his appearing frightened the one to whom he appeared (1:12, 29). Fourth, Gabriel reassured the one to whom he appeared (1:13, 30). Fifth, Gabriel promised a son (1:13, 31).

Sixth, Gabriel gave the son's name (1:13,31), and described his greatness (1:15–17, 32–33). Seventh, there was an objection (Zacharias's unbelief [1:18]; Mary' lack of understanding [1:34]). Finally, Gabriel gave a sign that what he had spoken would come true (1:19–20,35–36).

Luke's brief description of Mary's meeting with Elizabeth emphasizes God's confirmation of His promise to Mary that she would conceive a Son while still a virgin. The account reveals three aspects of that confirmation: personal confirmation, physical confirmation, and prophetic confirmation.

Personal Confirmation

Now at this time Mary arose and went in a hurry to the hill country, to a city of Judah, and entered the house of Zacharias and greeted Elizabeth. (1:39–40)

Eager to see the promised sign, Mary wasted no time in setting out to visit her older relative Elizabeth. The phrase **at this time** refers to the time of Gabriel's visit. That and Luke's note that she **went in a hurry** indicates that Mary immediately dropped everything to make the trip south to Judea to see Elizabeth, who was by that time six months pregnant (v. 36). Since she stayed with Elizabeth for three months (v. 56), Mary evidently returned home around the time of the birth of John the Baptist (v. 57).

Travel to **the** Judean **hill country** near Jerusalem would have taken three or four days. Such a journey by a girl of Mary's age was highly unusual in a culture where young girls were carefully shielded and protected. In addition, though the Bible nowhere mentions the exact moment of her conception, Mary no doubt was already pregnant when she made the trip. Some have even suggested that the reason she went was to hide her pregnancy. But her pregnancy would not have been evident that soon after conception. And if that were Mary's intent, she would hardly have returned home three months later when her condition would have been obvious to all. It is doubtful that Joseph was aware that Mary was pregnant. The account of Joseph's awareness of Mary's pregnancy, his response, and the next angelic visit is given by Matthew (1:18–25).

The exact location of the **city** (village) **of Judah** where Zacharias and Elizabeth lived is unknown, although a sixth-century tradition places it about five miles from Jerusalem. After arriving there Mary **entered the house of Zacharias and greeted Elizabeth** (cf. vv. 41, 44). Unlike the brief, casual, even flippant greetings common today, a greeting in the Ancient Near East was an extended social event, involving a lengthy dialogue. Moses' encounter with his father-in-law, Jethro, illustrates such a greeting:

> Then Moses went out to meet his father-in-law, and he bowed down and kissed him; and they asked each other of their welfare and went into the tent. Moses told his father-in-law all that the Lord had done to Pharaoh and to the Egyptians for Israel's sake, all the hardship that had befallen them on the journey, and how the Lord had delivered them. Jethro rejoiced over all the goodness which the Lord had done to Israel, in delivering them from the hand of the Egyptians. (Ex. 18:7–9)

Similarly, Mary and Elizabeth no doubt shared all the details of their remarkable stories with each other. Elizabeth would have told Mary of the amazing events that culminated in her pregnancy, starting with Gabriel's appearance to Zacharias in the temple. Mary likewise would have related to Elizabeth the story of her visit from Gabriel a short time earlier. The remarkable similarities in the two accounts, noted above, would have thrilled and amazed them as they realized that the long-awaited Messiah was about to arrive, and that God had chosen these two obscure women to be the miraculous bearers of these two sons.

Mary would share her wonderful news with Elizabeth, confident that she was the one person Mary could count on to believe her story. Others might have viewed her account as a far-fetched attempt to cover up her sexual immorality and resulting pregnancy. Even Joseph, who knew her well, did not believe Mary's account, and intended to divorce her (Matt. 1:19). It was not until he heard the truth from an angel (vv. 20–21, 24–25) that he accepted what had really happened. Therefore, the text does not reveal what, if anything Mary said to him, her family, or her friends; it says only that she told Elizabeth, since she too had experienced a miraculous conception. Hearing Elizabeth's account, and even more seeing her condition, also confirmed to Mary that God would keep His word to her.

PHYSICAL CONFIRMATION

When Elizabeth heard Mary's greeting, the baby leaped in her womb; . . . For behold, when the sound of your greeting reached my ears, the baby leaped in my womb for joy. (1:41a, 44)

The confirmation Mary received from talking with Elizabeth was reinforced in a wondrous manner. At some point in the lengthy conversation that comprised the **greeting** (no doubt after Mary recounted Gabriel's words to her), Elizabeth's **baby leaped in her womb.** Clearly this was not merely the normal movement of the baby in her womb that she felt frequently. Elizabeth's exclamation to Mary, **"When the sound of your greeting reached my ears, the baby leaped in my womb for joy"** clearly reveals that her baby's movement was not the familiar kind, but one she identified with joy at Messiah's anticipated coming.

This life would be born to be the forerunner (1:17) and herald (3:4–6) of the Messiah, and this silent prophecy was His first announcement. It was to enable Him to make this involuntary supernatural prophecy that John was "filled with the Holy Spirit while yet in his mother's womb" (v. 15). As will be seen later, the filling of the Spirit (an expression describing the power of the Holy Spirit taking control and effecting service to God by word or deed) is often connected with prophecy.

This was not the first time that movement in a pregnant woman's womb had prophetic significance. Centuries earlier, during Rebekah's pregnancy, there was an incident with far-reaching implications:

> Isaac prayed to the Lord on behalf of his wife, because she was barren; and the Lord answered him and Rebekah his wife conceived. But the children struggled together within her; and she said, "If it is so, why then am I this way?" So she went to inquire of the Lord. The Lord said to her, "Two nations are in your womb; and two peoples shall be separated from your body; and one people shall be stronger than the other; and the older shall serve the younger." (Gen. 25:21–23)

The children were Jacob and Esau, whose descendants, Israel and the Arabs, have been in conflict for millennia.

The joy that began in his mother's womb would set the tone for John's entire life and ministry. In John 3:29, he declared, "He who has the bride is the bridegroom; but the friend of the bridegroom, who stands and hears him, rejoices greatly because of the bridegroom's voice. So this joy of mine has been made full."

The baby's leap for joy provided the fulfillment of the promised confirmation to Mary. But unlike her unborn son, Elizabeth could speak, and she added her voice to the unspoken prophecy.

PROPHETIC CONFIRMATION

and Elizabeth was filled with the Holy Spirit. And she cried out with a loud voice and said, "Blessed are you among women, and blessed is the fruit of your womb! And how has it happened to

**me, that the mother of my Lord would come to me? . . . And
blessed is she who believed that there would be a fulfillment of
what had been spoken to her by the Lord."** (1:41*b*–43,45)

Like her unborn son, **Elizabeth** too **was filled with the Holy
Spirit.** As mentioned earlier, such filling was often connected to speaking a message from God. In 2 Samuel 23:2, David declared, "The Spirit of
the Lord spoke by me, and His word was on my tongue." After John's birth
"Zacharias was filled with the Holy Spirit, and prophesied" (1:67; cf. vv.
68–79). Simeon

> came in the Spirit into the temple; and when the parents brought in the
> child Jesus, to carry out for Him the custom of the Law, then he took
> Him into his arms, and blessed God, and said, "Now Lord, You are releas-
> ing Your bond-servant to depart in peace, according to Your word; for
> my eyes have seen Your salvation, which You have prepared in the pres-
> ence of all peoples, a light of revelation to the Gentiles, and the glory
> of Your people Israel." (2:27–32)

Acts 2:4 records that on the day of Pentecost the believers "were all filled
with the Holy Spirit and began to speak with other tongues [recognized
foreign languages; vv. 8–11], as the Spirit was giving them utterance." Later
in Acts,

> Peter, filled with the Holy Spirit, said to them, "Rulers and elders of the
> people, if we are on trial today for a benefit done to a sick man, as to
> how this man has been made well, let it be known to all of you and to
> all the people of Israel, that by the name of Jesus Christ the Nazarene,
> whom you crucified, whom God raised from the dead—by this name
> this man stands here before you in good health. He is the stone which
> was rejected by you, the builders, but which became the chief corner
> stone. And there is salvation in no one else; for there is no other name
> under heaven that has been given among men by which we must be
> saved." (Acts 4:8–12)

After Peter and John were threatened and released by the Sanhedrin,
the believers "were all filled with the Holy Spirit and began to speak the
word of God with boldness" (Acts 4:31). The writers of Scripture were
"men moved by the Holy Spirit [who] spoke from God" (2 Peter 1:21).

After being filled with the Spirit Elizabeth **cried out with a loud**
(a term associated with the speaking of divine truth in such passages as
John 1:15; 7:28; 37; Rom. 9:27) **voice.** She literally shouted out the message God gave her, both from excitement over its content, and to emphasize its authority. What followed was a hymn of praise, the first of five

associated with Christ's birth that Luke records (cf. 1:46–55, 67–79; 2:14, 25–32). This hymn of praise pronounced blessing on Mary, her child, Elizabeth herself, and ultimately everyone who believes God's word.

The phrase **blessed are you among women** is a Hebrew superlative expression that describes Mary as the most blessed of all women (cf. Judg. 5:24). In Hebrew culture, a woman's status was based to a great extent on her children; her significance was directly tied to their significance. Thus, when a woman wanted to honor Mary, she called out to Jesus, "Blessed is the womb that bore You and the breasts at which You nursed" (Luke 11:27). Elizabeth's point was that Mary was the most blessed woman of all because she would bear the greatest child. Although Gabriel had informed Zacharias that their own son would be great, Elizabeth humbly acknowledged that Mary's would be greater. Elizabeth's child would be Messiah's forerunner, but Mary's was the Messiah. Thus, Elizabeth acknowledged that Mary had received the greater privilege and the greater honor. Being a righteous woman (1:6), she was thrilled not only at the privilege of bearing Messiah's forerunner, but even more so that Messiah was coming.

Elizabeth then blessed Mary's Son, crying out, **"Blessed is the fruit of your womb!"** That familiar Old Testament phrase (cf. Gen. 30:2; Deut. 7:13; Ps. 127:3; Isa. 13:18), used only here in the New Testament, refers to the holy Child that Mary would bear. He is the Messiah (John 4:25–26); the Savior of the world (John 4:42; 1 John 4:14); the recipient of all of heaven's praise (Heb. 1:6); the one who is "holy, innocent, undefiled, separated from sinners and exalted above the heavens" (Heb. 7:26); the one whom "God highly exalted …and bestowed on Him the name which is above every name" (Phil. 2:9); the one who will inherit all that the Father possesses (John 16:15; 17:10); the Lord of glory (1 Cor. 2:8).

Elizabeth's exclamation of wonder and awe, **"And how has it happened to me, that the mother of my Lord would come to me?"** is in effect a pronouncement of blessing on herself. In her true humility, she felt unworthy to be in the presence of such an honored person (cf. Luke 5:8). That Elizabeth, still speaking under the control of the Holy Spirit, referred to Mary's Son as **my Lord** attests to His deity. **Lord** is a divine title, used more than two dozen times in the first two chapters of Luke's gospel to refer to God. Therefore, to call Jesus Lord is first to call Him God (cf. John 20:28). Later the emphasis will include the consequent total submission to His sovereign lordship (6:46).

Despite the teaching and liturgy of the Roman Catholic Church, the New Testament nowhere gives Mary the title "mother of God." God, being eternal (Gen. 21:33; Deut. 33:27; Ps. 90:2; Isa. 40:28; Hab. 1:12; Rom. 16:26), was never conceived or born, but has always existed. Mary was the mother of the human Jesus, not His eternal divine nature.

Elizabeth's closing statement, **"blessed is she who believed that there would be a fulfillment of what had been spoken to her by the Lord,"** supplements her earlier blessing of Mary. Mary was blessed not only because of her privilege in being the mother of the Messiah, but also because of her faith in believing **that there would be a fulfillment of what had been spoken to her by the Lord.** But Elizabeth's use of the third person pronoun **she** broadens the blessing beyond Mary to encompass all who believe that God fulfills His promises.

Mary is not the mother of God, or the queen of heaven. She plays no role in the redemption of sinners, and does not intercede for them or hear their prayers. But she is a model of faith, humility, and submission to God's will. She is an example to all believers of how to respond obediently, joyfully, and worshipfully to the Word of God. Therein lies her true greatness.

Mary's Praise
(Luke 1:46–55)

7

And Mary said: "My soul exalts the Lord, and my spirit has rejoiced in God my Savior. For He has had regard for the humble state of His bondslave; for behold, from this time on all generations will count me blessed. For the Mighty One has done great things for me; and holy is His name. And His mercy is upon generation after generation toward those who fear Him. He has done mighty deeds with His arm; He has scattered those who were proud in the thoughts of their heart. He has brought down rulers from their thrones, and has exalted those who were humble. He has filled the hungry with good things; and sent away the rich empty-handed. He has given help to Israel His servant, in remembrance of His mercy, as He spoke to our fathers, to Abraham and his descendants forever." (1:46–55)

Here is a rich offering of praise from Mary. It is remarkable for its theology and use of the Old Testament. She was a young girl, perhaps about thirteen years old who, like all the people of her day, had no personal copy of the Scriptures. Her familiarity with the Word of God must have come from hearing it read regularly in the synagogue (cf. 4:16). It settled in her heart and was readily on her mind when she opened her mouth in worshipful praise. What a benediction it would be for the church today if the young could be so biblically literate and devout.

The New Testament ultimately stresses the priority of worship. To Satan's blasphemous temptation to worship him, Jesus replied, "Go, Satan! For it is written, 'You shall worship the Lord your God, and serve Him only'" (Matt. 4:10). Hebrews 10:24–25 urges believers to come together to "stimulate one another to love and good deeds," since they, "as living stones, are being built up as a spiritual house for a holy priesthood, to offer up spiritual sacrifices acceptable to God through Jesus Christ" (1 Peter 2:5).

Because God created them to worship Him, all people are inherently worshipers. The object of one's worship determines his or her eternal destiny. The Old Testament condemns idolatry, that is, the worship of anyone other than the true God (e.g., Ex. 20:3, 23; 34:14; Pss. 81:9; 106:35–36), and makes it clear that it was Israel's persistent idolatry (e.g., Judg. 2:12–13, 17, 19; 3:5–7; 10:6; 1 Kings 15:12; 16:13; 21:25–26) that eventually led to the nation's destruction and captivity (cf. 2 Kings 17:6–12; 21:11–14). The New Testament reveals idolatry to be the inevitable response of those who deny the true God (Rom. 1:18–23). But the worship of false deities is not the only form of idolatry. There are idols in the heart of even the most hardened atheist, such as acceptance, fame, health, power, prestige, and wealth, among many others.

Idolatry, however, is not limited to the worship of false gods; it also encompasses attempting to worship the true God in an unacceptable manner. Moses's receiving of the Ten Commandments on Mount Sinai was interrupted by a shocking display of idolatry:

> Then the Lord spoke to Moses, "Go down at once, for your people, whom you brought up from the land of Egypt, have corrupted themselves. They have quickly turned aside from the way which I commanded them. They have made for themselves a molten calf, and have worshiped it and have sacrificed to it and said, 'This is your god, O Israel, who brought you up from the land of Egypt!'" (Ex. 32:7–8)

The Israelites were not worshiping a pagan deity, but had reduced the true God to an image—something God strictly forbids (Deut. 4:14–18). The result was a threat of deadly judgment (Ex. 32:10) and its execution (vv. 28–35).

Instead of following the prescribed regulations for worship, Aaron's sons Nadab and Abihu (probably while drunk; cf. Lev. 10:9) "offered strange fire before the Lord, which He had not commanded them" (Lev. 10:1). God was not pleased with their innovative worship, "and fire came out from the presence of the Lord and consumed them, and they died before the Lord" (v. 2).

After anxiously watching the Philistine forces mustering for battle while his own men were deserting him, Saul finally took matters into his own hands. Samuel had instructed the king to wait seven days, until he came to offer sacrifices (1 Sam. 10:8). But when the seven days were up and Samuel had not appeared, Saul rationalized that "the Philistines will come down against me at Gilgal, and I have not asked the favor of the Lord." Therefore, usurping the role of a priest, Saul "forced [himself] and offered the burnt offering" (1 Sam. 13:12). That willful failure to worship God properly was to cost Saul everything:

> Samuel said to Saul, "You have acted foolishly; you have not kept the commandment of the Lord your God, which He commanded you, for now the Lord would have established your kingdom over Israel forever. But now your kingdom shall not endure. The Lord has sought out for Himself a man after His own heart, and the Lord has appointed him as ruler over His people, because you have not kept what the Lord commanded you." (vv. 13–14)

Twenty years after the Philistines returned the ark of the covenant to Israel (1 Sam. 7:1), David decided to transport it to Jerusalem. Ignoring God's instructions on how to carry the ark (it was to be carried on poles; cf. Num. 4:5–6), the people placed it on an ox cart (2 Sam. 6:3) and celebrated as the ark set out for Jerusalem (v. 5). But the joyous mood was abruptly shattered when Uzzah "reached out toward the ark of God and took hold of it, for the oxen nearly upset it. And the anger of the Lord burned against Uzzah, and God struck him down there for his irreverence; and he died there by the ark of God" (vv. 6–7). Uzzah's seeming reverence for the Lord was actually a direct violation of His command not to touch the ark on pain of death (Num. 4:15). The drastic consequence of Uzzah's disobedience graphically illustrates that God does not accept any variant or, self-styled alteration of His instructions for worship (cf. Isa. 1:11–20; Amos 5:21–27; Hos. 6:4–7; Mal. 1:6–14; Matt. 15:1–9; 23:23–28; Mark 7:6–7).

The redeemed, on the other hand, manifest acceptable worship. They are, according to Philippians 3:3, those who "worship in the Spirit of God and glory in Christ Jesus and put no confidence in the flesh" (cf. John 4:23). Worship that is acceptable to God has many elements. In Romans 15:16, Paul used the language of worship to describe his evangelistic ministry to the lost, calling himself "a minister of Christ Jesus to the Gentiles, ministering as a priest the gospel of God, so that [his] offering of the Gentiles may become acceptable, sanctified by the Holy Spirit." Leading a "tranquil and quiet life in all godliness and dignity" (1 Tim. 2:2) is also an act of worship, since it is "good and acceptable in the sight of God our Savior" (v. 3).

Central to worshiping God is praise. The writer of Hebrews exhorts his readers to "continually offer up a sacrifice of praise to God, that is, the fruit of lips that give thanks to His name" (Heb. 13:15). Worship also includes "doing good and sharing, for with such sacrifices God is pleased" (v. 16). The apostle Paul notes that even the seemingly mundane act of meeting financial needs is an act of worship. Thanking the Philippians for their gift he wrote, "But I have received everything in full and have an abundance; I am amply supplied, having received from Epaphroditus what you have sent, a fragrant aroma, an acceptable sacrifice, well-pleasing to God" (Phil. 4:18).

True worship as defined by our Lord has two components: it is, He said, to be "in spirit and truth" (John 4:23–24). Worship in spirit is genuine, unfeigned, from the heart, as opposed to mere outward ritual. In his classic work *The Existence and Attributes of God,* the seventeenth-century English Puritan Stephen Charnock wrote,

> Without the heart it is no worship; it is a stage play; an acting a part without being that person really which is acted by us: a hypocrite, in the notion of the word, is a stage player. . . . We may be truly said to worship God, though we [lack] perfection; but we cannot be said to worship him, if we [lack] sincerity. (Reprint; Grand Rapids: Baker, 1979, 1:225–26)

"Bless the Lord, O my soul," wrote David, "and all that is within me, bless His holy name" (Ps. 103:1; cf. 51:15–17). In Romans 1:9, Paul wrote, "God, whom I serve in my spirit in the preaching of the gospel of His Son, is my witness as to how unceasingly I make mention of you."

The Bible reveals a number of prerequisites for worshiping in spirit. First and foremost, a true worshiper must be controlled and empowered by the Holy Spirit. That, of course, presupposes salvation, since those who are not saved do not have the indwelling Holy Spirit (Acts 5:32; Rom. 8:5–9), and thus cannot worship God. Second, to worship in spirit requires that the thoughts be focused on God. Worship flows out of an undivided (Ps. 86:11) mind filled with and meditating on the truth of God's Word (Josh. 1:8; Pss. 1:2; 4:4; 63:6; 77:6, 12; 119:15, 23, 48, 78, 97, 99, 148). Third, worship in spirit requires repentance, since sin hinders fellowship and communion with God. Thus David prayed, "Search me, O God, and know my heart; try me and know my anxious thoughts; and see if there be any hurtful way in me, and lead me in the everlasting way" (Ps. 139:23–24). Finally, to worship God in spirit requires humbly accepting His will no matter what the circumstances (cf. Abraham's willingness to sacrifice his son; Gen. 22:1–18).

Worship must also be in truth. As noted above, God rejects self-styled worship that is inconsistent with His revealed truth. The only source of that truth is His Word (John 17:17; cf. Ps. 119:142, 160), so only worship consistent with Scripture is acceptable to Him.

Hebrews 10:22 summarizes the approach of true worshipers to God: They are sincere (they "draw near with a sincere heart"), faithful ("in full assurance of faith"), humble ("having ... hearts sprinkled clean from an evil conscience"), and pure (having "bodies washed with pure water"). As a result of such worship God will be glorified (Ps. 50:23), believers purified (Ps. 24:3–4), and the lost evangelized (Acts 2:47).

As noted in the previous chapter of this volume, Mary is an example to all believers of faith, humility, and submission to God's will. This section of Luke's gospel reveals that she also modeled true, acceptable worship. After hearing the astonishing news from the angel Gabriel that she was to be the mother of the Messiah (see chapters 4 and 5 of this volume), Mary immediately went to visit her older relative Elizabeth, who was six months pregnant with John the Baptist (1:36). There God confirmed that His promise to her through Gabriel would indeed come to pass (see the exposition of 1:39–45 in chapter 6 of this volume). God's confirmation erased Mary's doubts, answered her questions, and strengthened her faith. Verses 46–55, known as the Magnificat (from the first word of the Latin text), record her outburst of praise and worship in response.

Mary's hymn is filled with allusions to Scripture, revealing that her heart and mind were saturated with the Old Testament. It echoes Hannah's prayers (1 Sam. 1:11; 2:1–10) and prayers in the Pentateuch, the Psalms, and the writings of the prophets.

For example, Mary began in verse 46 by saying, **"My soul exalts the Lord,"** which echoes Psalm 34:2, "My soul shall make its boast in the Lord." Her reference to God as her Savior (v. 47) is reminiscent of such Old Testament passages as 2 Samuel 22:3; Isaiah 43:11; 45:21; 49:26; 60:16; and Hosea 13:4, while her statement, **"For He has had regard for the humble state of His bondslave"** (v. 48) reflects Hannah's prayer in 1 Samuel 1:11 (cf. Ps. 136:23). Mary's exclamation, **"for behold, from this time on all generations will count me blessed"** echoes Leah's words in Genesis 30:13. Her declaration, **"For the Mighty One has done great things for me"** has Old Testament roots (cf. Ps. 126:3), as does the following statement, **"holy is His name"** (cf. Pss. 99:3; 111:9).

Mary's hymn also reveals that she was well-versed in the history of Israel. She spoke of God's having **"done mighty deeds with His arm"** (v. 51), including **"scatter[ing] those who were proud in the thoughts of their heart**" (v. 51), **"[bringing] down rulers from their thrones"** (v. 52), **"exalt[ing] those who were humble"** (v. 52), **"fill[ing] the hungry with good things; and [sending] away the rich empty-handed"** (v. 53).

Mary also understood the rich theological truth of the Abrahamic covenant. She knew that God **"has given help to Israel His servant, in remembrance of His mercy,"** in keeping with the promise He made **"to Abraham and his descendants forever"** (vv. 54–55). Jesus taught that "the mouth speaks out of that which fills the heart" (Matt. 12:34), and Mary's words were the outflow of a heart steeped in God's Word.

Mary's praise is the expression of her faith in God, her love for Him, and her deep understanding of Scripture. The result is an example of worship for all believers to emulate, as she displays the attitude, object, and motive of worship.

THE ATTITUDE OF WORSHIP

And Mary said: "My soul exalts the Lord, and my spirit has rejoiced in God my Savior. For He has had regard for the humble state of His bondslave; (1:46–48*a*)

Mary's example of the proper attitude of worship unfolds in four points.

First, worship is internal. Mary's worship was with her **soul** and **spirit.** The two terms are interchangeable, and refer to the inner person. True worship, worship in spirit (John 4:24), involves the whole inner being—mind, emotion, and will. Like the instruments in a great orchestra, all of Mary's thoughts and emotions came together in a crescendo of praise.

On the other hand shallow, superficial worship is intolerable to God. In Isaiah 29:13, the Lord rebuked the people of Israel for their external, ritualistic perversion of true worship, declaring that they "draw near with their words and honor Me with their lip service, but they remove their hearts far from Me, and their reverence for Me consists of tradition learned by rote." Jesus applied this passage to the hypocritical worshipers of His day (Matt. 15:7–9). In Isaiah 48:1, God declared, "Hear this, O house of Jacob, who are named Israel and who came forth from the loins of Judah, who swear by the name of the Lord and invoke the God of Israel, but not in truth nor in righteousness." Jeremiah complained to God regarding his fellow Israelites, "You are near to their lips but far from their mind" (Jer. 12:2). "They come to you as people come," the Lord cautioned Ezekiel, "and sit before you as My people and hear your words, but they do not do them, for they do the lustful desires expressed by their mouth, and their heart goes after their gain" (Ezek. 33:31). Through the prophet Amos God declared to Israel,

I hate, I reject your festivals, nor do I delight in your solemn assemblies. Even though you offer up to Me burnt offerings and your grain offerings, I will not accept them; and I will not even look at the peace offerings of your fatlings. Take away from Me the noise of your songs; I will not even listen to the sound of your harps. But let justice roll down like waters and righteousness like an ever-flowing stream. (Amos 5:21–24)

True worship is not only internal, but also intense. **Exalts** translates a form of the verb *megalunō,* which literally means, "to make great," "to magnify" (hence Magnificat) or "to enlarge"; figuratively it means, "to extol," "to exalt," "to celebrate," "to esteem highly," "to praise," or "to glorify." **Rejoiced,** from the verb *agalliaō,* is another intense word. It is an expression of supreme joy; in Luke 10:21 and Acts 16:34, it is translated "rejoiced greatly" (cf. 1 Peter 1:6, 8). True worship is spontaneous, not staged; heartfelt, not artificial; God-centered, not self-focused; mental, not just emotional; it seeks to honor God, not to manipulate Him. Mary praised God not only for what He was doing in her life, but also for all that He was going to accomplish through the coming of Messiah.

A third characteristic of genuine worship is that it is habitual; it is a way of life. The present tense form of the verb *megalunō* (**exalts**) suggests that worship happened naturally, continuously in the flow of Mary's life. Fluctuating circumstances do not affect true worship, because God does not change (Mal. 3:6), neither does His word (Mark 13:31), His purposes (Isa. 43:13), His promises (2 Cor. 1:20), or His salvation (Heb. 5:9; 7:25). Nor is believers' responsibility to give thanks in everything (Eph. 5:20; 1 Thess. 5:18) contingent on satisfaction with life's circumstances. No matter what was happening in his life, David could say, "I have set the Lord continually before me" (Ps. 16:8). No one exemplified that attitude of continuous worship more than Paul, whose goal, as he wrote to the Philippians, was that "Christ [would always] be exalted in [his] body, whether by life or by death" (Phil 1:20).

Finally, genuine internal worship is marked by humility. The two great hindrances of worship are ignorance, which makes it feeble and ineffectual, and pride, which renders it hypocritical. Those with a shallow, superficial knowledge of God cannot worship Him in the fullest sense because they do not grasp His greatness. But the proud cannot truly worship Him at all, since pride is in reality the worship of self. God tolerates no rivals, which is why the first of the Ten Commandments is, "You shall have no other gods before Me" (Ex. 20:3; cf. Isa. 42:8). Thus "God is opposed to the proud, but gives grace to the humble" (James 4:6), because "everyone who is proud in heart is an abomination to the Lord" (Prov. 16:5; cf. 15:25; Ps. 31:23; Isa. 2:11–12; 13:11; 1 Peter 5:5).

Proud people find it difficult to be thankful because they always think they deserved better. They remember the wrongs (real or imagined) done to them and seek revenge. Constantly mulling over their alleged mistreatment fills them with a spirit of bitterness, which is incompatible with true worship.

The humble, on the other hand, knowing they deserve nothing, recognize their spiritual bankruptcy, mourn over their sin, and hunger and thirst for righteousness from God, knowing they have none of their own. They have a profound sense of gratitude toward and love for God, which results in worship.

Mary was such a humble person. Her exclamation, **"He has had regard for the humble state of His bondslave,"** expressed her wonder and amazement that God would choose to bless her. She knew that she was a sinner, in need of God's mercy and grace. Far from viewing herself as the exalted, quasi-deified queen of heaven Roman Catholicism imagines her to be, Mary viewed herself as a lowly **bondslave** (cf. v. 38). The Greek word is *doulē*, the feminine form of the word meaning "slave." She is the first in the New Testament to identify herself as the Lord's slave—a designation that becomes the norm for the saints (cf. 2:29; 1 Cor. 7:22; Eph. 6:6; Rev. 1:1)

Giving further evidence of her humility, Mary expressed amazement that God would have **regard for** her **humble state.** Socially, she was an ordinary girl from an insignificant Galilean village (Nazareth) scorned by other Israelites (cf. John 1:46). Mary was thus far removed from society's elite in Judea and Jerusalem. Even after becoming the mother of the Messiah, she never became prominent. Jesus treated her with respect, but made it clear that she had no special claim on Him (John 2:4; Matt. 12:46–50). Nor did the early church elevate her to a special position, or bestow any particular honors on her. The only New Testament reference to her after the scene at the cross (John 19:25–27) was as just another one of the believers gathered in Jerusalem (Acts 1:14).

This ordinary young woman was engaged to a very ordinary young man. Though Joseph, like Mary, was of the line of David, he was merely a common laborer. It was because they viewed His family as nothing more than plain, average people that the villagers of Nazareth took offense at Jesus' claims (Matt. 13:54–57).

But Mary's **humble state** involved more than just her standing in Jewish society; it had to do with her spiritual character. She acknowledged that she, like everyone, was a sinner, in need of a **Savior.** Like all true worshipers, Mary had a lofty view of the Lord and a lowly view of herself. If she was the most exalted of women (cf. the exposition of 1:42 in the previous chapter of this volume), she at the same time was the most humble of women (cf. Luke 14:11). It is such humility that God requires and blesses (cf. James 4:6). In Isaiah 57:15 God said, "Thus says the high and exalted One who lives forever, whose name is Holy, 'I dwell on a high and holy place, and also with the contrite and lowly of spirit in order to revive the spirit of the lowly and to revive the heart of the contrite.'"

So Mary demonstrated the proper attitude in worship. She was joyful and grateful because of God's mercy to her. Her humble awareness of her utter unworthiness and God's marvelous grace to her produced praise and worship from her grateful heart.

THE OBJECT OF WORSHIP

the Lord . . . God my Savior (1:46*b*, 47*b*)

Mary's worship of **the Lord** centered primarily on His role as her **Savior.** The central theme of all believers' worship must be the reality that God is the Savior from sin and judgment. If that were not so, it would be impossible to worship Him, as impossible as it is for all who live in eternal torment in hell. If God were not a saving, redeeming, forgiving God, people might dread Him and attempt to pacify or appease Him, but not worship Him.

Mary knew that the coming of Messiah marked the apex of redemptive history. Her Son would "save His people from their sins" (Matt. 1:21; cf. John 1:29), because the purpose for His coming was "to seek and to save that which was lost" (Luke 19:10). The thrilling reality that through her the Messiah would be born into the world prompted Mary to praise and worship her Redeemer.

THE REASONS FOR WORSHIP

For behold, from this time on all generations will count me blessed. For the Mighty One has done great things for me; and holy is His name. And His mercy is upon generation after generation toward those who fear Him. He has done mighty deeds with His arm; He has scattered those who were proud in the thoughts of their heart. He has brought down rulers from their thrones, and has exalted those who were humble. He has filled the hungry with good things; and sent away the rich empty-handed. He has given help to Israel His servant, in remembrance of His mercy, as He spoke to our fathers, to Abraham and his descendants forever." (1:48*b*–55)

Three reasons or motives for Mary's praise emerge from her magnificent hymn.

Mary was motivated first because **the Mighty One** had **done great things for** her (cf. 1:30–35)—things so staggering and wonderful that all succeeding **generations** would **count** her **blessed.** To be the mother of the Messiah was an honor greater than any bestowed on any woman before or since. And, as noted above, the reality that she, an unworthy sinner, saved only by God's grace could also bear the Son of God prompted her worship. That the One whose **name** is **holy** would condescend to save wretched sinners will be the theme of believers' worship throughout eternity (cf. Rev. 5:9).

Mary's praise went beyond herself to embrace all that God would do for others in the future. Once again demonstrating her familiarity with the Old Testament, she quoted Psalm 103:17: **"And His mercy is upon generation after generation toward those who fear Him."** She praised God for the common salvation (cf. Jude 3) offered to all who **fear** Him—the saved, who are filled with a deep, reverent regard for the person and will of God and are committed to glorifying Him.

The final section of Mary's hymn recounts what God had done for His people in the past (cf. the seven aorist tense verbs in vv. 51–54). Consistent with Jewish worship, which not only recited God's attributes, but also recounted His **mighty deeds,** Mary praised Him for what He had done for Israel. As she did so, she noted first that God had **scattered those who were proud in the thoughts of their heart.** Perhaps she had in mind Pharaoh's arrogance (Ex. 5:2) and God's subsequent destruction of his army and deliverance of His people (Ex. 15:1–21). Mary may also have been thinking of Nebuchadnezzar, who "when his heart was lifted up and his spirit became so proud that he behaved arrogantly, he was deposed from his royal throne and his glory was taken away from him" (Dan. 5:20). Afterwards the thoroughly chastened king acknowledged that the Lord "is able to humble those who walk in pride" (Dan. 4:37). God had also **brought down rulers from their thrones** (perhaps a reference to the Canaanite rulers defeated by Joshua; [e.g., Josh. 10:23–26; cf. Job 34:24; Ps. 107:40; Ezek. 21:25–26]), and **exalted those who were humble** (cf. 14:11; 18:14; Gen. 45:26; 1 Sam. 2:6–8; Job 5:11; Pss. 78:70–71; 113:7–8). In His mercy and grace, God **filled the hungry with good things** (cf. Pss. 34:10; 107:8–9; 146:7); in judgment He **sent away the rich empty-handed** (cf. 6:24; 18:24–25).

Mary's overview of Israel's history reveals that God repeatedly overturned the normal order, illustrating the truth He expressed in Isaiah 55:8–9: "'For My thoughts are not your thoughts, neither are your ways My ways,' declares the Lord. 'For as the heavens are higher than the earth, so are My ways higher than your ways and My thoughts than your thoughts.'"

Throughout the nation's history, He gave **help to Israel His servant** (cf. 1:71; Pss. 98:3; 106:10) because of **His mercy** (v. 72; Isa. 63:9; Jer. 31:20; 33:25–26; Ezek. 39:25).

Mary viewed all of redemptive history as the outworking of the covenant which He **spoke to** the **fathers, to Abraham and his descendants forever** (Gen. 12:1–3; Ex. 2:24; Lev. 26:42; 2 Kings 13:23; 1 Chron. 16:14–16; Ps. 105:9; Acts 3:25). The salvation promised in that covenant would be clarified in the new covenant (Jer. 31:31–34) and would be ratified through the death of the very Child she carried in her womb. For it is only through the sacrificial death of the Lord Jesus Christ that all the sins of the redeemed—past, present, and future—are atoned for (Matt. 20:28; John 10:15; Rom. 3:24–26; Gal. 3:13; Eph. 1:7; 5:2; 1 Tim. 2:6; Titus 2:14; Heb. 7:27; 9:26, 28; 10:12; 1 Peter 1:18–19; 2:24; 3:18; Rev. 1:5). That covenant reality forms a fitting conclusion to Mary's hymn of praise.

The Revelation of God in the Birth of John the Baptist (Luke 1:56–66)

8

And Mary stayed with her about three months, and then returned to her home. Now the time had come for Elizabeth to give birth, and she gave birth to a son. Her neighbors and her relatives heard that the Lord had displayed His great mercy toward her; and they were rejoicing with her. And it happened that on the eighth day they came to circumcise the child, and they were going to call him Zacharias, after his father. But his mother answered and said, "No indeed; but he shall be called John." And they said to her, "There is no one among your relatives who is called by that name." And they made signs to his father, as to what he wanted him called. And he asked for a tablet and wrote as follows, "His name is John." And they were all astonished. And at once his mouth was opened and his tongue loosed, and he began to speak in praise of God. Fear came on all those living around them; and all these matters were being talked about in all the hill country of Judea. All who heard them kept them in mind, saying, "What then will this child turn out to be?" For the hand of the Lord was certainly with him. (1:56–66)

First and foremost, the Bible is God's revelation of Himself to mankind. It presents Him as the sovereign ruler of the universe, who not only created man, but also made His divine power manifest to him in His creation (Rom. 1:18ff.) and revealed His person as knowable in Scripture. The Bible reveals the triune God's nature, character, works, purposes, will, and provision of salvation; He is the one revealed in Scripture. Thus, Scripture is called "the testimony of the Lord" (Ps. 19:7); Jesus said of the Scriptures, "It is these that testify about Me" (John 5:39); Peter said of Jesus, "Of Him all the prophets bear witness" (Acts 10:43); and an angel told the apostle John that "the testimony of Jesus is the spirit of prophecy" (Rev. 19:10). God revealed Himself in Scripture as the Sovereign and Savior through the written or spoken words of angels, prophets, apostles, and others; and through visions, signs, wonders, and miracles.

Because the person and work of God permeate Scripture, every passage discloses something about Him. This passage is no exception, as its concluding phrase, **for the hand of the Lord was certainly with him** (John the Baptist), indicates. Everything in the story of John evidences the mighty presence of God. The hand of the Divine One was seen in the angel Gabriel's announcement of his birth to Zacharias in the temple, in Zacharias being struck deaf and dumb for not believing Gabriel's words, in Zacharias and Elizabeth conceiving a child when both were past childbearing years, and in Zacharias's hearing and speech being restored when John was named.

As he began his gospel, Luke, the divinely inspired historian, was especially concerned that his readers see the unfolding of the plan of redemption as the work of God. He focused on the staggering supernatural event that launched the most important era of redemptive history: the miraculous intervention that brought into the world the Messiah's forerunner.

The birth of a child is always cause for great joy and celebration —but especially, in Israel, if it was a boy to carry on the family line. Though John never married or fathered children, friends, neighbors, family members, and even hired musicians would have gathered with normal expectations and hopes to celebrate the joyous event. The news that Elizabeth had given birth to a boy was made all the more joyous because of her barrenness, the couple's age, and the child's status as Messiah's forerunner.

But as great as their joy was at John the Baptist's birth, ours is even greater, because we know the answer to their question, **"What then will this child turn out to be?"** The Gospels record the powerful impact of his life and preaching (Matt. 3:1). They note that huge crowds from Jerusalem and Judea flocked to the wilderness to hear him (v. 5); that in preparation for Messiah's coming (v. 3) people confessed their sins and demonstrated the genuineness of their repentance by being baptized (v. 6); that John announced Jesus as "the Lamb of God who takes away the sin of the world!" (John 1:29); and that his fearless confrontation of sinners (Matt. 3:7–10)—even those in high places (Matt. 14:3–4)—would eventually cost him his life (Matt. 14:6–10).

As he continues to interweave the birth narratives of John and Jesus, Luke's record of the birth of John reveals three truths about God: His promise is veracious, His purpose is gracious, and His power is wondrous.

THE PROMISE OF GOD IS VERACIOUS

And Mary stayed with her about three months, and then returned to her home. Now the time had come for Elizabeth to give birth, and she gave birth to a son. Her neighbors and her relatives heard that the Lord had displayed His great mercy toward her; and they were rejoicing with her. (1:56–58)

Luke's note that **Mary stayed with** Elizabeth **about three months, and then returned to her home** forms a transition from Mary's hymn of praise recorded in verses 46–55 to the account of John's birth in this passage. Since she came to stay with Elizabeth and Zacharias when Elizabeth was sixth months pregnant (1:26), Mary evidently **returned to her home** (her parents' home, since she and Joseph were not yet married) shortly before John's birth.

Among the comforting realities in Scripture is that God's promises are veracious; that is, they are true, and will certainly come to pass. Joshua 21:45 notes that "not one of the good promises which the Lord had made to the house of Israel failed; all came to pass" (cf. 1 Kings 8:56). "For as many as are the promises of God," Paul reminded the Corinthians, "in Him [Christ] they are yes" (2 Cor. 1:20) because, as the writer of Hebrews notes, "He who promised is faithful" (Heb. 10:23). There can be no doubt that God will keep His promises, since "God is not a man, that He should lie, nor a son of man, that He should repent; has He said, and will He not do it? Or has He spoken, and will He not make it good?" (Num. 23:19); Paul writes that "God . . . cannot lie" (Titus 1:2), and the writer of Hebrews declares that "it is impossible for God to lie" (Heb. 6:18). God is the "God of truth" (Ps. 31:5; Isa. 65:16), who is "abundant in . . . truth" (Ps. 86:15) and whose "word is truth" (John 17:17).

Through His angelic messenger Gabriel, God had promised Zacharias, "Your wife Elizabeth will bear you a son, and you will give him the name John. You will have joy and gladness, and many will rejoice at his birth" (1:13–14). In fulfillment of that promise, **Elizabeth . . . gave birth to a son. Her neighbors and her relatives heard that the Lord had displayed His great mercy toward her; and they were rejoicing with her.** Luke's matter of fact statement that **the time had come** marks the beginning of the apex of redemptive history. The birth of Messiah's forerunner would be followed by the birth of the Messiah, the Lord Jesus Christ, who would accomplish the work of redemption and ratify the New covenant, providing the sacrifice that brought forgiveness of sins and eternal life to all believers from Adam on.

The birth of the long-awaited child who would remove the stigma of her barrenness caused Elizabeth to rejoice, and her friends and relatives **were rejoicing with her.** Perhaps she even laughed for joy, as did Sarah, another older, barren woman, when she gave birth to Isaac (Gen. 21:6; Isaac means, "to laugh" in Hebrew). Certainly Elizabeth and the rest of those present praised God for **His great mercy.** God's mercy is His loving action toward undeserving sufferers, such as this old, childless couple stigmatized by barrenness, and is a major theme in this context (cf. vv. 50, 54, 72, 78).

THE PURPOSE OF GOD IS GRACIOUS

And it happened that on the eighth day they came to circumcise the child, and they were going to call him Zacharias, after his father. But his mother answered and said, "No indeed; but he shall be called John." And they said to her, "There is no one among your relatives who is called by that name." And they made signs to his father, as to what he wanted him called. And he asked for a tablet and wrote as follows, "His name is John." And they were all astonished. (1:59–63)

God is a God of grace who delights in being gracious to sinners (Isa. 30:18). He finds His joy in giving His people the blessings they do not deserve, and withholding the chastening they do deserve (cf. Luke 15:7, 10, 20–27). He has, according to Ephesians 1:9, kind intentions toward the elect, who "are not under law but under grace" (Rom. 6:14), and upon whom He will pour out the "surpassing riches of His grace" for all eternity (Eph. 2:7). God is the "God of all grace" (1 Peter 5:10), who gives grace (Ps. 84:11; Pr. 3:34; James 4:6; 1 Peter 5:5), and sits on the "throne of grace" (Heb. 4:16). The Bible describes God's grace as great (cf. James 4:6), surpassing (2 Cor. 9:14), sovereign (2 Tim. 1:9), rich (Eph. 1:7; 2:7), manifold (1 Peter 4:10), all-sufficient (2 Cor. 12:9), abundant (Acts 4:33; 1 Tim. 1:14), and glorious (Eph. 1:6).

God's grace manifested itself in a surprising way in this passage —through a conflict over the naming of Elizabeth's son. The setting was **the eighth day** after the baby's birth when **they came to circumcise the child.** Circumcision was required of all Jewish males (Gen. 17:9–14; Lev. 12:3), and was instituted by God for three reasons. First, it had health benefits, particularly in the ancient world where the danger of bacteria was undiscovered and standards of hygiene were largely unknown, so infection was more easily passed from a man to a woman. Eliminating the outer skin diminished the potential of such infection, so that historically, Jewish women have had low rates of cervical cancer and other diseases because Jewish husbands were circumcised. Circumcision was thus one of the many dietary and sanitary regulations God gave to protect and perpetuate the Jewish people. More significantly, circumcision was the sign of the Abrahamic covenant (Gen. 17:10), and thus a mark of Israel's national identity. Finally, circumcision serves as a spiritual object lesson, graphically illustrating man's need for cleansing from the depravity of sin, which is passed on to each succeeding generation through procreation (Deut. 10:16; Jer. 4:4; Ezek. 44:7, 9; Rom. 4:11).

Circumcision surgery was usually performed by the father or another appointed person. (On at least one occasion, it was performed by a woman—Moses's wife Zipporah [Ex. 4:25].) According to later Jewish tradition, there had to be at least ten witnesses present. They could, if need be, later attest that the circumcision had been performed. The practice of naming the child on the eighth day, the day of circumcision, is not prescribed in the Old Testament. By the first century A.D. it had become a common practice (how widespread is not known), perhaps based on the tradition that Moses was named and circumcised on the eighth day after his birth. In addition, Abraham received his new name on the day he was circumcised (Gen. 17:5, 23).

The people who had gathered to witness the circumcision of Elizabeth's child decided to get involved in naming him. For a group to participate in the naming of a child was not unusual; according to Ruth 4:17, "The neighbor women gave him [the son of Boaz and Ruth] a name, saying, 'A son [i.e., descendant] has been born to Naomi!' So they named him Obed. He is the father of Jesse, the father of David." To honor the faithful priest, who had endured so much suffering and sorrow due to his and Elizabeth's childlessness, **they were going to call** the boy **Zacharias, after his father.** Naming firstborn sons after their fathers was not unknown, though naming them after their grandfathers was more common.

In Jewish culture, names were meant to be descriptive. Sometimes they reflected a person's physical characteristics; for example, Esau means, "hairy," and Jacob, "one who grabs the heel"—an obvious reference to what he did at his birth (Gen. 25:26). Other names expressed the parents' joy over their child's birth, such as Saul and Samuel, both of which mean "asked for." Other names, such as Elijah ("Yahweh is God"), reflected the parents' faith.

The well-intentioned attempt to name the child after his father, however, provoked an immediate, forceful reaction from **his mother.** *Ouchi* (**no indeed**) is an emphatic, strengthened form of the negative adverb *ou,* and could be translated, "not so," "by no means," "not at all," or, in contemporary idom, "no way." Instead of being named after his father, Elizabeth insisted adamantly that her son was to **be called John,** just as the angel Gabriel had commanded Zacharias (1:13). There was to be no discussion; this was not going to be a group decision.

The reason the baby's name was nonnegotiable was because God Himself, as He had done in the cases of Isaac (Gen. 17:19), Isaiah's son (Isa. 8:3), Hosea's children (Hos. 1:4, 6, 9), and would shortly do in the case of Jesus (Matt. 1:21), had chosen it. *Iōannēs* (**John**) is the Greek form of the Hebrew name *Jehohanan* (or *Johanan*), which means, "God is gracious." The name reflects God's gracious salvation, in which John would figure prominently as Messiah's forerunner. The names of his parents also unfold aspects of the plan of redemption. "Zacharias" means, "God remembers" (i.e., is faithful to His promises), while "Elizabeth" may mean, "my God has sworn" or "my God is an oath," in other words, He is "the Absolutely Reliable One" (William Hendriksen, *The Gospel of Luke* [Grand Rapids: Baker, 1978], 65). Both of those possible meanings of Elizabeth's name also refer to God's faithfulness.

Taken aback by Elizabeth's vehement rejection of their choice of a name and her insistence on naming the baby John, those gathered **said to her, "There is no one among your relatives who is called by that name."** By giving her son a name not shared by any of her or Zacharias's relatives, Elizabeth had gone against Jewish custom. Perhaps feeling that as a woman she had overstepped her bounds, they decided to go over Elizabeth's head to her husband, Zacharias.

Still under God's chastening for doubting what Gabriel had said to him in the temple (1:20), Zacharias was unable to speak or hear (the word translated "mute" in 1:22 [*kōphos*] refers to those who are deaf in 7:22; Matt. 11:5; Mark 7:32, 37; 9:25]). That **they made signs to** him asking Zacharias **what he wanted** his son to be **called** also argues that he was unable to hear, or else they would simply have spoken to him.

In response to their inquiry, Zacharias **asked for a tablet.** *Pinakidion* (**tablet**), used only here in the New Testament, refers to a small, wooden, wax-covered writing tablet. On this tablet, which had been his only means of communicating for the last several months, Zacharias **wrote as follows, "His name is John."** His reply was terse and emphatic; Elizabeth had said that the child "shall be called John"

(v. 60), but Zacharias declared that his name is John. As far as he was concerned, that had been the child's name since Gabriel announced it to him. His decision, therefore, was final, and left those present **astonished.**

But if the choice of the child's name surprised those present, what happened next would utterly amaze them.

THE POWER OF GOD IS WONDROUS

And at once his mouth was opened and his tongue loosed, and he began to speak in praise of God. Fear came on all those living around them; and all these matters were being talked about in all the hill country of Judea. All who heard them kept them in mind, saying, "What then will this child turn out to be?" For the hand of the Lord was certainly with him. (1:64–66)

Zacharias's affirmation that his son would indeed be given the name prescribed by Gabriel was followed by a startling display of divine power. Zacharias had been deaf and unable to speak for the whole nine months. But immediately **his mouth was opened and his tongue loosed, and he began to speak in praise of God.**

From beginning to end, the Bible extols God's power. Genesis records His creation of the universe out of nothing (Gen. 1–2; cf. Jer. 10:12; 27:5; 32:17; 51:15; Rev. 4:11), and Revelation declares that God will destroy the present universe and create a new heaven and a new earth (Rev. 21–22; cf. 2 Peter 3:7–12). God, in the person of the Lord Jesus Christ, "upholds all things by the word of His power" (Heb. 1:3). Psalm 62:11 declares that "power belongs to God," one of whose names is El Shaddai—God Almighty (cf. Gen. 17:1; 28:3; 35:11; Ex. 6:3; Ezek. 10:5). God's power is limitless (Num. 11:23); therefore, "with God all things are possible" (Matt. 19:26) and "nothing will be impossible with God" (Luke 1:37; cf. Gen. 18:14). His power is great (Ex. 14:31; Nah. 1:3), majestic (Ex. 15:6), exalted (Job 37:23), and mighty (Isa. 8:11).

The phrase **at once,** as it (or the related term "immediately") does frequently in Luke's gospel, is associated with a divine miracle (cf. 4:39; 5:25; 8:44, 47, 55; 13:13; 18:43). Unlike the so-called miracles of today's faith healers, New Testament healings were instantaneous. (For a further discussion of this point, see John MacArthur, *Charismatic Chaos* [Grand Rapids: Zondervan, 1992], 211, 213–14, and the exposition of 4:38–44 in chapter 25 of this volume.) Immediately, Zacharias's **mouth was opened and his tongue loosed**—just as Gabriel had predicted (1:20). All the pent-up emotions of the past nine months burst forth, **and**

he began to speak in praise of God. Some of what he said is recorded in verses 67–79.

As a result of the shocking display of God's power demonstrated in Zacharias's miraculous healing, **fear came on all those living around them; and all these matters were being talked about in all the hill country of Judea.** All the details of the incredible story of John's birth—the angel Gabriel appearing to Zacharias in the temple, Zacharias becoming deaf and mute as a result of his unbelief, Elizabeth conceiving a child despite her and Zacharias's advanced age, the birth of their child, who was to be the forerunner of Messiah, Zacharias's sudden, miraculous healing—were a hot topic of conversation throughout the region. Not just those present at John's birth, but also **all who heard** of these incredible events **kept them in mind** (cf. 2:19, 51; 3:15), **saying, "What then will this child turn out to be?"** The speculation was rampant about John's future. Uppermost in people's minds was the thought that if he was to be Messiah's forerunner, then the arrival of Messiah Himself was imminent. What was undeniable to all was that **the hand of the Lord** (a phrase symbolizing God's powerful presence; cf. Ex. 9:3; Deut. 2:15; Josh. 4:23–24; 1 Sam. 5:6, 9; 7:13; 1 Kings 18:46; Ezra 7:28; Isa. 19:16) **was certainly with** John from the outset.

The inescapable conclusion to be drawn from this account of the birth of John the Baptist is that God acts graciously and savingly in human history. His veracity, grace, and power shine clearly through the events recorded here. The display of those attributes prompted Zacharias's rich and instructive outburst of praise, which Luke recorded in the next section of his gospel.

Zacharias's Song of Salvation—Part 1: The Davidic Covenant (Luke 1:67–71)

9

And his father Zacharias was filled with the Holy Spirit, and prophesied, saying: "Blessed be the Lord God of Israel, for He has visited us and accomplished redemption for His people, and has raised up a horn of salvation for us in the house of David His servant—as He spoke by the mouth of His holy prophets from of old—salvation from our enemies, and from the hand of all who hate us; (1:67–71)

One expression of the joy that marks the redeemed (cf. Neh. 8:10; Ps. 16:11; Rom. 14:17; Gal. 5:22; 1 Peter 1:8) is "singing and making melody with [the] heart to the Lord" (Eph. 5:19; cf. Col. 3:16). That theme runs throughout Scripture. Psalm 5:11 declares, "Let all who take refuge in You be glad, let them ever sing for joy"; in Psalm 13:6, the psalmist exults, "I will sing to the Lord, because He has dealt bountifully with me"; Psalm 30:4 exhorts, "Sing praise to the Lord, you His godly ones"; and Psalm 92:1 affirms that "it is good to give thanks to the Lord and to sing praises to Your name, O Most High" (cf. v. 4; 7:17; 9:2, 11; 18:49; 27:6; 28:7; 33:1–3; 40:3; 47:6–7; 57:7; 59:16–17; 61:8; 63:7; 66:2; 68:4; 69:30; 71:22–23; 75:9; 81:1; 84:2; 89:1; 90:14; 95:1; 96:1–2; 98:1; 104:33; 105:2; 108:1, 3; 119:54, 72; 132:9, 16; 135:3; 138:1; 144:9; 146:2; 147:1, 7; 149:1, 3, 5;

Ex. 15:1, 21; Judg. 5:3; 2 Sam. 22:50; 1 Kings 4:32; 1 Chron. 16:9, 23; Ezra 3:11; Isa. 12:2,5; 42:10; Jer. 20:13; Zech. 2:10; Rev. 5:9; 14:3; 15:3-4).

In addition to those exhortations to sing praise, the Bible records numerous songs of praise to God. After God miraculously delivered them from the pursuing Egyptians by drowning Pharaoh's army in the Red Sea, Moses and the Israelites sang a song celebrating that deliverance (Ex. 15:1-21). Deborah and Barak also sang of God's deliverance of His people, this time from the Canaanite forces led by Sisera (Judg. 5:1-31). At the dedication of the temple

> all the Levitical singers, Asaph, Heman, Jeduthun, and their sons and kinsmen, clothed in fine linen, with cymbals, harps and lyres, standing east of the altar, and with them one hundred and twenty priests blowing trumpets in unison when the trumpeters and the singers were to make themselves heard with one voice to praise and to glorify the Lord, and when they lifted up their voice accompanied by trumpets and cymbals and instruments of music, and when they praised the Lord saying, "He indeed is good for His lovingkindness is everlasting," then the house, the house of the Lord, was filled with a cloud, so that the priests could not stand to minister because of the cloud, for the glory of the Lord filled the house of God. (2 Chron. 5:12-14)

Hannah sang a song of praise to the Lord for delivering her from the stigma of barrenness (1 Sam. 2:1-10). The book of Psalms, Israel's hymn book, is filled with songs celebrating the delivering, saving, redeeming acts of God toward His people. The book of Revelation records songs of praise sung in heaven (5:9-10; 15:3-4).

In the first two chapters of his gospel, Luke records five tributes of praise: those of Elizabeth (1:41-45), Mary (1:46-55), Zacharias (1:67-79), the angels who announced Christ's birth (2:13-14), and Simeon (2:25-32). And though her words were not recorded the devout "prophetess, Anna" (2:36), who "never left the temple, serving night and day with fastings and prayers" (v. 37), gave "thanks to God [for the infant Jesus], and continued to speak of Him to all those who were looking for the redemption of Jerusalem" (v. 38). We have no information as to whether they were ever sung, or intended to be sung, but they were clearly outbursts of praise.

Verses 67-79 of chapter 1 comprise the third of those five anthems, that of Zacharias. Mary's praise, the Magnificat, emphasized personal salvation; Zacharias's praise, known as the Benedictus (from the first word in the Latin Vulgate), focuses on collective salvation. It is a tribute of praise to God for the salvation of sinners, and, therefore, omits any mention of divine judgment. As was fitting for a priest, who devoted his life to the study and teaching of the law, Zacharias's praise, like Mary's, was deeply rooted in the Old Testament. It focused especially on the three great covenants: the Davidic, Abrahamic, and New covenants, and thus is a major bridge from the Old Testament to the New. Zacharias's words plainly reveal that Christianity is not a new religion, but rather the fulfillment of everything promised in the Old Testament through the power and work of the Messiah, the Lord Jesus Christ.

Zacharias's outburst of praise and worship was prompted by the astounding events that had just taken place. Briefly summarizing, about nine months earlier the angel Gabriel had appeared to Zacharias while he was ministering in the temple. Gabriel made the stunning announcement that Zacharias and Elizabeth, who were barren and well past childbearing age, would nevertheless have a child—and not just any child, but the forerunner of the Messiah. When Zacharias's skeptical reply revealed his lack of faith, he became, at Gabriel's word, deaf and unable to speak. But Elizabeth became pregnant, just as God had promised through Gabriel. Eight days after she gave birth to their son, Zacharias was asked what to name him. When he wrote emphatically, "His name is John" (Luke 1:63; cf. v. 13), "at once his mouth was opened and his tongue loosed, and he began to speak in praise of God" (v. 64). Zacharias's Benedictus in verses 68–79 is an expression of that praise.

But Zacharias's song was not merely a reflection of his understandable joy at becoming a father when all hope seemed to have long vanished. It expressed the far more significant truth that the redemption God promised in the Old Testament was about to be accomplished. Zacharias's son, John, would be the forerunner announcing the coming Messiah, through whom God would deliver Israel and fulfill His covenants. Those promises and covenants were, no doubt, part of his teaching through the years, so he was very familiar with the texts of the Old Testament that contain them. That fact becomes obvious as his praise unfolds. It is with three of those covenants that Zacharias's reflections are chiefly concerned.

There are six covenants in the Old Testament that are specifically referred to by that term. Three of them, the Noahic (Gen. 9:9–17), Mosaic (Ex. 19:5; 24:7–8; 34:27–28; Deut. 4:13), and the Priestly (Num. 25:10–13) covenants, are non-salvific; eternal, spiritual salvation is not in view in any of them. The other three covenants, the Davidic, Abrahamic, and New, do relate to salvation. The Davidic covenant is universal; it involves the eternal rule of Jesus Christ over all. The Abrahamic covenant is national; it designates God's promised blessing of Israel. The New covenant is personal; it refers to God forgiving sin in the lives of individuals. Of course no one will enter into the full blessings of the Davidic and Abrahamic covenants apart from the salvation provided in the New covenant.

It was important for Luke to include this anthem of praise at the outset of his gospel story since, as noted above, it inseparably links Christianity to the Old Testament salvation covenants. More specifically, the coming of Messiah's forerunner, John the Baptist, announced the fulfillment of God's covenant promise of redemption through the Messiah, Jesus Christ.

Like his wife (1:41) and son (1:15) before him, **Zacharias was filled with the Holy Spirit.** The divine power of the Spirit of God came upon him so that he **prophesied.** The verb translated **prophesied** (*prophēteuō*) means, "to speak forth," "to proclaim and expound God's Word." Zacharias was filled with and inspired by the Holy Spirit so that what he spoke was the very Word of God.

Zacharias's introductory phrase, **"Blessed be the Lord God,"** was a common way to introduce praise in the Old Testament (e.g., Gen. 9:26; 24:27; Ex. 18:10; Ruth 4:14; 1 Sam. 25:32,39; 2 Sam. 18:28; 1 Kings 1:48; 8:15,56; 1 Chron. 16:36; 29:10; Ezra 7:27; Pss. 28:6; 31:21; 41:13; 66:20; 68:19; 72:18–19; 89:52; 106:48; 113:2; 124:6; 135:21; Dan. 2:19–20; cf. Luke 2:28; Rom. 1:25; 2 Cor. 1:3; Eph. 1:3; 1 Peter 1:3).

Zacharias rightly viewed God's plan of redemption as the unfolding of His promises to **Israel.** The Lord reminded a Samaritan woman that "salvation is from the Jews" (John 4:22), while Paul wrote that to the "Israelites ... [belong] the adoption as sons, and the glory and the covenants and the giving of the Law and the temple service and the promises, [and] whose are the fathers, and from whom is the Christ according to the flesh, who is over all, God blessed forever" (Rom. 9:4–5).

Zacharias praised God first because He had **visited** His people. The concept of God visiting His people, whether for judgment (cf. Ex. 32:34; Job 35:15) or for blessing (cf. Ruth 1:6; 1 Sam. 2:21; Jer. 29:10) is a familiar Old Testament theme. Heaven had come down to earth; the supernatural had invaded the natural; God was working out His eternal plan.

Specifically, Zacharias glorified God because He had **accomplished redemption for His people** (cf. 2:38; 24:21). *Lutrōsis* (**redemption**) and its related terms comprise one of the word groups used in the New Testament to express the rich theological truth of salvation. It refers to the payment of a price to release someone from bondage. (Another word group, *agoradzō* and its related terms, adds the idea of ownership, that God redeems sinners for Himself.) Redemption frees sinners from slavery to sin (John 8:34; Rom. 6:6,17,20), the curse of the law (Gal. 3:13; 4:5), the sinful ways of fallen men (1 Cor. 7:23), false religion (Gal. 4:3), and Satan, who wielded the power of death (Heb. 2:14–15) subject to God's will (Job 2:6). The purchase price paid to redeem the elect was the sacrificial death of the Lord Jesus Christ (Rom. 3:24; 1 Cor. 1:30; Eph. 1:7; Col. 1:14; Titus 2:14; Heb. 9:12; 1 Peter 1:18–19).

When Zacharias spoke these words, redemption had long been granted, but the covenant that secured it had not been ratified. His son, Messiah's forerunner, was only eight days old. And the Messiah, the Lord Jesus Christ, was not even born yet. But Zacharias was so certain that God would do what He had promised that he spoke of redemption as if it had already taken place. He knew that the birth of his son, John, signaled that God was about to visit His people and bring the provision that made salvation possible.

The people of Israel fervently longed for Messiah to come and deliver them from their bondage to Rome, as God had delivered their ancestors from slavery in Egypt (cf. Ps. 106). They viewed their deliverance primarily in earthly, political terms, expecting Messiah to establish His earthly kingdom and fulfill the promised blessings to David and Abraham. They overlooked the reality that those blessings would not be fulfilled apart from the forgiveness of sin provided in the New covenant. Sadly, when John and Jesus preached the necessity of that personal salvation, the majority of the people rejected their message. Zacharias, of course, had no way of knowing that would happen, and rejoiced as he saw the day of redemption dawning.

Zacharias described redemption as God's raising **up a horn of salvation.** That picturesque Old Testament expression (cf. 1 Sam. 2:10; 2 Sam. 22:3; Pss. 18:2; 89:17, 24; 92:10; 112:9; 132:17; 148:14; Mic. 4:13) spoke of power to conquer and kill, like that of a large, horned beast. Here Zacharias used it to refer to the Messiah, picturing Him as a powerful animal, who would lower His horns, drive out His enemies, and deliver His people.

This was the greatest moment in Israel's history, the culmination of all redemptive hope and anticipation. And at the center of that monumental moment in the unfolding saga of redemption was a common, ordinary priest from a small, insignificant village. As befits a man steeped in the Old Testament, Zacharias's anthem of praise considers first the Davidic covenant, revealing its background, promise, and fulfillment.

THE BACKGROUND OF THE DAVIDIC COVENANT

in the house of David His servant (1:69*b*)

Zacharias knew that the Old Testament clearly taught that Messiah would be from **the house of David.** Through Jeremiah the prophet, God said, "'Behold, the days are coming,' declares the Lord, 'When I will raise up for David a righteous Branch; and He will reign as king and act wisely and do justice and righteousness in the land'" (Jer. 23:5). In Jeremiah

33:15, He repeated that promise: "In those days and at that time I will cause a righteous Branch of David to spring forth; and He shall execute justice and righteousness on the earth." In addition, Isaiah 11:1 and 10 speak of Messiah as a descendant of David's father, Jesse (cf. Rom. 15:12), while Psalm 132:17 refers to Messiah as "the horn of David" ("Mine anointed"; cf. Ps. 2:2).

Zacharias would also have known that Jesus' mother, Mary, was of the line of David. She had stayed with him and Elizabeth for three months and had undoubtedly told them of Gabriel's promise to her: "Behold, you will conceive in your womb and bear a son, and you shall name Him Jesus. He will be great and will be called the Son of the Most High; and the Lord God will give Him the throne of His father David" (1:31–32). Since she was a descendant of David (see the discussion of 3:23–38 in chapter 21 of this volume), Mary passed the royal bloodline to Jesus.

David, God's **servant** (cf. 2 Sam. 3:18; 7:5, 8; 1 Kings 8:66; 11:13, 38; 14:8; Pss. 18:1; 36:1; 89:3; Jer. 33:21–22), the man after God's own heart (1 Sam. 13:14), and the "sweet psalmist of Israel" (2 Sam. 23:1), was arguably Israel's greatest king. The kingdom of Israel began under his predecessor, Saul, and declined under his successor, Solomon, splitting shortly after the latter's death. It was the fervent hope and expectation of the Jewish people that Messiah would fulfill the Davidic covenant and restore the kingdom of Israel to its former glory.

THE PROMISE OF THE DAVIDIC COVENANT

as He spoke by the mouth of His holy prophets from of old (1:70)

In the closing decade of his forty-year reign David, having finished building his palace, wanted to build a temple to house the ark of the covenant. Accordingly, "the king said to Nathan the prophet, 'See now, I dwell in a house of cedar, but the ark of God dwells within tent curtains'" (2 Sam. 7:2). What David had in mind sounded good to Nathan so he gave the project his blessing: "Nathan said to the king, 'Go, do all that is in your mind, for the Lord is with you'" (v. 3). But neither Nathan nor David had consulted God, who had something else in mind:

> But in the same night the word of the Lord came to Nathan, saying, "Go and say to My servant David, 'Thus says the Lord, "Are you the one who should build Me a house to dwell in? For I have not dwelt in a house since the day I brought up the sons of Israel from Egypt, even to this day; but I have been moving about in a tent, even in a tabernacle. Wherever I have gone with all the sons of Israel, did I speak a word with

one of the tribes of Israel, which I commanded to shepherd My people Israel, saying, 'Why have you not built Me a house of cedar?' " ' " (vv. 4–7)

Instead of David building a house for God, God would build a house for David:

"Now therefore, thus you shall say to My servant David, 'Thus says the Lord of hosts, "I took you from the pasture, from following the sheep, to be ruler over My people Israel. I have been with you wherever you have gone and have cut off all your enemies from before you; and I will make you a great name, like the names of the great men who are on the earth. I will also appoint a place for My people Israel and will plant them, that they may live in their own place and not be disturbed again, nor will the wicked afflict them any more as formerly, even from the day that I commanded judges to be over My people Israel; and I will give you rest from all your enemies. The Lord also declares to you that the Lord will make a house for you." ' " (vv. 8–11)

Those verses record God's irrevocable, unconditional covenant promise to David and his household (though it is not called a covenant here, it is in 2 Sam. 23:5). God **spoke by the mouth of His holy prophets** concerning this covenant repeatedly in the Old Testament; it has been estimated that more than forty other passages are directly related to these verses (e.g., Pss. 89, 110, 132). Isaiah alone has much to say about the future Davidic kingdom that will be ruled by the Messiah (cf. the discussion of 2 Sam. 7:12–13 below). According to Isaiah's prophecy the Lord will restore the faithful remnant of Israel to the land to inhabit the kingdom. He will defeat all of Israel's enemies, providing protection for His people. In the kingdom, Israel will enjoy great prosperity of many kinds. The city of Jerusalem will rise to world preeminence. Israel will be the center of world attention, and her mission will be to glorify the Lord. Gentiles in the kingdom will receive blessing through the channel of faithful Israel. Worldwide peace and righteousness will prevail under the rule of the Prince of Peace. Moral and spiritual conditions in the kingdom will reach their highest plane since the fall of Adam. Governmental leadership will be superlative with the Messiah, the perfect dictator who is just and true, in charge. Righteousness will prevail as the King swiftly judges overt sin. Humans will enjoy long lives; those who die at one hundred years of age will be considered mere youths. Knowledge of the Lord will be universal. The world of nature will enjoy a great renewal. Wild animals will be tame; the lion will lie down with the lamb, and children play with poisonous snakes. Sorrow and mourning will not exist. Finally, an eternal kingdom as part of God's new creation will follow the millennial kingdom. (For further information, including verse references for the above points, see the chart "Isaiah's Description of Israel's Future Kingdom" in John MacArthur, author and gen. ed., *The MacArthur Study Bible* [Nashville: Thomas Nelson, various publication dates], in the notes to Isa. 65.)

THE FULFILLMENT OF THE DAVIDIC COVENANT

salvation from our enemies, and from the hand of all who hate us; (1:71)

Like many Old Testament predictions, the Lord's promise to David in 2 Samuel 7:12–14 has both a near and a distant fulfillment. In the short term, David's descendant, whose kingdom God promised to establish (v. 12) was his son Solomon. He was granted the privilege of building the temple that was denied to David (v. 13*a*).

But neither Solomon's kingdom nor the temple he built were to last. As Solomon grew old, he sank deeper and deeper into sin. As a result, after his death the kingdom split into two kingdoms: the northern kingdom of Israel, and the southern kingdom of Judah. Eventually, after centuries of rebellion and disobedience, Israel was destroyed by the Assyrians (722 B.C.). Little more than a century later Judah fell to the Babylonians, who in 586 B.C. destroyed Solomon's magnificent temple.

God's covenant promise, however, did not fail. It extends to the One greater than Solomon (Luke 11:31)—the Lord Jesus Christ. It is His kingdom that God promised to establish forever (2 Sam. 7:13, 16). He will one day return to establish His earthly kingdom in fulfillment of the promise made to David, and "there will be no end to the increase of His government or of peace, on the throne of David and over his kingdom, to establish it and to uphold it with justice and righteousness from then on and forevermore" (Isa. 9:7).

It was that messianic kingdom, with its hope and expectation of **salvation from** Israel's **enemies, and from the hand of all who hate** the Jewish people (cf. Ps. 106:10), that elicited Zacharias's praise. As noted above, he believed the kingdom's arrival was imminent (as indeed did Jesus' own disciples, even after His resurrection [Acts 1:6]); he knew that his son was the forerunner of the Messiah, and that Mary was pregnant with the Messiah. Zacharias did not foresee that the unthinkable would happen—that Israel would reject and execute her King.

But Israel's disobedience cannot nullify the promises of God (Rom. 3:1–3). The King will one day return to establish His earthly kingdom, just as God promised David. In that day the remnant of Israel will come to repentance and faith and, says the Lord, "will look on Me whom they have pierced; and they will mourn for Him, as one mourns for an only son, and they will weep bitterly over Him like the bitter weeping over a firstborn" (Zech. 12:10). They will cry out joyously, "Blessed is He who comes in the name of the Lord!" (Matt. 23:39). "In that day," Zechariah prophesied, "His feet will stand on the Mount of Olives, which is in front of Jerusalem on the east" (Zech. 14:4). The most detailed description of the triumphant return of Jesus Christ to judge His enemies and establish His earthly kingdom is found in Revelation 19:11–21:

> And I saw heaven opened, and behold, a white horse, and He who sat on it is called Faithful and True, and in righteousness He judges and wages war. His eyes are a flame of fire, and on His head are many diadems; and He has a name written on Him which no one knows except Himself. He is clothed with a robe dipped in blood, and His name is called The Word of God. And the armies which are in heaven, clothed in fine linen, white and clean, were following Him on white horses. From His mouth comes a sharp sword, so that with it He may strike down the nations, and He will rule them with a rod of iron; and He treads the wine press of the fierce wrath of God, the Almighty. And on His robe and on His thigh He has a name written, "King of kings, and Lord of lords." Then I saw an angel standing in the sun, and he cried out with a loud voice, saying to all the birds which fly in midheaven, "Come, assemble for the great supper of God, so that you may eat the flesh of kings and the flesh of commanders and the flesh of mighty men and the flesh of horses and of those who sit on them and the flesh of all men, both free men and slaves, and small and great." And I saw the beast and the kings of the earth and their armies assembled to make war against Him who sat on the horse and against His army. And the beast was seized, and with him the false prophet who performed the signs in his presence, by which he deceived those who had received the mark of the beast and those who worshiped his image; these two were thrown alive into the lake of fire which burns with brimstone. And the rest were killed with the sword which came from the mouth of Him who sat on the horse, and all the birds were filled with their flesh.

The hope of Zacharias and the future remnant of Jews, as well as all true believers, is sure and will certainly come to pass. God will not forget His covenant with David. The redeemed will experience the blessed joy of serving and worshiping the King during the millennial kingdom and the eternal kingdom that will follow it. Only then will the fervent longing of the children of Israel for **salvation from** their **enemies, and from the hand of all who hate** them be realized.

Zacharias's Song of Salvation—Part 2: The Abrahamic Covenant (Luke 1:72–75)

10

To show mercy toward our fathers, and to remember His holy covenant, the oath which He swore to Abraham our father, to grant us that we, being rescued from the hand of our enemies, might serve Him without fear, in holiness and righteousness before Him all our days. (1:72–75)

If one were to ask historians to name the single most important event in history, the one with the most far-reaching implications and that made the greatest impact, there would be no consensus. Some might suggest a major battle or war that reshaped the balance of power, or the influence of a great military or political ruler, such as an Alexander the Great, Pharaoh, Caesar, king, prime minister, president, or general. Others might suggest the rise to power of a major civilization or nation, such as Egypt, Babylon, Greece, Rome, China, the British Empire, or the United States. Conversely, some might point to the fall of a major civilization, such as Babylon, Rome, or the decline of contemporary Western civilization.

Other historians might argue that a scientific invention or discovery made the greatest impact. Inventions such as the wheel, telegraph, telephone, automobile, airplane, radio, and computer, the harnessing of electricity, and the discoveries of modern medical science have unquestionably helped make our world what it is today.

Many would insist that it is ideas and beliefs that exert the greatest influence on history. They would point out the impact of thinkers such as Socrates, Plato, Aristotle, Augustine, Aquinas, Hume, Kant, Hegel, Kierkegaard, and Nietzsche; religious leaders such as Buddha, Confucius, Lao Tzu, and Muhammed; and of ideas such as evolution, communism, democracy, capitalism, and postmodernism. Nor can the significance of major movements or events, such as the Renaissance, Reformation, Enlightenment, the American Revolution, or the French Revolution, be underestimated.

But while historians might debate history's most significant event, history itself has already answered the question. The most monumental event of all was the coming of the Lord Jesus Christ into the world. The division of history into B.C. ("before Christ") and A.D. (Anno Domini, "in the year of our Lord") reveals the unsurpassed significance of Christ's incarnation; it is history's great dividing point.

God created mankind to serve, worship, and glorify Him. To that end, He placed Adam and Eve in the perfect environment of the garden of Eden. Tragically, Satan's lies led to the corruption of that perfect world as the fall plunged the human race into sin and depravity. But what Satan meant for evil, God used for His glory. He saved lost sinners, putting on display His otherwise unknowable attributes of grace, mercy, forgiveness, and compassion. The Father redeemed a people, and presented them to His beloved Son as a gift of His love. They will serve, praise, and worship Him forever.

The pinnacle of God's redemptive plan was the coming of the Lord Jesus Christ into the world. After living a sinless life of perfect obedience to God's law, He died on the cross bearing the sins of His people. Because He treated Jesus as if He had lived their sinful lives, God is able through His grace to treat the redeemed as if they had lived Jesus' perfectly righteous life. The incarnation, substitutionary atonement, and resurrection of Jesus Christ are the Bible's overarching themes. The Old Testament (most notably in Isa. 53) anticipates the death of Messiah as the ultimate sacrifice that the Old Testament sacrificial system pointed to. The Gospels give the record of Jesus' sinless life and sacrificial death. Acts and the Epistles are a commentary on the theological significance of His life, death, and resurrection. Revelation gives the details of His return and millennial reign on earth, and His eternal reign in the new heaven and new earth.

In Zacharias's day, the Jewish people were eagerly awaiting Messiah's arrival. They longed for Him to come, set up His kingdom, and restore their land to them. Zacharias was one of those "who were looking for the redemption of Jerusalem" (2:38). The birth of his son filled him with anticipation; the angel Gabriel had told him that John would "go as a forerunner before [the Messiah, Jesus Christ] in the spirit and power of Elijah, to turn the hearts of the fathers back to the children, and the disobedient to the attitude of the righteous, so as to make ready a people prepared for the Lord" (1:17). Zacharias knew that if His forerunner had just been born, Messiah's coming was imminent. That knowledge prompted his magnificent hymn of praise and worship. As befits a priest, a man who had devoted his life to studying and teaching God's law, Zacharias's hymn is saturated with Old Testament covenant texts. Specifically, he centers on the three covenants of salvation and blessing —the Davidic, Abrahamic, and New covenants. Having referred to the Davidic covenant in verses 67–71 (see the exposition of those verses in the previous chapter of this volume), Zacharias now turns to the Abrahamic covenant, noting its background, promise, and fulfillment in the coming Messiah.

THE BACKGROUND OF THE ABRAHAMIC COVENANT

To show mercy toward our fathers, (1:72*a*)

The Abrahamic covenant, which God made to the **fathers** of the nation of Israel (Abraham, Isaac, Jacob), is a foundational element of biblical interpretation. A correct understanding of it is essential to properly comprehending all of redemptive history. In contrast to the Davidic covenant, which was universal in scope, the Abrahamic covenant is national, promising blessings to Israel (though Gentiles can enter into those blessings through faith; see the discussion of Gal. 3:6–7 and Rom. 4:11–12 below).

The Abrahamic covenant is preeminently a covenant of **mercy,** revealing that God is gracious and compassionate to undeserving people. The stream of mercy that began with God's blessing of Abraham flows down through the centuries to provide forgiveness, redemption, and eternal blessing to all who have faith in the Messiah, the Lord Jesus Christ.

After beginning with universal themes, such as God's creation of the universe in six days, the entrance of sin into the world, and the worldwide flood of Noah's day and its aftermath, the book of Genesis narrows its focus to one individual and his descendants: Abraham (then known as Abram), who is introduced at the end of chapter 11. He was a native of the sophisticated and powerful Chaldean city of Ur (v. 31), located in Mesopotamia (Acts 7:2). What his connection with the true God was is not clear, since according to Joshua 24:2 he was an idolater. But God sovereignly called him while he was still living in Ur, commanding him, "Leave your country and your relatives, and come into the land that I will show you" (Acts 7:3). Later, after Abraham had settled in Haran with his father, Terah (Gen. 11:31), God repeated His call to him:

> Now the Lord said to Abram, "Go forth from your country, and from your relatives and from your father's house, to the land which I will show you; and I will make you a great nation, and I will bless you, and make your name great; and so you shall be a blessing; and I will bless those who bless you, and the one who curses you I will curse. And in you all the families of the earth shall be blessed." (Gen. 12:1–3)

In obedience to the Lord's command "Abram went forth as the Lord had spoken to him ...and came to the land of Canaan" (vv. 4, 5).

THE PROMISE OF THE ABRAHAMIC COVENANT

and to remember His holy covenant, the oath which He swore to Abraham our father, (1:72b–73)

The **holy covenant, the oath which God swore to Abraham,** though first mentioned in Genesis 12, would not actually be ratified until chapter 15 (see the discussion below). Having called Abraham to leave his home for another land which He would show him (Gen. 12:1), God promised to make of his descendants a great nation, protect and bless them, through them bless the world (vv. 2–3), and give them that land (v. 7). The Lord's promise to make a great nation from Abraham was humanly impossible, since his wife, Sarah (then known as Sarai), was barren (Gen. 11:30). The beginning of the fulfillment of that promise would be a conception miracle and the birth of Isaac (Gen. 18:9–15; 21:1–8).

God's promise to make Abraham a "great nation" (Gen. 12:2) has indeed come to pass. The Jewish people have made profound contributions in such fields as medicine, the arts, education, literature, science, and finance. But more significantly, through the nation of Israel "all the families of the earth [would] be blessed" (v. 3) spiritually. The Jewish people "were entrusted with the oracles of God" (Rom. 3:2), the Old Testament Scriptures, whose Holy Spirit-inspired writers were all Jewish. They received the "adoption as sons" (Rom. 9:4); that is, Israel was sovereignly called by God to be His special witness nation and to receive "the glory and the covenants and the giving of the Law and the temple service and the promises" (v. 4). Most important of all, "from [Israel] is the Christ according to the flesh" (v. 5; cf. Rom. 1:3). All the blessings of salvation came through the Jewish people, leading Jesus to declare that "salvation is from the Jews" (John 4:22).

But while Israel has been the channel through which God's revelation and blessings have flowed to the world, the nation has rarely shared in those blessings. Disobedience; idolatry; empty, ritualistic, outward worship; and, most heinous of all, rejecting the Messiah, have led to chastening from God instead of blessing. But despite their rebellion and resulting punishment, God has protected the Jewish people. They have survived exile to Babylon, the attempt by Antiochus Epiphanes during the intertestamental period to eradicate their religion and culture, the destruction of Jerusalem by the Romans, being dispersed from Palestine and forced to live in Gentile lands, and centuries of pogroms and persecution, culminating in the twentieth century with the madness of the Holocaust. Yet Israel still exists as a nation, occupying part of the land God promised to Abraham. And in the future God will continue to preserve the Jewish people, sealing 144,000 evangelists, 12,000 from each tribe (Rev. 7:4–8), during the tribulation, rescuing the nation from Antichrist's furious attempt to annihilate it (Rev. 12:13–17), and redeeming the believing remnant at the end of the tribulation (Rom. 11:25–27). But the Jews as a nation have yet to experience the complete fulfillment of God's promises to Abraham.

Underscoring its crucial significance in the flow of redemptive history, the Abrahamic covenant is reiterated eight times in the book of Genesis (chapters 12, 13, 15, 17, 22, 26, 28, and 35). As noted above, God announced the terms of the covenant in chapter 12, but the covenant was not actually set until chapter 15. That is clear from 15:18, which records, "On that day the Lord made a covenant with Abram." God sealed that covenant in a very dramatic way, one which emphasized its unilateral, unconditional nature.

In verse 7, God repeated the promise He had made to Abraham in chapter 12 regarding the land He would give to him and his descendants: "I am the Lord who brought you out of Ur of the Chaldeans, to give you this land to possess it." Seeking reassurance Abraham replied, "O Lord God, how may I know that I will possess it?" (v. 8). The ensuing ceremony, which was in keeping with Ancient Near Eastern custom, ratified the covenant:

> So [God] said to [Abraham], "Bring Me a three year old heifer, and a three year old female goat, and a three year old ram, and a turtledove, and a young pigeon." Then he brought all these to Him and cut them in two, and laid each half opposite the other; but he did not cut the birds. The birds of prey came down upon the carcasses, and Abram drove them away. Now when the sun was going down, a deep sleep fell upon Abram; and behold, terror and great darkness fell upon him. God said

to Abram,"Know for certain that your descendants will be strangers in a land that is not theirs, where they will be enslaved and oppressed four hundred years. But I will also judge the nation whom they will serve, and afterward they will come out with many possessions. As for you, you shall go to your fathers in peace; you shall be buried at a good old age. Then in the fourth generation they shall return here, for the iniquity of the Amorite is not yet complete." It came about when the sun had set, that it was very dark, and behold, there appeared a smoking oven and a flaming torch which passed between these pieces. (vv. 9–17)

Killing animals symbolized the seriousness of a covenant. The two parties making it would walk between the pieces of the dead animals, thus affirming that the same thing should happen to them if they broke the covenant. But in this case only the "smoking oven" and "flaming torch," which represented God's presence, passed between the parts of the slain animals; Abraham was divinely anesthetized. The covenant, therefore, was unilateral; an irrevocable pledge made by God alone and not dependant on Abraham.

Israel has never possessed all the land promised to Abraham (vv. 18–21). Only when the Lord Jesus Christ takes the throne of David and establishes His earthly kingdom will Israel experience the full blessings of the Abrahamic covenant.

Genesis 17 reveals another important component of God's covenant with Abraham. In verse 2, God said to him, "I will establish My covenant between Me and you, and I will multiply you exceedingly," then repeated that promise in verse 4: "You shall be the father of a multitude of nations." To further reinforce that point, the Lord changed his name from Abram ("exalted father") to Abraham ("father of a multitude"), because, God declared again, "I will make you the father of a multitude of nations" (v. 5).

In keeping with that promise Abraham became not only the father of the Jewish people, but also of the Arabs. Earlier Sarah, despairing of ever having a child herself, "took Hagar the Egyptian, her maid, and gave her to her husband Abram as his wife" (Gen. 16:3). The child born from that union was Ishmael (v. 11), the ancestor of the Arab people. But Ishmael was not the child through whom the covenant blessings would come:

> Then God said to Abraham, "As for Sarai your wife, you shall not call her name Sarai, but Sarah shall be her name. I will bless her, and indeed I will give you a son by her. Then I will bless her, and she shall be a mother of nations; kings of peoples shall come from her." Then Abraham fell on his face and laughed, and said in his heart, "Will a child be born to a man one hundred years old? And will Sarah, who is ninety years old, bear a child?" And Abraham said to God, "Oh that Ishmael might live

> before You!" But God said, "No, but Sarah your wife will bear you a son, and you shall call his name Isaac; and I will establish My covenant with him for an everlasting covenant for his descendants after him. As for Ishmael, I have heard you; behold, I will bless him, and will make him fruitful and will multiply him exceedingly. He shall become the father of twelve princes, and I will make him a great nation. But My covenant I will establish with Isaac, whom Sarah will bear to you at this season next year." (Gen. 17:15–21; cf. Rom. 9:7; Gal. 4:28)

Three times in this chapter (vv. 7, 13, 19) God described His covenant with Abraham as an everlasting covenant. It will never be abrogated, but will ultimately be fulfilled when Christ reigns during the millennial kingdom.

Although the Abrahamic covenant was enacted unilaterally by God and is thus unconditional and irrevocable, the enjoyment of its blessings comes only through faith. Genesis 22 illustrates that principle. In keeping with His promise, God had given Abraham and Sarah a son (Gen. 21:1–3). Years later (cf. Gen. 21:34), when Isaac was a young man, God gave Abraham a shocking command: "Take now your son, your only son, whom you love, Isaac, and go to the land of Moriah, and offer him there as a burnt offering on one of the mountains of which I will tell you" (Gen. 22:2). Humanly speaking, this was incomprehensible. Isaac was the son through whom God had promised to make of Abraham a great nation. Would not his death, therefore, abrogate God's covenant with Abraham? But Abraham's faith did not fail, and he set off with Isaac to obey God's command. According to Hebrews 11:19, Abraham believed that after he sacrificed Isaac, God would raise him from the dead. But as he was about to plunge the knife into his son,

> the angel of the Lord called to him from heaven and said, "Abraham, Abraham!" And he said, "Here I am." He said, "Do not stretch out your hand against the lad, and do nothing to him; for now I know that you fear God, since you have not withheld your son, your only son, from Me" (vv. 11–12).

Abraham's faith that God would keep His promise is a model for all believers to follow (cf. Gal. 3:9).

THE FULFILLMENT OF THE ABRAHAMIC COVENANT

to grant us that we, being rescued from the hand of our enemies, might serve Him without fear, in holiness and righteousness before Him all our days. (1:74–75)

In one of the most dramatic incidents in all of redemptive history, God's covenant with Abraham was confirmed by his faith, expressed in his willingness to offer his son Isaac as a sacrifice to God. Israel, unlike Abraham, has through history failed to respond in faith to the revealed will of God, even when Messiah came. As a result, the promised blessings of the Abrahamic covenant, like those of the Davidic covenant, have not been realized. Not until the Jewish people acknowledge Jesus as the Messiah who comes in the name of the Lord (Luke 13:35), look with penitent remorse on the One they pierced and mourn their rejection of Him (Zech. 12:10), will the believing remnant be saved (Rom. 11:26) and the nation experience all the blessings of the Abrahamic covenant in the millennial kingdom. Only then will Zacharias's fervent hope that the children of Israel, **being rescued from the hand of** their **enemies, might serve** God **without fear, in holiness and righteousness before Him all** their **days,** be realized.

As is the case with the Davidic covenant (see chap. 9 of this volume), Gentile believers will also experience the vast blessings of the Abrahamic covenant. In a spiritual sense, all Christians share in the promises of salvation blessing in this covenant, and so in the sense of salvation are called children of Abraham, as the apostle Paul notes in Galatians 3:6–7: "Even so Abraham believed God, and it was reckoned to him as righteousness. Therefore, be sure that it is those who are of faith who are sons of Abraham." Looking ahead to the cross, God applied the righteousness of Jesus Christ to Abraham's account. Those who believe the gospel and in faith embrace Jesus Christ "are blessed with Abraham, the believer" (v. 9). Even if they are not descended from Abraham physically, all who believe share the principle of faith with Abraham and thus are in that sense his spiritual descendants. The salvation blessings of the Abrahamic covenant are for all who believe in the Lord Jesus Christ, both Jews and Gentiles. To the Romans Paul wrote,

> and he [Abraham] received the sign of circumcision, a seal of the righteousness of the faith which he had while uncircumcised, so that he might be the father of all who believe without being circumcised, that righteousness might be credited to them, and the father of circumcision to those who not only are of the circumcision, but who also follow in the steps of the faith of our father Abraham which he had while uncircumcised. (Rom. 4:11–12)

That all believers become Abraham's children spiritually does not mean that the church is the new Israel, cancelling all the promises to the nation. That kind of "replacement theology" is unacceptable in light of the unconditional Old Testament promises of God and the New Testament reiteration of them. Paul says with regard to Israel, "the gifts and the calling of God are irrevocable" (Rom. 11:29). Israel has not been permanently set aside as a nation; God would not perpetuate and protect the Jewish people through the centuries unless He had a definite purpose for doing so. The apostle Paul recoiled in horror at the thought that God had permanently rejected Israel: "I say then, God has not rejected His people, has He? May it never be! [Gk., *mē genoito,* a very strong negation] ... God has not rejected His people whom He foreknew" (Rom. 11:1–2). Though Israel stumbled into disobedience, "they did not stumble so as to fall, did they? May it never be [*mē genoito*]! But by their transgression salvation has come to the Gentiles, to make them jealous" (v. 11). Gentiles, like a wild olive branch, are grafted into the rich root of Abrahamic blessing (v. 17). But the natural branches (the Jews), "if they do not continue in their unbelief, will be grafted in, for God is able to graft them in again" (v. 23). Indeed, after "the fullness of the Gentiles has come in" (v. 25), "all Israel [i.e., the believing remnant] will be saved" when Jesus returns at the end of the tribulation to set up the millennial kingdom (v. 26).

It is then that the Abrahamic covenant, anticipated by members of the believing remnant such as Zacharias, Simeon, and Anna, but rejected by the unbelieving nation when it rejected the Messiah, will be fully realized. Through redeemed Israel, its blessings will flow to the world in the earthly kingdom of the Lord Jesus Christ. (For further discussion of this critical issue, see *Romans 9–16,* The MacArthur New Testament Commentary [Chicago: Moody, 1994], chapters 1–10, and the excursus to chapter 11 of this volume.)

Zacharias's Song of Salvation—Part 3 The New Covenant (Luke 1:76–80)

11

"And you, child, will be called the prophet of the Most High; for you will go on before the Lord to prepare His ways; to give to His people the knowledge of salvation by the forgiveness of their sins, because of the tender mercy of our God, with which the Sunrise from on high will visit us, to shine upon those who sit in darkness and the shadow of death, to guide our feet into the way of peace." And the child continued to grow and to become strong in spirit, and he lived in the deserts until the day of his public appearance to Israel. (1:76–80)

Of the several covenants God has given for the outworking of redemptive history, the New covenant is unique. As noted in previous chapters of this volume, three of those covenants, the Noahic, Priestly, and Mosaic, are non-salvific; that is, they are not promises associated with salvation. The Noahic covenant is God's pledge not to destroy the world again by water, while the Priestly covenant is a "a covenant of a perpetual priesthood" (Num. 25:13) promising that all legitimate high priests would come from the family line of Phinehas. Nor is salvation in view in the Mosaic covenant, "because by the works of the Law no flesh will be justified in His sight; for through the Law comes the knowledge of sin" (Rom.

3:20; cf. v. 28; Gal. 2:16; 3:11; 5:4). And though the Abrahamic and Davidic covenants require salvation for their blessings to be realized, nothing in them provides it.

There is a barrier, insurmountable by any human effort, which prevents everyone, including Israelites, from experiencing the benefits of the Abrahamic and Davidic covenants—sin. For those covenant blessings to be realized requires a new, different, and superior covenant—one that provides total forgiveness of sin (Heb. 7:22; 8:6). That is precisely the point the writer of Hebrews makes in Hebrews 8:7–13:

> For if that first covenant had been faultless, there would have been no occasion sought for a second. For finding fault with them, He says, "Behold, days are coming, says the Lord, when I will effect a new covenant with the house of Israel and with the house of Judah; not like the covenant which I made with their fathers on the day when I took them by the hand to lead them out of the land of Egypt; for they did not continue in My covenant, and I did not care for them, says the Lord. For this is the covenant that I will make with the house of Israel after those days, says the Lord: I will put My laws into their minds, and I will write them on their hearts. And I will be their God, and they shall be My people. And they shall not teach everyone his fellow citizen, and everyone his brother, saying, 'know the Lord,' for all will know Me, from the least to the greatest of them. For I will be merciful to their iniquities, and I will remember their sins no more." When He said, "A new covenant," He has made the first obsolete. But whatever is becoming obsolete and growing old is ready to disappear.

Commenting on the significance of God's making a new covenant the Puritan theologian John Owen wrote, "Had it not been of the greatest importance to the glory of God and the good of the souls of men, God would not, for the sake of it, have laid aside one covenant and made another....All this was done that we might be pardoned (*The Forgiveness of Sin* [Reprint; Grand Rapids: Baker, 1977], 179).

The most basic problem people face is not psychological or social. It is not how they act, think, or speak. Those things merely reflect (cf. Luke 6:45) the true problem; that is, that all are sinners (Rom. 3:23), with evil, sin-defiled hearts (Jer. 17:9). The apostle Paul gave a comprehensive description (drawn from Old Testament passages) of mankind's endemic, systemic sinfulness when he wrote to the Romans,

> There is none righteous, not even one; there is none who understands, there is none who seeks for God; all have turned aside, together they have become useless; there is none who does good, there is not even one. Their throat is an open grave, with their tongues they keep deceiving, the poison of asps is under their lips; whose mouth is full of curs-

ing and bitterness; their feet are swift to shed blood, destruction and misery are in their paths, and the path of peace they have not known. There is no fear of God before their eyes. (Rom. 3:10–18)

Paul referred to sin's pervasive presence as the "law of sin" (Rom. 7:23, 25), graphically expressing the power, authority, constraint, and influence that sin exerts. The apostle's use of the term "law" was metaphorical; he was not speaking of a standard to be lived up to, but of a force to be reckoned with. Sin is an operative reality in man's nature that has the power to drive and compel behavior, much like hunger, thirst, sexual desire, fear, anger, and sorrow do. Indwelling sin manipulates and controls behavior from the inside, unlike external standards or rules.

Since neither the promised blessings of the Davidic and Abrahamic covenants, nor the threatened curses for violating the Mosaic law can change the heart, they cannot overpower the law of sin. No amount of willpower or determination to obey can enable a sinner to keep the Ten Commandments (or even Jesus' summary of the law [Mark 12:28–31]). The law both demonstrates to sinners their inability to obey and their need for mercy, grace, and forgiveness, and even exacerbates sin and leads to death (Rom. 7:8–11). It displays our sin and helplessness in order, as Paul wrote, to become "our tutor to lead us to Christ, so that we may be justified by faith" (Gal. 3:24).

Israel's experience illustrates that truth. The people had the best intentions, vowing obedience to God's law and sealing their commitment with blood as recorded in Exodus 24:4–8:

> Moses wrote down all the words of the Lord. Then he arose early in the morning, and built an altar at the foot of the mountain with twelve pillars for the twelve tribes of Israel. He sent young men of the sons of Israel, and they offered burnt offerings and sacrificed young bulls as peace offerings to the Lord. Moses took half of the blood and put it in basins, and the other half of the blood he sprinkled on the altar. Then he took the book of the covenant and read it in the hearing of the people; and they said, "All that the Lord has spoken we will do, and we will be obedient!" So Moses took the blood and sprinkled it on the people, and said, "Behold the blood of the covenant, which the Lord has made with you in accordance with all these words."

But it proved impossible for them to overcome their sinful natures and soon they were breaking the commandments with a level of idolatry and immorality that led to divine judgment (Ex. 32).

In his farewell address to the nation nearly forty years later as the wilderness wandering ended, Moses described the blessings that would come from obedience (Deut. 28:1–14), and warned of the consequences of disobedience (vv. 15–68). As an object lesson, Moses commanded that after Israel entered the Promised Land, half the tribes were to recite the promised blessings of obedience from Mount Gerizim and the other six pronounce the threatened curses for disobedience from Mount Ebal (Deut. 27:11–26). After the conquest of the land of Canaan, Joshua, like Moses, also challenged Israel to obey:

> If it is disagreeable in your sight to serve the Lord, choose for yourselves today whom you will serve: whether the gods which your fathers served which were beyond the River, or the gods of the Amorites in whose land you are living; but as for me and my house, we will serve the Lord. (Josh. 24:15)

In response "the people answered and said, 'Far be it from us that we should forsake the Lord to serve other gods'" (v. 16). When Joshua further cautioned them, "If you forsake the Lord and serve foreign gods, then He will turn and do you harm and consume you after He has done good to you" (v. 20) they protested, "No, but we will serve the Lord.... We will serve the Lord our God and we will obey His voice" (vv. 21, 24).

Again, those good intentions were not enough to keep the people from slipping into apostasy. "The people served the Lord all the days of Joshua, and all the days of the elders who survived Joshua, who had seen all the great work of the Lord which He had done for Israel" (Judg. 2:7). But after

> All that generation also were gathered to their fathers ... there arose another generation after them who did not know the Lord, nor yet the work which He had done for Israel. Then the sons of Israel did evil in the sight of the Lord and served the Baals, and they forsook the Lord, the God of their fathers, who had brought them out of the land of Egypt, and followed other gods from among the gods of the peoples who were around them, and bowed themselves down to them; thus they provoked the Lord to anger. So they forsook the Lord and served Baal and the Ashtaroth. The anger of the Lord burned against Israel, and He gave them into the hands of plunderers who plundered them; and He sold them into the hands of their enemies around them, so that they could no longer stand before their enemies. Wherever they went, the hand of the Lord was against them for evil, as the Lord had spoken and as the Lord had sworn to them, so that they were severely distressed. (vv. 10–15)

Israel's situation thus seemed hopeless. Were they never to receive the promised blessings of the Abrahamic and Davidic covenants? Could they somehow be forgiven for violating the Mosaic covenant and granted the means to obey? What they desperately needed was for God to provide another covenant that would provide both forgiveness and the power to obey. That reality underscores the need for the New covenant—the personal work of God to forgive sin, cleanse the heart, and provide spiritual power. (For a detailed exposition of the theological aspects of the New covenant, see *2 Corinthians*, The MacArthur New Testament Commentary [Chicago: Moody, 2003], 93–117.)

Zacharias, a true believer in the Lord God, and a student of the Old Testament Scripture, understood the covenants and their fulfillment through the Messiah to come. His response to the announcement of a son to be Messiah's forerunner was to break out in praise for the inevitable fulfillment of the messianic covenants. He had already referred to the Davidic and Abrahamic covenants (see the discussion of vv. 67–75 in chapters 9 and 10 of this volume). Now as he concluded his magnificent hymn of praise, he turned to the crucial New covenant, relating its promise, source, and blessings. But before discussing the New covenant Zacharias addressed his newborn son, John. He was to be the forerunner of the Messiah, whose sacrificial death would ratify that New covenant (Luke 22:20; 1 Cor. 11:25; cf. Heb. 8:6; 9:15; 12:24; 13:20).

John would **be called the prophet of the Most High.** Through John's prophetic ministry **the Most High** (a term that stresses God's absolute sovereignty; cf. the discussion of *El Elyon* ["Most High"] in chapter 4 of this volume) God would end four centuries of revelatory silence. John's ministry would be to **go on before the Lord to prepare His ways,** in fulfillment of God's promise through Malachi, "Behold, I am going to send My messenger, and he will clear the way before Me" (Mal. 3:1; cf. 4:5). He was "the one referred to by Isaiah the prophet when he said, 'The voice of one crying in the wilderness, "make ready the way of the Lord, make His paths straight!"'" (Matt. 3:3). John's mission was to prepare the people for Messiah's arrival. To that end he "preach[ed] a baptism of repentance for the forgiveness of sins" (Luke 3:3), and his uncompromising message was that the people should "repent, for the kingdom of heaven is at hand" (Matt. 3:2). John also challenged the legitimacy of some of his hearers' repentance:

> But when he saw many of the Pharisees and Sadducees coming for baptism, he said to them, "You brood of vipers, who warned you to flee from the wrath to come? Therefore bear fruit in keeping with repentance; and do not suppose that you can say to yourselves, 'We have Abraham for our father'; for I say to you that from these stones God is able to raise up children to Abraham. The axe is already laid at the root of the trees; therefore every tree that does not bear good fruit is cut down and thrown into the fire." (vv. 3:7–10)

John's message ran counter to the popular conception of the Messiah. The people were looking for a conquering hero, who would defeat their enemies, establish his throne, and usher in the promised blessings of the Abrahamic and Davidic covenants. That is why the crowd wanted to make Jesus king after He miraculously fed the five thousand (John 6:14–15). But before realizing the blessings of those covenants they needed to face the reality of their sin, repent, and seek the forgiveness provided only in the New covenant, already in operation, though ratified by our Lord on the cross. In God's timeless, eternal view He applied the death of the Savior through all redemptive history to those who repented and sought His salvation by grace.

THE PROMISE OF THE NEW COVENANT

to give to His people the knowledge of salvation by the forgiveness of their sins (1:77)

As noted above, to experience the promised blessings of the Abrahamic and Davidic covenants (as well as to escape the threatened curses for violating the Mosaic covenant) requires that God sovereignly **give to His people the knowledge of salvation.** The **knowledge** in view here is not theological or theoretical, but the personal knowledge that comes **by the forgiveness of . . . sins.**

Moses, the giver of the law, recognized the need for this covenant. As he reiterated the principles of the Mosaic covenant to the new generation about to enter the Promised Land, Moses spoke of another covenant "besides the covenant which [God] had made with them at Horeb [the Mosaic covenant]" (Deut. 29:1). That the people of Israel would be unable to keep the Mosaic covenant is evident from Deuteronomy 30:1–3:

> So it shall be when all of these things have come upon you, the blessing and the curse which I have set before you, and you call them to mind in all nations where the Lord your God has banished you, and you return to the Lord your God and obey Him with all your heart and soul according to all that I command you today, you and your sons, then the Lord your God will restore you from captivity, and have compassion on you, and will gather you again from all the peoples where the Lord your God has scattered you.

The reference to their banishment and captivity makes it clear that the people of Israel were not going to obey the law of Moses. God promised to regather them from the nations to which He had scattered them—but only when they returned to Him and obeyed Him with all their hearts and souls. (It should be noted that Israel's reconstitution as a nation in 1948 is not the regathering in view in this passage; modern Israel is a thoroughly secular state, whose people as a whole have not returned to the Lord with all their hearts and souls. The regathering predicted here refers to Israel's national salvation [Rom. 11:25–26]).

Before anyone can turn to the Lord and be saved, God must first circumcise their hearts (Deut. 30:6). Here is the essence of the New covenant—a spiritual surgery performed on the sinful heart of man. Only such a radical transformation (cf. 2 Cor. 5:17), can break the power of the law of sin and enable people to keep the law of God. Since the Mosaic, Davidic, and Abrahamic covenants did not have the power to change the heart, God provided the New covenant.

The most explicit Old Testament description of the New covenant is in Jeremiah 31:31–34:

> "Behold, days are coming," declares the Lord, "when I will make a new covenant with the house of Israel and with the house of Judah, not like the covenant which I made with their fathers in the day I took them by the hand to bring them out of the land of Egypt, My covenant which they broke, although I was a husband to them," declares the Lord. "But this is the covenant which I will make with the house of Israel after those days," declares the Lord, "I will put My law within them and on their heart I will write it; and I will be their God, and they shall be My people. They shall not teach again, each man his neighbor and each man his brother, saying, 'Know the Lord,' for they shall all know Me, from the least of them to the greatest of them," declares the Lord, "for I will forgive their iniquity, and their sin I will remember no more."

By Jeremiah's time, Israel's situation was desperate. The northern kingdom (Israel) had already fallen to the Assyrians, and the days of the southern kingdom (Judah) were numbered. The people were apostate, and Jeremiah's dire warnings of impending judgment and calls for repentance went unheeded. In the short term, then, the people's forsaking of the Mosaic covenant had rendered their situation hopeless. But God through Jeremiah promised a new covenant—the one Moses had spoken of centuries earlier (see the discussion of Deut. 30 above)—His unconditional, unilateral, eternal, irrevocable promise to redeem lost sinners from judgment and hell.

The promised New covenant would "not [be] like the [Mosaic] covenant which [God] made with their fathers" (v. 32). In sharp contrast to the external law code of the Mosaic covenant, God promised that in the New covenant He would "put [His] law within them and [write it] on their heart" (v. 33), thus granting sinners a new heart (Ezek. 36:26). The powerful spiritual dynamic provided in the New covenant provides deliverance from the power, penalty, and, ultimately, the presence of sin. God irresistibly draws sinners to Himself (John 6:44), and to those who come (John 6:37) He promises, "I will forgive their iniquity, and their sin I will remember no more" (Jer. 31:34; Ezek. 36:25). The New covenant thus provides the essential things that all the other covenants lacked—a new heart, power to obey God, fellowship with God, the Holy Spirit (Ezek. 36:27), and the forgiveness of sin. Those are the keys that unlock all the promised blessings of the Abrahamic and Davidic covenants and cancel the condemnation of the Mosaic law (cf. Rom. 8:1–2).

The New covenant is personal, promising the salvation of individual sinners through faith in the sacrificial death of Jesus Christ, the "Lamb of God who takes away the sin of the world" (John 1:29). Everyone who ever has or ever will be saved has come to salvation under the terms of the New covenant (John 14:6; Acts 4:12; cf. Acts 10:42–43; Matt. 1:21; 1 Tim. 2:5–6).

But the New covenant also has national implications for Israel. The irrevocable promises of God that Israel would be saved and blessed, that Messiah's kingdom will come, and that their land be restored all hinge on the nation's believing in Jesus Christ. In the future, the believing remnant of the Jewish people will "look on Me whom they have pierced; and they will mourn for Him, as one mourns for an only son, and they will weep bitterly over Him like the bitter weeping over a firstborn" (Zech. 12:10), and as a result "all Israel will be saved" (Rom. 11:26). Until that time of national repentance and acceptance of the New covenant and the One whose death made it possible, Israel cannot receive the blessings of the Abrahamic and Davidic covenants.

THE SOURCE OF THE NEW COVENANT

because of the tender mercy of our God, (1:78*a*)

It is God's **tender mercy** that moves Him to show compassion to lost sinners. **Tender** translates *splagchna,* which literally refers to the inner parts of the body, such as the intestines, heart, liver, and lungs (cf. Acts 1:18). Figuratively, it describes the affections and the heart as the seat of those affections (2 Cor. 6:12; 7:15; Phil. 1:8; 2:1; Col. 3:12; Philem. 7, 12, 20; 1 John 3:17). In combination with *eleos* (**mercy**) it vividly depicts the intensity of God's compassionate concern for sinners.

Mercy is a glorious attribute of God, celebrated throughout Scripture. He is "merciful and gracious" (Ps. 86:15; cf. 145:8), and "full of compassion and . . . merciful" (James 5:11; cf. Luke 6:36). The outworking of that mercy results in God showing kindness to sinners. Speaking of His tender mercy toward Israel, Isaiah wrote, "In all their affliction He was afflicted, and the angel of His presence saved them; in His love and in His mercy He redeemed them" (Isa. 63:9). In Jeremiah 33:26, God said of downtrodden Israel, "I will restore their fortunes and will have mercy on them" (cf. Ezek. 39:25). Mary rejoiced that God's "mercy is upon generation after generation toward those who fear Him" (Luke 1:50) and that "He has given help to Israel His servant, in remembrance of His mercy" (v. 54). Earlier in his hymn of praise, Zacharias also spoke of God's past mercy to Israel (v. 72). Ephesians 2:4 declares that it is because God is "rich in mercy" that He redeems lost sinners, while in 1 Timothy 1:13 and 16, Paul praised God for His mercy in saving him. Titus 3:5 declares that God "saved us, not on the basis of deeds which we have done in righteousness, but according to His mercy" (cf. 1 Peter 1:3; 2:10).

In his classic exposition of the attributes of God, *The Knowledge of the Holy*, A. W. Tozer expressed the wonder that all the redeemed should feel when they contemplate God's mercy toward them:

> When through the blood of the everlasting covenant we children of the shadows reach at last our home in the light, we shall have a thousand strings to our harps, but the sweetest may well be the one tuned to sound forth most perfectly the mercy of God.... We who earned banishment shall enjoy communion; we who deserve the pains of hell shall know the bliss of heaven. And all through the tender mercy of our God, whereby the Dayspring from on high hath visited us. ([New York: Harper & Row, 1975], 96)

There was nothing inherently wrong with the Mosaic covenant; "the Law is holy, and the commandment is holy and righteous and good" (Rom. 7:12). It was an absolutely perfect reflection of God's righteous character. Had God merely enforced the terms of the Mosaic covenant and condemned all sinners to eternal punishment for violating His law, He would have glorified Himself by displaying His justice. But God chose to have mercy on hopeless, helpless sinners in the misery of their fallen state and institute the New covenant, with its promise of forgiveness, righteousness, and full eternal acceptance with God.

THE BLESSINGS OF THE NEW COVENANT

with which the Sunrise from on high will visit us, to shine upon those who sit in darkness and the shadow of death, to guide our feet into the way of peace." (1:78b–79)

Zacharias anticipated the coming of the One whose death would procure the blessings of the New covenant—the Messiah. He identified Him using a metaphor rich in Old Testament messianic theology and symbolism. *Anatolē* (**Sunrise**) literally means "rising," and refers here to the first light of dawn. **On high** (lit., "out of" or "from the height") refers symbolically to heaven. Zacharias thus depicts the Messiah as a great light from heaven, who will **shine** the light of salvation **upon those who sit in darkness and the shadow of death** (cf. Isa. 9:2; Ps. 107:10, 14; John 12:46). He is the "the sun of righteousness [who] will rise with healing in its wings" (Mal. 4:2), shining into the deep darkness of sin and ending the soul's long night. Second Peter 1:19 speaks of the time when "the day dawns and the morning star arises in your hearts," while in Revelation 22:16, the Lord Jesus Christ called Himself "the bright morning star."

Darkness in Scripture can be used metaphorically in two ways. Intellectually, it refers to ignorance and error (e.g., Ps. 82:5; Eccl. 2:14; Eph. 4:18). Morally, darkness symbolizes sin (e.g., Prov. 2:13; 4:19; John 3:19; Rom. 13:12; 2 Cor. 6:14; Eph. 5:8, 11), and the realm of Satan (e.g., Luke 22:53; Eph. 6:12; Col. 1:13). God is light (1 John 1:5), and consequently Jesus, God incarnate, came into the world as the Light of the world (John 1:9; 3:19; 8:12; 9:5; 12:46). He is "a light to the nations, to open blind eyes, to bring out prisoners from the dungeon and those who dwell in darkness from the prison" (Isa. 42:6–7).

To a lost world groping in the darkness and desperately hoping for light (Isa. 59:9–10), God, knowing there was no human solution to sin's dilemma (v. 16), sent "a Redeemer … to those who turn from [their] transgression" (v. 20; cf. 53:4–6, 8, 10–12). Speaking of the New covenant that would bring that about, God declared, "'As for Me, this is My covenant with them,' says the Lord: 'My Spirit which is upon you, and My words which I have put in your mouth shall not depart from your mouth, nor from the mouth of your offspring, nor from the mouth of your offspring's offspring,' says the Lord, 'from now and forever'" (v. 21).

The light of salvation will continue to shine in the millennial kingdom, as Isaiah 60:1–5 reveals:

> Arise, shine; for your light has come, and the glory of the Lord has risen upon you. For behold, darkness will cover the earth and deep darkness the peoples; but the Lord will rise upon you and His glory will appear upon you. Nations will come to your light, and kings to the brightness of your rising. Lift up your eyes round about and see; they all gather together, they come to you. Your sons will come from afar, and your daughters will be carried in the arms. Then you will see and be radiant, and your heart will thrill and rejoice.

Indeed, throughout eternity the light of God's glory will illuminate the New Jerusalem:

> No longer will you have the sun for light by day, nor for brightness will the moon give you light; but you will have the Lord for an everlasting light, and your God for your glory. Your sun will set no more, neither will your moon wane; for you will have the Lord for an everlasting light, and the days of your mourning will be over. (60:19–20)

Not only would the Messiah bring the light of salvation to His people, He would also **guide** their **feet into the way of peace.** Lost sinners, stumbling around in the darkness, know nothing of true peace (Rom. 3:17). But peace is one of the elements of the New covenant. In Isaiah 54:10, God said, "'For the mountains may be removed and the hills may shake, but My lovingkindness will not be removed from you, and My covenant of peace will not be shaken,' says the Lord who has compassion on you." "Peace I leave with you;" Jesus promised, "my peace I give to you; not as the world gives do I give to you. Do not let your heart be troubled, nor let it be fearful" (John 14:27). Peace, Paul wrote, begins with salvation: "Therefore, having been justified by faith, we have peace with God through our Lord Jesus Christ" (Rom. 5:1). The kingdom of God is characterized by "righteousness and peace and joy in the Holy Spirit" (Rom. 14:17). Peace is one of the fruits of the Spirit (Gal. 5:22), and the "peace of God, which surpasses all comprehension, will guard [believers'] hearts and [their] minds in Christ Jesus" (Phil. 4:7).

With the end of Zacharias's song of praise, the curtain falls on the life of John the Baptist, not to be raised again until the beginning of his public ministry in chapter 3. The Bible passes over his childhood in silence, revealing even less details about it than it does of Jesus' childhood. All that is known of John during the long years between his circumcision and the beginning of his public ministry is that he **continued to grow and to become strong in spirit, and he lived in the deserts until the day of his public appearance to Israel.** He then assumed the role predicted for him as Messiah's forerunner, proclaiming the New covenant of which his father so eloquently and passionately spoke.

Excursus:
Why Every
Self-respecting
Calvinist Must
Be a Premillennialist

This material is taken from a message delivered by the author at the March, 2007 Grace Community Church Shepherds' Conference. It has been lightly edited, but no effort has been made to remove the marks of the original spoken message. It is included here as an expansion of a theme introduced in the discussion of the covenants in chapters 9–11 of this volume. A proper interpretation of the biblical data leads to the conclusion that God's promises to Israel will be literally fulfilled to the nation of Israel and not transferred to the church. That reality logically leads to premillennialism.

It is one of the strange ironies in the church and Reformed theology that those who love the doctrine of sovereign election most supremely and sincerely, and who are most unwavering in their devotion to the glory of God, the honor of Christ, the work of the Spirit in regeneration and sanctification, the veracity and inerrancy of Scripture, and who are the most fastidious in hermeneutics, and who are the most careful and intentionally biblical regarding categories of doctrine, and who see themselves as guardians of biblical truth, and are not content to be wrong at all, and who agree most heartily on the essential matters of Christian truth so that they labor with all their powers to examine in a Berean fashion every relevant text to discern the true interpretation of all matters of divine revelation are in varying degrees of noninterest in applying those same passions and skills to the end of the story, and are rather content to be in a happy and even playful disagreement regarding the vast biblical data on eschatology, as if the end didn't matter much.

But it does matter that Calvinists care about eschatology and get it right—and we will if we get Israel right. We get Israel right when we get the Old Testament covenants and promises right. We get the Old Testament covenants and promises right when we get the interpretation of Scripture right. We get the interpretation of Scripture right when we're faithful to a legitimate hermeneutic and God's integrity is upheld. We get our hermeneutics right, we'll get the Old Testament promises right. Get the promises right, we'll get Israel right. Get Israel right, we'll get eschatology right.

The Bible calls God the God of Israel more than 200 times. There are more than 2,000 references to Israel in Scripture, and not one of them means anything but Israel, including Romans 9:6 and Galatians 6:16, which are the only two passages that amillennialists go to, to try to convince us that those cancel out the other 2,000. There is no difficulty in interpreting those verses as simply meaning Jews who were believers, the Israel of God. Israel always means Israel, never means anything but Israel. Seventy-three New Testament uses of Israel always mean Israel.

Seventy percent of Scripture is the story of Israel. And, I think, the whole point of the story is to get to the ending—and it doesn't go up in smoke. So here's how to get the foundation for an accurate understanding of eschatology. Get election right and get Israel right. Those two go together; they're inseparable. How is it that we've come to get number one right and totally miss number two so often? I'm confident that God did not reveal prophetic truth in such detail to hide or obscure the truth, but to reveal it for our blessing, our motivation, and ultimately His glory.

But there is a theology concerning Israel and the end times—popular in many Reformed and Calvinistic circles today—that I believe does not get things right concerning Israel. It is replacement theology, and scholastically it's often referred to as supersessionism. This view demands that all the Old Testament promises to Israel be viewed through the lens of the New Testament and ultimately get transferred to the church. Replacement theology, an integral part of amillennialism, also creates a strange dichotomy, since all the curses promised to Israel came to Israel. Literally, and they're still coming. If one wonders whether the curses in the Old Testament were literal, they're going on right now. Israel right now is not under divine protection. They are under the promise of God that they will be perpetuated as an ethnic people, but this current group of Jews that live in the world today and in the nation of Israel are not now under divine protection—they're apostate. They've rejected their

Messiah. They are under divine chastening. But they are still a people and will be to the end.

What a staggering apologetic that is for the truthfulness of Scripture. We can't abandon that without a huge loss of confidence in Scripture. All the curses promised to Israel for disobedience to God came true, literally on Israel. And now, all of a sudden, we're supposed to split all those passages that give blessing and cursing and say all the blessings promised to Israel aren't coming to Israel; they're coming to the church instead? Where's the textual justification for such a split interpretation? And wouldn't we think that whatever way the curses were fulfilled would set the standard for whatever way the blessings would be fulfilled? Or to put the question in another context, Wouldn't we expect that all the prophecies that came to pass when Jesus came in a literal fashion would set the pattern for how the prophecies connected to His second coming would come to pass? There's no place for splitting up these interpretations.

Thus the Old Testament cannot be amillennial. If we affirm a normal hermeneutic—the perspicuity of the Old Testament—of course it pronounces clearly covenants and promises and a kingdom to come to Israel.

The Old Testament must be interpreted, preached, and taught as clear revelation from God that is to be understood, believed, and applied by the people to whom it was given. So what did God promise Israel? Look at the twelfth chapter of Genesis, and obviously this is a study beyond our capability to dig into all the details. But it's clear and straightforward; it's not difficult. I want us to see the connection between these covenants and divine, electing sovereignty.

Genesis 12:1 says, "The Lord said to Abram, 'Go forth from your country, and from your relatives and from your father's house.'" Now here we have a great illustration of election. That's almost like a Damascus Road experience, isn't it? What did Abraham, or Abram as he's called here, do to set this in motion? Nothing. Abram plays no part in this covenant.

Follow the use of the expression "I will" in verses 2–3: "And I will make you a great nation, and I will bless you, and make your name great; and so you shall be a blessing; and I will bless those who bless you, and the one who curses you, I will curse. And in you all the families of the earth will be blessed." I will, I will, I will, I will, I will—five times. It is sovereign, unilateral, unconditional election.

That's prophecy. God later puts Abram to sleep and says this is what is going to happen: "I will also judge the nations whom they will serve, and afterward they will come out with many possessions. As for you, you shall go to your fathers in peace; you will be buried at a good old age" (Gen. 15:14–15).

Then in verse 17: "It came about when the sun had set, that it was very dark, and behold, there appeared a smoking oven and a flaming torch which passed between these pieces." God put Abram out, anesthetized him, and He alone went through the pieces—a unilateral, unconditional, irrevocable promise that God made with Himself. There were no conditions for Abram to fulfill. On that day, the Lord made a covenant with him.

It is to be a covenant that does not end. Chapter 17, verse 7 says, "I will establish My covenant between Me and you and your descendants after you throughout their generations for an everlasting covenant, to be God to you and to your descendants after you." God elected Abram, elected the nation that would come out of his loins, made a covenant and a promise with them to be their God. This is the foundational covenant in the Bible—foundational, biblical covenant—the promise of God, unilateral and unconditional.

God's decision to set His love on Israel was in no way determined by Israel's performance. It was not determined by Israel's national worthiness. It was based purely on His independent, uninfluenced, sovereign grace (see Deut. 7:7–8). He chose them because He predetermined to set His love on them, for no other reason but election. The survival of the kingdom of Judah, despite the blatant sin of its rulers, depended on covenant promises God had made (read Pss. 89 and 132, where these are reiterated). God's unilateral covenant declares that the Lord alone is the party responsible to fulfill the obligations. There are no conditions that Abraham or any other Jew could fulfill on his own. It's no different from our salvation—we were divinely chosen. But we didn't come to Christ on our own. We were given life by the Spirit of God in God's time. God's unilateral covenant declares that the Lord is the sole party responsible to fulfill the obligations to preserve Israel.

Obedience is not the condition that determines fulfillment. Divine, sovereign power is the condition that determines obedience, which leads to fulfillment. When God gave Israel the unilateral covenant, He knew He would have to produce the obedience in the future, according to His plan.

Then God gave the Davidic covenant, 2 Samuel 7, where the promise comes to David that he'll have a greater Son who will have an everlasting kingdom. That is an expansion, by the way, of the Abrahamic covenant. Verse 12 says, "I will establish his kingdom. He shall build a house for My name, and I will establish the throne of his kingdom forever." God promises to Abraham a seed, a land, a nation, and now, of course that embodies a kingdom, and now comes the promise of a King. This is an expansion of the Abrahamic covenant. And what's notable here, again, in 2 Samuel 7:12–13, "I will raise up your descendant ... I will establish his kingdom...I will establish the throne of his kingdom forever." I will ...I will ...I will ...again.

This is not to say the Abrahamic covenant is only for Israel. We all participate in its blessings spiritually—and we will millennially. The Abrahamic and the Davidic covenants—we all will participate in them, even those not of Israel, because we'll participate in salvation and be in the kingdom.

There's a third covenant, the New covenant. Jeremiah 31—there can be no fulfillment of the promises God gave to Abraham or David apart from salvation. Throughout history there has always been an Israel of God, there's always been a remnant, there have always been those who didn't bow the knee to Baal. God always has had a chosen people. But not all Israel is Israel. That is to say, not all Israel is the true Israel of God, true believers. But God has always had a remnant, always had a people— always, as Isaiah 6 says, a stump, a holy seed throughout history. But in the future there will be a salvation of ethnic Israel on a national level. And that's the message of Jeremiah 31. Here is the New covenant given to Israel.

We like to talk about the New covenant because we participate in the salvation provision of the New covenant, ratified in the death of Christ. But the application of the New covenant is in a special way given to a future generation of Jews. Jeremiah 31:31 says, "'Behold, days are coming,' declares the Lord, 'when I will make a New covenant with the house of Israel and with the house of Judah [that is unmistakable], not like the covenant which I made with their fathers in the day I took them by the hand to bring them out of the land of Egypt, My covenant which they broke, although I was a husband to them,' declares the Lord. 'But this is the covenant which I will make with the house of Israel'" (vv. 32–33).

What warrant is there to say that doesn't mean Israel? It does mean Israel. I will ...I will ...I will ...I will ...I will make a covenant with the house of Israel. "I will put My law within them and on their heart I will write it; and I will be their God and they shall be My people ...I will forgive their iniquity, and their sin I will remember no more" (vv. 33–34). Did we ever see so many "I wills"?—unconditional, unilateral, sovereign, gracious, and irrevocable.

We could say, "Well, maybe God changed His mind." Go to verse 35: "Thus says the Lord, who gives the sun for light by day and the fixed order of the moon and the stars for light by night, who stirs up the sea so that its waves roar; the Lord of hosts is His name: 'If this fixed order departs from before Me,' declares the Lord, 'then the offspring of Israel also shall cease.'" I haven't noticed that that's happened. If it doesn't mean what it just said, it's incomprehensible.

And the New covenant promises the salvation that then includes the reception of all the promises in the Abrahamic covenant, Davidic covenant, and all the extended promises throughout the whole Old Testament.

What is the key feature of this? "I will put My law within them and on their heart I will write it; and I will be their God....I will forgive their iniquity."

Notice how sovereign that is: "I will do it; I will do it in My time."

Look at Ezekiel 36, because this is a parallel; but I think it's good just to be reminded. Ezekiel 36:24–27, "For I will take you from the nations, gather you from all the lands and bring you into your own land. Then I will sprinkle clean water on you, and you will be clean; I will cleanse you from all your filthiness and from all your idols. Moreover, I will give you a new heart and put a new spirit within you; and I will remove the heart of stone from your flesh and give you a heart of flesh. I will put My Spirit within you,"—It's overwhelming, isn't it?—"and cause you to walk in My statutes, and you will be careful to observe My ordinances."

How could anybody walk in His statutes and obey and observe His ordinances? Only if He caused them to do it. "You will live in the land that I gave to your forefathers; so you will be My people, and I will be your God."

And then verse 32, just a good reminder: "'I am not doing this for your sake,' declares the Lord God, 'let it be known to you. Be ashamed and confounded for your ways, O house of Israel!'" For whose sake is He doing it? His own sake.

Go to the end of verse 38. When God does this, "Then they will know that I am the Lord" (see also v. 37).

So when God gave unilateral, unconditional-as-primary-cause, sovereign, gracious promises to an elect people, they are guaranteed by divine faithfulness to be fulfilled like all His salvation work. And when God says such covenant promises are irrevocable, we cannot, with impunity for any seemingly convenient idea or assumption, say these are void. Why?

Someone may say, "Well, what about Israel's apostasy? Doesn't that cancel the promises? Doesn't Israel's apostasy cancel the promises?" But do we understand that the New covenant promises given in Jeremiah and Ezekiel were given to Israel at the time when they were under divine judgment for apostasy. They weren't given to them when all was well and they were living and flourishing in obedience to God. They were so apostate, they were out of their land and *then* the covenant was given to them. And God was saying, "Don't get the idea that what's going on by way of apostasy changes My promises."

Someone else may say, "Well wait a minute, didn't they reject their Lord and Messiah? That did it. They rejected Him. They killed Jesus." That's in the plan. One of the wacky ideas of old-line dispensationalism is that Jesus came and offered a kingdom; and because the Jews didn't accept it and killed Him, He went to the church and came up with plan B.

The cross is not plan B. What is Zechariah 12:10 saying when it declares, "They look on Him whom they have pierced" (see Ps. 22 and Isa. 53)? It's in the main plan. And then 13:1 says, "In that day a fountain will be opened for the house of David." Israel will be saved. The New covenant will be fulfilled. Keep reading into chapter 14: "The Lord will be king over all the earth" (v. 9). There is no other way to interpret Zechariah 12–14.

So is the Old Testament amillennial? No. Were the Jews in Jesus' day amillennial? No. Emile Schurer's helpful *Study of Jewish Eschatology in the Day of Jesus*, published in 1880 by T. & T. Clarke in Edinburgh (a new edition of it was published by Hendrickson Publishing in 1998), does a great job of studying the Jewish messianic, eschatological mind-set at the time of Jesus. They believed the Messiah was coming, preceded by a time of trouble. They believed that before Messiah, Elijah the prophet would come. They believed that when Messiah came, He would be the personal Son of David. He would have special powers to set up His kingdom, and all Abrahamic and Davidic covenant promises would be fulfilled. They also believed that Israel would repent and be saved at the coming of Messiah. They believed the kingdom would be established in Israel, with Jerusalem at the center, and would extend across the world. They believed that peace and righteousness would dominate the world. All people would worship the Messiah. There would be no war, only gladness and health. They believed in a reinstituted temple worship; and the fulfillment of the covenants included the renovation of the world, a general resurrection, final judgment, and after that the eternal state. That's Jewish pre-New Testament eschatology.

That's what Zacharias, the priestly father of John the Baptist, believed. Read Zacharias's great *Benedictus* in Luke 1:67 to the end of the chapter. And what is he saying? Every single phrase comes from an Old Testament text on the Abrahamic covenant, the Davidic covenant, or the New covenant—every single one of them. He knew what was happening. The covenants were to be fulfilled.

Was Jesus an amillennialist? Acts 1 is the first postresurrection account "about all that Jesus began to do and teach, until the day when He was taken up to heaven, after He had by the Holy Spirit given orders to the apostles whom He had chosen" (vv. 1–2). There's election again.

So He had spent time before His ascension with the apostles. Now verse 3 says, "To these He also presented Himself alive after His suffering, by many convincing proofs, appearing to them over a period of forty days." Literally, "appearing to them over forty days." It must have been intense. Can we imagine the level of teaching a resurrected Jesus would give His own over a forty-day period? What kind of a seminary education would that be? And what was He talking about?—"speaking of the things concerning the kingdom of God."

For forty days He talks about the kingdom of God. This is His moment. If Jesus is an amillennialist, this is where He has to tell them. The Jews' apostasy—that's a given. The rejection of the Messiah, that's a given. The execution of the Messiah, that's a given. This is the perfect place for Jesus to launch amillennialism.

Verse 6 says, "So when they had come together, they were asking Him, saying, 'Lord, is it at this time You are restoring the kingdom to Israel?'" Now what did He say? "Where did you get such a stupid idea? Where did you ever come up with that concept? Haven't you been listening for forty days? I'm an amillennialist. What a bizarre thought, that I'm going to restore the kingdom to Israel? You don't listen." This is it. If Jesus is amillennialist, this is His moment. He's got to say, "No, the church is the new Israel."

The disciples ask if this is the time the Father is going to restore *apokathistanō* (according to Jewish sources, a technical eschatological term for the end time). They were using a term that was a part of their eschatology. "Is this the end time when You are restoring the kingdom to Israel?" Forty days of instruction on the kingdom and they knew one thing for sure: the kingdom for Israel was still coming. And all they wanted to know was, When? That's all.

"He said to them, 'It is not for you to know times or epochs'" (v. 7a). We can't know timing. He didn't say, "Wait, wait, wait. There isn't going to be a kingdom." He said, "It's not for you to know times and epochs [seasons]."

By the way, "which the Father has fixed by His own authority" (v. 7b). There's that sovereign election again. It's sovereign. The disciples knew that when they asked, "Lord, is it at this time You are restoring the kingdom?" (v. 6). They knew it was a divine work to do it. This was a perfect opportunity for Jesus to straighten things out.

Let's dig a little into the text of verse 7: "which the Father has fixed [*tithēmi*, 'set, appointed']." "Fixed" is in the aorist middle—"fixed for Himself." It's about His glory. It's about His exaltation. It's about the whole world finally seeing paradise regained. It's about God finally being glorified—who is so dishonored throughout human history. It's about the glory of God and the honor of Jesus Christ. And God the Father has fixed for Himself that time by His own authority—it is singular, unilateral. There is no other way to understand it.

There's no replacement theology in the theology of Jesus. There's no supersessionism, which is a movement to establish that there is no earthly kingdom for Israel. That is absolutely foreign to the Old Testament and completely foreign to the New Testament. Jesus didn't say, "Where did you get that crazy idea? Haven't you been listening?"

They just couldn't know the seasons, the time. The cross was always the plan. He said, you remember, in the eighteenth chapter of Luke, also recorded in Matthew and Mark, "Behold, we are going up to Jerusalem" (v. 31). And what's going to happen, if we put those three accounts together? "I [Jesus] am going to be betrayed. I'm going to be handed over to the chief priests and the scribes. They're going to condemn Me. They're going to hand Me over to the Gentiles because they can't execute Me. All this is in exact order. Then when I'm handed over to the Gentiles, I'm going to be mocked, mistreated, spit on, scourged, crucified, and I'm rising again" (see vv. 32–33).

That's not plan B. In fact, if we think that's plan B, we're fools. And Jesus used that terminology: "O foolish men and slow of heart to believe in all that the prophets have spoken!" (Luke 24:25). So, wherever this amillennial thing came from, it didn't come from the Old Testament, it didn't come from New Testament Jews, and it didn't come from Jesus.

We might say, "Well, were the apostles amillennialists?" How about Peter; was Peter an amillennialist? In Acts 3, Peter is preaching away: "Men of Israel," and so forth. Verse 13: "The God of Abraham, Isaac and Jacob, the God of our fathers, has glorified His servant Jesus, the One whom you delivered [there's that primary and secondary element] and disowned in the presence of Pilate, when he had decided to release Him. But you disowned the Holy and Righteous One and asked for a murderer to be granted to you, but put to death the Prince of life" (vv. 13–15). What an indictment! They [the Jews] couldn't be any worse, any more horrific.

Verse 18: "But the things which God announced beforehand by the mouth of all the prophets, that His Christ should suffer, He has thus fulfilled." That's literal, isn't it? "Therefore repent and return, so that your sins may be wiped away, in order that times of refreshing may come from the presence of the Lord ['the times of refreshing' is a kingdom phrase] and that He may send Jesus, the Christ appointed for you [set for you, fixed for you], whom heaven must receive until the period of restoration [another kingdom term] of all things about which God spoke by the mouth of His holy prophets from ancient time" (vv. 19–21).

And then I specially love verses 25–27, "It is you who are the sons of the prophets and of the covenant which God made with your fathers." Does Peter cancel the covenant? What does he say? "You...are the sons of the covenant which God made with your fathers, saying to Abraham, 'And in your seed all the families of the earth shall be blessed.' For you first, God raised up His Servant and sent Him to bless you by turning everyone of you from your wicked ways [and He will do that; you're still the sons of the covenant]." That was a perfect opportunity to cancel those promises.

How about James, the head of the Jerusalem church? Was he amillennial in his view? Acts 15—"James answered, saying, 'Brethren, listen to me. Simeon has related how God first concerned Himself about taking from among the Gentiles a people for His name. With this the words of the Prophets agree, just as it is written, "After these things I will return, and I will rebuild the tabernacle of David which has fallen, and I will rebuild its ruins, and I will restore it, so that the rest of mankind may seek the Lord, and all the Gentiles who are called by My name, says the Lord, who makes these things known from long ago" '" (vv. 13–18).

The acceptance of the Gentiles is not the cancellation of promises to Israel. After Gentile conversion, after the times of the Gentiles are over, God will rebuild the tabernacle of David that is fallen—rebuild its ruins and restore it. Davidic covenant promises and Messianic promises will be fulfilled.

Maybe the writer of Hebrews was an amillennialist: "When God made the promise to Abraham, since He could swear by no one greater, He swore by Himself, saying, 'I will surely bless you and I will surely multiply you'" (6:13)—I will, I will; no hesitation. And he calls on our understanding of swearing. "Men swear by one greater than themselves, and with them an oath given as confirmation is an end of every dispute. In the same way God, desiring even more to show to the heirs of the promise the unchangeableness of His purpose, interposed with an oath" (vv. 16–17). God swears, or makes an oath. And "it is impossible," the next verse says, "for God to lie."

Maybe the apostle Paul was the first amillennialist: "What advantage has the Jew? Or what is the benefit of circumcision? Great in every respect. First of all, that they were entrusted with the oracles of God. What then? If some did not believe, their unbelief will not nullify the faithfulness of God, will it? May it never be!" (Rom. 3:1–4). And this is where Paul [the amillennialist] would have said, "Absolutely ... absolutely; it nullifies the promise of God; unquestionably, it nullifies the promise of God." But it doesn't say that.

Romans 9:6–8 says, "But it is not as though the Word of God has failed. For they are not all Israel who are descended from Israel [that is to say, they're not all true Israel, that is, believers]; nor are they all children because they are Abraham's descendants, but 'through Isaac your descendants will be named.' That is, it is not the children of the flesh who are children of God, but the children of promise are regarded as descendants." There are children God has elected to fulfill His promise in. And He goes on to describe it, saying something as blatant as this: "Jacob I loved," verse 13, "but Esau I hated." Verse 15: "I will have mercy on whom I have mercy, and I will have compassion on whom I have compassion." Verse 16: "It does not depend on the man who wills or the man who runs, but on God who has mercy." Verse 18: "He has mercy on whom He desires, and He hardens whom He desires." This is back to the whole idea of sovereignty again.

Just because there are some Jews who don't believe does not nullify the faithfulness of God. Just because there are some that God chooses, doesn't mean that He's not going to choose a whole duly constituted generation of Jews to fulfill His promises.

And then perhaps most notable, Romans 11:26*a*, "All Israel will be saved." How can we interpret that? One way. Someone tells me that's not Israel? Where in the text does it say it's not Israel? I would understand if it said, "And God has cancelled His promises to Israel." But verses 26–27 say, "All Israel will be saved; just as it is written, 'The deliverer will come from Zion, He will remove ungodliness from Jacob. This is My covenant with them, when I take away their sins.'"

Yes, they are enemies at the present time. But that is for the sake of the Gentiles, verse 29, "the gifts and the calling of God are irrevocable," which brings us back to where we started.

If it depended on the Jews to obey on their own, it was impossible from the start. Only the One who made the promise can enable the obedience that is connected to the fulfillment of the promise.

So when Jonathan Edwards wrote this: "Promises that were made by the prophets to the people of Israel concerning their future prosperity and glory are fulfilled in the Christian church according to their proper intent," I say, "Where did he get that? Where did that come from?" It didn't come from any passage that I can find.

Let me just conclude with some effects. I'd suggest for your reading, *Israel and the Church* by Ronald Diprose. It first appeared in Italian as a Ph.D. dissertation and has no connection to traditional dispensationalism. It's a really, really fine work on replacement theology. It shows the effect of this idea upon the church of the Dark Ages, explaining how the church went from the New Testament concept of the church to the sacerdotal, sacramental, institutional system of the Dark Ages that we know as Roman Catholicism. Diprose lays much of that at the feet of replacement theology, which rises out of Augustine and a few before him.

Where did the church ever come up with altars? There's no altar in the New Testament. Where did the church ever come up with sacrifices? Where did the church ever come up with a parallel sign to circumcision? Where did the church ever come up with a priesthood? Where did the church ever come up with ceremony and ritual and symbolism? Where did the church ever come up with the idea that we should reintroduce mystery by speaking in a language that the people there couldn't understand? And we replace preaching with ritual?

From the formation of the church in those early centuries to the system of Roman Catholicism, all the trappings fit Old Testament Judaism. And the hierarchical, institutional, nonpersonal, nonorganic, sacerdotal approach to the church, Diprose traces largely to the influence of causing the church to be the new Israel. Replacement theology justifies bringing in all the trappings of Judaism.

Another effect of replacement theology is the damage it does to Jewish evangelism. Here's a little scenario. Someone is talking to a Jew and saying,"Jesus is the Messiah."

"Really; where's the kingdom?"

"Oh, it's here."

"Oh, it is? Well why are we being killed all the time? Why are we being persecuted and why don't we have the land that was promised to us? And why isn't the Messiah reigning in Jerusalem, and why isn't the peace and joy and gladness dominating the world? And why isn't the desert blooming?"

"Oh no, you don't understand. All that's not going to happen. You see, the problem is you're not God's people anymore. We are."

"Oh, I see. But this is the kingdom and Jews are being killed and hated and Jerusalem is under siege. This is the kingdom? If this is the kingdom, Jesus is not the Messiah. Can't be. It's ludicrous."

No matter how many wonderful Jewish-Christian relationships we try to have with rabbis, this is a huge bone in the throat. Why can't Jesus be the Messiah? Because this isn't the kingdom. Unless we can say to a Jew,"God will keep every single promise He made to you, and Jesus will fulfill every single promise. And that is why there are still Jews in the world, and that is why Jews are in the land and God is preparing for a great day of salvation in Israel. And Jesus is your Messiah. But look at Psalm 22, Isaiah 53, and Zechariah 12:10 and understand that He had to come and die to ratify the New covenant before He could forgive sin— but the kingdom is coming."

That we have a chance to communicate. The rest doesn't make sense. Now if we get election right—the divine, sovereign, gracious, unconditional, unilateral, irrevocable election—then we get God right. And we get Israel right. And we get eschatology right. And guess what?— then we can just open our Bibles and preach our hearts out of the text and say what it says. We don't have to scramble around and find some bizarre interpretation.

Get it right and God is glorified. Get it right and Christ is exalted. Get it right and the Holy Spirit is honored. Get it right and Scripture is clear. Get it right and the greatest historical illustration of God's work in the world is visible. Get it right and the meaning of mystery in the New

Testament is maintained. Get it right and normal language is intact—Scripture wasn't written for mystics. Get it right and the chronology of prophetic literature is intact. Get it right and we shut out imagination from exegesis. Get it right and the historical worldview is complete. Get it right and the practical benefit of eschatology is released for our people. Get it right.

Kingdom theology of the eschaton is the only view that honors sovereign, electing grace; honors the truthfulness of God's promises; honors the teaching of the Old Testament prophets and the teaching of Jesus and the New Testament writers, which will allow Christ to be honored as supreme ruler over His creation, now temporarily in the hands of Satan. And the earthly, millennial kingdom, established at Christ's return, is the only and necessary bridge from temporary human history to eternal divine glory. Let's make our churches second coming churches and make our lives second coming lives.

Jesus' Birth in Bethlehem (Luke 2:1–7)

12

Now in those days a decree went out from Caesar Augustus, that a census be taken of all the inhabited earth. This was the first census taken while Quirinius was governor of Syria. And everyone was on his way to register for the census, each to his own city. Joseph also went up from Galilee, from the city of Nazareth, to Judea, to the city of David which is called Bethlehem, because he was of the house and family of David, in order to register along with Mary, who was engaged to him, and was with child. While they were there, the days were completed for her to give birth. And she gave birth to her firstborn son; and she wrapped Him in cloths, and laid Him in a manger, because there was no room for them in the inn. (2:1–7)

Luke's simple, straightforward, unembellished language describes the most profound birth, with the most far-reaching implications, in the history of the world. On a night like any other night, in an obscure village in Israel, unnoticed by the world, a child was born. But while His birth was like that of every other child, the child was unlike any other child ever born, either before or since. For this child was the Son of God, the Lord Jesus Christ, deity in human flesh, Israel's long-awaited Messiah, the

Savior of the world. In His birth God entered human society as an infant; the creator of the universe became a man; the eternal "Word became flesh, and dwelt among us" (John 1:14).

This chapter, which provides the most detailed look at the events of the first Christmas, is perhaps the most widely known chapter in the Bible. Its familiar story has inspired music, cards, books, and pageants over the centuries. But the world celebrates the birth of Jesus Christ for all the wrong reasons. Christmas has become an excuse for self-indulgence, materialism, and partying; it has degenerated into a secularized social event that misses entirely its true meaning.

For the first few centuries of its existence, the church did not celebrate Christ's birth. Some of the early fathers, most notably Origen, even argued against celebrating the birthdays of saints and martyrs (including Jesus). They reasoned that such people should be honored instead on the day of their martyrdom. Noting that the only birthdays mentioned in the Bible are those of Pharaoh (Gen. 40:20) and Herod (Matt. 14:6), they viewed birthday celebrations as a pagan custom. By the second century, the actual date of Christ's birth had been forgotten, as evidenced by the numerous dates proposed for it (e.g., January 2, 6; March 21, 25; April 18, 19; May 20, 28; November 17, 20).

Exactly when the early church settled on December 25 is not known. The first recorded reference to that date as the day of Christ's birth is found in the writings of Sextus Julius Africanus early in the third century. The earliest evidence of the church celebrating Christmas on December 25 comes from the fourth-century manuscript known as the Chronography or Calendar of 354. According to that document Christmas was being celebrated on December 25 by the church at Rome no earlier than A.D. 336. That date was gradually adopted by the church as a whole over the next several centuries.

Why the church finally decided to celebrate the birth of Jesus on December 25 is also not known for certain. Some believe that it was to offer a Christian alternative to the popular pagan holiday known as *Dies Natalis Solis Invicti* ("the birthday of the unconquered sun"), which was celebrated on December 25. That festival was inaugurated late in the third century to honor several sun gods, chief of which was Mithras, whose worship (Mithraism) posed a serious threat to the Christian church. Others hold that the date was chosen because it is nine months after March 25, the day that some in the early church believed (without biblical warrant) was the date of Jesus' conception.

Over the centuries the trappings now commonly associated with Christmas gradually seeped into the celebration. Gift giving was an integral part of the pagan winter festivals, and became firmly associated with Christmas by the end of the eighteenth century. Mistletoe was sacred to the ancient Druids, who attributed to it both magical and medicinal powers. Kissing under the mistletoe may derive from a Druid or Scandinavian custom that enemies who met under mistletoe were to cease fighting and observe a truce. The crèche, or manger scene, originated with St. Francis of Assisi in the thirteenth century. The practice of singing carols also originated in the Middle Ages. The city of Riga in Latvia claims to be the home of the first Christmas tree, dating from the year 1510. Others legends attribute the first Christmas tree to Martin Luther, who allegedly brought an evergreen tree into his house and decorated it. There is, however, no contemporary record of his having done so. Christmas trees became popular in Germany in the seventeenth century, and first appeared in America early in the nineteenth century. The first commercial Christmas cards were sold in London in 1843.

Santa Claus, the secular symbol of Christmas, derives from the fourth-century Saint Nicholas, bishop of Myra in modern Turkey. Though little is known of his life, Nicholas was remembered for his generosity and kindness. According to one legend, he rescued three daughters of a poor family from being forced into prostitution by providing dowries for them so they could marry. After doing their laundry, the girls hung their stockings by the fireplace to dry. That night Nicholas tossed a small bag of gold coins into each girl's stocking. The custom of hanging Christmas stockings derives in part from that story. Settlers from the Netherlands, where Nicholas is popular, brought his tradition with them to America. Nicholas's Dutch name, Sinterklaas, or Sinte Klaas, eventually became Anglicized into "Santa Claus."

All of those extrabiblical elements only obscure the simple, yet unfathomably profound, meaning of Christmas. No less a theologian than Martin Luther confessed,

> When I am told that God became man, I can follow the idea, but I just do not understand what it means. For what man, if left to his natural promptings, if he were God, would humble himself to lie in the feedbox of a donkey or to hang upon a cross? God laid upon Christ the iniquities of us all. This is that ineffable and infinite mercy of God which the slender capacity of man's heart cannot comprehend and much less utter—that unfathomable depth and burning zeal of God's love toward us. . . . Who can sufficiently declare this exceeding great goodness of God? (cited in Roland H. Bainton, *Here I Stand* [Nashville: Abingdon, 1950], 223)

For the moment, the curtain has fallen in Luke's narrative on the story of John the Baptist (1:80), and is about to rise on the story of Jesus Christ. The promise made to Mary by Gabriel (1:31–35) is about to be fulfilled. As Luke picks up the story of Jesus' birth, he demonstrates how

God sovereignly orchestrated events to bring about a direct fulfillment of Old Testament prophecy. Divine intervention was required, because in the normal course of events, Jesus would not have been born in Bethlehem as the Old Testament predicted (Mic. 5:2), since Joseph and Mary lived in Nazareth.

Before describing the birth of the Savior, Luke gave three settings for it: the world, national, and personal. Those settings are fitting for the One who is the Savior of the world, the fulfillment of Old Testament prophecy, and the redeemer of individuals who humbly put their trust in Him.

THE WORLD SETTING

Now in those days a decree went out from Caesar Augustus, that a census be taken of all the inhabited earth. This was the first census taken while Quirinius was governor of Syria. And everyone was on his way to register for the census, each to his own city. (2:1–3)

To fulfill the prophecy that Messiah would be born in Bethlehem God in His providence moved the heart of the most powerful man in the world—the ruler of the mighty Roman Empire. The emperor, seated on his throne in the imperial capital at Rome, was far removed from the tiny hamlet of Bethlehem. He was even further removed from an understanding of the purposes and plans of God, being utterly ignorant of His Word. Yet he played a crucial role in fulfilling God's design concerning the birth of His Son. I. Howard Marshall writes, "The census ... serves to place the birth of Jesus in the context of world history and to show that the fiat of an earthly ruler can be utilized in the will of God to bring his more important purposes to fruition" (*The Gospel of Luke*, The New International Greek Testament Commentary [Grand Rapids: Eerdmans, 1978], 97–98).

Luke noted first that Messiah's birth took place **in those days;** that is, "in the days of Herod, king of Judea" (1:5). Herod, the Idumean (Edomite) vassal king under Rome, was nearing the end of his long reign and would die soon after Christ's birth. Those were also the days of the hated Roman occupation of Israel, which the Jews found especially galling for several reasons. First, the Romans were Gentiles, whom the Jews viewed as unclean, and outside of God's covenants (cf. Eph. 2:12). As much as possible, the Jews avoided contact with them. Peter told the Gentiles gathered in the house of Cornelius, "You yourselves know how unlawful it is for a man who is a Jew to associate with a foreigner or to visit him" (Acts 10:28). After hearing of his visit to Cornelius's house some of the Jewish believers in Jerusalem said in shock and disbelief, "You went to uncircumcised men and ate with them" (Acts 11:3). The Jews also abhorred the Romans' blatant idolatry; they had been cured of their own penchant for idolatry by the Babylonian captivity. They also found the Romans' taxation oppressive, and hated both it and those Jews (such as Matthew and Zaccheus) who helped collect the taxes (cf. Luke 18:11–13).

Though in other places (e.g., 3:1) Luke was precise in his dating, here he gave only a general time frame. Thus it is impossible to deduce the exact date of Christ's birth from this passage. Another clue in the text, however, helps make the time a little more specific. Luke connected the Lord's birth with a particular **decree** or imperial edict, which was handed down by the emperor and binding on his subjects (cf. Acts 17:7 where the same Greek word is used; see also Acts 18:2).

This particular decree was issued by the reigning emperor, **Caesar Augustus.** That was not his name, but rather his title; **Caesar** means "emperor," while **Augustus** means, "revered," "honored," or "esteemed," and reflects the great respect that he commanded. Augustus's ascension to the throne marked the beginning of the Roman Empire. He restored unity and orderly government after a long period of destructive civil wars, and ushered in the Pax Romana, an era of peace and prosperity throughout the Greco-Roman world that lasted for two centuries. He is arguably the most significant person in Roman history.

Augustus was born Gaius Octavius on September 23, 63 B.C. His grandmother was Julius Caesar's sister, making Octavius his grand-nephew. After Julius's assassination in 44 B.C., Octavius learned that Caesar had adopted him and made him his heir. In keeping with Roman custom, he then took the name Gaius Julius Caesar Octavianus (usually shortened in English to Octavian).

After Caesar's murder Octavian shrewdly used his status as Caeasar's adopted son to build up his power. After initially clashing with Mark Antony, Octavian joined with him and Lepidus to form the Second Triumvirate (the First Triumvirate had consisted of Julius Caesar, Pompey, and Crassus). They then attacked Caesar's assassins, Brutus and Cassius. The forces of the Triumvirate decisively defeated their armies near Philippi, after which Brutus and Cassius committed suicide.

The Second Triumvirate lasted for less than a decade. While Antony was in the east fighting the Parthians, Octavian forced Lepidus from power. Then in 32 B.C. Antony divorced Octavian's sister, Octavia, whom he had married to cement his political alliance with Octavian. He then resumed his affair with Cleopatra (with whom he had had two children before he married Octavia). This affront to his sister naturally infuriated Octavian.

Even worse, Antony declared Caesarion, Cleopatra's son from her affair with Julius Caesar, to be Caesar's legitimate son and heir, thus undercutting Octavian's position as Caesar's heir. War broke out between the two rivals and Octavian decisively defeated the forces of Antony and Cleopatra in the naval battle of Actium (31 B.C.), after which Antony and Cleopatra committed suicide. Octavian was now the sole ruler of the Roman world. In 27 B.C., the Senate conferred on him the titles Augustus (see the discussion of this term above) and Princeps, or "first citizen." Octavian's immense wealth, the respect he commanded, and his control of the army made his rule absolute.

Octavian died in A.D. 14, and was succeeded by his stepson Tiberius, who was the emperor during the ministry of Jesus Christ. Octavian left a legacy of peace, prosperity, wise administration, and a commitment to public works. There is an element of truth in the boast he made on his deathbed that he found Rome brick and left it marble. The network of roads he developed aided in the spread of the gospel by Christian missionaries. Octavian was intelligent, decisive, bold, and not afraid to take risks when necessary. He was a patron of the arts, a friend of such noted writers as Ovid, Horace, Virgil, and Livy. Such was the respect that he commanded that his loyal subjects deified him after his death.

Of all the decrees Octavian issued during his long reign, Luke is concerned with one mandating that **a census be taken of all the inhabited earth** (i.e., the Roman Empire; cf. Acts 17:6; 19:27). Such censuses (or enrollments) were generally taken either to register young men for military service or for purposes of taxation. This census was for the latter reason, since the Jews were exempt from Roman military service.

Seeking to deny the truthfulness of Luke's account, anti-Scripture critics maintain that there is no existing record of an empire-wide census during Octavian's reign. But that argument from silence is undercut by the many censuses known to have been carried out at about that same time in various parts of the empire (cf. Darrell L. Bock, *Luke 1:1–9:50*, Baker Exegetical Commentary on the New Testament [Grand Rapids: Baker, 1994], 904). Nor were such censuses merely one-time occurrences. In Egypt, for example, censuses were taken every fourteen years, beginning no later than A.D. 20 and running through at least A.D. 258 (William Ramsay, *Was Christ Born at Bethlehem?* [London: Hodder and Stoughton, 1898], 132; *The Bearing of Recent Discovery on the Trustworthiness of the New Testament* [2nd edition; London: Hodder and Stoughton 1915], 256). Ramsay argued that the practice of taking recurring censuses was not limited to Egypt, but was empire-wide (*The Bearing of Recent Discovery on the Trustworthiness of the New Testament*, 257; cf. William Hendriksen, *The Gospel of Luke*, New Testament Commentary [Grand Rapids: Baker, 1978], 138–39). Further, the second-century church father Clement of Alexandria wrote that the same cycle of periodic censuses existed in the province of Syria (which included Palestine). Clement also stated that the first census taken in Syria was the one connected with Christ's birth (A. T. Robertson, *Luke the Historian in the Light of Research* [New York: Scribner, 1920], 122–29).

Thus, to charge Luke with error for speaking of two censuses in Palestine (see the discussion below), one in A.D. 6 (referred to in Acts 5:37 and by the first-century Jewish historian Josephus) and this one fourteen years earlier in 8 B.C., ignores the historical evidence. Luke's readers knew all about the census system he was describing, so for him to have invented the story would have been foolish:

> No historian of any kind or class would state a falsehood whose falsity was obvious to every reader. …The conclusion was evident. Luke trusted to his readers' familiarity with the facts and the census-system. He spoke of the first census, knowing how much that would imply to them. They knew the system as it was carried out in the Roman Empire. (Ramsay, *The Bearing of Recent Discovery on the Trustworthiness of the New Testament*, 239)

Luke further indentified this census as **the first census taken while Quirinius was governor of Syria.** The mention of **Quirinius** introduces a further difficulty, since he is known to have governed Syria from A.D. 6–9. As governor, Quirinius administered the census of A.D. 6. That cannot, however, be the census in view here, because it took place more than a decade after Herod's death, while Herod was still alive when Jesus was born (Matt. 2:1–3). Many possible solutions have been proposed (see the discussion in Bock, *Luke 1:1–9:50*, 906–909; Harold Hoehner, *Chronological Aspects of the Life of Christ* [Grand Rapids: Zondervan, 1977], 18–22; Marshall, *The Gospel of Luke*, 102–104). Perhaps the best solution is the one championed by Sir William Ramsay. Based on inscriptional evidence, Ramsay argued that Quirinius had twice held an important position in the province of Syria (*Was Christ Born at Bethlehem?* 227–48). It should be noted that the Greek word translated **governor** is a nontechnical term for a person in authority, "hence the word, as employed by Luke, might be applied to any Roman official holding a leading and authoritative position in the province of Syria" (Ramsay, *Was Christ Born at Bethlehem?* 229). At the time of the first census in 8 B.C., "Varus was controlling the internal affairs of Syria while Quirinius was commanding its armies and controlling its foreign policy" (Ramsay, *Was Christ Born at Bethlehem?* 244).

The 8 B.C. date for the decree also presents a problem, since scholars generally agree that Jesus was born no earlier than 6 B.C., and more likely closer to 4 B.C. Evidently there was a delay in carrying out the decree in Palestine, to which a number of factors may have contributed. First, ancient communication was slow, and implementation slowly enforced. The latter years of Herod's reign were also a time of turmoil and upheaval. Herod was ill, and his sons were fighting over who would succeed him. Herod executed three of them and changed his will three times. He also fell out of favor with Octavian. That instability, coupled with Jewish resistance to Roman taxation, and the logistic difficulties inherent in carrying out a census in those days, could easily have delayed the implementation of the emperor's decree.

Eventually, however, the census was taken, and thus **everyone** went **to register for the census, each to his own city.** Obviously a deadline had been imposed, or else Joseph and Mary would not have made the long trip from Nazareth to Bethlehem in the winter and so near the end of her pregnancy. Some have questioned why Joseph and Mary went to Bethlehem, noting that the Romans generally had people register where they were currently living. Those owning property in another district, however, were required to go there to register (Marshall, *The Gospel of Luke,* 101). Although Luke does not mention it, Joseph may have owned some property in the vicinity of Bethlehem. Another possibility is that the Romans acquiesced to Jewish custom, which stressed the importance of one's ancestral home (cf. Lev. 25:10). Further, an early second-century document from Egypt indicates that the Egyptians were also required to return to their homes for the census just as Joseph and Mary did (Robertson, *Luke the Historian,* 125–26). That shows that the Romans were flexible on such matters of local custom.

God providentially arranged the world setting to get Joseph and Mary to Bethlehem so His Son would be born where the Old Testament predicted He would be. As He had with Artaxerxes (Ezra 7:21–26), Tiglath-pileser (Isa. 10:5–7), and Cyrus (Isa. 45:1–4), God directed the mind of the most powerful man on earth, Caesar Augustus, to accomplish His purposes (cf. Prov. 21:1).

THE NATIONAL SETTING

Joseph also went up from Galilee, from the city of Nazareth, to Judea, to the city of David which is called Bethlehem, because he was of the house and family of David, in order to register along with Mary, who was engaged to him, and was with child. (2:4–5)

The nation of Israel is inseparably linked with the Old Testament Scriptures, which clearly predicted where Messiah would be born.

Centuries earlier the prophet Micah had written, "But as for you, Bethlehem Ephrathah [Bethlehem's original name; cf. Gen. 35:19], too little to be among the clans of Judah, from you One will go forth for Me to be ruler in Israel. His goings forth are from long ago, from the days of eternity" (Mic. 5:2). Although Bethlehem was a small, insignificant village, "too little to be among the clans of Judah," God declared that it would produce a ruler in Israel. The only king who came from Bethlehem was David, but he cannot be in view in this passage. David died long before Micah's day, but the ruler of whom the prophet wrote was yet to come. Micah's reference is to the Messiah, whose "goings forth are from long ago, from the days of eternity"—a statement that could not apply to any human, since only God has existed from all eternity.

Luke wrote that **Joseph . . . went up from Galilee, from the city of Nazareth, to Judea, to the city of David which is called Bethlehem,** because **Bethlehem,** located in **Judea** (southern Israel) very near Jerusalem, is higher in elevation than **Nazareth,** which was located in **Galilee** (northern Israel). Though in the Old Testament, the **city of David** was a title given to Mount Zion in Jerusalem, because David actually reigned there (cf. 2 Sam. 5:7–9; 1 Chron. 11:7), Luke used the term to identify the town where he was born and raised (cf. 1 Sam. 17:12, 15; 20:6). Joseph went to Bethlehem **because he was of the house and family of David** (1:27), **in order to register** for the census (see the discussion above) **along with Mary.** God sovereignly directed the couple to where they needed to be to fulfill Micah's prophecy.

Some have questioned whether it was necessary for Mary to make the long (at least seventy mile) trip from Nazareth to Bethlehem, especially since she **was with child.** As head of the family, they argue, Joseph alone needed to register. There is, however, evidence that in Syria (the province that included Israel) women twelve years and older were subject to a poll tax (Marshall, *The Gospel of Luke,* 102). Thus Mary may also have been required to register. Several personal considerations may also help explain why she went to Bethlehem with Joseph. Perhaps she was uncomfortable staying behind in Nazareth where her unexpected and —humanly speaking—unexplained pregnancy was undoubtedly the subject of a good deal of gossip. Joseph certainly would not have wanted to miss the birth of the Son of God, whom the angel had told him was conceived in Mary by the Holy Spirit (Matt. 1:20–21). Finally, as devout Jews, Joseph and Mary were familiar with Micah's prophecy and knew their child needed to be born in Bethlehem. Whatever human factors may have influenced Mary to travel to Bethlehem, ultimately she did so to fulfill God's purpose. Leon Morris writes,

We should perhaps reflect that it was the combination of a decree by the emperor in distant Rome and the gossiping tongues of Nazareth that brought Mary to Bethlehem at just the time to fulfil the prophecy about the birthplace of the Christ (Mi. 5:2). God works through all kinds of people to effect His purposes. (*The Gospel According to St. Luke,* The Tyndale New Testament Commentaries [Grand Rapids: Eerdmans, 1975], 84)

Luke wrote that Mary **was engaged to** Joseph, while Matthew 1:24 states that Joseph had already married her. There is no contradiction between the two accounts, however. First, it must be remembered that the distinction in Jewish culture between engagement and marriage was not as clear-cut as it is today. Engagement was a legally binding contract, though the physical union was not consummated. For example, to end their engagement, as he contemplated doing after discovering that she was pregnant, Joseph would have had to divorce Mary (Matt. 1:19. Note that Matthew in that same verse refers to Joseph as Mary's husband before they were married.) Since a covenant to be married had taken place, Matthew could properly refer to the couple as married. But since the marriage was not physically consummated until after Jesus' birth (Matt. 1:24–25), Luke could refer to them as engaged, since they were conducting their relationship as appropriate to the betrothal period.

THE PERSONAL SETTING

While they were there, the days were completed for her to give birth. And she gave birth to her firstborn son; and she wrapped Him in cloths, and laid Him in a manger, because there was no room for them in the inn. (2:6–7)

Luke described the most profoundly significant event in all of history up to that point—the birth of the God-man, Jesus Christ—in startlingly simple, straightforward, unembellished, even sparse language. **While** Joseph and Mary **were** in Bethlehem, **the days were completed for her to give birth.** Luke did not say how long they had been in Bethlehem, or whether they were still waiting to register, or stayed there after registering because Mary's time to give birth was near. He gave no description of where the birth took place, except to say that it was not in the inn (see the discussion below). Luke simply said that Mary **gave birth to her firstborn son.** No angels appeared, as they later would to the shepherds. No heavenly trumpets rang. No voice from heaven announced the birth of the Son of God. Alone except for her young husband, far from her family and friends, in the most primitive of conditions, a young girl gave birth. Thus did the second person of the Trinity step from eternity into time and space.

Luke carefully noted that Jesus was Mary's **firstborn** (*prōtotokos*), not her only (*monogenēs*) **son** (cf. his use of *monogenēs* to refer to an only child in 7:12; 8:42; 9:38). The teaching of the Roman Catholic Church that Jesus was Mary's only child and that she remained a perpetual virgin until her death, is clearly a denial of Scripture. Matthew 1:25 says that Joseph "kept her a virgin *until* she gave birth to a Son" (emphasis added). That strongly implies that after Christ's birth, they had normal marital relations. It is also revealed that Mary gave birth to other children, Jesus' half brothers and sisters (Matt. 12:46–47; 13:55–56; John 2:12; 7:3, 5, 10; Acts 1:14). As the firstborn, Jesus had the primary right to the family inheritance (cf. Gen. 43:33; Deut. 21:15–17; 1 Chron. 5:1; 2 Chron. 21:3). Joseph was not wealthy (cf. the discussion of 2:21–24 in chapter 14 of this volume), and had no great estate to bequeath to his firstborn son. But what he did pass along was the right to the throne of Israel (Matt. 1:1–16).

As was customary, Mary **wrapped** her baby **in cloths.** Strips of fabric were used to bind a baby snugly for warmth, security, and to keep the limbs straight. The point is that Jesus was treated like any other baby. He was not dressed in royal robes but in the normal wrappings that other babies wore.

Having borne her Son and wrapped Him, Mary **laid Him in a manger.** The reference to a manger has given rise to the tradition that Jesus was born in a stable. The Bible nowhere states that, however. *Phatnē* (**manger**) is the word for a feeding trough. Such troughs could be found anywhere animals were kept, not only in stables. The Bible does not specifically say where Mary gave birth to Jesus although a tradition, dating back to the middle of the second century, says that it was in a cave. While that is possible, since caves were sometimes used to shelter animals, there is no way to verify it.

Wherever the couple stayed, it was not in the inn, **because there was no room for them** there. Part of the Christmas legend is the heartless innkeeper who turns away a young woman about to give birth. But *kataluma* (**inn**) is not the normal Greek word for an inn (*pandocheion*, which Luke used in 10:34), but rather a general term for a shelter, or lodging place (it is translated "guest room" in 22:11). Exactly what that lodging place was is not clear, but it may have been a public shelter or campground, perhaps a place where caravans stopped. But with the overcrowding brought about by the census, there was no room for Joseph and Mary even in such a makeshift shelter. As a result, Mary was forced to give birth in the only place available—the place where the travelers' animals were kept.

When Jesus came into the world, He was born in the most comfortless conditions—a smelly, filthy, chilly shelter, surrounded by noisy animals. It was a fitting entrance for the "Son of Man [who had] nowhere to lay His head" (Luke 9:58); the one who "was in the world, and the world was made through Him, and the world did not know Him" (John 1:10); for the one "who, although He existed in the form of God, did not regard equality with God a thing to be grasped, but emptied Himself, taking the form of a bond-servant, and [was] made in the likeness of men" (Phil. 2:6–7); for the "Son of Man [who] did not come to be served, but to serve, and to give His life a ransom for many" (Matt. 20:28) by bearing "our sins in His body on the cross, so that we might die to sin and live to righteousness" (1 Peter 2:24). His humble birth was appropriate for Jesus, who came to die as a substitute in the place of lowly, humble, wretched sinners. As the writer of the hymn "Ivory Palaces" put it,

> Out of the ivory palaces,
> Into a world of woe,
> Only His great, eternal love
> Made my Savior go.

The Announcement of Jesus' Birth (Luke 2:8–20)

13

In the same region there were some shepherds staying out in the fields and keeping watch over their flock by night. And an angel of the Lord suddenly stood before them, and the glory of the Lord shone around them; and they were terribly frightened. But the angel said to them, "Do not be afraid; for behold, I bring you good news of great joy which will be for all the people; for today in the city of David there has been born for you a Savior, who is Christ the Lord. This will be a sign for you: you will find a baby wrapped in cloths and lying in a manger." And suddenly there appeared with the angel a multitude of the heavenly host praising God and saying, "Glory to God in the highest, and on earth peace among men with whom He is pleased." When the angels had gone away from them into heaven, the shepherds began saying to one another, "Let us go straight to Bethlehem then, and see this thing that has happened which the Lord has made known to us." So they came in a hurry and found their way to Mary and Joseph, and the baby as He lay in the manger. When they had seen this, they made known the statement which had been told them about this Child. And all who heard it wondered at the things which were told them by the shepherds. But Mary treasured all

these things, pondering them in her heart. The shepherds went back, glorifying and praising God for all that they had heard and seen, just as had been told them. (2:8–20)

The Scripture says that in His incarnation the Lord of glory (1 Cor. 2:8) "emptied Himself, taking the form of a bond-servant, and [was] made in the likeness of men" (Phil. 2:7). All the adjectives and exclamations in language could never say enough about that reality. Yet, paradoxically, history's most notable birth happened under the most obscure, nondescript, humble circumstances imaginable—Jesus was born in the place where the animals of those staying in a public shelter were kept. No one in the sleepy little village of Bethlehem realized the significance of what had happened, except, to a certain degree, the Child's parents. But that was about to change; the silence regarding the Savior's birth would be broken in a most supernaturally dramatic way.

If the announcement of Jesus' birth had been part of a humanly planned public relations campaign, it would have been handled very differently. The announcement would have targeted the powerful and influential in Israel: the high priest, the members of the Sanhedrin, the priests, Levites, scribes, Sadducees, and Pharisees. Instead God chose to reveal this glorious truth first of all to members of a lowly, despised group (see the exposition of v. 8 later in the chapter).

The theme of this passage is found in the angel's declaration in verse 11, **"there has been born for you a Savior."** That statement is the heart of the gospel message that the church proclaims to the world: all people are sinners, and in need of a Savior. But the concept of a savior is by no means limited to the New Testament. The idea that there is a radical disconnect between the supposedly angry, hostile, vengeful God of the Old Testament and the compassionate, loving, saving Christ of the New Testament is a figment of the skeptics' imagination.

The truth is that in the Old Testament God was known to His people as a Savior and a deliverer. That is in sharp contrast to the false gods worshiped by Israel's neighbors. When the prophets of Baal, one of the chief Canaanite deities, confronted Elijah on Mount Carmel, they tried for hours to get Baal's attention. But "there was no voice and no one answered" (1 Kings 18:26). That prompted Elijah to say mockingly, "Call out with a loud voice, for he is a god; either he is occupied or gone aside, or is on a journey, or perhaps he is asleep and needs to be awakened" (v. 27). Even after they in desperation mutilated themselves (v. 28), "there was no voice, no one answered, and no one paid attention" (v. 29). At the other end of the spectrum from Baal's indifference was Molech's cruelty and hostility, which his worshipers desperately attempted to appease by the unspeakable atrocity of infant sacrifice (Lev. 18:21, 20:2–5; 2 Kings 23:10; Jer. 32:35).

Unlike the false gods of Israel's pagan neighbors, the God of Israel, the only true, eternal, and living God, is by nature "compassionate and gracious, slow to anger, and abounding in lovingkindness'" (Ex. 34:6; cf. Neh. 9:17; Ps. 103:8; Joel 2:13; Jonah 4:2). The Jewish people understood, therefore, that it was in keeping with God's nature to save His people. In Deuteronomy 20:4 Moses reminded Israel, "The Lord your God is the one who goes with you, to fight for you against your enemies, to save you." David called God "my savior, [the one who] save[s] me from violence" (2 Sam. 22:3); the "God of [his] salvation" (Ps. 25:5); and the "Savior of those who take refuge at [His] right hand" (Ps. 17:7). Psalm 106:21, Isaiah 45:15; 63:8–9; and Jeremiah 14:8 also refer to God as Israel's Savior, as does God Himself (Isa. 43:3, 11; 45:21; 49:26; 60:16; Hos. 13:4). Reflecting their understanding of that key Old Testament truth, Mary (Luke 1:47), Zacharias (Luke 1:68–69, 77), and Simeon (Luke 2:30) all spoke of God as Savior, as does the rest of the New Testament (1 Tim. 1:1; 2:3; 4:10; Titus 1:3; 2:10; 3:4; Jude 25). Since God alone is the Savior (Isa. 43:11; Hos. 13:4), the New Testament's repeated use of that title for the Lord Jesus Christ (e.g., Luke 2:11; Acts 5:31; 13:23; Phil. 3:20; 2 Tim. 1:10; Titus 1:4; 2:13; 3:6; 2 Peter 1:2, 11; 2:20; 3:18; 1 John 4:14) is a strong affirmation of His full deity and equality with the Father.

What allows God to be the Savior of lost sinners is the propitiatory, sacrificial, substitionary death of the Messiah, the Lord Jesus Christ. The Old Testament describes Messiah's sacrificial death most thoroughly in Isaiah 53:

> Surely our griefs He Himself bore, and our sorrows He carried; yet we ourselves esteemed Him stricken, smitten of God, and afflicted. But He was pierced through for our transgressions, He was crushed for our iniquities; the chastening for our well-being fell upon Him, and by His scourging we are healed. All of us like sheep have gone astray, each of us has turned to his own way; but the Lord has caused the iniquity of us all to fall on Him. (vv. 4–6)

> By oppression and judgment He was taken away; and as for His generation, who considered that He was cut off out of the land of the living for the transgression of my people, to whom the stroke was due? (v. 8)

> But the Lord was pleased to crush Him, putting Him to grief; if He would render Himself as a guilt offering, He will see His offspring, He will prolong His days, and the good pleasure of the Lord will prosper in His hand. As a result of the anguish of His soul, He will see it and be satisfied; by His knowledge the Righteous One, My Servant, will justify the many, as He will bear their iniquities. Therefore, I will allot Him a portion

with the great, and He will divide the booty with the strong; because He poured out Himself to death, and was numbered with the transgressors; yet He Himself bore the sin of many, and interceded for the transgressors. (vv. 10–12)

All the redeemed, both in the Old Testament and the New Testament eras, were saved by God's placing their sins on Jesus Christ. He alone (Acts 4:12) is the source of salvation since, as Peter wrote, "He Himself bore our sins in His body on the cross, so that we might die to sin and live to righteousness; for by His wounds you were healed" (1 Peter 2:24; cf. 3:18; John 1:29; 2 Cor. 5:21; Gal. 3:13; Eph. 5:2; Heb. 9:28; 1 John 2:1–2).

God revealed Himself as a Savior to Israel in two ways. Temporally, God saved the people by delivering them from bondage in Egypt and preserving them through the ensuing forty years of wandering in the wilderness (Isa. 63:9; cf. Num. 10:9; Deut. 23:14; 33: 29; Judg. 2:18; 8:34; 2 Sam. 3:18; 22:1, 4; 2 Kings 17:39; Ps. 106:10; Ezra 8:31). Through common grace, God, in His "kindness and tolerance and patience," gives sinners an opportunity to repent (Rom. 2:4); He is "the Savior of all men" in a temporal sense and "especially of believers" in a spiritual sense (1 Tim. 4:10). God delivers people generally from the just and immediate temporal and physical consequences of their sin, but more importantly delivers believers from sin's spiritual and eternal consequences as well. Thus the believing remnant of Israel (Rom. 9:27; 11:5) enjoyed not only God's temporal salvation like the rest of the nation, but also spiritual salvation.

The angelic announcement of His birth set forth at the outset the purpose of Jesus' life and ministry. He did not come into the world to be an example of nobility and integrity. He was not merely a Jewish sage, a teacher of morality and ethics. Still less was He a passive, nonviolent social reformer; a sort of first-century Gandhi. He was and is "the Savior of the world" (John 4:42; 1 John 4:14), who came "to seek and to save that which was lost" (Luke 19:10) by "sav[ing] His people from their sins" (Matt. 1:21). Jesus did come to fulfill the Abrahamic and Davidic covenants (see chaps. 9 and 10 of this volume). The fulfillment of those covenants, however, is predicated on the fulfillment of the New covenant (see chapter 11 of this volume), which was initiated by His sacrificial death (Matt. 26:28).

The announcement of the birth of Jesus Christ heralds the greatest good news that the world has ever heard. From the narrative of that announcement and its aftermath, five truths about the good news emerge: the proclamation of the good news, the pervasiveness of the good news, the person of the good news, the purpose of the good news, and the picture of the good news.

THE PROCLAMATION OF THE GOOD NEWS

In the same region there were some shepherds staying out in the fields and keeping watch over their flock by night. And an angel of the Lord suddenly stood before them, and the glory of the Lord shone around them; and they were terribly frightened. But the angel said to them, "Do not be afraid; for behold, I bring you good news of great joy (2:8–10a)

The good news of the Savior's birth came first to a most unlikely group of people. **Shepherds** were near the bottom of the social ladder. They were uneducated and unskilled, increasingly viewed in the post-New Testament era as dishonest, unreliable, unsavory characters, so much so that they were not allowed to testify in court. Because sheep required care seven days a week, shepherds were unable to fully comply with the man-made Sabbath regulations developed by the Pharisees. As a result, they were viewed as being in continual violation of the religious laws, and hence ceremonially unclean.

That is not to say, however, that being a shepherd was an illegitimate or disreputable occupation. Two of the greatest figures in Israel's history, Moses (Ex. 3:1) and David (1 Sam. 16:11–13), were shepherds at some point in their lives. Moreover, the Old Testament refers metaphorically to God as the "Shepherd of Israel" (Ps. 80:1; cf. 23:1; Isa. 40:11), while Jesus described Himself as the "good shepherd" (John 10:11, 14; cf. Heb. 13:20; 1 Peter 2:25; 5:4). Shepherds were, however, lowly, humble people; they certainly were not the ones who would be expected to receive the most significant announcement in history. That they were singled out to receive this great honor suggests that these shepherds were devout men, who believed in the true and living God. Such people are later described as those who were "looking for the consolation of Israel" (2:25) and the "redemption of Jerusalem" (2:38).

God's choice of shepherds to receive the announcement of His Son's birth is in keeping with Old Testament prophecy concerning Messiah's ministry. Isaiah 61:1 prophetically put these words in the mouth of the Messiah: "The Spirit of the Lord God is upon me, because the Lord has anointed me to bring good news to the afflicted; He has sent me to bind up the brokenhearted, to proclaim liberty to captives and freedom to prisoners." After reading that passage in the synagogue at Nazareth, Jesus declared, "Today this Scripture has been fulfilled in your hearing" (Luke 4:21). The Messiah's ministry would not be to the self-righteous (Luke 5:32)—especially the religious leaders (John 7:48), or the self-sufficient wealthy (Luke 18:24). Instead, He would seek out the poor, the lowly, the afflicted, the outcasts of society (cf. Luke 1:52; 1 Cor. 1:26). Throughout

His ministry Jesus attracted such people (cf. Matt. 9:10–13; 11:19; Luke 15:1–2), who were broken over their sin and humbled themselves in repentance (cf. Luke 7:37–38; 18:13–14).

These particular shepherds were watching their sheep in the **region** around Bethlehem, about six miles south of Jerusalem. They were **staying out in the fields** with their flocks, something typically done in Israel from April to November. That does not mean, however, that Jesus could not have been born in the winter, since winters in Israel are often mild. Further, as Leon Morris notes, the rabbinic writings speak of sheep being pastured between Jerusalem and Bethlehem in February (*The Gospel According to St. Luke*, The Tyndale New Testament Commentaries [Grand Rapids: Eerdmans, 1975], 84). According to rabbinic law, sheep were to be kept in the wilderness, and any animal found between Jerusalem and the vicinity of Bethlehem was subject to being used as a sacrifice in the temple. It may be, then, that the sheep these shepherds were caring for were destined for that very purpose.

Sheep were kept out in the fields during the day. In the evening they were moved into sheepfolds, where the shepherds could take turns **keeping watch over their flock** during the **night.** Inside the fold the sheep could more easily be guarded from predators and thieves.

But the tranquil normalcy of the shepherds' nightly routine was abruptly shattered in a most amazing, dramatic, unexpected way. While they were doing what they normally did during the long hours spent watching their flock **an angel of the Lord suddenly stood before them.** The angel is not identified, but in light of his earlier appearances to Zacharias and Mary, it may have been Gabriel. Adding immeasurably to the shepherds' shock and terror at the angel's unexpected appearance, **the glory of the Lord** blazed forth out of the darkness and **shone around them.**

Throughout Scripture, God's glorious presence was manifested in brilliant light (e.g., Ex. 24:17; 33:22–34:5; Deut. 5:24; 2 Chron. 7:1–3; Ezek. 1:27–28; 43:2; Luke 9:28–32; Rev. 21:23; cf. Ex. 34:29, 35; Ps. 104:1–2; Hab. 3:3–4; Rev. 1:13–16). The glory of God first appeared in the garden of Eden, where Adam and Eve had intimate fellowship with God and enjoyed His presence. But after they sinned, God banished them forever from the garden and posted an angel with a flaming sword at the entrance to keep them out. God's glory manifested itself to Israel in the wilderness (Ex. 24:16–17), especially at the dedication of the tabernacle (Ex. 40:34–35), as it would later appear at the dedication of the temple (1 Kings 8:10–11).

But after centuries of sin and rebellion, the glory of God left the temple (Ezek. 9:3; 10:4, 18, 19; 11:22–23), symbolizing its withdrawal from Israel. It would not appear again until this very night, where it signified that God's presence had once again entered the world through the birth of the Lord Jesus Christ. Later in His life Jesus would reveal His divine glory to Peter, James, and John on the Mount of Transfiguration (Matt. 17:1–2). The next visible manifestation of God's glory to the world will be at the second coming, when "the sign of the Son of Man will appear in the sky, and …all the tribes of the earth will mourn, and they will see the Son of Man coming on the clouds of the sky with power and great glory" (Matt. 24:30). Heaven will be lit by the all-pervasive glory of God throughout eternity (Rev. 21:10–11, 23).

The shepherds understandably **were terribly frightened** by the appearing of the angel and the manifestation of God's glory. Fear was the normal response whenever anyone in Scripture either encountered an angel (cf. Dan. 8:15–18; 10:7–9, 16–17; Matt. 28:2–4; Luke 1:12, 26–30) or saw the glory of God manifest (Isa. 6:1–5; Ezek. 1:28; 3:23; Matt. 17:5–6; Mark 4:41; 5:33; Acts 9:4; Rev. 1:17). Those who experience the presence of the holy God are acutely aware of their sinfulness. Isaiah cried out, "Woe is me, for I am ruined! Because I am a man of unclean lips, and I live among a people of unclean lips; for my eyes have seen the King, the Lord of hosts" (Isa. 6:5), and Peter exclaimed after witnessing a miracle performed by the Lord, "Go away from me Lord, for I am a sinful man, O Lord!" (Luke 5:8).

Seeing the shepherds' obvious terror, **the angel said to them, "Do not be afraid."** The sequence of events in the angel's appearance to the shepherds is the same as in Gabriel's appearances to Zacharias and Mary: the angel appeared, those to whom he appeared were frightened, the angel spoke words of comfort, delivered his message, and promised a sign.

There is a sense in which it is right to fear God; the Bible declares that "the fear of the Lord is the beginning of wisdom" (Prov. 9:10; cf. 1:7; 15:33; Job 28:28; Ps. 111:10; Mic. 6:9), and godly men are marked by reverence for Him (Gen. 22:12; 42:18; Ex. 18:21; Neh. 7:2; Job 1:9; Ps. 66:16; Eccl. 5:7; 8:12; 12:13; Matt. 10:28; 1 Peter 2:17). But the redeemed need not be terrified of God. "For you have not received a spirit of slavery leading to fear again," Paul reminded the Romans, "but you have received a spirit of adoption as sons by which we cry out, 'Abba! Father!'" (Rom. 8:15; cf. Gal. 4:6–7). God says to His people, as He did to Abraham, "Do not fear" (Gen. 26:24; cf. Judg. 6:23; Isa. 43:1, 5; 44:2; Jer. 46:27–28; Lam. 3:57; Dan. 10:12, 19; Matt. 14:27; 17:7; 28:5, 10; Luke 5:10; 12:32; Rev. 1:17).

The shepherds did not need to fear, for the angel had come bearing **good news.** His message was not one of judgment, but rather that "the Father has sent the Son to be the Savior of the world" (1 John 4:14). *Euangelizō* ("to proclaim **good news**) is one of Luke's favorite terms; he used it more than any other New Testament writer (cf. 1:19; 3:18; 4:18, 43; 7:22; 8:1; 9:6; 16:16; 20:1; Acts 5:42; 8:4, 12, 25, 35, 40; 10:36; 11:20; 13:32; 14:7,

15, 21; 15:35; 16:10; 17:18). The good news of the gospel is that the saving God sent the Savior to redeem sinners. That news produces **great joy;** the joy that Peter described as "inexpressible and full of glory" (1 Peter 1:8), which is reserved for those whose sins have been forgiven through faith in the Lord Jesus Christ.

THE PERVASIVENESS OF THE GOOD NEWS

which will be for all the people; (2:10*b*)

The good news the angel proclaimed is **for all the people.** *Laos* (**people**) refers first to Israel (1:68; 7:16; 19:47; 21:23; 22:66; 23:5, 14), since "salvation is from the Jews" (John 4:22; cf. Rom. 1:16). But the promise of salvation is not for them only. Praising God after seeing the baby Jesus in the temple, Simeon said, "For my eyes have seen Your salvation, which You have prepared in the presence of all peoples, a light of revelation to the Gentiles, and the glory of Your people Israel" (2:30–32). Significantly, *laos* in verse 31 is plural, while it is singular in verse 32. Simeon's words reflect the truth expressed in Isaiah's prophecy:

> Arise, shine; for your light has come, and the glory of the Lord has risen upon you. For behold, darkness will cover the earth and deep darkness the peoples; but the Lord will rise upon you and His glory will appear upon you. Nations will come to your light, and kings to the brightness of your rising. (60:1–3; cf. 9:2; 42:6; 49:6–9; 51:4)

The good news of salvation, having been proclaimed first to Israel, is now proclaimed throughout the world (Matt. 28:19–20).

THE PERSON OF THE GOOD NEWS

for today in the city of David there has been born for you a Savior, who is Christ the Lord. This will be a sign for you: you will find a baby wrapped in cloths and lying in a manger. (2:11–12)

Having reassured the stunned and frightened shepherds that he came bearing good news, the angel then gave them the details of that good news. That very day, in the fullness of time (Gal. 4:4), history's most significant birth had taken place. It had happened in the most unlikely of places—**in the city of David** (the tiny hamlet of Bethlehem; see the discussion of 2:4 in chap. 12 of this volume). The angel prefaced his threefold description of the newborn Child by telling the shepherds that the One of whom he spoke had **been born for** them. Collectively, as noted above, Jesus is the Savior of both Jews and Gentiles; individually, He is the Savior of everyone who believes in Him (John 3:16). The angel did not give the Child's earthly name; Savior, Christ and Lord are all titles. But since the name "Jesus" means "the Lord is salvation," its meaning is encompassed by the term **Savior.**

The description of Jesus as **Savior** is an apt one, since the reason He was born was to "save His people from their sins" (Matt. 1:21; cf. Luke 19:10). That obvious truth is often obscured in contemporary presentations of the gospel. Too often Jesus is presented as the One who will rescue people from unfulfillment in their marriages, families, or jobs; from a debilitating habit they cannot overcome on their own; or from a sense of purposelessness in life. But while relief in those areas may be a by-product of salvation, it is not its primary intent. Mankind's true problem, of which those issues are only symptoms, is sin. Everyone (Rom. 3:10, 23) is guilty of breaking God's holy law and deserves eternal punishment in hell. The true gospel message is that Jesus Christ came into the world to rescue people from sin and guilt—not psychological, artificial guilt feelings, but true, God-imposed guilt that damns to hell.

Christ is an exalted title for a baby born in such humble circumstances. The name and its Old Testament counterpart, Messiah (Dan. 9:25–26), both mean "anointed one"; one placed in a high office and worthy of exaltation and honor. Jesus was anointed first in the sense that He is God's appointed King, the "King of kings" (Rev. 17:14; 19:16), who will sit on David's throne and reign forever, as Gabriel told Mary (1:32–33). He was also anointed to be the great High Priest (Heb. 3:1) for His people; the mediator between them and God (1 Tim. 2:5) who makes intercession for them (Heb. 7:25). Finally, Jesus was anointed as a prophet, God's final and greatest spokesman (Heb. 1:1–2).

Lord in a human sense is a term of respect and esteem, given to someone in a position of leadership and authority. Especially it was the title borne by slave owners; *kurios* (Lord) and *doulos* (slave) were connected. To call someone Lord was to acknowledge your subservience. In the New Testament Sarah called Abraham lord, acknowledging his authority over her as her husband (1 Peter 3:6).

But in this context Lord is no mere elevated human designation; it is a divine title. To say that this Child is Lord is to say that He is God. When used in reference to Jesus Christ, *kurios* (**Lord**) conveys all that is implied by the tetragrammaton YHWH ("Yahweh," which the Septuagint translates *kurios*)—the name of God (cf. Ex. 3:14–15). The most fundamental and basic confession of Christianity is, "Jesus is Lord" (1 Cor. 12:3). No one who does not affirm Christ's full deity and equality with God the

Father can be saved for, as He warned the Jews, "Unless you believe that I am [God], you will die in your sins" (John 8:24. For a discussion of the "I am" statements in John's gospel in reference to Christ's deity, see *John 1–11,* The MacArthur New Testament Commentary [Chicago: Moody, 2006], 14, 348). Romans 10:9 declares that "if you confess with your mouth Jesus as Lord, and believe in your heart that God raised Him from the dead, you will be saved."

The angel then gave the shepherds a **sign** by which they could recognize this remarkable Child: they would **find** the **baby wrapped in cloths and lying in a manger.** That the **baby** would be **wrapped in cloths** would not single out Jesus for the shepherds, since that was done to all Jewish babies (see the discussion of 2:7 in the previous chapter of this volume). To fail to properly care for a newborn baby, including wrapping it, was unthinkable (cf. Ezek. 16:1–5). But Jewish mothers did not usually put their newborn babies **in a manger,** so that would narrow the shepherds' search to the Child of whom the angel spoke. The stark contrast between Jesus' exalted status as Savior, Messiah, and God and the humble circumstances of His birth emphasizes the magnitude of His "[emptying] Himself, taking the form of a bond-servant, and being made in the likeness of men" (Phil. 2:7).

THE PURPOSE OF THE GOOD NEWS

And suddenly there appeared with the angel a multitude of the heavenly host praising God and saying, "Glory to God in the highest, and on earth peace among men with whom He is pleased." (2:13–14)

While the angel was speaking to the shepherds something even more amazing took place. **Suddenly** (cf. v. 9; Mal. 3:1; Mark 13:36; Acts 2:2; 9:3; 1 Thess. 5:3) **there appeared with the angel a multitude of the heavenly host.** How many of the millions of holy angels ("myriad" is the Greek word for 10,000, the highest number for which there was a word, hence the use of the expression "myriads of myriads" to indicate more [Rev. 5:11]) appeared is not revealed, but the term **multitude** signifies a large group. The appearance of so many angels at once is unprecedented in Scripture.

These angels were doing what angels constantly do, **praising God** (cf. Rev. 5:11–12; 7:11–12). All heaven broke loose with rejoicing at the birth of the Son of God. The angels knew Him as the second person of the Trinity before His incarnation, where they saw His ineffable glory. They understood that the fall had transformed the human race into sinful rebels against God, but they also knew that God had provided a way of salvation for man. Their deep concern for the salvation of sinners causes there to be "joy in the presence of the angels of God over one sinner who repents" (Luke 15:10). The angelic chorus of praise reflects the transcendent pinnacle of all thought and action; the highest of all truths; the supreme reason for all that exists—the glory of God. The ultimate purpose of the good news of salvation is to save sinners so they can join the angels in glorifying God.

The angels ascribed **glory to God in the highest;** that is, heaven. **On earth,** the lowest place in comparison with heaven, they proclaimed **peace among men with whom He is pleased.** The **peace** of which the angels spoke is the peace with God that results from salvation (Rom. 5:1; cf. Acts 10:36). Through faith in the Messiah, the "Prince of Peace," God and sinners are reconciled (Rom. 5:10; 2 Cor. 5:18–19; Eph. 2:16; Col. 1:20–22).

The peace of which the angels spoke is only for **men with whom** God **is pleased.** That does not, of course, mean that He gives salvation to those who please Him by their good works, since salvation is "not as a result of works, so that no one may boast" (Eph. 2:9). The Greek text literally reads, "men of His good pleasure." As Marshall explains, "The phrase means 'those upon whom God's will/favour rests', and expresses the thought of God's free choice of those whom he wills to favour and save" (*The Gospel of Luke,* The New International Greek Testament Commentary [Grand Rapids: Eerdmans, 1978], 112). Salvation peace belongs to those to whom God is pleased to give it; it is not a reward for those who have good will, but a gracious gift to those who are the objects of God's good will.

THE PICTURE OF THE GOOD NEWS

When the angels had gone away from them into heaven, the shepherds began saying to one another, "Let us go straight to Bethlehem then, and see this thing that has happened which the Lord has made known to us." So they came in a hurry and found their way to Mary and Joseph, and the baby as He lay in the manger. When they had seen this, they made known the statement which had been told them about this Child. And all who heard it wondered at the things which were told them by the shepherds. But Mary treasured all these things, pondering them in her heart. The shepherds went back, glorifying and praising God for all that they had heard and seen, just as had been told them. And when eight days had passed, before His circumcision, His name was

then called Jesus, the name given by the angel before He was conceived in the womb. (2:15–21)

How long the angels lingered is not known, but eventually they returned to heaven to resume their praise and worship before the throne of God (cf. Rev. 5:11–14). After **the angels had gone away from them into heaven, the shepherds** immediately started discussing the amazing event they had just witnessed, and what they should do next. Although the angel had not specifically commanded them to do so, they excitedly **began saying to one another, "Let us go straight to Bethlehem then, and see this thing that has happened which the Lord has made known to us."** Understandably, they wanted to get to Bethlehem as soon as possible. But since they were responsible for the sheep under their care, they could not just drop everything and leave. Either some of them had to remain with the sheep, or they had to find other shepherds to watch over them. As soon as those details were worked out, the shepherds went at once to Bethlehem.

The shepherds' response illustrates the first two things involved in a person's coming to Christ: they heard the revelation from God that the Savior had come, and they believed that revelation. In Romans 10:14 Paul described those same two steps (in reverse order): "How then will they call on Him in whom they have not believed? How will they believe in Him whom they have not heard?" As noted earlier, these shepherds were most likely devout worshipers of the true God, who were looking for the redemption of Israel. Their hearts were prepared so that when they heard the revelation of the Savior's birth they believed it.

After making provision for their sheep to be cared for, the shepherds **came in a hurry and found their way to Mary and Joseph, and the baby.** The traditional site of the field where the shepherds were watching their sheep is about two miles from Bethlehem. Luke does not describe how the shepherds found Mary, Joseph, and the baby Jesus. However, there would not have been many babies born in a small village like Bethlehem on any given night. Certainly news of any birth would have spread rapidly by word of mouth, especially since Mary gave birth in a semipublic place (see the discussion of v. 7 in the previous chapter of this volume). When the shepherds saw the Child **as He lay in the manger,** the angel's prophecy was confirmed and their faith verified.

The shepherds' seeking out Mary, Joseph, and Jesus illustrates the next step in the salvation process. Those who truly believe the revelation of God in Christ will come to Him. They will accept His invitation, "Come to Me, all who are weary and heavy-laden, and I will give you rest. Take My yoke upon you and learn from Me, for I am gentle and humble in heart, and you will find rest for your souls. For My yoke is easy and My burden is light" (Matt. 11:28–30; cf. John 5:40; 6:37, 44; 7:37).

There must have been an interesting dialog between the shepherds and Mary and Joseph between verses 16 and 17. The young couple was no doubt overwhelmed by the shepherds' recounting of the amazing event they had just witnessed. The words of the angel provided further confirmation to Mary and Joseph of who their Child was. And Mary's account of Gabriel's appearance to her (1:26–38), coupled with Joseph's account of his dream (Matt. 1:20–23) could only have increased the shepherds' amazement.

The angels' appearance to them and their conversation with Mary and Joseph made the shepherds privy to information no one else had. Their enthusiastic response was to make **known the statement which had been told them about this Child.** They went everywhere proclaiming the news that the Savior, Israel's long-awaited Messiah, had been born. The shepherds thus became the first New Testament evangelists.

Once they had heard, believed, and acted on the truth, the shepherds could not help but tell others about it. Their witness to the good news they had received reveals something else that happens in the life of a newborn soul. The response of those who come to Christ is to tell others about Him. Usually the most bold and passionate people in proclaiming the gospel are the newest Christians; the longer people are saved, the less excited they seem about their salvation, and the less eager they are to share their faith. But true spiritual commitment is determined by the quality and tenacity of believers' long-term joy over their salvation. One measure of that joy is how eagerly they share the gospel. Lack of the zeal and passion that compels believers to tell others about Christ betrays a sinful heart of indifference and ingratitude.

The shepherds did not have that problem. The astounding nature of their message, coupled with the eagerness and enthusiasm with which they shared it, caused **all who heard it** to wonder **at the things which were told them by the shepherds.** *Thaumazō* (**wondered**) appears frequently in Luke's writings (cf. 1:21, 63; 2:33; 4:22; 7:9; 8:25; 9:43; 11:14, 38; 20:26; 24:12, 41; Acts 2:7; 3:12; 4:13; 7:31; 13:41). From the very beginning the life and ministry of Jesus Christ caused people to marvel and be amazed. Unfortunately then, as now, much of that amazement produced not commitment, but merely curiosity. When the shepherds heard the good news of the Savior's birth, they immediately sought Him out. But all that is said of those to whom they witnessed is that they **wondered.** After their initial amazement wore off, most of them probably just went on with their lives as if nothing had happened.

In contrast to the shallow, superficial reaction of many who heard the news, **Mary treasured all these things, pondering them in**

her heart. She reflected deeply on the significance of the birth of God's Son, and on what that birth portended for her and Joseph as His earthly parents. In addition to the normal thoughts that go through the mind of any new mother, Mary had many other things to think about. She considered God's redemptive purpose, how just as He had promised, He had sent a Savior to redeem His people. But that redemption would come at a fearful cost. As Simeon would later warn Mary, "Behold, this Child is appointed for the fall and rise of many in Israel, and for a sign to be opposed—and a sword will pierce even your own soul—to the end that thoughts from many hearts may be revealed" (2:34–35). Years later, Mary would watch her Son die on the cross bearing God's wrath against sin (John 19:25–27).

Mary's deep meditation on the Savior illustrates another aspect of what it means to truly embrace Christ. Salvation's initial euphoria and excitement deepens into a richer, fuller, more profound understanding of the person and work of the Lord Jesus Christ. The apostle John described the Christian life as a progression from being a spiritual child, who only knows God as Father and forgiver of sins, to being a spiritual young man, well grounded in biblical truth, to being a spiritual father, with a deep understanding of God's person (1 John 2:12–14). But no Christian will ever be satisfied with the level of knowledge they have attained. Paul, many years into his Christian pilgrimage, yearned to know Christ even better. He expressed to the Philippians his desire to "know Him and the power of His resurrection and the fellowship of His sufferings, being conformed to His death" (Phil. 3:10).

The shepherds had had an amazing evening, one that forever changed their lives. But life goes on, and eventually the shepherds went back to their flock, **glorifying and praising God** (cf. 1:64; 5:25–26; 7:16; 13:13; 17:15; 18:43; 23:47; 24:52–53) **for all that they had heard and seen, just as had been told them.** Their hopes and longings that the Redeemer would come had been realized, and their lives were marked by a newfound attitude of praise and worship. That same attitude characterizes all who know and love the Lord Jesus Christ (cf. Ps. 22:26; 30:4; 33:1; 34:1; 100:4; Acts 16:25; Heb. 13:15), whom Paul describes as "the true circumcision, who worship in the Spirit of God and glory in Christ Jesus" (Phil. 3:3).

Testifying to Jesus—Part 1: Joseph and Mary (Luke 2:21–24)

14

And when eight days had passed, before His circumcision, His name was then called Jesus, the name given by the angel before He was conceived in the womb. And when the days for their purification according to the law of Moses were completed, they brought Him up to Jerusalem to present Him to the Lord (as it is written in the Law of the Lord, "Every firstborn male that opens the womb shall be called holy to the Lord"), and to offer a sacrifice according to what was said in the Law of the Lord, "A pair of turtledoves or two young pigeons." (2:21–24)

A basic legal principle requires a person's testimony to be confirmed by multiple witnesses. The Mosaic law declared that "a single witness shall not rise up against a man on account of any iniquity or any sin which he has committed; on the evidence of two or three witnesses a matter shall be confirmed" (Deut. 19:15; cf. 17:6; Matt. 18:16; 2 Cor. 13:1; 1 Tim. 5:19; Heb. 10:28). In his gospel, Luke testified that Jesus Christ was born the Son of God; that He was Israel's long-awaited Messiah, conceived in a virgin through the power of the Holy Spirit; that He is God in human flesh, the Redeemer, who will save His people from their sins.

Such an amazing, unprecedented claim came with verification, as Luke presented the testimony of several witnesses to corroborate it. Because a person's testimony is only as credible as his or her character, Luke was careful to establish that the witnesses he presented were righteous people.

At the time of Jesus' birth four groups, whose teachings were inimical to true biblical righteousness, dominated Jewish society. The Sadducees were the theological liberals of the time, denying the resurrection of the body and the existence of angels (Acts 23:8). Their arch-rivals, the Pharisees, were legalists, who believed they could earn their way to heaven by observing rituals and ceremonies (Matt. 23:1ff.). The Zealots were political revolutionaries, advocating the violent overthrow of Roman rule and the recovery of Israel's sovereignty (cf. Acts 21:38). The last group, the Essenes, were ascetic hermits, living in the wilderness in isolation from the rest of society.

In contrast, the righteous were a small remnant in Israel. Luke has already introduced some of them—Zacharias, Elizabeth, Joseph, Mary, and the shepherds who received the announcement of Jesus' birth. In this section of his narrative (2:21–38) Luke called four members of that righteous remnant to testify as witnesses to Jesus' true identity and mission: Joseph and Mary, Simeon, and Anna. The setting of this passage is closely connected with two Old Testament themes. The scene for most of the passage is the temple and involves the rituals prescribed by the Mosaic law. The passage also borrows richly from the writings of Isaiah, particularly chapters 40–66.

Fittingly, the first to give testimony to Jesus were His parents, Joseph and Mary. That Joseph was a righteous man is explicitly stated in Matthew 1:19, while Mary's righteousness is evident from her declaration in Luke 1:47 that God was her Savior. Five times in chapter 2 of his gospel Luke affirmed the couple's righteousness by noting their commitment to the law of God (vv. 22, 23, 24, 27, 39). Genuine righteousness, the righteousness that comes from God by saving faith, inevitably manifests itself in obedience, since "faith without works is dead" (James 2:26; cf. John 3:36; Acts 5:32; 6:7; Rom. 1:5; 15:18; 16:26; 2 Thess. 1:8; Heb. 5:9; 1 Peter 1:1–2). Obedience is also the mark of true love for God (John 14:15, 21, 23; 15:10, 14).

Two acts of obedience reveal Joseph and Mary's testimony to Jesus as Messiah and Savior of the world: the circumcision and naming, and the purification and presenting.

THE CIRCUMCISION AND NAMING

And when eight days had passed, before His circumcision, His name was then called Jesus, the name given by the angel before He was conceived in the womb. (2:21)

In obedience to the law's requirement (Gen. 17:9–14; Lev. 12:3) Joseph and Mary circumcised their newborn Son **eight days** after His birth. As noted in the discussion of 1:59 in chapter 8 of this volume, God instituted **circumcision** for three purposes. First, along with the other dietary and sanitary regulations prescribed in the law, circumcision had health benefits. As the sign of the Abrahamic covenant, circumcision was also the mark of Israel's national identity. Finally, circumcision was a spiritual object lesson of the need for cleansing from the depravity of sin, which is passed to each succeeding generation through procreation. Circumcision was a physical symbol of the spiritual cleansing of the heart that takes place at salvation (cf. Deut. 10:16; 30:6; Jer. 4:4).

But why was Jesus circumcised, since He was sinless (Isa. 53:9; John 8:46; 2 Cor. 5:21; Heb. 4:15; 1 Peter 2:22; 1 John 3:5) and did not need to have His heart cleansed? The answer lies in understanding that He came to fulfill the law. In the words of the apostle Paul, Jesus was "born of a woman, born under the Law" (Gal. 4:4). Like His baptism, Jesus' circumcision served to "fulfill all righteousness" (Matt. 3:15). He could say with David, "I delight to do Your will, O my God; Your Law is within my heart" (Ps. 40:8), and He alone kept God's law perfectly throughout His life. Only because He did so could His righteousness be credited to believers. At the cross God treated Jesus as if He had lived their sinful lives. He is, therefore, able to treat them as if they had lived Jesus' perfectly righteous life.

In keeping with prevailing Jewish custom (see the discussion of 1:59 in chapter 8 of this volume), the Child's **name was then** (at His circumcision) **called Jesus, the name given by the angel before He was conceived in the womb.** The name **Jesus** is the Greek equivalent of the Hebrew name "Joshua," which means, "Yahweh saves." It is a fitting name for the One who was born to "save His people from their sins" (Matt. 1:21).

One of the most egregious misrepresentations of biblical truth by the Roman Catholic Church is its portrayal of God as a reluctant Savior. The implication of Catholic theology is that Father is angry, vengeful, and hostile toward sinners. Jesus is slightly more sympathetic, but the truly gentle, compassionate, approachable one is Mary. Sinners are thus well advised to approach her for salvation because Jesus cannot resist His mother's requests. So pervasive is this view that Rome elevates Mary to the status of co-redemptrix with Jesus.

Such a portrayal of God is completely false, since the Bible reveals Him to be a saving God by nature. In Deuteronomy 33:29, Moses said, "Blessed are you, O Israel; who is like you, a people saved by the Lord." David referred to God as the "God of our salvation" (1 Chron. 16:35), while in Psalm 7:10 he exclaimed, "My shield is with God, who saves the upright in heart." Psalm 106:21 chided Israel because "they forgot God their Savior, who had done great things in Egypt." Isaiah called

God the "Savior of Israel," who has saved His people "with an everlasting salvation" (Isa. 45:15,17; cf. 45:22; 59:1; 63:1,8). Jeremiah described Him as the "Hope of Israel, its Savior in time of distress" (Jer. 14:8).

In the New Testament Mary referred to God as her Savior (Luke 1:47). Paul described Him as "God our Savior, who desires all men to be saved and to come to the knowledge of the truth" (1 Tim. 2:3–4; cf. 4:10; Titus 1:3; 2:10; Jude 25) and affirmed that it is "God who has saved us" (2 Tim. 1:8–9; cf. Titus 3:4–5). Nowhere in the New Testament is God's tender, compassionate, saving nature more clearly depicted than in the case of the prodigal son (Luke 15:11–32).

Even more significant than what others said about Him are God's repeated declarations that He is a Savior. "For I am the Lord your God," He said in Isaiah 43:3, "the Holy One of Israel, your Savior." In verse 11, He added emphatically, "I, even I, am the Lord, and there is no savior besides Me." In Isaiah 45:21, God described Himself as "a righteous God and a Savior" (cf. 49:26; 60:16; Hos. 13:4).

The ultimate proof that God is a saving God is the reality that He "so loved the world, that He gave His only begotten Son, that whoever believes in Him shall not perish, but have eternal life" (John 3:16; cf. 1 John 4:14). In the Old Testament Isaiah predicted that God would be "pleased to crush Him [Christ], putting Him to grief" (Isa. 53:10). To the Romans Paul wrote, "For while we were still helpless, at the right time Christ died for the ungodly" (Rom. 5:6) and, "He who did not spare His own Son, but delivered Him over for us all, how will He not also with Him freely give us all things?" (Rom. 8:32). In 2 Corinthians 5:21, the apostle described the profound theological implications of God's sacrifice of His Son: "He made Him who knew no sin to be sin on our behalf, so that we might become the righteousness of God in Him." "In this is love," wrote the apostle John, "not that we loved God, but that He loved us and sent His Son to be the propitiation for our sins" (1 John 4:10).

The Father's choice of the name "Jesus" for His Son is appropriate, reflecting the reality that He is "a righteous God and a Savior" (Isa. 45:21).

THE PURIFICATION AND PRESENTING

And when the days for their purification according to the law of Moses were completed, they brought Him up to Jerusalem to present Him to the Lord (as it is written in the Law of the Lord, "Every firstborn male that opens the womb shall be called holy to the Lord"), and to offer a sacrifice according to what was said in the Law of the Lord, "A pair of turtledoves or two young pigeons." (2:22–24)

As was the case with Jesus' circumcision, Mary's **purification** (the word **their** merely reflects the presence of Joseph and Jesus) and the presenting of the baby Jesus were done strictly in keeping with the **law of Moses.** Like circumcision, a woman's purification after childbirth illustrated the need for cleansing from sin. Leviticus 12:1–5 describes the purification process:

> Then the Lord spoke to Moses, saying, "Speak to the sons of Israel, saying, 'When a woman gives birth and bears a male child, then she shall be unclean for seven days, as in the days of her menstruation she shall be unclean. On the eighth day the flesh of his foreskin shall be circumcised. Then she shall remain in the blood of her purification for thirty-three days; she shall not touch any consecrated thing, nor enter the sanctuary until the days of her purification are completed. But if she bears a female child, then she shall be unclean for two weeks, as in her menstruation; and she shall remain in the blood of her purification for sixty-six days.'"

The uncleanness in view here is ceremonial uncleanness, the first part of which lasted for seven days, like that of menstruation (Lev. 15:19). While she was unclean, a woman could not touch anything sacred or holy, nor could she go to the temple. Her ceremonial uncleanness tempered the natural joy of bringing a new life into the world (John 16:21) with the sober reality that the child, like its parents, was a sinner (Ps. 51:5).

After a male child's circumcision on the eighth day, the mother was ceremonially unclean for another thirty-three days. Interestingly, the time of her impurity was doubled if the child was a girl, to two weeks initially followed by a subsequent sixty-six days. The Bible does not explain the reason for that additional time of uncleanness, but there are at least two possibilities. First, as noted above, when a male child was born circumcision served as an illustration of sin and depravity. It may be that God intended the extra period of uncleanness involved in the birth of a female child to take the place of circumcision. Second, doubling the length of purification may reflect the stigma on women stemming from Eve's leading the human race into sin (1 Tim. 2:14). That stigma is removed in Christ; while a woman led humankind into sin, godly women, through their influence on their children, have the privilege of leading many out of sin into godliness (v. 15).

After **the days for** Mary's **purification . . . were completed** and she was again permitted to enter the temple, the couple **brought** Jesus **up to Jerusalem to present Him to the Lord.** Though it did not have to be done at **Jerusalem** or the temple, the **Law of the Lord** given through Moses declared that **every firstborn male that opens the womb shall be called holy to the Lord** and set apart to Him. In Exodus

13:1–2, "the Lord spoke to Moses, saying, 'Sanctify to Me every firstborn, the first offspring of every womb among the sons of Israel, both of man and beast; it belongs to Me.'" Elaborating on that commandment Moses said to Israel,

> Now it shall come about when the Lord brings you to the land of the Canaanite, as He swore to you and to your fathers, and gives it to you, you shall devote to the Lord the first offspring of every womb, and the first offspring of every beast that you own; the males belong to the Lord. But every first offspring of a donkey you shall redeem with a lamb, but if you do not redeem it, then you shall break its neck; and every firstborn of man among your sons you shall redeem. And it shall be when your son asks you in time to come, saying, "What is this?" then you shall say to him, "With a powerful hand the Lord brought us out of Egypt, from the house of slavery. It came about, when Pharaoh was stubborn about letting us go, that the Lord killed every firstborn in the land of Egypt, both the firstborn of man and the firstborn of beast. Therefore, I sacrifice to the Lord the males, the first offspring of every womb, but every firstborn of my sons I redeem." (vv. 11–15)

The setting apart of the firstborn was not for priestly service, because priests came only from the tribe of Levi (Jesus was from the tribe of Judah [Heb. 7:14]). Joseph and Mary, then, were not presenting Jesus for priestly service, but rather dedicating His life to God.

The Levites took the place of the firstborn of the rest of the tribes by being devoted to the service of God. In Numbers 3:12–13, God said to Moses,

> Now, behold, I have taken the Levites from among the sons of Israel instead of every firstborn, the first issue of the womb among the sons of Israel. So the Levites shall be Mine. For all the firstborn are Mine; on the day that I struck down all the firstborn in the land of Egypt, I sanctified to Myself all the firstborn in Israel, from man to beast. They shall be Mine; I am the Lord. (cf. vv. 41, 44–45)

But in return for their being exempted from priestly duty, a redemption price had to be paid for the firstborn from the other tribes. In Numbers 18:15–16, God said to Aaron,

> Every first issue of the womb of all flesh, whether man or animal, which they offer to the Lord, shall be yours; nevertheless the firstborn of man you shall surely redeem, and the firstborn of unclean animals you shall redeem. As to their redemption price, from a month old you shall redeem them, by your valuation, five shekels in silver.

Israel was to a great extent a theocracy, with the priests and Levites doing much of the work of governing the country. The five shekels (a significant amount of money) paid by the families of the firstborn sons of the other tribes helped defray the costs of running the government.

Though it is not explicitly stated in the text, it is safe to assume that Joseph and Mary paid the five-shekel redemption fee for Jesus, since they "performed everything according to the Law of the Lord" (v. 39). That fee, coupled with the expense of traveling to Bethlehem and staying there for an extended period of time, was a significant financial burden for this young couple. As the discussion of Mary's sacrifice below reveals, Joseph and Mary were not wealthy. But like all the righteous, they found great joy in obeying the law of God (cf. Pss. 1:1–2; 40:8; 119:70,77,92,174).

After his parenthetical statement in verse 23, Luke returned to the other reason Joseph, Mary, and Jesus went to the temple. After her forty days of uncleanness following the birth of her Son, Mary had **to offer a sacrifice according to what was said in the Law of the Lord.** This again reveals her righteous character and commitment to obeying the law of God.

Just as her ceremonial uncleanness pictured sin, so Mary's **sacrifice** symbolized the ultimate sacrifice for sin that her own Son would make on the cross. That sacrifice granted direct access to God (symbolized by the tearing of the temple veil [Matt. 27:51]) by fully satisfying His wrath and atoning for the sins of all who put their faith in the Lord Jesus Christ.

The normal sacrifice was "a one year old lamb for a burnt offering and a young pigeon or a turtledove for a sin offering" (Lev. 12:6). For those whose means were not sufficient for such an offering an alternative was provided: "But if she cannot afford a lamb, then she shall take two turtledoves or two young pigeons, the one for a burnt offering and the other for a sin offering; and the priest shall make atonement for her, and she shall be clean" (v. 8). Having made her offering, Mary was once again ceremonially clean. That she offered the alternative offering, **a pair of turtledoves or two young pigeons,** showed that she and Joseph were poor. It also indicates that they had not yet seen the wise men (Matt. 2:11), since the valuable gifts they brought would have allowed Joseph and Mary to afford a lamb for the sacrifice. That Mary offered a sin offering is consistent with the reality that she was a sinner in need of a Savior (cf. 1:47). The Catholic dogma that Mary was immaculately conceived and lived a sinless life finds no support in Scripture.

Joseph and Mary's obedience to the law of God shines forth throughout the narrative of Christ's birth. Giving Him the name Jesus in obedience to the angel's command (Matt. 1:21), presenting Him in the temple, paying the fee required for a firstborn son, and Mary's scrupulous observance of the law of purification demonstrate that they, like Zacharias and Elizabeth,"were both righteous in the sight of God, walking blamelessly in all the commandments and requirements of the Lord" (Luke 1:6). That righteousness validates their confirming testimony to their Son, the Lord Jesus Christ.

Testifying to Jesus—Part 2 Simeon and Anna
Luke 2:25–38

15

And there was a man in Jerusalem whose name was Simeon; and this man was righteous and devout, looking for the consolation of Israel; and the Holy Spirit was upon him. And it had been revealed to him by the Holy Spirit that he would not see death before he had seen the Lord's Christ. And he came in the Spirit into the temple; and when the parents brought in the child Jesus, to carry out for Him the custom of the Law, then he took Him into his arms, and blessed God, and said, "Now Lord, You are releasing Your bond-servant to depart in peace, according to Your word; for my eyes have seen Your salvation, which You have prepared in the presence of all peoples, a light of revelation to the Gentiles, and the glory of Your people Israel." And His father and mother were amazed at the things which were being said about Him. And Simeon blessed them and said to Mary His mother, "Behold, this Child is appointed for the fall and rise of many in Israel, and for a sign to be opposed—and a sword will pierce even your own soul—to the end that thoughts from many hearts may be revealed." And there was a prophetess, Anna the daughter of Phanuel, of the tribe of Asher. She was advanced in years and had lived with her husband seven years after her marriage,

and then as a widow to the age of eighty-four. She never left the temple, serving night and day with fastings and prayers. At that very moment she came up and began giving thanks to God, and continued to speak of Him to all those who were looking for the redemption of Jerusalem. (2:25–38)

All the promises in Scripture will certainly be fulfilled, because God is "the faithful God" (Deut. 7:9; cf. Hos. 11:12), the "God of faithfulness" (Deut. 32:4) whose every "work is done in faithfulness" (Ps. 33:4). "His faithfulness is a shield and bulwark" to His people (Ps. 91:4), causing them to exclaim, "Great is Your faithfulness" (Lam. 3:23). Such passages as Psalms 36:5; 40:10; 89:8; 100:5; 119:90; Romans 3:3; 1 Corinthians 1:9; 10:13; 2 Corinthians 1:18; 1 Thessalonians 5:24; 2 Thessalonians 3:3; Hebrews 10:23; 1 Peter 4:19; and 1 John 1:9 also attest to God's faithfulness.

God promised Abraham and Sarah that they would have a son despite their advanced age (Gen. 17:15–19; 18:10, 14; cf. Rom. 9:9), and she bore Isaac (Gen. 21:1–2). He promised to give Israel the land of Canaan (Gen. 12:7; 13:14–17; 15:7, 18; 17:8; 26:3; 28:13; 35:12; 50:24; Ex. 12:25; 33:1; Num. 32:11; Deut. 1:8; 6:10; Josh. 23:5; cf. Heb. 11:9), and "not one of the good promises which the Lord had made to the house of Israel failed; all came to pass" (Josh. 21:45; cf. 1 Kings 8:56). The Lord promised David, "Your house and your kingdom shall endure before Me forever; your throne shall be established forever" (2 Sam. 7:16; cf. v. 28; 1 Kings 2:4; 8:24–25; 9:5). That promise will ultimately be fulfilled in the Lord Jesus Christ, who will sit "on the throne of David and [reign] over his kingdom, to establish it and to uphold it with justice and righteousness from then on and forevermore" (Isa. 9:7; cf. Luke 1:32–33).

But the most significant of all God's trustworthy promises is the promise that He would send His Son, the Messiah and Savior, into the world. In 2 Corinthians 1:20, Paul wrote, "For as many as are the promises of God, in [Christ] they are yes." "For the testimony of Jesus," the apostle John added, "is the spirit of prophecy" (Rev. 19:10). In keeping with that truth, the Old Testament is filled with hundreds of prophecies of the coming Messiah. Many of those were fulfilled at the first coming of Jesus Christ, and the remainder will be fulfilled when He returns in glory.

Immediately after the fall, God promised to send a Redeemer (Gen. 3:15) and "when the fullness of the time came, God sent forth His Son, born of a woman, born under the Law" (Gal. 4:4). The Old Testament said that the Messiah would be a descendant of Abraham (Gen. 22:18) and David (2 Sam. 7:12–13; Ps. 89:3–4; Jer. 23:5), and Jesus was (Acts 3:25; Gal. 3:16; Acts 13:22–23; Rom. 1:3). The Old Testament predicted that the Messiah would be born of a virgin (Isa. 7:14), and Jesus was (Matt. 1:22–23). According to Micah 5:2, the Messiah would be born in Bethlehem, and Jesus was (Matt. 2:1). Isaiah (40:3) and Malachi (3:1) predicted that Messiah would be preceded by a forerunner, and John the Baptist fulfilled that role for Jesus Christ (Matt. 3:1–3; Luke 1:17). Jesus was the prophet like Moses (Deut. 18:15–18; cf. Acts 3:20–22); the "priest forever according to the order of Melchizedek" (Ps. 110:4; cf. Heb. 5:5–6); the suffering Servant who bore the sins of His people (Isa. 53:4–6; cf. 1 Peter 2:24); the ruler of the nations (Ps. 2:6–9; Isa. 9:6; cf. Rev. 19:15–16); and the one exalted to the Father's right hand (Ps. 110:1; cf. Acts 2:32–36; Heb. 1:3; 10:10–12). Those are but a few of the numerous Old Testament prophecies the Lord Jesus fulfilled (cf. Ps. 2:7 with Heb. 1:5; Isa. 11:2; 61:1 with Matt. 3:16; Acts 10:38; Zech. 9:9 with Matt. 21:1–5; Isa. 53:9 with 1 Peter 2:22; Heb. 4:15; Ps. 41:9 with John 13:18; Zech. 13:7 with Matt. 26:31, 56; Zech. 11:12–13 with Matt. 27:3–10; Isa. 53:7 with Matt. 26:63; John 1:29; Isa. 52:14; 53:3 with Matt. 26:67; John 19:3; Isa. 50:6 with Mark 14:65; John 19:1; Ps. 22:16; with Matt. 27:35; John 20:25, 27; Ps. 22:1 with Matt. 27:46; Ps. 22:7–8 with Matt. 27:39–44; Ps. 22:18 with Luke 23:34; Isa. 53:12 with Luke 22:37; Ex. 12:46 with John 19:33, 36; Zech. 12:10 with John 19:34, 37; Isa. 53:9 with Matt. 27:57–60; Ps. 16:10 with Acts 2:25–31; 13:35; Isa. 29:18 with Matt. 11:5).

But despite the clear testimony to the Lord Jesus Christ in the Old Testament (cf. Luke 24:25–27, 44–47; John 5:39) only a small, believing remnant in Israel were prepared to recognize Him when He arrived. Among them was an old couple, a common priest named Zacharias and his barren wife, Elizabeth, who became the parents of Messiah's forerunner (Luke 1:5ff.). Also a part of that small believing remnant was a young couple just beginning their life together, Joseph and Mary, Jesus' earthly father and the virgin in whom He was conceived by the Holy Spirit (Luke 1:34–35). The shepherds who received the angelic announcement of Jesus' birth (Luke 2:8–20) were also members of the believing remnant. All of them were humble people, far from the elite circles of Jewish thought, education, or religion. Yet they were chosen by God for monumental service in connection with the birth of the Messiah.

In verses 25 to 38, Luke introduced two more members of the believing remnant, who further testified to the infant Jesus' true identity and mission: Simeon and Anna. Both were advanced in years, lived in Jerusalem, were associated with the temple, and were "looking for the consolation of Israel" (v. 25) along with "all those who were looking for the redemption of Jerusalem" (v. 38). They, like John the Baptist would later be, were burning and shining lamps (John 5:35) in the spiritual darkness of a hypocritical and apostate nation.

SIMEON

And there was a man in Jerusalem whose name was Simeon; and this man was righteous and devout, looking for the consolation of Israel; and the Holy Spirit was upon him. And it had been revealed to him by the Holy Spirit that he would not see death before he had seen the Lord's Christ. And he came in the Spirit into the temple; and when the parents brought in the child Jesus, to carry out for Him the custom of the Law, then he took Him into his arms, and blessed God, and said, "Now Lord, You are releasing Your bond-servant to depart in peace, according to Your word; for my eyes have seen Your salvation, which You have prepared in the presence of all peoples, a light of revelation to the Gentiles, and the glory of Your people Israel." And His father and mother were amazed at the things which were being said about Him. And Simeon blessed them and said to Mary His mother, "Behold, this Child is appointed for the fall and rise of many in Israel, and for a sign to be opposed—and a sword will pierce even your own soul—to the end that thoughts from many hearts may be revealed." (2:25–35)

Luke's account of his testimony to Jesus reveals five things about Simeon: his character, theology, anointing, proclamation, and warning.

SIMEON'S CHARACTER

And there was a man in Jerusalem whose name was Simeon; and this man was righteous and devout, (2:25a)

Simeon, who appears only here in Scripture, evidently lived **in Jerusalem** and was most likely an old man (cf. vv. 26, 29). His name, which means,"God has heard" (cf. Gen. 29:33), was a common name, one he shared with one of the twelve sons of Jacob (Gen. 34:25) and the tribe named after him (Num. 1:23), an ancestor of Jesus (Luke 3:30), one of the teachers in the church at Antioch (Acts 13:1), and Peter, whose Hebrew name was Simeon (Acts 15:14).

But what is known about him reveals Simeon to have been spiritually qualified to testify about the Messiah. Luke's description of him as **righteous and devout** is loaded with meaning. To say that Simeon was **righteous** means that he, like Abraham (Gen. 15:6), had righteousness imputed to him by faith (cf. 1:6; 14:14; Matt. 13:49; 25:46; Acts 10:22; 24:15; Rom. 1:17; Gal. 3:11; Heb. 12:23). *Eulabēs* (**devout**) has the meaning of "cautious" in classical Greek. It appears in the New Testament only in Luke's writings (cf. Acts 2:5; 8:2; 22:12), where it describes those who are "reverent toward God," "God-fearing," or "pious." It conveys the idea of being careful to obey and honor God so as to lead an exemplary life before others. Those two terms indicate that Simeon not only was justified, but also sanctified. The two are inseparably linked since, as John Calvin put it, "Christ . . . justifies no man without also sanctifying him" *(Institutes,* III, 16, 1). In the words of the apostle Paul, Simeon was "not a Jew who is one outwardly . . . [but] a Jew who is one inwardly" (Rom. 2:28–29). Simeon had received the salvation benefits promised in the prophet Isaiah 55:6–7: "Seek the Lord while He may be found; call upon Him while He is near. Let the wicked forsake his way and the unrighteous man his thoughts; and let him return to the Lord, and He will have compassion on him, and to our God, for He will abundantly pardon" (cf. Mic. 7:18–19).

SIMEON'S THEOLOGY

looking for the consolation of Israel; (2:25*b*)

Like the rest of the believing remnant, Simeon eagerly awaited the coming of Messiah, who would bring **the consolation of Israel.** *Paraklēsis* (**consolation**) has in this context the connotation of "comfort," "encouragement," or "solace." Simeon was both looking for the personal consolation of salvation for himself, and for the national deliverance promised in the Davidic and Abrahamic covenants.

Simeon was a man who cared deeply about his people. He was like the apostle Paul, who was so passionately concerned about the salvation of his fellow Israelites that he wrote, "I could wish that I myself were accursed, separated from Christ for the sake of my brethren, my kinsmen according to the flesh" (Rom. 9:3). Simeon's concern for his people was heightened by the distressing circumstances in which the nation found itself, chafing under the occupation of the hated Romans. Such trying times intensified the believing remnant's longing for Messiah to come and deliver them. They yearned for deliverance from their Gentile oppressors, the restoration of their national sovereignty, and the national blessings promised in the Davidic and Abrahamic covenants. But most of all they eagerly awaited the realization of the New covenant, with its promise of forgiveness of sin, a new, cleansed heart, and the indwelling of the Holy Spirit (Jer. 31:31–34).

The Messiah was the embodiment of the nation's hope of consolation; the only one who could bring consolation to Israel was the Consoler. Thus the rabbis sometimes referred to the Messiah as Menachem, which means "Comforter" or "Consoler." Isaiah in particular emphasized Messiah's role as a comforter. In Isaiah 40:1, he wrote, "'Comfort, O comfort My people,' says your God." In verse 10, the prophet identified the comforter: "Behold, the Lord God will come with might, with His arm ruling for Him. Behold, His reward is with Him and His recompense before Him." Several other passages in Isaiah also emphasize that God will comfort His people:

> Thus says the Lord, "In a favorable time I have answered You, and in a day of salvation I have helped You; and I will keep You and give You for a covenant of the people, to restore the land, to make them inherit the desolate heritages; saying to those who are bound, 'Go forth,' to those who are in darkness, 'Show yourselves.' Along the roads they will feed, and their pasture will be on all bare heights. They will not hunger or thirst, neither will the scorching heat or sun strike them down; for He who has compassion on them will lead them and will guide them to springs of water. I will make all My mountains a road, and My highways will be raised up. Behold, these shall come from afar; and lo, these will come from the north and from the west, and these from the land of Sinim. Shout for joy, O heavens! And rejoice, O earth! Break forth into joyful shouting, O mountains! For the Lord has comforted His people and will have compassion on His afflicted." (49:8–13)

> Indeed, the Lord will comfort Zion; He will comfort all her waste places. And her wilderness He will make like Eden, and her desert like the garden of the Lord; joy and gladness will be found in her, thanksgiving and sound of a melody. . . . I, even I, am He who comforts you. (51:3, 12)

> Break forth, shout joyfully together, you waste places of Jerusalem; for the Lord has comforted His people, He has redeemed Jerusalem. (52:9)

> O afflicted one, storm-tossed, and not comforted, behold, I will set your stones in antimony, and your foundations I will lay in sapphires. (54:11)

> I have seen his ways, but I will heal him; I will lead him and restore comfort to him and to his mourners. (57:18)

> The Spirit of the Lord God is upon me, because the Lord has anointed me to bring good news to the afflicted; He has sent me to bind up the brokenhearted, to proclaim liberty to captives and freedom to prisoners; to proclaim the favorable year of the Lord and the day of vengeance of our God; to comfort all who mourn. (61:1–2)

> "Be joyful with Jerusalem and rejoice for her, all you who love her; be exceedingly glad with her, all you who mourn over her, that you may nurse and be satisfied with her comforting breasts, that you may suck and be delighted with her bountiful bosom." For thus says the Lord, "Behold, I extend peace to her like a river, and the glory of the nations

like an overflowing stream; and you shall be nursed, you shall be carried on the hip and fondled on the knees. As one whom his mother
comforts, so I will comfort you; and you will be comforted in
Jerusalem." (66:10–13)

Jeremiah (Jer. 31:13), Ezekiel (Ezek. 14:22–23), and Zechariah (Zech.
1:17) also speak of God's comforting of His people. Simeon's theology
was consistent with the Old Testament promises that God would console
His people through the coming of Messiah.

SIMEON'S ANOINTING

**and the Holy Spirit was upon him. And it had been revealed to
him by the Holy Spirit that he would not see death before he had
seen the Lord's Christ. And he came in the Spirit into the temple;
and when the parents brought in the child Jesus, to carry out for
Him the custom of the Law,** (2:25c–27)

A common misconception about the Holy Spirit is that His ministry in the lives of God's people began on the day of Pentecost. That is
not the case, however. All those who were saved before the cross and Pentecost were saved in the same way as those who were saved afterward—
by grace through faith (Eph. 2:8–9). And no sinner, "dead in ... trespasses
and sins" (Eph. 2:1), can come to repentance and faith apart from the
work of the Holy Spirit. "The heart is more deceitful than all else," wrote
Jeremiah, "and is desperately sick; who can understand it?" (Jer. 17:9). Sinners can no more change their hearts by their own efforts than people
can change their skin color, or animals the pattern of their fur (Jer. 13:23).
"Who can say, 'I have cleansed my heart, I am pure from my sin'?"
Solomon asked rhetorically (Prov. 20:9). The obvious answer is no one,
since "there is none righteous, not even one; there is none who under-
stands, there is none who seeks for God; all have turned aside, together
they have become useless; there is none who does good, there is not
even one" (Rom. 3:10–12; cf. Job 15:14; 1 Kings 8:46; Eccl. 7:20; Rom. 3:23).

The Holy Spirit convicted people in the Old Testament of their
sin, prompted repentance, gave life, elicited faith, and drew them to God.
Apart from His work, no person in any age can ever be justified, sanctified, empowered for service and witness, understand Scripture, or pray in
the will of God. There is, however, a new dimension to the Spirit's work in
the lives of believers after Pentecost. As Jesus told the disciples in John
14:17 concerning the increased degree of the Spirit's ministry to them,
"He abides with you and will be in you." Under the old covenant, the
Spirit was present in power and person *with* believers. But under the

New covenant, His presence was *in* those who believed and is expressed in an unprecedented way (cf. Ezek. 36:26–27). There was to come for believers a giving of the Spirit by which unique power would be provided for ministry and evangelism. That happened on the day of Pentecost, when the Spirit was given to believers in a new fullness that became normative for all believers since (Rom. 8:9; 1 Cor. 12:13).

Luke's note that **the Holy Spirit was upon** Simeon reflects the Spirit's pre-Pentecost empowering of people to serve and speak for God (cf. Ex. 31:2–3; Num. 11:25; 27:18; Judg. 3:9–10; 11:29; 13:24–25; 14:6, 19; 15:14; 1 Sam. 16:13; 2 Chron. 15:1; 20:14–17; 24:20; Mic. 3:8; Zech. 7:12). He has already recorded the Holy Spirit's filling of John the Baptist (1:15), Elizabeth (1:41), and Zacharias (1:67). As a result of the Spirit's coming upon Simeon **it had been revealed to him by the Holy Spirit that he would not see death before he had seen the Lord's Christ** (i.e., the Messiah). A revelation from God had granted a very unusual privilege to this noble saint. That revelation must have heightened Simeon's messianic hope to a fever pitch, since he knew that it would be realized in his lifetime. He must have lived in a constant state of joyous expectation, knowing that each new day might bring the Messiah he longed to see. That knowledge must also have had a sobering effect on him, motivating him to lead a godly life.

On the divinely appointed day, forty days after Jesus' birth, Simeon **came in the Spirit** (that is, under the Spirit's leading; cf. Rev. 1:10; 4:2; 17:3; 21:10) **into the temple.** Unlike *naos,* which refers to the inner sanctuary, the Holy Place and the Holy of Holies (cf. its use in 1:9, 21, 22), *hieron* (**temple**) refers to the temple complex as a whole. It was there, most likely in the Court of the Women, that Simeon met Joseph and Mary when they **brought in the child Jesus, to carry out for Him the custom of the Law** (cf. the exposition of 2:22–24 in the previous chapter of this volume). Luke does not give the details of how they met, since neither party was looking for or knew the other. The temple, where God met with His people, was a fitting location for Him to providentially arrange for Simeon to meet the God-man, Jesus Christ.

SIMEON'S PROCLAMATION

then he took Him into his arms, and blessed God, and said, "Now Lord, You are releasing Your bond-servant to depart in peace, according to Your word; for my eyes have seen Your salvation, which You have prepared in the presence of all peoples, a light of revelation to the Gentiles, and the glory of Your people Israel." And His father and mother were amazed at the things which

were being said about Him. (2:28–33)

Having met Joseph, Mary, and Jesus, Simeon **took** Jesus **into his arms.** It is hard to imagine how thrilled he must have been as he realized that God's promises had come true. Salvation had come to Israel, and he was holding the consolation of Israel, the Messiah, in his arms. Overwhelmed with joy and gratitude, Simeon **blessed God.**

His song of praise (cf. 1:41–45, 46–55, 67–79; 2:13–14, 38) is known as the Nunc Dimittis (**Now Lord**), from the first two words of the hymn in Latin. God was **releasing** His **bond-servant to depart** (die) **in peace, according to** His **word** of promise revealed to Simeon by the Holy Spirit. His hope fulfilled, his joy complete, his heart at peace, Simeon was content to die. With his own **eyes** he had **seen** God's **salvation,** personified in the infant Jesus (cf. 1:69; 2:11). He understood that salvation for Israel involved much more than the national deliverance promised by the Abrahamic and Davidic covenants, whose blessings will not be fully realized until the millennial kingdom. In the incarnation, Jesus came not to save His people from their enemies, but from their sins (Matt. 1:21; cf. Acts 4:12).

Simeon's next statement would shock Jewish sensibilities. Fiercely proud of their status as God's chosen, covenant people, the Jews believed Messiah was their deliverer. They assumed He would establish their kingdom, which would then rule over the infidel Gentiles. The truth that God had **prepared** salvation **in the presence of all peoples,** and that Messiah would be **a light of revelation to the Gentiles** (cf. Acts 26:23), as well as **the glory of** God's **people Israel** (cf. Isa. 46:13; 45:25), ran counter to all their preconceptions. Even after the resurrection, the apostles still did not understand. Shortly before the Lord ascended to heaven "they were asking Him, saying, 'Lord, is it at this time You are restoring the kingdom to Israel?' " (Acts 1:6).

Centuries of animosity toward the idolatrous Gentiles, whose corrupting influence had contributed to Israel's downfall, was not easily set aside. The Jewish believers in Jerusalem were horrified that Peter "went to uncircumcised men and ate with them" (Acts 11:3) because, as Peter reminded the Gentiles gathered in Cornelius's house, "You yourselves know how unlawful it is for a man who is a Jew to associate with a foreigner or to visit him" (Acts 10:28). But salvation is offered to all people, Jews and Gentiles alike, since Christ "made both groups into one and broke down the barrier of the dividing wall" (Eph. 2:14) and "there is neither Jew nor Greek, there is neither slave nor free man, there is neither male nor female; for [believers] are all one in Christ Jesus" (Gal. 3:28). Thus the Lord directed that "repentance for forgiveness of sins would be proclaimed in His name to all the nations, beginning from Jerusalem"

(Luke 24:47; cf. Matt. 28:19–20).

Speaking prophetically of Messiah's ministry Isaiah wrote,

> But there will be no more gloom for her who was in anguish; in earlier
> times He treated the land of Zebulun and the land of Naphtali with
> contempt, but later on He shall make it glorious, by the way of the sea,
> on the other side of Jordan, Galilee of the Gentiles. The people who
> walk in darkness will see a great light; those who live in a dark land, the
> light will shine on them. (Isa. 9:1–2; cf. Matt. 4:12–16)

According to Isaiah 42:6, Messiah would be "a light to the nations," while
in 49:6, the Lord said to Him, "It is too small a thing that You should be My
Servant to raise up the tribes of Jacob and to restore the preserved ones
of Israel; I will also make You a light of the nations so that My salvation
may reach to the end of the earth." In Isaiah 51:4–5, God declared, "A law
will go forth from Me, and I will set My justice for a light of the peoples.
My righteousness is near, My salvation has gone forth, and My arms will
judge the peoples; the coastlands will wait for Me, and for My arm they
will wait expectantly." Isaiah 52:10 notes that "the Lord has bared His holy
arm in the sight of all the nations, that all the ends of the earth may see
the salvation of our God." In Isaiah 60, God once again addressed His Servant, the Messiah:

> Arise, shine; for your light has come, and the glory of the Lord has risen
> upon you. For behold, darkness will cover the earth and deep darkness
> the peoples; but the Lord will rise upon you and His glory will appear
> upon you. Nations will come to your light, and kings to the brightness
> of your rising. (60:1–3)

With each confirmation of their Son's true identity, Joseph and
Mary's astonishment grew. After hearing Simeon's song of praise, they
were amazed at the things which were being said about Him.
Their son, in every sense a normal human baby, was the Divine Savior of
the world, the Messiah who would fulfill all the Old Testament promises
of salvation and blessing.

SIMEON'S WARNING

**And Simeon blessed them and said to Mary His mother, "Behold,
this Child is appointed for the fall and rise of many in Israel, and
for a sign to be opposed—and a sword will pierce even your own
soul—to the end that thoughts from many hearts may be**

revealed." (2:34–35)

After he finished his hymn of praise, Simeon turned to the young couple and **blessed** them. But the euphoria Joseph and Mary were experiencing was abruptly tempered by a shocking warning given by Simeon—the first negative note in Luke's gospel. It foreshadows the opposition Jesus would face, culminating in His rejection by the nation and crucifixion.

Simeon addressed his words to **Mary.** It was particularly important for her to hear them so she would not be surprised when the hostility to her Son manifested itself. Joseph apparently would not be around to witness that hostility. After the incident at Passover when Jesus was twelve (Luke 2:41–51), Joseph disappears from the Gospels' account of Jesus' life and ministry. Whenever Mary appears (e.g., John 2:1–11) she is without Joseph. Further, when Jesus was rejected by the people of His hometown of Nazareth, they mentioned His mother, brothers, and sisters, but not His father (Matt. 13:55–56). The presumption, then, is that Joseph died before Jesus' public ministry began.

Simeon spoke first of separation, declaring that **this Child is appointed for the fall and rise of many in Israel.** He is destined to be the determiner of people's destiny (cf. John 1:9–13). As He solemnly warned, "Do you suppose that I came to grant peace on earth? I tell you, no, but rather division" (Luke 12:51; cf. John 3:36; 8:24; 14:6; Acts 4:12; 1 Cor. 3:11; 1 Tim. 2:5–6; 1 John 5:11–12). Not only would some Gentiles be saved, but also some Jews would stumble over Him and **fall** into judgment and perdition, thus fulfilling Isaiah's prophecy:

> It is the Lord of hosts whom you should regard as holy. And He shall be your fear, and He shall be your dread. Then He shall become a sanctuary; but to both the houses of Israel, a stone to strike and a rock to stumble over, and a snare and a trap for the inhabitants of Jerusalem. Many will stumble over them, then they will fall and be broken; they will even be snared and caught. (Isa. 8:13–15; cf. Matt. 21:42–44; Rom. 9:32–33; 1 Peter 2:7–8)

Only the believing remnant would **rise** to eternal life in heaven:

> [God] raised us up with Him, and seated us with Him in the heavenly places in Christ Jesus, so that in the ages to come He might show the surpassing riches of His grace in kindness toward us in Christ Jesus. For by grace you have been saved through faith; and that not of yourselves, it is the gift of God. (Eph. 2:6–8)

Not only would Jesus bring separation, but He would also be **a**

sign to be opposed. As in Matthew 25:31, the **sign** is the Son of Man—signaling the arrival of kingdom presence, power, and person. **Opposed** translates a form of the verb *antilegō*, which means "to speak against," "to reject," "to deny," or "to contradict"—all of which aptly describe the insults, abuse, mockery, and hatred, culminating in His crucifixion, that Jesus faced from unbelieving Israel. Israel's rejection of Jesus Christ is an important theme of Luke's gospel (4:28–30; 13:31–35; 19:47; 20:14–20).

The nation's violent rejection of her Son would cause Mary to suffer. Simeon graphically pictured the pain and grief she would endure when he said to her, **"a sword will pierce even your own soul."** Mary's suffering began when her Son began to distance Himself from her. When His worried parents finally found Him after three days of searching, Jesus "said to them, 'Why is it that you were looking for Me? Did you not know that I had to be in My Father's house?'" (Luke 2:49). At the wedding in Cana, He did not address her as "mother," but with the polite but formal term "woman" (John 2:4). When told that Mary and His brothers wanted to see Him, Jesus replied, "'Who is My mother and who are My brothers?' And stretching out His hand toward His disciples, He said, 'Behold My mother and My brothers! For whoever does the will of My Father who is in heaven, he is My brother and sister and mother'" (Matt. 12:48–50). Mary's suffering culminated at the cross, as she watched her Son suffer and die (John 19:25).

The **end** result of Israel's rejection of Jesus was **that** the evil **thoughts from many hearts** would **be revealed.** "This is the judgment," Jesus said to Nicodemus, "that the Light has come into the world, and men loved the darkness rather than the Light, for their deeds were evil" (John 3:19). Jesus was the light shining in the darkness (cf. John 1:5), who exposed the evil of men's hearts.

In contrast to those who rejected Jesus when they saw His works, Simeon knew, when He had done none of them, that He was the Messiah and testified to that glorious truth.

ANNA

And there was a prophetess, Anna the daughter of Phanuel, of the tribe of Asher. She was advanced in years and had lived with her husband seven years after her marriage, and then as a widow to the age of eighty-four. She never left the temple, serving night and day with fastings and prayers. At that very moment she came up and began giving thanks to God, and continued to speak of Him to all those who were looking for the redemption of Jerusalem. (2:36–38)

The next testimony to Jesus was given by **a prophetess** named

Anna. Her name is the Greek form of the Hebrew name Hannah, which means "grace." Like the Old Testament Hannah, **Anna** was characterized by prayer and fasting (cf. 1 Sam. 1:7, 10–16). That she was a **prophetess** does not mean that she predicted the future, but that God had used her to speak His word.

The Old Testament mentions five women who are called prophetesses. But neither Miriam, the sister of Moses and Aaron (Ex. 15:20), Deborah (Judg. 4:4), or Huldah (2 Kings 22:14) had an ongoing prophetic ministry as Isaiah, Jeremiah, Ezekiel, and the other male prophets did. A fourth, Noadiah (Neh. 6:14), was a false prophetess. Isaiah's wife was described as a prophetess (Isa. 8:3) because she gave birth to a son who was given a prophetic name. Among the New Testament women, only the daughters of Philip are called "prophetesses" (Acts 21:9), with no explanation beyond that. Anna may have been called a prophetess because, as noted above, she was a teacher of the Word. Or she may have been a prophetess more like Isaiah's wife because she testified that this Child was the Messiah.

That Anna was a member **of the tribe of Asher** is noteworthy. **Asher** was one of the ten tribes that formed the northern kingdom and were taken captive by Assyria in 722 B.C. But the so-called ten lost tribes were in fact not lost. Before the fall of the northern kingdom, in response to letters from King Hezekiah of Judah (2 Chron. 30:6), "some men of Asher, Manasseh and Zebulun humbled themselves and came to Jerusalem" (v. 11). Their descendants would be among those who were carried away captive to Babylon, and returned to Israel after the exile.

While Simeon's old age is inferred, the text explicitly states that Anna **was advanced in years.** Luke explained that she **had lived with her husband seven years after her marriage, and then as a widow to the age of eighty-four.** Some interpret the last phrase to mean that Anna lived as a widow for eighty-four years after the death of her husband, which would mean that she was more than one hundred years old. Both translations are possible and both support Luke's statement that she was **advanced in years.** That **she never left the temple** suggests that Anna lived in the temple complex, perhaps in one of the apartments in the outer court normally occupied by priests doing their two weeks of annual service. She was not idle, but spent her time at the temple **serving night and day with fastings and prayers.** Prayer is often associated with fasting in Scripture (cf. 5:33; 2 Sam. 12:16; Ezra 8:23; Neh. 1:4; Ps. 35:13; Dan. 9:3; Acts 13:3; 14:23); fasting is the self-denial that accompanies passionate prayer. Anna was singularly and completely devoted to the service and worship of God; such a devout, godly woman was a fitting witness to Jesus.

In God's providential timing, **at that very moment**—while

Simeon was uttering his prophetic hymn of praise—**she came up** to the little group. In his typical understated way, Luke gave no details of the meeting or of what transpired between the time Anna arrived and when she began giving thanks. Certainly Simeon, whom she most likely knew, along with Joseph and Mary, must have told her who the Child was. But Luke merely noted that Anna **began giving thanks to God** for the baby Jesus. All the long years of passionately petitioning God gave way to an outburst of joyous praise. Hers, though the words were not recorded, is the final hymn of praise in Luke's account of Christ's birth, along with those of Elizabeth (1:41–45), Mary (1:46–55), Zacharias (1:67–79), the angels (2:13–14), and Simeon.

Anna's testimony to Jesus did not end with this incident. Instead, from her place inside the temple, she **continued to speak of Him to all those who were looking for the redemption of Jerusalem;** that is, the believing remnant, everyone who anticipated that the Lord would visit His people with salvation, who believed that the promises given through the prophets would be fulfilled, and looked for the blessings of the Abrahamic, Davidic, and New covenants to be realized.

The Amazing Child Who Was God
(Luke 2:39–52)

16

When they had performed everything according to the Law of the Lord, they returned to Galilee, to their own city of Nazareth. The Child continued to grow and become strong, increasing in wisdom; and the grace of God was upon Him. Now His parents went to Jerusalem every year at the Feast of the Passover. And when He became twelve, they went up there according to the custom of the Feast; and as they were returning, after spending the full number of days, the boy Jesus stayed behind in Jerusalem. But His parents were unaware of it, but supposed Him to be in the caravan, and went a day's journey; and they began looking for Him among their relatives and acquaintances. When they did not find Him, they returned to Jerusalem looking for Him. Then, after three days they found Him in the temple, sitting in the midst of the teachers, both listening to them and asking them questions. And all who heard Him were amazed at His understanding and His answers. When they saw Him, they were astonished; and His mother said to Him, "Son, why have You treated us this way? Behold, Your father and I have been anxiously looking for You." And He said to them, "Why is it that you were looking for Me? Did you not know that I had to be in My Father's house?" But they

did not understand the statement which He had made to them. And He went down with them and came to Nazareth, and He continued in subjection to them; and His mother treasured all these things in her heart. And Jesus kept increasing in wisdom and stature, and in favor with God and men. (2:39–52)

History has recorded some truly amazing children, child prodigies who performed astonishing feats. Early in the eighteenth century Jean Louis Cardiac, known as the "wonder child," was said to have recited the alphabet at the age of three months. By the age of four, he read Latin, Greek, and Hebrew, and translated Latin into English and French. Christian Friedrich Heinecken, known as the "infant of Lubeck," was a contemporary of Cardiac. He reportedly knew the major events recorded in the Bible by the time he was a year old. At the age of three, he was familiar with world history and geography, as well as Latin and French. No doubt the most famous child prodigy of the time was the composer Wolfgang Amadeus Mozart. The young Mozart began playing the keyboard by ear at the age of three. By the time he was six, he had begun composing his own pieces. At that same age Mozart, along with his older sister, began touring Europe, giving both private concerts for the nobility, and also public concerts. At eight, he composed his first symphony.

The noted nineteenth-century philosopher John Stuart Mill was also a child prodigy. Under the rigorous tutelage of his father, John learned Greek at the age of three. At the age of eight, he began learning Latin, geometry, and algebra. Another nineteenth-century child phenomenon was Truman Henry Safford, noted for his remarkable powers of calculation. When the ten-year-old Safford was challenged to calculate the square of 365,365,365,365,365,365 in his head, he did so in less than a minute. At about that same age Safford devised a new method for calculating the moon's risings and settings that was significantly faster than the existing one.

William James Sidis (1898–1944) was the son of a Harvard-trained psychologist. He is regarded as one of the most intelligent persons who ever lived, with an IQ estimated to have been well over 200. According to his biographer, Sidis was reading the *New York Times* at the age of eighteen months, and had taught himself Latin, Greek, French, Russian, German, Hebrew, Turkish, and Armenian by the time he was eight. At eleven he entered Harvard, where he lectured the Harvard Mathematical Society on four-dimensional bodies.

One of the most noted contemporary child prodigies is Kim Ung-Yong, born in South Korea in 1963. By the time he was four, he was able to read Korean, Japanese, German, and English, and at that same age solved complicated calculus problems on Japanese television. Kim came to the

United States at the age of seven at the invitation of NASA, and earned a PhD in physics before he turned sixteen.

But the accomplishments of these and all other child prodigies combined pale into insignificance compared to one twelve-year-old boy named Jesus. No human genius, no IQ in excess of 200, no precocious feats of learning can compare with the infinite mind and capabilities of the child who was God incarnate. In a dramatic and moving account of the only recorded incident of Jesus' childhood, Luke revealed from His own words that the child was God.

Luke has already presented compelling testimony that Jesus Christ was the Son of God (1:35), the One through whom God would redeem and save His people (1:68–69, 78–79; 2:10–11, 27–32, 34, 38). But in this passage he turned from the testimony of others to the testimony of the child Himself. Luke's account reveals plainly that at the age of twelve, Jesus already possessed a complete understanding of His nature and mission; He was God the Son, come to do the Father's will.

In this the only recorded incident from Jesus' childhood, we have the only words He is recorded to have said before the start of His public ministry. Luke's inclusion of it signifies its monumental importance. Jesus' identity as the Son of God incarnate was not something thrust upon Him by Jewish messianic expectations, or invented by His followers. Nor was it something He assumed for Himself when He began His public ministry. It was His true identity, which He had become aware of by the age of twelve—eighteen years before His public ministry began.

After presenting the testimonies of Simeon and Anna (2:25–38), Luke noted that **when they** (Joseph and Mary) **had performed everything according to the Law of the Lord** (cf. vv. 22–24) they **returned to Galilee, to their own city of Nazareth.** But between verses 38 and 39 a very important part of the birth narrative took place. It was after their encounter with Simeon and Anna in the temple and before their return to Nazareth that the wise men visited Joseph, Mary, and Jesus (Matt. 2:1–12) and they fled to Egypt to escape Herod's murderous rage (vv. 13–15), which culminated in his brutal slaughter of the male infants in the vicinity of Bethlehem (vv. 16–18). It was only after Herod's death that Joseph, Mary, and Jesus returned to Nazareth (vv. 19–23).

This one brief passage contains everything that is known about the life of Jesus Christ from His infancy to the outset of His public ministry. Two statements summarizing the silent years of His childhood and His adult years at Nazareth bracket the incident at Jerusalem when He was twelve, which is the main thrust of this passage.

THE SILENT YEARS OF CHILDHOOD

The Child continued to grow and become strong, increasing in wisdom; and the grace of God was upon Him. (2:40)

Scripture passes over Jesus' childhood in silence, in contrast to the fanciful legends recorded in the apocryphal inventions of a fantasy childhood. The latter range from having Jesus perform magician's tricks (e.g., turning clay birds into live ones) or malicious acts completely inconsistent with His character as revealed in the Bible (e.g., killing another child who bumped into Him, then striking the child's parents blind for complaining to Joseph and Mary).

The statement that **the Child continued to grow** demonstrates that Jesus was fully human. He developed as all children develop, though unaffected by sin. The phrase **become strong** should be taken grammatically with the following phrase, **increasing in wisdom.** To be sure, Jesus possessed a unique physical strength because of His sinlessness. But Luke's primary emphasis is on Jesus' spiritual development, as He matured in wisdom until, as the Greek text literally reads, He was "filled with wisdom," the profound wisdom of the mind of God. Jesus did not possess all of that knowledge as an infant, toddler, or young child. But by the time He was twelve, the fullness of divine wisdom had come to fruition in His mind. A feature of Christ's incarnation was that He relinquished control of His use of His divine prerogatives to the Holy Spirit, who mediated between His deity and His humanity. By the time He reached twelve, the Spirit had disclosed the understanding of His identity and mission.

Hebrews 5:8 reveals that much of His increase in wisdom came as Jesus "learned obedience from the things which He suffered." At every stage of His development, Jesus faced the full, unabated onslaught of temptation, so that He was "tempted in all things as we are, yet without sin" (Heb. 4:15).

Not only was Jesus filled with the wisdom of God, but also **the grace of God was upon Him.** John describes Him as "full of grace" (1:14). The **grace** in view here is not, of course, the saving, redeeming grace that God grants to undeserving sinners, since Jesus was sinless. Instead, it was the favor of God granted to His "beloved Son, in [whom He is] well-pleased" (Luke 3:22). He was both the recipient of grace as favor deserved and the giver of grace as favor undeserved.

By the time Jesus turned twelve, He had a complete grasp of His true identity. He fully understood the wisdom of God and its application to the mission for which God had sent Him into the world. William Hendriksen writes, "The development of this child was therefore perfect, and this along every line: physical, intellectual, moral, spiritual; for from beginning to end progress was unimpaired and unimpeded by sin,

whether inherited or acquired. Between the child Jesus and his Father …
there was perfect harmony, limitless love" (*The Gospel of Luke,* New Testament Commentary [Grand Rapids: Baker, 1978], 180).

THE INCIDENT AT AGE TWELVE

**Now His parents went to Jerusalem every year at the Feast of the
Passover. And when He became twelve, they went up there
according to the custom of the Feast; and as they were returning,
after spending the full number of days, the boy Jesus stayed
behind in Jerusalem. But His parents were unaware of it, but supposed Him to be in the caravan, and went a day's journey; and
they began looking for Him among their relatives and acquaintances. When they did not find Him, they returned to Jerusalem
looking for Him. Then, after three days they found Him in the
temple, sitting in the midst of the teachers, both listening to them
and asking them questions. And all who heard Him were amazed
at His understanding and His answers. When they saw Him, they
were astonished; and His mother said to Him, "Son, why have
You treated us this way? Behold, Your father and I have been anxiously looking for You." And He said to them, "Why is it that you
were looking for Me? Did you not know that I had to be in My
Father's house?" But they did not understand the statement
which He had made to them. And He went down with them and
came to Nazareth, and He continued in subjection to them; and
His mother treasured all these things in her heart.** (2:41–51)

The incident that comprises the bulk of the passage finds Jesus
on the brink of adulthood, twelve years after His presentation in the temple
(2:22–38). It is a powerful and poignant story, and a profound testimony
by Jesus to His true identity as God the Son (v. 49); yet there is nothing
miraculous or supernatural about it.

The incident began at Passover during Jesus' twelfth year. Joseph
and Mary, as a devout couple, **went to Jerusalem every year at the
Feast of the Passover** to celebrate with the nation God's deliverance
from bondage in Egypt (Ex. 12:1–51). Passover was one of the three
major annual feasts in Israel, along with Pentecost and Tabernacles.
Immediately following Passover day was the seven-day long Feast of Unleavened Bread. The entire eight-day period eventually became known
collectively as Passover.

According to Exodus 23:17; 34:22–23; and Deuteronomy 16:16, all
Jewish men were required to attend the three major feasts. But by the

first century, the dispersion of many Jewish people outside of Palestine had made that impractical. Consequently, many Jewish men came to Jerusalem only for Passover. Women were not required by the law to attend (though some rabbis strongly encouraged them to do so); for a woman to attend the feast was considered a sign of unusual spiritual devotion.

As they did every year, the year that Jesus **became twelve** Joseph and Mary went up to Jerusalem **according to the custom of the Feast.** The trip from Nazareth was an arduous one of about eighty miles, lasting three or four days. They did not travel alone, but with a large company of people in a **caravan** (v. 44). To journey to Jerusalem in a group offered both the opportunity for fellowship and protection from the threat of highway robbers. Such caravans would also include children, since the rabbis taught that Passover should be a family celebration (cf. Ex. 12:26–27).

When they arrived in Jerusalem, Joseph, Mary, and Jesus would have found the city teeming with hundreds of thousands of fellow pilgrims, who would have been trying to find lodging and a place to celebrate the Passover meal, along with purchasing their sacrificial animals. The city would have been filled with the noise of hundreds of thousands of sheep, which the priests would have been busy butchering. Beggars, no doubt decked out in their most ragged clothes, would have been out in force. Roman soldiers would have been on patrol, jostling with the crowds and trying to keep some semblance of order. Joseph would have taken the family's lamb to be sacrificed, and one can only imagine what went through Jesus' mind, knowing that He was the "Lamb of God who takes away the sin of the world" (John 1:29). The whole frenetic scene in Jerusalem must have made a profound impression on Him.

This particular Passover was especially significant for Jesus. Jewish boys became accountable to the law of God at thirteen, a transition later marked by the ceremony known as Bar Mitzvah ("son of the law" or "covenant"). The last couple of Passovers before a boy turned thirteen were particularly important in preparing him for his responsibility to the law.

Luke did not describe any features of that Passover but picked up the story afterward, when Joseph, Mary, and Jesus **were returning** to Nazareth. The seeming aside that Joseph and Mary left Jerusalem **after spending the full number of days** there is actually another affirmation of their devotion to the things of God. In contrast to most people, who stayed for only part of the eight-day celebration, Joseph and Mary stayed the entire time.

Instead of returning with the others, **the boy Jesus stayed behind in Jerusalem.** Nothing was said to **His parents, who were unaware of it, but supposed Him to be in the caravan.** It was not until the end of the first **day's journey** that Joseph and Mary realized that Jesus was missing **and they began looking for Him among their relatives and acquaintances.** But their worst fears were confirmed; Jesus was not with the caravan. **When they did not find Him,** Joseph and Mary spent an anxious night before **they returned** the next morning **to Jerusalem looking for Him.**

Jesus' staying behind was not an act of disobedience to His parents, nor was it irresponsibility on their part. They had never before known Him to do anything other than what they had expected Him to do. He was responsible, obedient, sensitive, thoughtful; in every way sinlessly perfect. This act, however, marked a transition. Jesus was moving from responsibility to His earthly parents to responsibility to God (see the discussion of v. 49 on the next page).

Finally, **after three** anxious **days** (one day's journey away from Jerusalem, one day back, and one day searching Jerusalem for Jesus) Joseph and Mary **found** Jesus **in the temple.** Incredibly, He was **sitting in the midst of the teachers, both listening to them and asking them questions.** This was a typical, traditional setting for teaching in Israel. The **teachers** would be seated, with the students, sitting in their midst. Only here does Luke use *didaskalos* to refer to Jewish **teachers;** in the rest of his gospel the term is reserved for John the Baptist (3:12) or Jesus. No one is called "teacher" after Jesus became the teacher.

Many eminent teachers would have been in Jerusalem for Passover. Jesus seized this opportunity, which would never have been afforded Him in tiny, insignificant Nazareth, to dialogue with some of the greatest minds in Judaism. He had a burning, passionate, consuming interest in the Word of God, and must have wanted to hear their views on the Old Testament, especially messianic prophecy, the sacrificial system, and the Law. The dialogue method was the customary pattern for teaching in Judaism and was employed by the apostle Paul (Acts 17:2; "reasoned" translates a form of the Greek verb *dialegomai,* "to discuss"). Students would gather around a teacher or teachers and stimulate the discussion by asking questions. Only here in the Gospels is Jesus portrayed as the student; after this He is always the teacher—who would ask questions for which the Jewish teachers had no adequate answers (cf. 11:19–20; 13:2–5; 20:41–44).

So impressive was Jesus' performance that **all who heard Him were amazed at His understanding and His answers.** Jesus' questions and answers were penetrating, insightful, and profound; His wisdom and knowledge far exceeded that of any twelve-year-old boy that they had ever known. This was not the first (cf. 2:18, 33), nor would it be the last time Jesus elicited wonder and amazement in Luke's gospel (cf. 4:22, 32, 36; 5:9; 8:25, 56; 9:43; 11:14; 20:26; 24:41).

Finally, after hours of anxious searching, Joseph and Mary found their missing son. **When they saw Him, they were astonished** along with everyone else, not so much by the dialogue, but by His location. Assuming that He was lost, they no doubt expected Him to be searching frantically for His parents. Instead, they found Him sitting calmly in the temple, dialoging with the elite teachers in Judaism.

As anxious as any parent would be under the circumstances, Mary was both relieved and upset. In exasperation she **said to Him, "Son, why have You treated us this way?"** Her question was designed to make Jesus feel guilty, as if He had intentionally caused His parents to suffer. Mary's next statement intensified her rebuke. **"Behold,"** she continued, **"Your father and I have been anxiously looking for You."** As mentioned above, Jesus' behavior in this incident was totally unlike anything Joseph and Mary had ever experienced and thus to them inexplicable.

Jesus, of course, had not intentionally defied or hurt His parents. What He had done was to make evident the necessary break that was to come between Him and His earthly family. As He would later say, Jesus had "come down from heaven, not to do [His] own will, but the will of [His Father] who sent [Him]" (John 6:38; cf. 4:34; 5:30). Although that break would not be fully realized for another eighteen years, it is made evident here.

Jesus' reply **to them, "Why is it that you were looking for Me? Did you not know that I had to be in My Father's house** (the temple)**?"** is not only the crux of the passage, but also expresses the definitive reality of Christian theology. This statement is the first time in Scripture that any individual claimed God as his personal father. The Jews viewed God as the Father of all in a creative sense, and the Father of Israel in a national sense. But no one had the audacity to claim God as his father in a personal, intimate sense, because of the profound implications of such a claim (see the discussion below). In this confession, Jesus made it clear that His first priority was to do the will of His heavenly Father. He also lifted Himself above the human realm. He was not in the ultimate sense Joseph's son, or Mary's son; He was the eternal Son of God, who came down from heaven (John 3:13; 6:38, 42). As such, He was under the authority of His heavenly Father, not His earthly parents.

The biblical teaching that Jesus is the Son of God is clear and unmistakable. The angel told Mary before Jesus' birth that He "shall be called the Son of God" (Luke 1:35). Jesus often referred to Himself as the Son of God or claimed that God was His Father (e.g., 10:21–22; John 6:39–40; 8:18–19, 28–29, 38, 49; Rev. 2:18). Mark opened his gospel with the words, "The beginning of the gospel of Jesus Christ, the Son of God" (Mark 1:1). John the Baptist (John 1:34), Nathanael (John 1:49), the twelve apostles (Matt. 14:33), Martha (John 11:27), Paul (Acts 9:20; Rom. 1:4; 2 Cor. 1:19; Gal. 2:20; Eph. 4:13), the writer of Hebrews (Heb. 4:14; 6:6; 7:3; 10:29), and the apostle John (John 20:31; 1 John 4:15; 5:5, 10, 12, 13, 20) all affirmed Jesus' divine sonship. Even Satan (Luke 4:3, 9), the demons (Matt. 8:29; Luke 4:41), and a Roman centurion (Matt. 27:54) acknowledged that Jesus is the Son of God.

It was Jesus' claim to be the Son of God above all else that infuriated His Jewish opponents and led to His execution. In John 5:17, Jesus defended His healing of a crippled man on the Sabbath by saying, "My Father is working until now, and I Myself am working." The Jewish authorities were outraged, and as John noted in verse 18: "For this reason therefore the Jews were seeking all the more to kill Him, because He not only was breaking the Sabbath, but also was calling God His own Father, making Himself equal with God." In John 10:36, they accused Him of blasphemy for calling Himself the Son of God. At Christ's mock trial it was His affirmation that He was the Son of God that gave the Sanhedrin the excuse to declare Him guilty of blasphemy and thus deserving of death (Matt. 26:63–66). After Pilate pronounced Jesus innocent "the Jews answered him, 'We have a law, and by that law He ought to die because He made Himself out to be the Son of God'" (John 19:7). And when Jesus was on the cross, they mocked His claim to be the Son of God (Matt. 27:40, 43).

The reason Jesus' claim to be the Son of God infuriated the Jewish leaders is that such a claim, as they understood perfectly, was a claim to deity, to full equality with God. The title Son of God describes Jesus as the second person of the Trinity, God incarnate. The full, rich meaning of the title Son of God is not evident from the English concept of sonship. In Jewish culture "son" denoted more than just a male offspring. A young, underage child was considered a boy; only when that boy had become an adult was he a son in the fullest sense. It was then that he became equal to his father under the law and in terms of adult responsibility, and received the privileges his father had reserved for him. "Son," in this more technical sense, came to mean "equal to" or "one with."

There are a number of examples in Scripture where "son" identifies a person's nature. Barnabas's name means "son of encouragement"; he was so much an encourager that he was identified with encouragement. Jesus called James and John "Sons of thunder" (Mark 3:17), identifying them with that term because of their bombastic personalities. Similarly, He described some people as "son[s] of hell" (Matt. 23:15) because they had the characteristics of those who are hell bound. In much the same way, both Judas (John 17:12) and the Antichrist (2 Thess. 2:3) are called sons of perdition or destruction (the same Greek word is used to describe both individuals), identifying them with their eternal destiny.

Ephesians 2:2 calls unbelievers "sons of disobedience," while Matthew 13:38 describes them as "sons of the evil one" (cf. John 8:44). Luke 16:8 and John 12:36 call believers "sons of light;" and Luke 20:36 calls them "sons of the resurrection."

"Son" in the above examples does not refer to origin, but to nature. The term is used to refer to Jesus Christ to establish His being of the same essence and nature, with the same rights and privileges, as God Himself. As noted above, the Jewish leaders understood perfectly that by claiming to be the Son of God, Jesus was claiming deity and full equality with the Father.

Some might argue that the terms "only begotten" (*monogenēs;* John 1:14, 18; 3:16, 18; 1 John 4:9) and "firstborn" (*prōtotokos;* Rom. 8:29; Col. 1:15, 18; Heb. 1:6; Rev. 1:5) indicate that Jesus came into existence, and thus was not God from all eternity. But neither of those terms refer to origin. *Monogenēs* means "one of a kind," and distinguishes Jesus as the unique Son of God from believers, who are sons of God in a different sense (cf. 1 John 3:2). The Bible calls Isaac Abraham's *monogenēs* (Heb. 11:17), even though Isaac was neither Abraham's oldest son nor his only son, because he alone was the son of the covenant (Gen. 21:12; cf. Rom. 9:7). *Prototokos,* when used of Christ, does not refer to chronology, but to preeminence. Both Colossians 1:18 and Revelation 1:5 call Jesus the "firstborn from the dead," because of all who will ever be resurrected, He is the preeminent one. In Exodus 4:22, God refers to Israel as His firstborn; though Israel was not the first nation to come into existence chronologically, she was the first among the nations in preeminence.

To argue that the terms "firstborn" and "only begotten" mean that Jesus was a created being is contradictory. Jesus could not be both the "only begotten" and the "first begotten." Nor could He be the creator of the universe (Col. 1:16) if He Himself were a created being.

Joseph and Mary **did not** fully **understand** the profound **statement which** Jesus **had made to them.** They understood that He was the Messiah, the Son of David, conceived in a virgin's womb by the power of the Holy Spirit. But the full meaning of His divine sonship eluded them. This would not be the last time that His followers would fail to grasp what Jesus was saying (cf. Luke 9:44–45; 18:34; John 10:6; 12:16).

But the time for Jesus to leave His parents' authority had not yet arrived, so **He went down with them and came to Nazareth, and He continued in subjection to them.** His relationship with His heavenly Father did not yet abrogate His responsibility to obey His earthly parents. His obedience to the fifth commandment was an essential part of Jesus' perfect obedience to the law of God.

Here was the first fulfillment of Simeon's warning to Mary in 2:35, as she **treasured all these things in her heart.** She had much to think about as she pondered Jesus' amazing reply. Mary had to realize that her Son was her Savior, and she would have to exchange her parental authority over Him for His divine authority over her. The sword would pierce her heart again later in her last appearance in Luke's gospel (8:19–21), when Jesus distanced Himself from His human relationship with her and His siblings (cf. 11:27–28). Ultimately, the sword would pierce Mary's heart as she watched her Son suffer and die on the cross.

THE ADULT YEARS IN NAZARETH

And Jesus kept increasing in wisdom and stature, and in favor with God and men. (2:52)

This summary statement reveals all that is known about the eighteen years Jesus spent in Nazareth from the age of twelve to the beginning of His public ministry at the age of thirty (3:23). **Increasing** translates a form of the verb *prokoptō,* which means "to progress" or "to advance." In the unfathomable mystery of the incarnation, when Jesus "emptied Himself, taking the form of a bond-servant, and [was] made in the likeness of men" (Phil. 2:7), and was "found in appearance as a man" (v. 8), He was subject to the normal process of human growth and development. Jesus grew in **wisdom** as His intellectual grasp of divine truth increased, physically in **stature,** and spiritually **in favor with God,** strengthened by His victories over the assaults of temptation (Heb. 4:15). The reference to His finding favor with **man** describes His increasing social maturity and the respect He commanded.

The question arises as to why Jesus needed to live all those years, instead of simply coming to earth, dying as a substitute for sin, rising from the dead, and ascending back to heaven. The answer is that He had to live a perfectly righteous life and "fulfill all righteousness" (Matt. 3:15), and thus prove to be the perfect sacrifice to take the place of sinners (1 Peter 3:18). Only then could His righteousness be imputed to believers and their sins placed on Him. When Paul wrote in 2 Corinthians 5:21 that God made "Him who knew no sin to be sin on our behalf, so that we might become the righteousness of God in Him," he expressed both aspects of Christ's substitutionary atonement. Not only did Jesus bear believers' sins, God also imputed His righteousness to them. To put it another way, God treated Christ as if He had lived believers' sinful lives, and believers as if they had lived His perfectly righteous life. Jesus lived a perfectly righteous life from childhood through adulthood, so that His righteous life could be imputed to believers. Salvation comes only to those who do not have a "righteousness of [their] own derived from the Law, but that which is through faith in Christ, the righteousness which comes from God on the basis of faith" (Phil.3:9).

It was not without purpose that the Holy Spirit–inspired account of the Savior's life in the four Gospels included only this episode from the years between His birth and the launch of His public ministry. This brief narrative, bookended by two sweeping summary statements, reveals Jesus Christ as the Son of God, whose perfectly sinless life qualified Him to be the only acceptable sacrifice for sin (1 Peter 1:18–19), both having believers' sins imputed to Him and providing a righteous life to be imputed to them.

Setting the Stage for Jesus (Luke 3:1–6)

17

Now in the fifteenth year of the reign of Tiberius Caesar, when Pontius Pilate was governor of Judea, and Herod was tetrarch of Galilee, and his brother Philip was tetrarch of the region of Ituraea and Trachonitis, and Lysanias was tetrarch of Abilene, in the high priesthood of Annas and Caiaphas, the word of God came to John, the son of Zacharias, in the wilderness. And he came into all the district around the Jordan, preaching a baptism of repentance for the forgiveness of sins; as it is written in the book of the words of Isaiah the prophet, "The voice of one crying in the wilderness, 'Make ready the way of the Lord, make His paths straight. Every ravine will be filled, and every mountain and hill will be brought low; the crooked will become straight, and the rough roads smooth; and all flesh will see the salvation of God.'" (3:1–6)

In chapters 1 and 2 of his gospel, Luke recorded the birth narratives of John the Baptist and Jesus Christ. As chapter 3 opens, eighteen years have passed since the last historical event recorded by Luke, the story of the twelve-year-old Jesus in the temple (2:41–51). The public ministries of the Baptist and Jesus are about to begin.

For thirty years each had lived in seclusion. John "lived in the deserts until the day of his public appearance to Israel" (1:80). Jesus lived in the obscure, out of the way, off the beaten path village of Nazareth, where "He continued in subjection" to His parents (2:51). Only a select few, those who were looking for the consolation and redemption of Israel (2:25, 38), knew the true identities of John and Jesus. Of that small group many, such as Zacharias, Elizabeth, Simeon, Anna, and Joseph, had most likely died by this time and gone on to glory. The angels who announced their births had long since returned to heaven. But the three decades of silence were about to end. The beginning of John the Baptist's public ministry would also mark the end of an even longer silence—the four centuries of prophetic silence since the time of the last prophet, Malachi (about 430 B.C.).

As the curtain rose on the ministries of John and Jesus, Israel was shrouded in deep darkness. It was the bleakest of times politically. The nation chafed under the oppressive rule of pagan idolaters. Israel, God's covenant nation, was now part of a minor province in a backwater region of the mighty Roman Empire. It was also the darkest of times spiritually. The Jewish people were crushed under the heavy burden of an apostate, legalistic, hypocritical religion dominated by corrupt, wicked spiritual leaders (cf. Matt. 23:1–33). Israel had not realized the promises of the Abrahamic and Davidic covenants; they possessed neither the land promised by the former, nor the kingdom promised by the latter. Engulfed in legalism, hypocrisy, and external ritual, the nation also failed to experience the New covenant blessings promised in Jeremiah 31:31–34 and Ezekiel 37:26.

The Old Testament closed with the promise of Messiah's coming (Mal. 3:1; 4:2), and throughout the ensuing centuries of political and religious darkness the Jewish people had clung to that hope. But before Messiah's ministry began, His forerunner was to appear to prepare the way for Him. Years earlier John the Baptist's father, Zacharias, had prophesied concerning him, "And you, child, will be called the prophet of the Most High; for you will go on before the Lord to prepare His ways" (Luke 1:76; cf. Mal. 3:1). Thus John, the first prophet in more than 400 years, appeared on center stage to introduce the main character of the story, the Lord Jesus Christ. His task was twofold: to prepare the people for the Messiah, and to present the Messiah to the people.

Like any good historian, Luke understood the importance of placing his historical account in its proper context. In this passage he gave four settings that provide the backdrop for the ministries of John and Jesus: the historical, geographical, theological, and prophetical settings.

The Historical Setting

Now in the fifteenth year of the reign of Tiberius Caesar, when Pontius Pilate was governor of Judea, and Herod was tetrarch of Galilee, and his brother Philip was tetrarch of the region of Ituraea and Trachonitis, and Lysanias was tetrarch of Abilene, in the high priesthood of Annas and Caiaphas, (3:1–2*a*)

Luke includes seven individuals, five Gentiles and two Jews, in providing the background for the ministries of John and Jesus. Luke's purpose in introducing them was not to provide an exact chronology, but rather a general historical context. The first name, **Tiberius Caesar,** illustrates that fact, because there are two plausible ways of determining **the fifteenth year of** his **reign.** Some argue that Tiberius's reign as emperor began at the death of his illustrious predecessor Augustus Caesar, Rome's first emperor (for more information on Augustus, see the exposition of 2:1 in chapter 12 of this volume). Since Augustus died on August 19, A.D. 14, that would mean John's ministry began in A.D. 29. The more traditional view counts the fifteen years not from Augustus's death in A.D. 14, but from A.D. 11, when Tiberius became his co-regent. John's ministry would then have commenced in A.D. 26

While it is impossible to be dogmatic, the latter view best harmonizes with the chronology of the New Testament (cf. *The Zondervan Pictorial Encyclopedia of the Bible,* s.v. "Chronology of the New Testament"; Lewis A. Foster, "The Chronology of the New Testament" in Frank E. Gaebelein, ed., *The Expositor's Bible Commentary,* vol. 1 [Grand Rapids: Zondervan, 1979]). There are also several specific arguments in favor of starting the fifteen years in A.D. 11 when Tiberius became co-regent.

First, his reference to the co-regency of Annas and Caiaphas as high priests (see the discussion below) suggests that Luke may also have had the co-regency of Augustus and Tiberius in mind.

Second, according to the first-century Jewish historian Josephus, Herod the Great began building the temple in 19 B.C. In John 2:20, the Jewish leaders said to Jesus, who was in Jerusalem for Passover, that the temple had been under construction for forty-six years. That would make the date of that Passover A.D. 27, which in turn places the start of Jesus' public ministry late in A.D. 26.

Finally, according to Luke 3:23, Jesus was about thirty years old when He began His public ministry. Since He was born shortly before the death of Herod in 4 B.C., Jesus would have been about thirty in A.D. 26.

Moving from the supreme ruler of the Roman Empire to the highest-ranking local Roman authority, Luke next introduced **Pontius Pilate,** who had been appointed the fifth **governor of Judea** by Tiberius in A.D. 26 and remained until he was removed from office in A.D. 36. The Gospels and extrabiblical sources portray Pilate as proud, arrogant, and cynical (cf. John 18:38), and also weak and vacillating. As governor, Pilate displayed insensitivity and brutality (cf. Luke 13:1). Reversing the policy of the earlier governors, Pilate marched his troops into Jerusalem carrying standards bearing images that the Jews viewed as idolatrous. Outraged, many protested heatedly against what they saw as a sacrilege. Pilate ignored their protests and ordered them, on pain of death, to stop bothering him. But they called his bluff and dared him to carry out his threat. Unwilling to massacre so many people, Pilate removed the offending standards. The story reveals his poor judgment, stubbornness, arrogance, and vacillating weakness. Pilate also enraged the Jews when he took money from the temple treasury to build an aqueduct to bring water to Jerusalem. In the ensuing riots, his soldiers beat and slaughtered many of the protesters.

Ironically, the incident that finally triggered Pilate's removal from office involved not the Jews, but their hated rivals the Samaritans. A group of them decided to climb Mount Gerizim in search of golden objects Moses had supposedly hidden on its summit. Mistakenly thinking the Samaritans were insurrectionists, Pilate ordered his troops to attack them, and many were killed. The Samaritans complained about Pilate's brutality to his immediate superior, the governor of Syria. He removed Pilate from office and ordered him to Rome to be judged by Tiberius, but Tiberius died before Pilate reached Rome. At that point, Pilate disappeared from history. Some accounts claim that he was banished, others that he was executed, still others that he committed suicide.

Two other local rulers of note were **Herod,** the **tetrarch of Galilee, and his brother Philip,** the **tetrarch of the region of Ituraea and Trachonitis.** These two were members of the notorious Herod family, sons of Herod the Great. When Herod died in 4 B.C., his domain was divided among three of his sons, Archelaus, Antipas, and **Philip.** Archelaus proved to be such an inept and brutal ruler that he was deposed in A.D. 6 and his territory (Judea, Samaria, and Idumea) was placed under the rule of Roman governors (as noted above, Pilate was the fifth of those governors). The **Herod** in view here is Antipas, who ruled Galilee from 4 B.C. to A.D. 39. He is the Herod referred to in the Gospels' accounts of Jesus' ministry. It was Antipas who imprisoned (Luke 3:20) and executed (Luke 9:9) John the Baptist, and played a role in the unjust trial of Jesus (Luke 23:7–12).

Antipas's brother **Philip** ruled **the region of Ituraea and Trachonitis** (northeast of Galilee) from 4 B.C. to A.D. 34. Philip has been considered the best of the Herodian rulers.

Little is known of the third local ruler mentioned by Luke,

Lysanias, the **tetrarch of Abilene** (northwest of Damascus). Rejecters of biblical inerrancy used to charge Luke with an historical blunder, claiming that the only Lysanias known to history had died years earlier in 36 B.C. Inscriptions have been found, however, that indicate another Lysanias had ruled during the reign of Tiberius (Darrell L. Bock, *Luke 1:1–9:50*, Baker Exegetical Commentary on the New Testament [Grand Rapids: Baker, 1994], 283).

Moving from the secular to the religious realm, Luke placed the outset of John's ministry **in the high priesthood of Annas and Caiaphas,** suggesting that in some sense they held the office jointly. Although no longer officially the high priest, **Annas** was nonetheless the most powerful figure in the Jewish religious establishment. He had been the high priest from A.D. 6 to A.D. 15, when he was removed from office by Valerius Gratus, Pilate's predecessor as governor. He could still properly be referred to as high priest (Acts 4:6), in much the same way that former presidents of the United States are still referred to as president after they leave office. Annas's title, however, was more than a mere courtesy. Many Jews, resentful of the Romans' meddling in their religious affairs, still considered him to be the true high priest (especially since according to the Mosaic law high priests served for life; cf. Num. 35:25). As Leon Morris notes, "There is little doubt but that . . . the astute old man at the head of the family exercised a good deal of authority. He was in all probability the real power in the land, whatever the legal technicalities" (*The Gospel According to John*, The New International Commentary on the New Testament [Grand Rapids: Eerdmans, 1979], 749).

Further, after his removal from office five of Annas's sons and one of his grandsons served as high priest, as did his son-in-law **Caiaphas,** who held the office from A.D. 18 to 36. Since high priests were appointed and deposed at the whim of the Romans, Caiaphas's unusually long tenure testifies to his skill as a politician. His ruthless determination to preserve his own status and power can be seen in his proposal that Jesus be executed (John 11:49–50)—an unwitting prophetic prediction of the atoning nature of His death (vv. 51–52).

Annas was proud, ambitious, and notoriously greedy. A major source of his income came from the temple. He received a share of the proceeds from the sale of sacrificial animals; only those for sale at the temple (for exorbitant prices) would be approved as an offering. Annas also got a cut of the fees the money changers charged to exchange foreign currency (only Jewish money could be used to pay the temple tax; cf. John 2:14). So notorious was his greed that the outer courts of the temple, where the business was conducted, became known as the Bazaar of Annas (Alfred Edersheim, *The Life and Times of Jesus the Messiah* [Reprint; Grand Rapids: Eerdmans, 1974], 1:371–72). Annas and Caiaphas especially hated Jesus because He twice disrupted their temple business operations (John 2:13–16; Matt. 21:12–13).

These two wretched individuals, as greedy and corrupt as the pagans they despised, exercised tremendous control over the people of Israel. Their rule was especially odious, since they corrupted their God-ordained authority (cf. Matt. 23:1–3). The epitome of their wickedness came during the mock trial of Jesus, in which they played the leading roles.

It was into the world of these seven men that John and Jesus came proclaiming the word of God. Four of them, Pilate, Herod, Annas, and Caiaphas, would play important roles in the unfolding drama of the Lord's life, ministry, and death. All of them symbolized the moral and spiritual darkness that the Light of the world (John 8:12) came to dispel.

The Geographical Setting

the word of God came to John, the son of Zacharias, in the wilderness. And he came into all the district around the Jordan, (3:2b–3a)

One could hardly have envisioned a less auspicious location for the beginning of the public ministry of **John** the Baptist, **the son of Zacharias,** than **the wilderness.** Surely the forerunner of the Messiah would be expected to make a dramatic appearance at the temple, or at least somewhere in Jerusalem. There was no more barren, desolate region in Israel than the **wilderness** of Judea (Matt. 3:1). It stretched from the hill country of Judah on the west to the shores of the Dead Sea on the east, and extended north into the Jordan River valley. According to one writer,

> It is difficult to describe adequately the foreboding desolation and howling barrenness along the shores of the Dead Sea. . . . If there could be fixed in one's mind the image of the almost-painful sterility of the Sahara or of Death Valley, and then multiply that by a factor of four or more, one might come close to capturing the geographical reality to which he is exposed along the shores of the Dead Sea. (Barry J. Beitzel, *The Moody Atlas of Bible Lands* [Chicago: Moody, 1985], 41).

It was in that harsh, unforgiving environment that John grew to manhood. Since his parents, Zacharias and Elizabeth "were both advanced in years" when he was born (Luke 1:7), John may have been orphaned at a young age, and then moved to the wilderness after the death of his parents. Despite the claims of some, however, there is no evidence that John ever lived at the famous religious community of Qumran, which was located in that region (cf. Bock, _Luke 1:1–9:50,_ 198). That John's entire ministry was spent in **the district around the Jordan** (cf. Matt. 3:6, 13; John 1:28; 3:23, 26; 10:40) in no way diminished his enormous popularity (cf. Matt. 3:5; Mark 1:5).

The phrase **the word of God came to John** does not imply that God revealed Scripture to him. Instead, the use of the more specific term _rhema_ (**word**) as opposed to the more general term _logos_ (cf. 5:1) suggests that John's call to a prophetic ministry is in view here (cf. Jer. 1:1–2; Ezek. 1:3; Hos. 1:1; Joel 1:1; Jonah 1:1; Mic. 1:1; Zeph. 1:1; Hag. 1:1). After years of isolation, John suddenly, dramatically stepped onto the public stage.

The location of John's ministry was a rebuke to the religious establishment, located primarily in Jerusalem. That John ministered in the wilderness symbolized God's disdain not only for Gentile idolatry, but also for hypocritical Jewish legalism. John kept his distance from both, remaining untouched and unpolluted by either. It also symbolized John's attack on the establishment (Matt. 3:7–12), and the necessity for truth seekers to leave it (Matt. 3:5–6). Finally, like the Messiah he heralded, John was humble. He did not minister in the temple, or a royal palace, but in the humblest of circumstances (cf. Matt. 11:8). That illustrates the truth that God chooses the humble and the lowly (1 Cor. 1:26–29). As the Jews had to be purged in the wilderness after they had left Egypt before entering the Promised Land, they would also be required to return to the wilderness again to be cleansed, baptized by John to prepare their hearts to receive Messiah's kingdom.

THE THEOLOGICAL SETTING

preaching a baptism of repentance for the forgiveness of sins; (3:3_b_)

John's message of repentance and forgiveness is the one proclaimed by every true preacher of God's truth. It is the good news that alone provides hope to a sin-cursed world. John's message would be readily understandable had he been preaching to Gentiles. But at first glance it seems an unnecessary one for Israel, whose people were steeped in the Old Testament.

The truth is, however, that Israel was religiously bankrupt and desperately needed to hear John's call to repentance. The Jewish people were cured of their penchant for idolatry by the Babylonian captivity. In its place, however, arose a legalistic religion, whose followers believed they could gain a right relationship to God by means of their own efforts.

The Lord Jesus Christ denounced that pernicious, false perspective in the Sermon on the Mount. He declared that no one can earn salvation by keeping the law, since the standard is the absolutely perfect holiness of God (Matt. 5:48; cf. v. 20). Focusing on external behavior instead of heart attitudes (vv. 21–47), making showy public displays of giving to the poor, praying, and fasting (6:1–18) all mark those on the broad way that leads to destruction (7:13). Those counting on such self-righteous achievements to earn their salvation are foolishly building a house on sand— one that will be washed away by the flood of divine judgment (vv. 26–27). But those who declare spiritual bankruptcy, humbly mourning their sin, yearning for a righteousness granted them by God (5:1–12; cf. Phil. 3:9), and trusting in the Lord Jesus (Matt. 10:32–33), will become sons of God and inherit the kingdom of God. The apostle Paul reminded the Romans that

> he is not a Jew who is one outwardly, nor is circumcision that which is outward in the flesh. But he is a Jew who is one inwardly; and circumcision is that which is of the heart, by the Spirit, not by the letter; and his praise is not from men, but from God. (Rom. 2:28–29)

Three important theological realities characterized John's **preaching.** He offered the hope of **forgiveness of sins.** As noted above, the Jewish people were caught up in a system of works righteousness. Salvation, they were taught, came from keeping the Law, observing the traditions, and performing the rituals. But the realization that they could not perfectly do those things laid a heavy burden of guilt on them. Jesus declared that the Jewish religious leaders "tie up heavy burdens and lay them on men's shoulders, but they themselves are unwilling to move them with so much as a finger" (Matt. 23:4). Defending the biblical truth that salvation is by grace alone through faith alone, Peter asked his fellow Jews at the Jerusalem council, "Now therefore why do you put God to the test by placing upon the neck of the disciples a yoke which neither our fathers nor we have been able to bear?" (Acts 15:10).

Yet the Jewish people knew that the New covenant promised forgiveness. In Jeremiah 31:34, God declared, "I will forgive their iniquity, and their sin I will remember no more" (cf. 33:8; 50:20; Ezek. 16:60–63). They also understood that God is by nature a forgiving God. The Lord described Himself to Moses as one "who forgives iniquity, transgression and sin" (Ex. 34:7). Interceding for rebellious Israel, Moses characterized God as "slow to anger and abundant in lovingkindness, forgiving iniquity and transgression" (Num. 14:18). Nehemiah called God "a God of forgiveness" (Neh. 9:17). In Psalm 32, David exalted,

> How blessed is he whose transgression is forgiven, whose sin is covered! How blessed is the man to whom the Lord does not impute iniquity, and in whose spirit there is no deceit! ... I acknowledged my sin to You, and my iniquity I did not hide; I said, "I will confess my transgressions to the Lord"; and You forgave the guilt of my sin." (vv. 1–2, 5).

"Iniquities prevail against me," David lamented, but then added, "as for our transgressions, You forgive them" (Ps. 65:3). In Psalm 86:5, he affirmed, "You, Lord, are good, and ready to forgive." In Psalm 103:12, he expressed the magnitude of God's forgiveness when he declared, "As far as the east is from the west, so far has He removed our transgressions from us," and in Psalm 130:3–4, he added, "If You, Lord, should mark iniquities, O Lord, who could stand? But there is forgiveness with You, that You may be feared." Daniel took comfort in the knowledge that "to the Lord our God belong compassion and forgiveness" (Dan. 9:9). Isaiah pictured God's forgiveness as washing sins so thoroughly that they are white as snow or wool (1:18), casting them behind His back (38:17; cf. Ps. 51:9), refusing to remember them (43:25), and covering them with a thick cloud and a heavy mist (44:22); Micah depicts forgiveness as God's trampling sins under His feet and casting them into the depths of the sea (Mic. 7:19).

Just as his father, Zacharias, had prophesied (Luke 1:76–77), the Baptist proclaimed God's forgiveness. His message offered hope to a people staggering under the weight of sin and guilt. As a result, multitudes flocked to the wilderness to hear the strange prophet with the profound, penetrating message that their burdened hearts so desperately needed to hear.

But forgiveness comes only to those who acknowledge and turn from their sins; hence John also proclaimed the need for **repentance.** That concept was also familiar to the Jewish people. Isaiah 55:6–7 commanded, "Seek the Lord while He may be found; call upon Him while He is near. Let the wicked forsake his way and the unrighteous man his thoughts; and let him return to the Lord, and He will have compassion on him, and to our God, for He will abundantly pardon." Ezekiel 18:30–32 also called upon the people to repent:

> "Therefore I will judge you, O house of Israel, each according to his conduct," declares the Lord God. "Repent and turn away from all your transgressions, so that iniquity may not become a stumbling block to you. Cast away from you all your transgressions which you have committed and make yourselves a new heart and a new spirit! For why will you die, O house of Israel? For I have no pleasure in the death of anyone who dies," declares the Lord God. "Therefore, repent and live." (cf. 33:19)

Repentance is not merely an intellectual change of mind about who Christ is, or superficial remorse over the consequences of sin. It is a radical turning from sin to God; a repudiation of the old life and a turning to God for salvation from the penalty and dominion of sin. In 1 Thessalonians 1:9, Paul wrote that the Thessalonians "turned to God from idols to serve a living and true God." Those who come to Him broken in spirit, humble, and mourning over their sins will experience God's forgiveness.

Saving repentance never exists except in partnership with faith. It is impossible to have true faith in Jesus Christ apart from true repentance from sin or true repentance from sin apart from true faith. They are two sides of the same work of the Holy Spirit to convict sinners of their sin and draw them to Christ.

It must be clearly understood that repentance is not a human work that earns salvation. Repentance is not a pre-salvation effort by sinners to set their lives right that God rewards by saving them. In repentance sinners recognize their dire condition, acknowledge that they are unable to save themselves, and turn to Jesus Christ as the only One who can save them. Left to themselves, the unregenerate will never come to that conclusion, since they love darkness rather than light (John 3:19), and are dead in their trespasses and sins (Eph. 2:1).

The conviction that produces repentance is a work of the Holy Spirit, who "convict[s] the world concerning sin and righteousness and judgment" (John 16:8). In Acts 5:31, Peter declared that, "God exalted [Jesus] to His right hand as a Prince and a Savior, to grant repentance to Israel, and forgiveness of sins." Acts 3:26; 11:18; and 2 Timothy 2:25 also affirm that God grants repentance to sinners.

In 2 Corinthinans 7:9–11, the apostle Paul captures the essence of repentance:

> I now rejoice, not that you were made sorrowful, but that you were made sorrowful to the point of repentance; for you were made sorrowful according to the will of God, so that you might not suffer loss in anything through us. For the sorrow that is according to the will of God produces a repentance without regret, leading to salvation, but the sorrow of the world produces death. For behold what earnestness this very thing, this godly sorrow, has produced in you: what vindication of yourselves, what indignation, what fear, what longing, what zeal, what avenging of wrong! In everything you demonstrated yourselves to be innocent in the matter.

He began by distinguishing remorse over sin's consequences from the sorrow that produces repentance, noting that the Corinthians "were made sorrowful to the point of repentance." Their sorrow was "according to the will of God"; that is, they viewed their sin the same way God does. That in turn "produce[d] a repentance without regret, leading to salvation," as opposed to the "sorrow of the world [that] produces death." Remorse over sin's consequences, which is little more than wounded pride stemming from being caught in a sin, cannot produce the genuine repentance that results in forgiveness.

Paul closed his description of true repentance by defining it in a series of words or phrases. The first mark of repentance is "earnestness," an eager pursuit of righteousness that ends a person's indifference to sin and complacency about his or her lost condition. "Vindication" describes the desire to clear one's name of the stigma attached to sin. "Indignation" is righteous anger at the dishonor sin brings to God's holy name. It goes hand in hand with "fear" of God's just judgment on sin and a "longing" to have one's relationship with Him restored. Repentance also produces "zeal," a passionate desire for righteousness that causes sinners to long to see justice done and the wrong of their sins avenged and atoned for. The Corinthians' desire "to be innocent in the matter" shows that the one who is truly repentant aggressively pursues holiness.

The **baptism** in view here is not Christian baptism, which symbolizes the death, burial, and resurrection of Jesus Christ, because it had not yet been instituted. Nor did John's baptism produce forgiveness, for no ritual can accomplish that. And while there were various ceremonial washings in Judaism (cf. Heb. 6:2), there was no baptism of Jews. But while there was no baptism of Jews in Judaism, the Jews did baptize Gentile converts to Judaism. Thus, those who "were being baptized by [John] in the Jordan River, as they confessed their sins" (Matt. 3:6), were publicly acknowledging they were no better than the Gentiles. Their sins had separated them from the true and living God (cf. Isa. 59:2) and cut them off from covenant blessings. For Jewish people to place themselves on the same level as the despised Gentiles was astonishing, and demonstrates the power of John's preaching.

Unfortunately, few being baptized by John were truly repentant. The nation would later reject Jesus when He failed to meet their expectations of a political Messiah, who would deliver them from the Romans. Others were superficial from the start. Thus when John

> saw many of the Pharisees and Sadducees coming for baptism, he said to them, "You brood of vipers, who warned you to flee from the wrath to come? Therefore bear fruit in keeping with repentance; and do not suppose that you can say to yourselves, 'We have Abraham for our father'; for I say to you that from these stones God is able to raise up children to Abraham [cf. John 8:37–40]. The axe is already laid at the root of the trees; therefore every tree that does not bear good fruit is cut down and thrown into the fire. As for me, I baptize you with water for

repentance, but He who is coming after me is mightier than I, and I am not fit to remove His sandals; He will baptize you with the Holy Spirit and fire. His winnowing fork is in His hand, and He will thoroughly clear His threshing floor; and He will gather His wheat into the barn, but He will burn up the chaff with unquenchable fire. (Matt. 3:7–12)

But those few (Matt. 7:13–14) who acknowledged their sinful condition and alienation from God and turned to Him in repentant faith were saved. (For more information on repentance, see the exposition of 3:7–17 in chapter 18 of this volume and my books *The Gospel According to Jesus* [Rev. ed.; Grand Rapids: Zondervan, 1994] and *The Gospel According to the Apostles* [Nashville: Thomas Nelson, 1993, 2000].)

THE PROPHETICAL SETTING

as it is written in the book of the words of Isaiah the prophet, "The voice of one crying in the wilderness, 'Make ready the way of the Lord, make His paths straight. Every ravine will be filled, and every mountain and hill will be brought low; the crooked will become straight, and the rough roads smooth; and all flesh will see the salvation of God.'" (3:4–6)

Nothing more convincingly demonstrates God's control over history than fulfilled prophecy. One such prophecy is Isaiah 40:3–5, the subject of these verses. It was **written in the book of the words of Isaiah the prophet** seven centuries before John's birth, and has immense theological and historical significance. John's fulfillment of this prophecy also shows the continuity between his ministry and the Old Testament, something critically important if the Jewish people were to accept him as a prophet of God.

John perfectly fulfilled this prophecy. He was **the voice . . . crying in the wilderness,** where he lived most of his life and where he ministered (see the discussion of the geographical setting above). In keeping with his role as Messiah's forerunner, John called on the people to **make ready the way of the Lord, to make His paths straight.** The imagery is of an Oriental monarch on a journey sending a messenger ahead of him to make sure the roads were cleared of debris or other hazards. In the process **ravine[s]** would **be filled** in, **mountain[s] and hill[s] brought low, crooked** paths made **straight, and . . . rough roads** made **smooth.**

Chapter 40, the source of this prophecy, is a pivotal point in the book of Isaiah. The first thirty-nine chapters focus largely on God's coming judgments on Israel and the surrounding nations. The opening words of chapter 40, "'Comfort, O comfort My people,' says your God," mark a dramatic change in tone. The message of Isaiah's prophecy changed from judgment to salvation, which is the theme of the rest of the book. The same God who judged Israel for her sins will one day have mercy on her; His ultimate purpose for the nation is not judgment but the salvation of the believing remnant, based on His unmerited grace (cf. Rom. 11:1–32). The theme of God's comforting of Israel runs throughout the last half of Isaiah's prophecy (cf. 40:6–11, 28–31; 41:8–10, 13; 49:14–16; 51:1–3, 12; 52:9; 54:4–8; 57:18; 61:2; 66:12–13).

Ultimately, God's comfort of Israel will culminate in the millennial kingdom. Human history will end when the Lord Jesus Christ establishes His earthly kingdom and reigns over the entire world (Ps. 2:6; Isa. 2:2; Jer. 33:15; Ezek. 34:23–24; Dan. 2:44–45; Hos. 3:5; Rev. 20:4–6). Politically, the millennial kingdom will be characterized by Christ's universal, absolute, and righteous rule. Physically, the curse will be lifted, resulting in abundant provision, health, and long life for all. Spiritually, knowledge of the Lord will be universal (Isa. 11:9), and the believing remnant of Israel will be saved (Zech. 13:1, 8).

The words of Isaiah's prophecy quoted here also serve as an analogy of the repentance John preached. The wilderness pictures the sinful heart, and repentance involves bringing to light the deep, dark things of the heart, pictured by filling in the ravines, and humbling human pride, depicted in the imagery of bringing low the mountains and hills. The crooked, deceitful, devious perverse things must be made straight, and any other rough places in the heart, whether self-love, love of money, love of the world, the lust of the flesh, indifference, or unbelief, must be smoothed out. Only then will the truly repentant **see the salvation of God.**

True Repentance: God's Highway to the Heart
(Luke 3:7–17)

18

So he began saying to the crowds who were going out to be baptized by him, "You brood of vipers, who warned you to flee from the wrath to come? Therefore bear fruits in keeping with repentance, and do not begin to say to yourselves, 'We have Abraham for our father,' for I say to you that from these stones God is able to raise up children to Abraham. Indeed the axe is already laid at the root of the trees; so every tree that does not bear good fruit is cut down and thrown into the fire." And the crowds were questioning him, saying, "Then what shall we do?" And he would answer and say to them, "The man who has two tunics is to share with him who has none; and he who has food is to do likewise." And some tax collectors also came to be baptized, and they said to him, "Teacher, what shall we do?" And he said to them, "Collect no more than what you have been ordered to." Some soldiers were questioning him, saying, "And what about us, what shall we do?" And he said to them, "Do not take money from anyone by force, or accuse anyone falsely, and be content with your wages." Now while the people were in a state of expectation and all were wondering in their hearts about John, as to whether he was the Christ, John answered and said to them all, "As for me, I baptize

**you with water; but One is coming who is mightier than I, and I
am not fit to untie the thong of His sandals; He will baptize you
with the Holy Spirit and fire. His winnowing fork is in His hand to
thoroughly clear His threshing floor, and to gather the wheat into
His barn; but He will burn up the chaff with unquenchable fire."**
(3:7–17)

Having set the scene for John's ministry in 3:1–6 (see the exposition of those verses in the previous chapter of this volume), Luke gave an
illustration of it in verses 7–17. The message John preached, and his dialogue with the crowd, the tax collectors, and the soldiers were not one-
time occurrences but were typical of what John routinely did. This brief
look at the ministry and message of the one whom Jesus called the greatest man who had ever lived up to his time (Matt. 11:11) is invaluable.
John's blunt, forceful, and uncompromising preaching is a model for all
who proclaim the good news of salvation in Jesus Christ.

First and foremost, John was a preacher of repentance, calling on
the people of Israel to turn from their sin and embrace the Messiah.
Repentance is at the heart of the gospel message; salvation is granted
only to those who repent of their sin and acknowledge Jesus Christ as
the only Savior and Lord (Acts 4:12). It is impossible to truly preach the
good news of forgiveness and grace without calling sinners to repent,
and a gospel message devoid of a call to repentance is foreign to the
New Testament (cf. 15:7, 10; 24:47; Acts 5:31; 11:18; 17:30; 2 Peter 3:9).

John's message stands in sharp contrast to the "cheap grace" and
"easy-believism" that characterizes much watered-down contemporary
preaching. Such deficient preaching strips the gospel of its warning that
sinners have violated God's law and face His wrath and judgment in eternal hell unless they repent. The predictable result of a shallow, superficial
gospel presentation devoid of a biblical call to repentance is a shallow,
superficial, nonsaving response. As a result, churches are filled with many
who profess to know Jesus Christ, but since they have never repented the
Lord will say to them, "I never knew you; depart from Me, you who practice lawlessness" (Matt. 7:23). Although they imagine themselves to be on
the narrow way that leads to eternal life, they are in reality on the broad
way that leads to eternal destruction (vv. 13–14; cf. 25:12; Acts 8:13, 18–23;
2 Tim. 3:5; Titus 1:16).

Even most who heard the powerful preaching of John the Baptist
and underwent his baptism failed to manifest genuine repentance. The
vast crowds (Matt. 3:5) came to see John and listen to his preaching
because they were eagerly anticipating the Messiah. Many even wondered if John himself might be the Messiah (see the discussion of v. 15
below)—a notion that John quickly dismissed (vv. 16–17). But when

Jesus did appear and was announced by John as the Messiah and the "Lamb of God" (John 1:29), in spite of being baptized by John, the people ultimately rejected Him.

In light of the ever-present danger of false repentance, it is crucial to be able to distinguish it from true repentance. Six progressive marks of true repentance emerge from this passage as necessary. True repenters must reflect on personal sin, recognize divine wrath, reject religious ritual, reveal spiritual transformation, renounce ancestry, and receive the Messiah.

TRUE REPENTERS REFLECT ON PERSONAL SIN

As noted in the discussion of 3:4–5 in the previous chapter of this volume, John's ministry as Messiah's forerunner involved preparing the hearts of the people to receive Him. In the words of Isaiah's prophecy, John was "the voice of one crying in the wilderness." His message, "Make ready the way of the Lord, make His paths straight" (v. 4) called on the people to prepare their hearts to receive the Messiah. The imagery of Isaiah's prophecy pictures the work of preparing a pathway through the wilderness of the heart. As noted in the previous chapter of this volume, filling in the ravines pictures bringing to light the hidden sins of the heart. Bringing down the mountains and hills symbolizes the abasement of sinful pride. Making the crooked things straight speaks of straightening out anything perverse, twisted, deceitful, or dangerous by confession and repentance. Finally, smoothing out the rough roads refers to removing any hindrance or obstacle, such as self-love, apathy, indifference, lust, or unbelief, that might obstruct the Lord's entrance into the heart. True repentance involves a complete and full dealing with sin in response to the convicting work of the Holy Spirit.

TRUE REPENTERS RECOGNIZE DIVINE WRATH

So he began saying to the crowds who were going out to be baptized by him, "You brood of vipers, (3:7*a*)

A legitimate motive for repentance is fear of God's wrath. Sin must be dealt with not merely because it creates problems in this life, but even more so because of its far-reaching, eternal consequences. John's message **to the crowds who were going out to be baptized by him** included warnings of God's coming wrath (cf. Rom. 2:5, 8; 5:9; Eph. 5:6; Col. 3:6; Rev. 6:16–17). The notion of some that the suffering in this world is all the hell anyone will ever know is terribly, tragically wrong. The Bible clearly and unmistakably teaches—in graphic terms—the reality of eternal punishment. Jesus, who preached more about hell then He did about heaven, described hell as the place "where their worm does not die, and the fire is not quenched" (Mark 9:48); "the outer darkness" (Matt. 8:12; cf. 22:13; 25:30); and "the furnace of fire" (Matt. 13:42, 50). In Luke 13:28 He warned His hearers, "In that place [hell] there will be weeping and gnashing of teeth when you see Abraham and Isaac and Jacob and all the prophets in the kingdom of God, but yourselves being thrown out." In hell the lost "will pay the penalty of eternal destruction, away from the presence of the Lord and from the glory of His power" (2 Thess. 1:9; cf. Matt. 25:41, 46). In that awful place "they will be tormented day and night forever and ever" (Rev. 20:10; cf. 14:10–11).

John's hearers were well aware of God's coming wrath, since it was a constant theme of the Old Testament prophets. The familiar term "the day of the Lord," which depicts God's catastrophic future judgment of the wicked, is mentioned explicitly nineteen times in the Old Testament (Isa. 2:12; 13:6, 9; Ezek. 13:5; 30:3; Joel 1:15; 2:1, 11, 31; 3:14; Amos 5:18 [two times], 20; Obad. 15; Zeph. 1:7, 14 [two times]; Zech. 14:1; Mal. 4:5). It is the time when God pours out His wrath on the wicked, which is why Scripture three times calls the day of the Lord "the day of vengeance" (Isa. 34:8; 61:2; 63:4).

The Old Testament passages dealing with the day of the Lord often convey a sense of imminence, nearness, and expectation: "Wail, for the day of the Lord is near!" (Isa. 13:6); "For the day is near, even the day of the Lord is near" (Ezek. 30:3); "For the day of the Lord is near" (Joel 1:15); "Let all the inhabitants of the land tremble, for the day of the Lord is coming; surely it is near" (Joel 2:1); "Multitudes, multitudes in the valley of decision! For the day of the Lord is near in the valley of decision" (Joel 3:14); "For the day of the Lord draws near on all the nations" (Obad. 15); "Be silent before the Lord God! For the day of the Lord is near" (Zeph. 1:7); "Near is the great day of the Lord, near and coming very quickly" (Zeph. 1:14).

Those imminent past historical days of the Lord were merely a prelude to the final eschatological day of the Lord, which will be far greater in extent and more terrible in its destruction. The Old Testament day of the Lord passages often have both a near and a far fulfillment. Isaiah 13:6 points to an historical day of the Lord, while verse 9 of that same chapter has the final, eschatological day of the Lord in view. Joel 1:15 and 2:1, 11 describe an historical day of the Lord; Joel 3:1–14 the eschatological day of the Lord. Obadiah 1–14 depicts the historical day of the Lord in which Edom was judged; verses 15–21 describe the eschatological day of the Lord. Zephaniah 1:7–14 predicts an imminent, historical day of the Lord judgment on Judah, which was fulfilled shortly afterward in the Babylonian captivity; 3:8–20 predicts the final day of the Lord.

John's decidedly non-sinner-friendly characterization of the crowds as a **"brood of vipers"** reflects the sobering truth that there is more to repentance than scrambling to avoid the fires of divine wrath. Led by their religious leaders (Matt. 3:7; cf. 12:34; 23:33), hordes of shallow, superficial repenters flocked to hear John. But as he was well aware, they were not interested in changing their nature. By denouncing them as a **brood of vipers,** John identified them with their father, Satan (John 8:44), whom Scripture depicts as a serpent (Gen. 3:1–5, 13–15; 2 Cor. 11:3; Rev. 12:9; 20:2). Their superficial repentance and their vicious, hostile, poisonous natures revealed that they were children of the devil.

TRUE REPENTERS REJECT RELIGIOUS RITUAL

who warned you to flee from the wrath to come? (3:7*b*)

The Jews hoped to gain right standing before God through their own self-righteous achievements. Keeping the Sabbath, celebrating the annual feasts, offering formal prayers, giving alms to the poor, and observing the law (at least externally), was the essence of their religion. Thus it was natural for them to see John's baptism as just another ritual to perform.

But that legalistic, external approach was antithetical to true repentance, and John boldly confronted them. **Who warned you to flee from the wrath to come?** in this manner, he demanded. Did they think they could escape the inferno of God's wrath by slithering into the Jordan River like snakes fleeing a brush fire?

God detests mere outward, ritualistic, hypocritical religion. In Isaiah 29:13 He said of Israel, "This people draw near with their words and honor Me with their lip service, but they remove their hearts far from Me, and their reverence for Me consists of tradition learned by rote." Later in Isaiah God rebuked His people because they "swear by the name of the Lord and invoke the God of Israel, but not in truth nor in righteousness" (48:1). Jeremiah lamented to God concerning his fellow Jews, "You are near to their lips but far from their mind" (Jer. 12:2; cf. Ezek. 33:31–32). In His masterful discourse on salvation commonly known as the Sermon on the Mount (Matt. 5–7), the Lord Jesus Christ destroyed any hope of salvation through human achievement. He attacked the works-righteousness religion of His day, denouncing its prayers as nothing but vain repetition, its almsgiving as the parading of self-righteous pride, and its outward keeping of the law while ignoring the inner attitudes of the heart as rank hypocrisy. In short, He pointed out the utter inability of all their ceremonies and rituals to earn salvation. After his conversion the zealous (Gal. 1:14), outwardly blameless Pharisee Saul of Tarsus acknowledged that all his self-righteousness amounted to nothing more than a heap of rubbish (Phil. 3:4–8).

Like the crowds that flocked to hear John, churches today are filled with people merely going through the motions. They may be baptized as infants, attend services, perform rituals, pray, read their Bibles, even serve as pastors and leaders in the church. But superficial penitence will not deliver anyone from divine wrath and judgment.

TRUE REPENTERS REVEAL SPIRITUAL TRANSFORMATION

Therefore bear fruits in keeping with repentance . . . Indeed the axe is already laid at the root of the trees; so every tree that does not bear good fruit is cut down and thrown into the fire." And the crowds were questioning him, saying, "Then what shall we do?" And he would answer and say to them, "The man who has two tunics is to share with him who has none; and he who has food is to do likewise." And some tax collectors also came to be baptized, and they said to him, "Teacher, what shall we do?" And he said to them, "Collect no more than what you have been ordered to." Some soldiers were questioning him, saying, "And what about us, what shall we do?" And he said to them, "Do not take money from anyone by force, or accuse anyone falsely, and be content with your wages." (3:8a, 9–14)

Genuine repentance will inevitably manifest itself in changed attitudes and behavior; **therefore** John challenged those coming to be baptized to **bear fruits in keeping with** their professed **repentance.** The apostle Paul also challenged people to prove the reality of their repentance. He described his ministry as one of "declaring both to those of Damascus first, and also at Jerusalem and then throughout all the region of Judea, and even to the Gentiles, that they should repent and turn to God, performing deeds appropriate to repentance" (Acts 26:20). Because the evidence of the repentance that leads to salvation is a changed life, God "will render to each person according to his deeds" (Rom. 2:6). That does not mean, of course, that people can earn salvation by good works, but rather that good works are the inevitable result of repentance. The repentance that God grants (Acts 11:18; 2 Tim. 2:25) does not take place in a vacuum, but in the context of the transformation brought about by conversion and regeneration (2 Cor. 5:17). As a result, the redeemed "are [God's] workmanship, created in Christ Jesus for good works, which God prepared beforehand so that we would walk in them" (Eph. 2:10).

None of this was new to the Jewish people. In Isaiah 1:4–5 the prophet lamented concerning Israel,

> Alas, sinful nation, people weighed down with iniquity, offspring of evil-doers, sons who act corruptly! They have abandoned the Lord, they have despised the Holy One of Israel, they have turned away from Him. Where will you be stricken again, as you continue in your rebellion? The whole head is sick and the whole heart is faint.

In verses 16 and 17, God commanded the people, "Wash yourselves, make yourselves clean; remove the evil of your deeds from My sight. Cease to do evil, learn to do good; seek justice, reprove the ruthless, defend the orphan, plead for the widow." If the presence of those deeds confirmed the genuineness of their repentance, God promised that "though [their] sins are as scarlet, they will be as white as snow; though they are red like crimson, they will be like wool" (v. 18). In 2 Chronicles 7:14, God declared, "[If] My people who are called by My name humble themselves and pray and seek My face and turn from their wicked ways, then I will hear from heaven, will forgive their sin and will heal their land" (cf. Ezek. 33:19; Jon. 3:10).

John followed his exhortation to repent with a warning of the severe consequences of failing to do so. **Indeed,** he declared, **the axe is already laid at the root of the trees; so every tree that does not bear good fruit is cut down and thrown into the fire.** (Jesus used the same graphic imagery to depict judgment in Matthew 7:19.) God's judgment was imminent, John warned; His **axe** was **already laid at the root of the trees. And every tree that does not bear good fruit** would be **cut down and thrown into the fire.** Those trees symbolize people whose repentance is demonstrably false, since they do **not bear good fruit**—the attitudes and actions that manifest righteousness, love for God, and obedience to His word. They will be **thrown into the fire;** "the eternal fire which has been prepared for the devil and his angels" (Matt. 25:41; cf. 18:8; Jude 6–7).

The judgment pictured here is of individuals, as the singular **every tree** suggests. But if enough individuals fail to repent, it becomes a national issue. That is what happened in Israel, when the vast majority of the Jewish people rejected Jesus Christ. A few decades later in A.D. 70 the axe of divine judgment fell. The Romans sacked Jerusalem, burned the temple, and slaughtered thousands of Jewish people, who were cast into the fire of eternal damnation. The same axe of divine judgment will fall on all who fail to repent, both Jew and Gentile alike (cf. Joel 3:1–2, 12–14; Zeph. 3:8).

John's sobering message prompted at least some in the crowd to reflect on their sinful lives. Wanting to know what specific actions they needed to take to manifest genuine repentance, they began **questioning him, saying, "Then what shall we do?"** John **would** habitually (as the imperfect tense of the verb translated **say** indicates) **answer** them by giving practical advice. He told the crowds in general, **"The man who has two tunics is to share with him who has none; and he who has food is to do likewise."** Though seemingly trivial, sharing such basic necessities as clothing and food with those in need fulfills the command to love one's neighbor (10:27; cf. Lev. 19:18; Rom. 13:8–10; Gal. 5:14; James 2:8)—which is second in importance only to the command to love God (Matt. 22:37–38).

Luke then recorded the questions of two specific groups. When **some tax collectors also came to be baptized** and asked him, **"Teacher, what shall we do?"** John **said to them, "Collect no more than what you have been ordered to."** **Tax collectors** were hated, vilified, and scorned because they collected taxes for the Roman oppressors. Despised as traitors and robbers, they were cut off from Jewish religious life and forbidden to testify in court. John did not order them to give up their jobs, since it is not wrong for a government to collect taxes (Matt. 22:17–21; Rom. 13:7). But he did tell them not to **collect** any **more than what** they had **been ordered to** collect. Tax collectors normally increased their profits by extorting exorbitant tolls beyond what was mandated by Rome (cf. Luke 19:8), and demanding kickbacks and bribes. They could manifest true repentance by treating people fairly and honestly and not abusing their authority. Some of the tax collectors took John's message to heart and repented (Matt. 21:31–32; Luke 19:1–10).

Soldiers were another group prone to abusing their authority for selfish gain. These **soldiers** could have been under the authority of Herod Antipas or Rome and may also have included some members of the Judean police. John gave them three ways to manifest genuine repentance. First, they were **not** to **take money from anyone by force.** The verb translated **take money by force** literally means "to shake violently." The soldiers were not, to use contemporary idiom, to shake people down for money through intimidation or force. Nor were they to **accuse anyone falsely.** They were not to abuse their authority to twist and pervert the evidence in an attempt to extort money from the innocent. Finally, John charged the soldiers to **be content with** their **wages,** since failing to do so might motivate them to abuse their power.

By selecting tax collectors and soldiers as examples of those who repented, John was making the general point that true repentance produces a life that is transformed from being characterized by sin to being benchmarked by virtue.

TRUE REPENTERS RENOUNCE ANCESTRY

and do not begin to say to yourselves, 'We have Abraham for our father,' for I say to you that from these stones God is able to raise up children to Abraham. (3:8*b*)

The Jewish people based their hope of salvation largely on their descent from Abraham. They were the people to whom God had promised blessing, heirs to the unilateral, irrevocable, unconditional, eternal promises made to Abraham and David. They counted on their Abrahamic descent to gain entrance for them into the kingdom. As some of them proudly said to Jesus, "We are Abraham's descendants" (John 8:33), and, "Abraham is our father" (v. 39).

But salvation is individual, not corporate. Jesus challenged those who claimed to be Abraham's children, "If you are Abraham's children, do the deeds of Abraham" (John 8:39). "For he is not a Jew who is one outwardly," Paul wrote, "but he is a Jew who is one inwardly" (Rom. 2:28–29). Later in that epistle he added, "For they are not all Israel who are descended from Israel; nor are they all children because they are Abraham's descendants, but: 'Through Isaac your descendants will be named'" (Rom. 9:6–7). To the Galatians he wrote, "Therefore, be sure that it is those who are of faith who are sons of Abraham. . . . And if you belong to Christ, then you are Abraham's descendants, heirs according to promise" (Gal. 3:7, 29). Being a descendant of Abraham is no defense against divine judgment, Jesus warned:

> Strive to enter through the narrow door; for many, I tell you, will seek to enter and will not be able. Once the head of the house gets up and shuts the door, and you begin to stand outside and knock on the door, saying, "Lord, open up to us!" then He will answer and say to you, "I do not know where you are from." Then you will begin to say, "We ate and drank in Your presence, and You taught in our streets"; and He will say, "I tell you, I do not know where you are from; depart from Me, all you evildoers." In that place there will be weeping and gnashing of teeth when you see Abraham and Isaac and Jacob and all the prophets in the kingdom of God, but yourselves being thrown out. (Luke 13:24–28)

Nor was the rich man in the story of the rich man and Lazarus delivered from hell by claiming Abraham as his father (Luke 16:24–26).

In keeping with that biblical truth, John cautioned his hearers **not** to **begin to say to** themselves, **We have Abraham for our father.** Then John pointed out **that from these stones God is able to raise up children to Abraham.** His caustic statement was a severe blow to their overweening pride. There was nothing worthy or deserving about them; God could, if He chose, make children of Abraham out of rocks. And apart from repentance and salvation, their hearts were hearts of stone anyway (Ezek. 11:19; 36:26). John's harsh tone, reminiscent of his earlier denunciation of them as snakes (v. 7), was warranted by the seriousness of the situation. Those who trust in their ethnic or religious heritage for salvation are deceived and headed for the fire of eternal judgment.

TRUE REPENTERS RECEIVE THE MESSIAH

Now while the people were in a state of expectation and all were wondering in their hearts about John, as to whether he was the Christ, John answered and said to them all, "As for me, I baptize you with water; but One is coming who is mightier than I, and I am not fit to untie the thong of His sandals; He will baptize you with the Holy Spirit and fire. His winnowing fork is in His hand to thoroughly clear His threshing floor, and to gather the wheat into His barn; but He will burn up the chaff with unquenchable fire." (3:15–17)

This final point moves beyond the things that accompany salvation to the One who alone can save, the Messiah, the Lord Jesus Christ. John's words powerfully attest that the coming one, the Messiah, is God, since He does things only God can do.

For centuries the Jewish people had longed for and eagerly anticipated the coming of Messiah. But now **the people were in a** heightened **state of expectation** because of John's ministry. Their speculation **as to whether he was the Christ,** though understandable, was misguided. It is true that John was a prophet (Luke 20:6), and the greatest man who had ever lived up to his time (Matt. 11:11). But John was not the Messiah (John 1:6–8), nor did he ever claim to be. On the contrary, "When the Jews sent to him priests and Levites from Jerusalem to ask him, 'Who are you?' [John] confessed and did not deny, but confessed, 'I am not the Christ'" (John 1:19–20; cf. 3:28).

John's disclaimer, **As for me, I baptize you with water; but One is coming who is mightier than I, and I am not fit to untie the thong of His sandals** not only made it clear that he was not the Messiah, but also that he was inferior to Him. John baptized them in the water of the Jordan River as an outward confession of their repentance. But the

the Messiah, the **One** who **is coming,** or "the Expected One" (Luke 7:19–20) is **mightier** than John. So superior is the Messiah that John deemed himself unfit even **to untie the thong of His sandals**—a menial task performed by the lowliest of slaves (cf. John 1:27). The Messiah would **baptize** them **with the Holy Spirit and fire.** That demonstrates the Messiah's superiority to John, for those two supernatural acts can only be performed by God. It is God alone who dispenses the **Holy Spirit** to those who repent and judgment to those who do not.

The Jews were well aware that under the New covenant, God would send the Spirit to indwell those who repent (Ezek. 36:27; 37:14). Nor does any human have the authority to immerse unrepentant sinners in the **fire** of eternal judgment. The Jews also knew that the Old Testament frequently associates fire with divine judgment (cf. Isa. 29:6; 30:33; 31:9; 66:15–16; Ezek. 38:22; Zeph. 1:18; 3:8). Malachi wrote that Messiah would come (3:1) bringing judgment, which caused the prophet to exclaim, "But who can endure the day of His coming? And who can stand when He appears? For He is like a refiner's fire and like fullers' soap" (v. 2). In 4:1, God used the metaphor of fire to picture future judgment: "'For behold, the day is coming, burning like a furnace; and all the arrogant and every evildoer will be chaff; and the day that is coming will set them ablaze,' says the Lord of hosts, 'so that it will leave them neither root nor branch.'" The New Testament also uses fire in reference to divine judgment (Matt. 7:19; 13:40, 42, 50; 18:8; 25:41; Luke 9:54; 12:49; 17:29; John 15:6; 2 Thess. 1:7; Heb. 10:27; 2 Peter 3:7; Jude 7; Rev. 14:10; 19:20; 20:10, 14–15; 21:8).

Verse 17 pictures the separation involved in judgment by using a familiar agricultural illustration. After the grain was harvested, it was dumped onto a hard, flat floor. It was then tossed into the air with a **winnowing fork,** and the breeze would blow the lighter **chaff** away from the heavier **wheat.** John's illustration pictures Messiah with **His winnowing fork . . . in His hand,** ready **to** so **thoroughly clear His threshing floor** that no traces of chaff are left. His judgment will be complete, and no one will be exempted from it. After the separation is accomplished, Messiah will **gather the wheat** (the repentant; cf. Matt. 13:25–30) **into His barn** (heaven); **but He will burn up the chaff** (the unrepentant; cf. Ex. 15:7; Pss. 1:4; 35:5; 83:13; Isa. 17:13; 29:5; Mal. 4:1) **with** the **unquenchable fire** of eternal hell (cf. Isa. 66:24; Matt. 18:8; 25:41, 46; Rev. 14:10–11).

John's powerful call for true repentance is just as relevant and needed today as when he first gave it. It is the duty of every true preacher of God's Word to warn his hearers of the danger of false, shallow, nonsaving repentance; repentance that is grounded in selfish regret over sin's consequences instead of a desire to be delivered from sin fails to subdue the love of sin and initiate a passion for holiness, leads to further sin in a hypocritical attempt to maintain the facade of self-righteousness, produces self-deception, leads to a deadly false security, and ultimately hardens the heart, and sears the conscience.

The Boldness of John the Baptist (Luke 3:18–20)

19

So with many other exhortations he preached the gospel to the people. But when Herod the tetrarch was reprimanded by him because of Herodias, his brother's wife, and because of all the wicked things which Herod had done, Herod also added this to them all: he locked John up in prison. (3:18–20)

Throughout redemptive history fearless preachers have paid the price for boldly confronting sin. It should come as no surprise then that the Lord Jesus Christ, the greatest preacher who ever lived (John 7:46; cf. Matt. 7:28–29), was executed by His enemies. According to traditions (of varying reliability) handed down from the early church, the same fate befell all of the apostles except for John, who was exiled to Patmos. Peter was crucified (upside down, at his request, because he felt unworthy to be crucified as his Lord had been [Eusebius, *Ecclesiastical History,* III, 1]). His brother Andrew reportedly was also crucified; tied instead of nailed to the cross to prolong his suffering. James the brother of John is the only apostle whose death is recorded in Scripture; he was executed by Herod Agrippa I (Acts 12:1–2). Philip was said to have been stoned to death in Asia Minor, but not before multitudes came to faith in Christ through his preaching. The traditions vary concerning how Philip's close

225

companion Nathanael (Bartholomew) died. Some say he was bound and thrown into the sea, others that he was crucified. Matthew may have been burned at the stake. Thomas likely reached India, where some traditions say he was killed with a spear. According to the apocryphal Martyrdom of James, James the son of Alphaeus was stoned to death by the Jews for preaching Christ. Simon the Zealot, according to some traditions, preached the gospel in Egypt, North Africa, and Persia, where he was martyred by being sawn in two. Other traditions place his ministry in Britain, where he was eventually crucified by the Romans. Thaddeus (also known as Judas the son of James [Luke 6:16]) reportedly took the gospel message to what is now modern Turkey, where he was clubbed to death. Paul was likely beheaded at Rome during Nero's persecution of the church. The New Testament also records the martyrdoms of the fearless evangelist Stephen (Acts 7:58–60) and Antipas, a faithful pastor of the church at Smyrna (Rev. 2:13).

In the postapostolic era faithful preachers continued to face martyrdom. Ignatius was martyred at Rome early in the second century. Diligently carrying out his ministry to the end, he wrote a series of letters to various churches while he was being taken to Rome for execution, exhorting them to stand firm in the faith. Polycarp, facing martydom at Smyrna in the middle of the second century, refused to renounce Christ. "Eighty and six years have I served Him, and He never did me any injury" he replied. "How then can I blaspheme my King and my Savior?" When the proconsul threatened to burn him alive Polycarp fearlessly replied, "You threaten me with fire which burns for an hour, and after a little is extinguished, but are ignorant of the fire of the coming judgment and of eternal punishment, reserved for the ungodly. But why tarry you? Bring forth what you will."

John Chrysostom, fourth-century bishop of Constantinople, was perhaps the greatest preacher of the early church (the nickname Chrysostom means "golden-mouthed"). He was exiled when his bold, uncompromising preaching offended many of the rich and powerful in Constantinople (especially the vain Empress Eudoxia). No longer able to preach, Chrysostom turned to writing. So powerful and effective was his continuing ministry that he was banished to a more remote location. Treated harshly by the soldiers escorting him, Chrysostom became ill and died along the way. Historian Justo Gonzalez describes the scene: "When he perceived that death was near, he asked to be taken to a small church by the roadside. There he took communion, bid farewell to those around him, and preached his briefest but most eloquent sermon: 'In all things, glory to God. Amen'" (*The Story of Christianity* [Peabody, Mass.: Prince, 1999], 1:199–200).

Two notable medieval forerunners to the Reformation were John

Wycliffe and Jan Huss. Wycliffe (1329–1384), sometimes called the "Morning Star of the Reformation," was an English reformer who affirmed the Bible to be the only authority in matters of doctrine and practice. He sought to translate it into English, so more people could read it. Wycliffe taught that Christ, not the pope, was the head of the church, denied the Roman Catholic doctrine of transubstantiation and (like Luther later would) opposed the granting of indulgences (remissions of some or all of the punishments of purgatory, often sold in the Middle Ages to raise money for the Catholic Church). Wycliffe and his followers, the Lollards, helped pave the way for the Reformation in England. For his bold opposition to the false teaching of his day, Wycliffe was condemned and forced to leave his position at Oxford.

Wycliffe's younger contemporary, the Czech reformer Jan Huss (1373–1415) paid a steeper price for opposing some of the false teaching of the Roman church. Huss, like Wycliffe, taught that the Bible, not the pope, was the supreme authority. He also rejected indulgences. When the pope issued a decree that forbade preaching in chapels such as the one Huss preached in, Huss ignored it and continued to preach. For doing so, he was excommunicated. Huss was summoned to appear before the Council of Constance (1415) and was promised safe conduct to and from the council by the emperor of the Holy Roman Empire. But Huss was condemned and burned at the stake, the emperor's guarantee of safe conduct notwithstanding.

Among the hundreds of Protestants martyred in England during the reign of Mary Tudor ("Bloody Mary") was the great preacher Hugh Latimer. As he was about to be burned at the stake along with fellow reformer Nicolas Ridley, Latimer said to him, "Be of good comfort, Master Ridley, and play the man; we shall this day light such a candle by God's grace in England as I trust shall never be put out."

In modern times many faithful preachers of God's Word have faced persecution or martyrdom in such places as China, the Middle East, parts of Africa and India, and elsewhere. Nevertheless, as Paul wrote during his own imprisonment for the cause of Christ, "the word of God is not imprisoned" (2 Tim. 2:9).

The first of many through the ages who would be martyred for faithfully testifying to Christ was His forerunner, John the Baptist. By human standards, John's career does not appear to have been very successful. His brief ministry of about a year was spent in the Judean wilderness, and ended with a long stretch in prison followed by his being beheaded.

But such an evaluation of John's career is misguided. The truth is, he was eminently used by God to accomplish the task for which he was born (Luke 1:13–17, 76)—so much so that Jesus said of him, "Truly I say to you, among those born of women there has not arisen anyone greater than John the Baptist!" (Matt. 11:11). John accomplished precisely what God purposed him to.

Having given examples of his preaching and interacting with the crowds in verses 7–17, Luke closed out the story of John the Baptist with this brief summary of his ministry. It should be noted that Luke's insertion of this section here was not chronological, but thematic. John was not actually imprisoned until later in Jesus' ministry, but Luke pulls his imprisonment back to this point to conclude his account of John's ministry and set Jesus on center stage. For the rest of Luke's gospel John appears only in reference to Him.

Three words, "preaching," "personalizing," and "persecution," help unfold John's impact.

PREACHING

So with many other exhortations he preached the gospel to the people. (3:18)

As noted in the previous chapter of this volume, John ministered for many months in the Judean wilderness near the Jordan River. Large crowds flocked to hear him, and speculation was rampant that he might be Israel's long-awaited Messiah. John was not the Messiah, but he **preached the gospel to the people,** calling them to repent and baptizing those who did so in preparation for the Messiah's coming. His **exhortations** exposed the wickedness of their hearts, condemned their reliance on ritual and their Abrahamic heritage for salvation, and warned them that they would face God's wrath and judgment if they did not truly and evidently repent. His message was not confined to the Jewish **people,** however, as his condemnation of Herod, a non-Jew, indicates (see the exposition of v. 19).

John's ministry overlapped that of Jesus, continuing for as long as six months after he baptized Him. But as Jesus came to the forefront, His ministry eclipsed John's. In John 3:22–36, the apostle John recorded John the Baptist's final testimony to Jesus, as his ministry wound down to its conclusion. Verses 22–23 note that both Jesus (through His disciples; cf. 4:2) and John were baptizing, indicating the overlap in their ministries referred to above. Both Matthew (4:12) and Mark (1:14) move directly from Christ's temptation to John's imprisonment. John's gospel supplements the account of the Synoptic Gospels by revealing what took place between those two events.

Disturbed by their master's declining popularity, John's disciples "said to him, 'Rabbi, He who was with you beyond the Jordan, to whom you have testified, behold, He is baptizing and all are coming to Him'" (v. 26). Though his disciples may have lost sight of the purpose of John's ministry, which was to point Israel to the Messiah, John had not. "A man can receive nothing," he reminded them, "unless it has been given him from heaven. You yourselves are my witnesses that I said, 'I am not the Christ,' but, 'I have been sent ahead of Him'" (vv. 27–28). John saw Jesus' increasing popularity not as a threat to his ministry, but as its fulfillment. To make his point perfectly clear, John told his disciples, "He [Jesus] must increase, but I must decrease" (v. 30). Then in verses 31–36 John gave six reasons why Jesus was superior to him.

First, Jesus had a heavenly origin. He is the one "who comes from above [and] is above all" (v. 31; cf. 6:33, 38, 50–51, 58; 8:42; 13:3; 16:28; 17:8; 1 Cor. 15:47; Eph. 4:10), which affirms His deity.

Second, Jesus is omniscient. His teaching is superior to anyone else's because He is the source of divine revelation. "What He has seen and heard" in the heavenly realm, "of that He testifies" (v. 32).

Third, what Jesus said was always in complete harmony with God the Father, so that "he who has received His testimony has set his seal to this, that God is true" (v. 33). Conversely, to reject Jesus is to call God a liar (1 John 5:10).

Fourth, Jesus experienced the power of the Holy Spirit in an unlimited way; God gave Jesus "the Spirit without measure" (v. 34). That is in contrast to all others who spoke for God, even the prophets and the inspired writers of Scripture. Their ability to receive the Spirit's power was limited by their sinful, fallen human natures. But since in Christ "all the fullness of Deity dwells in bodily form" (Col. 2:9), there were no limits on the Spirit's power working in Him.

Fifth, Jesus has received all authority from the Father, who "has given all things into His hand" (v. 35). The Father's granting Him supreme authority over everything in heaven and earth (Matt. 11:27; 28:18; 1 Cor. 15:27; Eph. 1:22; Phil. 2:9–11; Heb. 1:2; 1 Peter 3:22) is a clear testimony to the Son's deity.

Finally, Jesus alone is the Savior (Acts 4:12), and "he who believes in the Son has eternal life; but he who does not obey the Son will not see life, but the wrath of God abides on him" (v. 36). Since in Isaiah 43:11 God declared, "I, even I, am the Lord, and there is no savior besides Me," to say that Jesus is Savior is to say that He is God.

Having given this final testimony to the Messiah, the Lord Jesus Christ, John faded from the scene. The work of the great prophet was over.

PERSONALIZING

But when Herod the tetrarch was reprimanded by him because of Herodias, his brother's wife, and because of all the wicked things which Herod had done, (3:19)

John's bold preaching was not only directed to large audiences, but also to specific individuals. Even **Herod** Antipas, **the tetrarch** of Galilee and Perea (see the discussion of 3:1 in chapter 17 of this volume) where John was ministering, did not escape being **reprimanded by him.** Antipas was a son of Herod the Great, and his long reign (4 B.C. to A.D. 39) encompassed the entire ministry of Jesus Christ. With the exception of the birth narratives (Matt. 2:1–19; Luke 1:5), Antipas is the Herod who appears in the gospel accounts. He was not a Jew; his father, Herod the Great, was an Idumean (Edomite) and his mother, Malthace, was a Samaritan. That he was descended from the despised Edomites and Samaritans did not endear Antipas to his Jewish subjects. Neither did his actions as ruler, in particular building Tiberias, his capital city, on the site of a Jewish cemetery. Because they considered the site to be defiled, Antipas had a hard time persuading any Jews to settle there.

Though some may have hesitated to rebuke a ruler of Herod's status, John was not deterred. The verb translated **reprimanded** is a present passive participle, indicating continuous action. John continually challenged the moral character of this ruler **because of all the wicked things which Herod had done.**

Of all of Herod's sins, one glaring one stood out publicly: his illicit marriage to **Herodias, his brother's wife.** Their sordid story was nothing less than a first-century soap opera. Marital problems were nothing new to the Herods; Antipas's father, Herod the Great, for example, had had ten wives. Antipas had married the daughter of Aretas, the king of Nabatea, a region located just south of Perea. While on a journey to Rome, Antipas visited his half brother Philip (not the Philip the tetrarch mentioned in 3:1). While staying with him, Antipas became infatuated with Philip's wife Herodias (who was also Antipas's niece, the daughter of another of his half brothers). The ambitious Herodias was eager to be the wife of a tetrarch (her husband, Philip, was a private citizen) and agreed to marry Antipas on the condition that he divorce Aretas's daughter. Aretas was outraged over this insult, and his smoldering resentment later led to war between him and Antipas. Antipas was defeated by Aretas and saved from disaster only by Roman intervention.

Herodias would ultimately prove to be Herod's downfall. After Emperor Caligula granted Herodias's brother Agrippa I (Acts 12:1) the title of king, she demanded that Herod go to Rome and obtain the same title. (The gospel references to him as king [Matt. 14:9; Mark 6:14, 22] reflect informal popular usage of the term.) But before Herod and Herodias reached Rome, a messenger from Agrippa accused Herod of wrong-doing. As a result, Caligula deposed Herod who, accompanied by Herodias, was banished permanently to a city in what is now France.

Antipas and Herodias are reminiscent of another ill-fated couple, Ahab and Jezebel. "Like Ahab," writes D. A. Carson, "Antipas was wicked but weak; and Herodias, like Jezebel, wicked and ruthless" (*Matthew*, in Frank E. Gaebelein, ed., The Expositor's Bible Commentary [Grand Rapids: Zondervan, 1984], 8:338). Antipas's weakness coupled with Herodias's ruthlessness ensured that eventually their sins could only bring disastrous consequences.

PRISON

Herod also added this to them all: he locked John up in prison.
(3:20)

Antipas's marriage to Herodias was wrong on several counts. First, they divorced their spouses to marry each other. Second, their relationship was also incestuous, since she was his niece. Finally, Antipas's marriage to her was a flagrant violation of the Mosaic law, which explicitly prohibited a man from marrying his brother's wife (Lev. 20:21). The only exception was to produce offspring if his brother died (levirate marriage). But Philip already had offspring (Salome; see the discussion below). Moreover, he was still alive.

Although he was calling Herod to repent out of concern for his soul, John's uncompromising rebuke of the couple's illicit marriage was explosive politically. As noted above, Aretas was already infuriated that Antipas had divorced his daughter to marry Herodias. Now the widely popular John the Baptist was denouncing his sin. Moving to silence the bold preacher, **Herod added** to his already lengthy list of iniquities the most public one of **them all: he locked John up in prison.**

Luke ends the story of John there, but Matthew and Mark record the grim final episode of his life. Wanting to execute John, but afraid of the people's reaction (Matt. 14:5), Herod kept him in prison. But mere imprisonment was not enough for the vindictive Herodias, who "had a grudge against [John] and wanted to put him to death" (Mark 6:19). Eventually, she found a way to manipulate her husband and get what she wanted. At a gala celebration of Antipas's birthday Herodias's daughter from her marriage to Philip (Josephus gives her name as Salome) performed a lewd and immoral dance before Herod and his guests. Seduced by her performance, wanting to play the magnanimous ruler before his guests, and probably more than a little drunk, Herod "promised with an oath to give her whatever she asked" (Matt. 14:7). Prompted by her vengeful mother, the girl replied, "Give me here on a platter the head of John the Baptist" (v. 8). Grieved over the outcome of his foolish promise but too proud to break it, Herod reluctantly ordered John's decapitation (Matt. 14:10).

In the end, killing John did not accomplish anything for Herod and Herodias. As noted above, they eventually lost everything and went into exile. And Herod was haunted by guilt over what he had done. Thus when reports of Jesus' ministry reached him, Herod exclaimed, "This is John the Baptist; he has risen from the dead, and that is why miraculous powers are at work in him" (Matt. 14:2). And Herod would add to his guilt by playing a role in the trial of Jesus (Luke 23:7–12).

John's humble acceptance of his subordinate role is an example for all preachers (and all believers) of humility. John confrontively and fearlessly spoke the truth, thus faithfully carrying out his ministry. He boldly called for repentance no matter what it cost him. In an age of ear-tickling preaching (2 Tim. 4:3) and self-promoting preachers (Phil. 1:17), the church desperately needs more bold, yet humble preachers like the Baptist.

The Messiah's Divine Confirmation (Luke 3:21–22)

20

Now when all the people were baptized, Jesus was also baptized, and while He was praying, heaven was opened, and the Holy Spirit descended upon Him in bodily form like a dove, and a voice came out of heaven, "You are My beloved Son, in You I am well-pleased." (3:21–22)

The central theme of both Old Testament prophecy and New Testament preaching is the Lord Jesus Christ. The Bible, particularly the Gospels, is filled with testimony to Him (Luke 24:44; John 5:39; Rev. 19:10). After her conversation with Jesus in which He revealed Himself to be the Messiah (John 4:26), the Samaritan woman went back to her village "and said to the men, 'Come, see a man who told me all the things that I have done; this is not the Christ, is it?'" (v. 29). As a result, "From that city many of the Samaritans believed in Him because of the word of the woman who testified, 'He told me all the things that I have done'" (v. 39). Jesus' supernatural knowledge of him moved Nathanael to testify, "Rabbi, You are the Son of God; You are the King of Israel" (John 1:49).

Not only His omniscient knowledge, but also His miraculous works testified to Jesus. In John 5:36 Jesus said to His opponents, "The works which the Father has given Me to accomplish—the very works that

I do—testify about Me, that the Father has sent Me" (cf. 10:25).

As befitting those chosen to be His witnesses (Acts 1:8), the apostles continually testified about Jesus Christ. In response to the Lord's query, "Who do you say that I am?" (Matt. 16:15) Peter replied, "You are the Christ, the Son of the living God" (v. 16). The apostle John twice recorded his testimony to Jesus: "And he who has seen has testified, and his testimony is true; and he knows that he is telling the truth, so that you also may believe" (John 19:35); "This is the disciple who is testifying to these things and wrote these things, and we know that his testimony is true" (John 21:24; cf. 1 John 1:2; 4:14; Rev. 1:1–2, 9). Jesus told the apostles, "You will testify... because you have been with Me from the beginning" (John 15:27), and the book of Acts records that they did just that (Acts 4:33; 10:42; 18:5; 20:21).

As has been noted in previous chapters of this volume, it was the mission of John the Baptist, the forerunner of the Messiah, to bear witness to Jesus. John "came as a witness, to testify about the Light" (John 1:7; cf v. 8); he "testified about Him and cried out, saying, 'This was He of whom I said, "He who comes after me has a higher rank than I, for He existed before me"' " (v. 15); "Behold, the Lamb of God who takes away the sin of the world!" ... I myself have seen, and have testified that this is the Son of God" (vv. 29, 34). Both John's disciples (John 3:26) and Jesus (John 5:33) referred to John's testimony to Jesus.

Holy angels gave testimony to the deity of our Lord (1:35; cf. Matt. 1:23). Even demons gave testimony to the Lord Jesus as God: "I know who You are—the Holy One of God!" said the demon in the synagogue in Capernaum (Mark 1:24; cf. v. 34).

Moving to the Trinity, the Holy Spirit has testified to Jesus. "When the Helper comes, whom I will send to you from the Father," Jesus told His disciples, "that is the Spirit of truth who proceeds from the Father, He will testify about Me" (John 15:26). In John 16:13–14, He added,

> When He, the Spirit of truth, comes, He will guide you into all the truth; for He will not speak on His own initiative, but whatever He hears, He will speak; and He will disclose to you what is to come. He will glorify Me, for He will take of Mine and will disclose it to you.

Peter and the apostles declared to the Sanhedrin, "He [Christ] is the one whom God exalted to His right hand as a Prince and a Savior, to grant repentance to Israel, and forgiveness of sins. And we are witnesses of these things; and so is the Holy Spirit, whom God has given to those who obey Him" (Act 5:31–32). Speaking of the Spirit's testimony to Jesus the apostle John wrote,

> This is the One who came by water and blood, Jesus Christ; not with the
> water only, but with the water and with the blood. It is the Spirit who tes-
> tifies, because the Spirit is the truth. For there are three that testify: the
> Spirit and the water and the blood; and the three are in agreement.
> (1 John 5:6–8)

But of all the historic New Testament witnesses to Jesus Christ
the most significant was God the Father. In John 5:37, Jesus said to the
Jewish leaders, "The Father who sent Me, He has testified of Me," and in
8:18, He added, "the Father who sent Me testifies about Me." Concerning
the Father's testimony to the Son, the apostle John wrote,

> The testimony of God is this, that He has testified concerning His Son.
> The one who believes in the Son of God has the testimony in himself;
> the one who does not believe God has made Him a liar, because he has
> not believed in the testimony that God has given concerning His Son.
> And the testimony is this, that God has given us eternal life, and this life
> is in His Son. (1 John 5:9*b*–11)

At the transfiguration the terrified disciples heard the Father's "voice out
of the cloud [saying], 'This is My beloved Son, with whom I am well-
pleased; listen to Him!'" (Matt. 17:5).

The Father also testified audibly concerning Jesus at His baptism. That testimony, recorded in verse 22, is the main point of this powerful, majestic passage. Though brief, it opens up a wide panorama of truth,
as it reveals the Spirit's and the Father's confirmation of Jesus as Messiah
and Savior.

These verses also mark the final transition from the story of John
the Baptist to Jesus. Everything up to this point has set the stage for the
ministry of Jesus Christ. That ministry, launched here at His baptism, will
be the theme and focus of the remainder of Luke's gospel.

This passage is also one of the most significant Trinitarian texts in
the New Testament, as the Father speaks, the Holy Spirit descends, and
Jesus is baptized. That all appear simultaneously refutes the heresy
known as modalism (or modalistic monarchianism. Modalism is also
known as Sabellianism after Sabellius, its most prominent advocate in
the early church). In modern times, it is the teaching of the so-called
"oneness" groups, the largest of which is the United Pentecostal Church.
Modalism denies the biblical teaching that God exists eternally in three
persons. It views Him as one person, the Father, who also manifests Himself at various times as the Holy Spirit, and on other occasions as the Son.
That view is untenable in light of this and other passages where the
members of the Trinity are clearly distinguished from each other (e.g.,

Matt. 10:32–33; 11:25–27; 17:1–5; 26:39, 42; 28:19; Luke 23:46; John 5:17–26; 11:41; 12:28; 16:28; 17:1–26; 20:17; Acts 7:55–56; Col. 3:1; Heb. 1:3; 8:1; 10:12; 12:2; 1 Peter 3:22; 2 Peter 1:17; 1 John 2:1).

This text may be approached by looking at it in relation to each of the persons of the Godhead: the Son's baptism, the Spirit's anointing, and the Father's testimony.

THE SON'S BAPTISM

Now when all the people were baptized, Jesus was also baptized, and while He was praying, heaven was opened, (3:21)

Jesus' baptism was not, as some imagine, a private affair; **when all the people were baptized, Jesus was also baptized.** His thirty years in obscurity were over, and the time had come for Him to publicly launch His ministry. **All** does not refer to the entire nation of Israel, or even to all who came out to hear John. Not everyone who heard John's message repented; in 7:30, Luke notes that "the Pharisees and the lawyers rejected God's purpose for themselves, not having been baptized by John." But all those who responded to John's preaching were baptized.

At the height of John's ministry Jesus came along with the crowds to be baptized. There was nothing to distinguish Him; He had done no miracles, there was no halo around His head, His divine glory was veiled, and He wore no special messianic vestments. Even John did not recognize Him at first (John 1:31); although they were cousins, they had lived in different regions: John in the Judean wilderness (Luke 1:80) and Jesus in Galilee. There is no indication in Scripture that they had ever met before this incident, which would in fact be their only meeting. John's ministry would continue only for about another six months before his imprisonment and execution (see the discussion in chapter 19 of this volume).

Matthew's account relates that John was extremely reluctant to baptize Jesus (the verb translated "to prevent" in Matt. 3:14 is an intense, compound verb, and the imperfect tense suggests a dialogue between John and Jesus), and exclaimed, "I have need to be baptized by You, and do You come to me?" (Matt. 3:14). John's baptism involved a public confession of sin and repentance (see the exposition of 3:3 in chapter 17 of this volume). John was unwilling to baptize Jesus because he knew that He was the holy Son of God, and thus did not need to undergo John's baptism of repentance. John may have been concerned that people not draw the wrong conclusion about Jesus and assume He was acknowledging Himself to be a sinner. John's defensiveness was groundless, as would shortly become evident.

Jesus had a specific purpose for being baptized. It was not, as the apocryphal Gospel According to the Hebrews claimed, to please His mother and brothers. Still less was it so that the "Christ spirit" could indwell the purely human Jesus, as the Gnostics falsely taught. Nor was it to affirm John's ministry, or to act as though He was a sinner to preview His work of sin-bearing on the cross. Jesus plainly stated His purpose in being baptized when He said to John, "Permit it at this time; for in this way it is fitting for us to fulfill all righteousness" (Matt. 3:15).

According to John 1:33, God commanded John the Baptist to baptize. Therefore, He wanted people to be baptized, and it was incumbent on the righteous to do so. And whatever God required the righteous to do, Jesus did—even things He personally did not need to do. For example, Jesus faithfully participated in the Passover celebration, which pictured God's deliverance of His people from sin. Yet He had no sin to be delivered from. Matthew 17:24–27 provides another illustration:

> When they came to Capernaum, those who collected the two-drachma tax came to Peter and said, "Does your teacher not pay the two-drachma tax?" He said, "Yes." And when he came into the house, Jesus spoke to him first, saying, "What do you think, Simon? From whom do the kings of the earth collect customs or poll-tax, from their sons or from strangers?" When Peter said, "From strangers," Jesus said to him, "Then the sons are exempt. However, so that we do not offend them, go to the sea and throw in a hook, and take the first fish that comes up; and when you open its mouth, you will find a shekel. Take that and give it to them for you and Me."

As the Son of God, Jesus was exempt from paying the temple tax. But to do what righteous people do, He paid it anyway.

Jesus' living a perfectly righteous life was not only a demonstration of His deity, but also was absolutely essential to our salvation. In 2 Corinthians 5:21, the apostle Paul explains, "He [the Father] made Him [the Son] who knew no sin to be sin on our behalf, so that we might become the righteousness of God in Him." God imputed the sins of all who would believe in Jesus to Him on the cross, and imputed Jesus' perfect righteousness to them. In other words, God treated Jesus as if He had lived believers' sinful lives and treated them as if they had lived His sinlessly perfect life. Obviously, if He had merely come down from heaven, been crucified, and raised three days later, there would have been no righteous life to impute to believers. It was because He did live such a life that Paul could speak of "not having a righteousness of [his] own derived from the Law, but that which is through faith in Christ, the righteousness which comes from God on the basis of faith" (Phil. 3:9).

Although all three of the Synoptic Gospels record Jesus' baptism and John refers to it, only Luke notes that Jesus **was praying.** During His baptism, as was the case throughout His life, Jesus was in unbroken communion with the Father—except for that moment on the cross when He cried out, "My God, My God, why have You forsaken Me?" (Matt. 27:46). From beginning to end Jesus' earthly ministry was marked by frequent times of prayer. He prayed at His baptism (Luke 3:21), during His first preaching tour (Mark 1:35; Luke 5:16), before choosing the twelve apostles (Luke 6:12–13), before feeding the 5,000 (Matt. 14:19), after feeding the 5,000 (Matt. 14:23), before feeding the 4,000 (Matt. 15:36), before Peter's confession of Him as the Christ (Luke 9:18), at the transfiguration (Luke 9:28–29), for some children brought to Him (Matt. 19:13), after the return of the seventy (Luke 10:21), before giving the Lord's Prayer (Luke 11:1), before raising Lazarus from the dead (John 11:41–42), as He faced the reality of the cross (John 12:28), at the Last Supper (Matt. 26:26–27), for Peter (Luke 22:31–32), in Gethsemane (Matt. 26:36–44), from the cross (Matt. 27:46; Luke 23:34, 46), with the disciples He encountered on the road to Emmaus (Luke 24:30), at the ascension (Luke 24:50–51) and, supremely, in His high priestly prayer in John 17.

Until this point Jesus' baptism had been done the same as everyone else's. But what happened next was utterly transcendent and unlike anything anyone there that day had ever seen. While Jesus was coming up out of the water, still praying, **heaven was opened.** Whenever that happened in Scripture, either God manifested Himself in some way, spoke, or both. In Ezekiel 1:1, "the heavens were opened and [Ezekiel] saw visions of God." Stephen "gazed intently into heaven and saw the glory of God, and Jesus standing at the right hand of God" (Acts 7:55), and cried out, "Behold, I see the heavens opened up and the Son of Man standing at the right hand of God" (v. 56). In Revelation 19:11, the apostle John "saw heaven opened, and behold, a white horse, and He who sat on it is called Faithful and True, and in righteousness He judges and wages war." At Christ's baptism, as at the transfiguration and in John 12:28, God spoke from heaven. But before He did, another dramatic event occurred.

THE SPIRIT'S ANOINTING

and the Holy Spirit descended upon Him in bodily form like a dove, (3:22*a*)

That **the Holy Spirit descended** and remained (John 1:32–33) **upon** Jesus does not imply that up to this point He did not have the Holy Spirit. The members of the Trinity have been eternally in communion with each other with no breach in their essential unity. Jesus and the

Holy Spirit have always been in perfect communion, so much so that Romans 8:9 calls the Holy Spirit the Spirit of Christ (cf. Acts 16:7; Gal. 4:6; Phil. 1:19; 1 Peter 1:11). The Spirit's descent here was merely a symbolic act, indicating publicly His empowerment for Jesus' life and ministry.

A way to understand this empowerment is to consider that the Son "emptied Himself" (Phil. 2:7) of the personal prerogative in the use of His divine attributes and allowed Himself to submit to the will of the Father and the power of the Spirit. In effect, the Spirit mediated between our Lord's divine and human natures.

Beginning with His miraculous conception (Luke 1:35; cf. Matt. 1:18, 20), the Spirit was involved in every aspect of Christ's life (cf. 4:1, 14; 10:21; Matt. 4:1; 12:28; Acts 10:38; Heb. 9:14). The Old Testament records many instances of the Spirit coming upon individuals to anoint them for special service, including Moses (Num. 11:17), Joshua (Num. 27:18), the seventy elders of Israel (Num. 11:25), Gideon (Judg. 6:34), Jephthah (Judg. 11:29), Samson (Judg. 13:25), Saul (1 Sam. 10:1, 6), David (1 Sam. 16:13), Elijah (1 Kings 18:12; 2 Kings 2:16), Azariah (2 Chron. 15:1), Zechariah (2 Chron. 24:20), Ezekiel (Ezek. 2:1–2), and Micah (Mic. 3:8). All those men, however, were limited in their ability to be empowered by the Spirit by their sinful, fallen human natures. But since Jesus was God in human flesh, God gave Him the Spirit without measure (John 3:34).

The Old Testament also taught that God would give the Spirit to the Messiah. Isaiah 11:1–2 predicted that "the Spirit of the Lord will rest on Him." In Isaiah 42:1, God said of the Messiah, "Behold, My Servant, whom I uphold; My chosen one in whom My soul delights. I have put My Spirit upon Him," while in Isaiah 61:1–2 the Messiah says,

> The Spirit of the Lord God is upon me, because the Lord has anointed me to bring good news to the afflicted; He has sent me to bind up the brokenhearted, to proclaim liberty to captives and freedom to prisoners; to proclaim the favorable year of the Lord and the day of vengeance of our God; to comfort all who mourn.

Throughout Christ's entire life, including His development (Luke 2:52), sinless obedience, triumph over temptation, preaching, healing, casting out demons, death (cf. Heb. 9:14), and resurrection (cf. Rom. 1:4), His deity was mediated to His humanity by the Holy Spirit. The Spirit's power was essential—in His humanity Christ would not have done the miraculous deeds He did, or say the divine words He spoke. The reason for that is found in Philippians 2:6–7, which says that "although [Christ] existed in the form of God, [He] did not regard equality with God a thing to be grasped, but emptied Himself, taking the form of a bond-servant, and being made in the likeness of men." Jesus voluntarily surrendered the independent use of His divine power, and submitted Himself completely to the will of the Father. And though His human nature was sinlessly perfect, it nevertheless did not have supernatural power. Thus Christ performed His miraculous deeds through the Spirit's power, so much so that to attribute His works to Satan is to blaspheme the Holy Spirit (Matt. 12:31–32). It must be stressed that that in no way limits Christ's full deity and equality with the Father (cf. Col. 2:9). But in the wonder and mystery of the incarnation, He set aside the independent use of His divine attributes.

That the Spirit **descended upon** Jesus **in bodily form like a dove** does not, as is commonly assumed, mean that the Spirit appeared in the physical form of a dove. The phrase does not describe a birdlike visible manifestation of the Spirit's presence, but rather that visible manifestation's manner of movement as it descended upon Jesus. "What was visible was not a dove, but rather what was seen is compared to a dove,... The manner of the Spirit's descent was like the way a dove floats gracefully through the air" (Darrell L. Bock, *Luke 1:1–9:50*, Baker Exegetical Commentary on the New Testament [Grand Rapids: Baker, 1994], 338). The visible reality of the Spirit's presence indicates His approval of and involvement in the Son's ministry.

The Father's Testimony

and a voice came out of heaven, "You are My beloved Son, in You I am well-pleased." (3:22b)

Grammatically, this is the main clause of the passage, and the ones that have preceded it are subordinate to it. The Father's testimony to the Son is the primary point of the passage. The Father's audible **voice** from **heaven** expressed His approval of His **beloved Son,** in whom He is continually **well-pleased.** The Father's expression of approval protects Jesus from any misunderstanding as to why He was baptized (see the discussion earlier in this chapter). If Jesus were not sinless, He would not have had God's approval, since His "eyes are too pure to approve evil, and [He] can not look on wickedness with favor" (Hab. 1:13).

As He did here, the Father would once again audibly state His approval of the holy perfection of Jesus at the transfiguration (Matt. 17:1–5). His reference to Jesus as His Son affirms that Jesus is of the same essence as Himself, and thus fully God (see the discussion of 2:49 in chapter 16 of this volume). It is also the fulfillment of Psalm 2:7, where God says to the Messiah, "You are My Son, today I have begotten You."

To have the Spirit descend on Him and the Father express love and approval for Him was the most auspicious way for Jesus to launch His public ministry. Their public confirmation should have been more than enough to compel belief in Jesus as the Messiah. Sadly, however, such was not to be the case. In spite of such manifest testimony and all the mighty words and works that followed, most of those there that day, along with the majority of the Jewish people, would ultimately reject Jesus and demand that He be crucified. But His sinless life and sacrificial death brings salvation to "as many as received Him, to [whom] He gave the right to become children of God, even to those who believe in His name" (John 1:12).

The Messiah's Royal Lineage
(Luke 3:23–38)

21

When He began His ministry, Jesus Himself was about thirty years of age, being, as was supposed, the son of Joseph, the son of Eli, the son of Matthat, the son of Levi, the son of Melchi, the son of Jannai, the son of Joseph, the son of Mattathias, the son of Amos, the son of Nahum, the son of Hesli, the son of Naggai, the son of Maath, the son of Mattathias, the son of Semein, the son of Josech, the son of Joda, the son of Joanan, the son of Rhesa, the son of Zerubbabel, the son of Shealtiel, the son of Neri, the son of Melchi, the son of Addi, the son of Cosam, the son of Elmadam, the son of Er, the son of Joshua, the son of Eliezer, the son of Jorim, the son of Matthat, the son of Levi, the son of Simeon, the son of Judah, the son of Joseph, the son of Jonam, the son of Eliakim, the son of Melea, the son of Menna, the son of Mattatha, the son of Nathan, the son of David, the son of Jesse, the son of Obed, the son of Boaz, the son of Salmon, the son of Nahshon, the son of Amminadab, the son of Admin, the son of Ram, the son of Hezron, the son of Perez, the son of Judah, the son of Jacob, the son of Isaac, the son of Abraham, the son of Terah, the son of Nahor, the son of Serug, the son of Reu, the son of Peleg, the son of Heber, the son of Shelah, the son of Cainan, the son of Arphaxad, the son of Shem,

the son of Noah, the son of Lamech, the son of Methuselah, the son of Enoch, the son of Jared, the son of Mahalaleel, the son of Cainan, the son of Enosh, the son of Seth, the son of Adam, the son of God. (3:23–38)

There is a rising interest today in genealogy, as people attempt to trace their ancestry and uncover the famous and infamous in their family trees. For most it is purely recreational, a hobby motivated by simple curiosity. Some, however, do it out of a desire to bring meaning to their disconnected lives and build their sense of self-esteem. It makes them feel better about themselves to know that even if they are not significant, they are connected to someone who was.

In pursuit of their ancestors, people pore over census data, obituaries, and other historical records. Some even travel to the hometowns or countries of their forefathers to do research, making genealogy an expensive hobby for them. Others, such as Mormons, have a religious motive for tracking their genealogies, spending vast sums of money and time researching their ancestors so they can be baptized by proxy for them. That is a prerequisite for the spirits of the dead to enter the celestial kingdom, the highest level of heaven in their cultic pseudo-theology.

Genealogies were legitimately critical to the people of Israel. First, ancestry determined the original division of the land of Canaan among the twelve tribes (cf. Num. 26:53–55). Second, ancestry also established the right of inheritance to property and all that went with it (servants, crops, buildings, etc.). Third, ancestry formed the basis of the principle of kinsman redemption. If a poor man was forced to sell his property, one of his near relatives was to purchase it (Lev. 25:25; cf. Ruth 4:1–6). Fourth, ancestry played a role in taxation. Thus Joseph and Mary had to return to Joseph's ancestral city of Bethlehem to register for the census (cf. the exposition of 2:4 in chapter 12 of this volume). Fifth, ancestry determined one's eligibility to serve as a priest (cf. Ezra 2:61–62). Last, and most important, any claim to be king or Messiah would have to be backed up by the genealogical records.

Genealogies play a significant role in Scripture by rooting the biblical account in history. Because of their importance, the Jews kept very careful genealogical records, which survived until the Romans sacked Jerusalem and burned the temple in A.D. 70. In fact, the genealogies recorded by both Matthew and Luke are likely based on those public records, which were still in existence when they wrote. In addition to the official public records, many families undoubtedly kept private genealogical records. The Old Testament contains numerous genealogies (e.g., Gen. 4; 5; 10; 11; 1 Chron. 1–9). The New Testament also alludes to the availability of genealogical records. For example, Anna is identified as a member of the tribe of Asher (Luke 2:36), Barnabas as a member of the tribe of Levi (Acts 4:36 [cf. Luke 10:32]), and Paul as a member of the tribe of Benjamin (Rom. 11:1; Phil. 3:5). Also, as noted above, Joseph knew that he had to go to Bethlehem for the census "because he was of the house and family of David" (Luke 2:4).

Because of the significance of genealogies in the ancient world, Luke's readers would have understood why he included the genealogy of Jesus Christ. It was an essential credential for one claiming to be the Messiah to be a descendant of David. Luke has already given several credentials that establish irrefutably that Jesus is the Messiah. The account of John the Baptist's miraculous birth to an elderly, barren couple introduced His prophesied forerunner (Luke 1:17; cf. Isa. 40:3–4; Mal. 3:1). Then the angel Gabriel announced to a young virgin named Mary that she was to be the mother of the Messiah (Luke 1:31–33). When Mary visited her older relative Elizabeth, John the Baptist's mother, "Elizabeth was filled with the Holy Spirit. And she cried out with a loud voice and said, 'Blessed are you among women, and blessed is the fruit of your womb! And how has it happened to me, that the mother of my Lord would come to me?'" (vv. 41–43). Her husband, Zacharias, also filled with the Holy Spirit (v. 67), prophesied that John the Baptist would be Jesus' forerunner. The angels who announced His birth to the shepherds (2:8–11) testified that Jesus was Savior, Messiah, and Lord (v. 11). Two righteous and godly individuals, Simeon and Anna, also added their testimony that Jesus was the Messiah, the one who would bring salvation to Israel (2:25–38). In 3:1–18, Luke recorded John the Baptist's testimony to Jesus (see especially vv. 15–17). Then at His baptism, the Holy Spirit and God the Father gave the ultimate affirmation that Jesus is the Son of God, and thus the Messiah and the Savior of the world.

The genealogies of Jesus recorded by Matthew and Luke prove that He was not a self-appointed Messiah; a misguided reformer caught up in popular acclaim who began to have delusions of grandeur. Nor was He merely a good teacher of morality and ethics, or a revolutionary out to overthrow Rome's rule. His genealogies, tracing His ancestry back through David and Abraham to Adam and ultimately to God Himself, show that Jesus was Israel's rightful king.

A comparison of the genealogies in Matthew and Luke reveals marked differences. Some reflect the writers' different purposes. Matthew placed his genealogy at the beginning of his gospel where it fits chronologically into the life of Christ. Luke, however, inserted Christ's genealogy later in the context of His messianic credentials (see the discussion above). There are no women in Luke's genealogy, while Matthew includes five (counting Mary). Luke's genealogy goes from the present to the past; Matthew's from the past to the present. Thus Matthew's genealogy begins with Abraham and moves forward in time, while Luke's begins with Jesus and moves backward in time to Adam. Matthew's genealogy begins with Abraham, while the first name (chronologically) in Luke's is Adam. The different starting points in their genealogies reflect the different purposes of the two Gospel writers. Matthew wrote primarily to the Jewish people, so it was natural for him to begin with Abraham, the father of the nation of Israel. Luke's approach was more universal. He was concerned to present Jesus as the Son of Man, and demonstrate His solidarity with the entire human race. Therefore, he took Christ's genealogy all the way back to Adam. Matthew's emphasis on Joseph (Matt. 1:16, 18, 19, 20, 24; 2:13, 14, 19–21) and Luke's on Mary (Luke 1:27, 30–56; 2:5, 16, 19, 34) in the early chapters of their gospels also reflects their complementary strategies.

Luke's genealogy, therefore, was longer than Matthew's, containing seventy-seven names as opposed to forty-two names in Matthew's genealogy. Neither genealogy was intended to be exhaustive, but rather both are compressed or abridged. Matthew's genealogy contains three groups of fourteen names, which was evidently done to make it easier to memorize. (It should be noted that the term "father" in Matthew's genealogy does not necessarily denote a father-son relationship; it can be used in the more general sense of "ancestor." See for example Matthew 1:5; several generations must have elapsed between Salmon, the husband of Rahab, who lived during the Israel's conquest of the Promised Land under Joshua, and Boaz, who lived much later during the period of the judges. Note also verse 1 where Jesus is referred to as the son [i.e., descendant] of David and Abraham.) Luke's genealogy also skips generations. The repeated term **son** does not appear in the Greek text; in each pair of names the first named individual is merely said to be a descendant in some sense of the second one (cf. also v. 38; Adam obviously was not the son of God in a physical sense).

Other differences are more significant. Luke identifies Jesus' grandfather as **Eli,** while Matthew calls him Jacob. Luke traces Jesus' ancestry through David's son **Nathan,** while Matthew traces it through his son Solomon. Finally, while the names from Abraham to David are identical in both genealogies (except that Matthew skips Admin), all but two of the names from David to Joseph are different. Two possible explanations for those differences have been proposed.

Some hold that both genealogies are Joseph's, noting that Mary's name does not appear in Luke's genealogy and that the Jews traced ancestry through the father's genealogy, not the mother's (but as Leon Morris points out, "We have no information as to how a genealogy would be reckoned when there was no human father. The case is unique" [*The Gospel According to St. Luke,* The Tyndale New Testament Commentaries (Grand Rapids: Eerdmans, 1975), 100]). They explain Jesus' different grandfathers (Eli in Luke and Jacob in Matthew), as well as the different names from David to Joseph, by invoking the principle of levirate marriage (Gen. 38:8; Deut. 25:5–7; Ruth 4:10). According to this view, **Eli** and Jacob were half brothers, having the same mother, but different fathers. One of the two died childless, and the surviving brother married his widow. That would make Joseph the biological son of the surviving brother, and the legal son of the deceased.

Though plausible, that view is based largely on utterly unprovable conjecture (that Eli and Jacob were half brothers, and that a levirate marriage took place). A far better explanation is that Matthew records Joseph's genealogy and Luke Mary's (Luke omitted her name in deference to Jewish custom). The two different names given for Jesus' grandfather actually refer to two different men, Joseph's father, and Mary's father. The differences in the names from David to Joseph are also to be expected, since the genealogies are those of two different people. Mary traced her ancestry through Nathan, while Joseph traced his through Solomon. This view is also consistent with the purposes of the two writers, as noted above. Matthew's desire to prove Jesus' legal claim to the throne of David led him to include Joseph's genealogy. Luke addressed a broader, largely Gentile audience and thus gave Jesus' actual, physical descent through Mary. Finally, this view explains how Jesus could legitimately be Israel's king despite being a descendant of Jeconiah (Matt. 1:11). Jesus was the legal, but not physical, descendant of Jeconiah through Joseph. That avoided the curse that the Lord pronounced on Jeconiah, that none of his descendants would ever be king (Jer. 22:24–30). (For further evidence that Luke presents Mary's genealogy, see Robert L. Thomas and Stanley N. Gundry, *A Harmony of the Gospels* [Chicago: Moody, 1978], appendix 9.)

The genealogies in Matthew and Luke establish beyond doubt that Jesus was a descendant of David. Not even His bitter enemies among the Jewish leaders denied that. They surely would have rejected His messianic claims out of hand had He not been, and silenced the crowds who enthusiastically cried out at the triumphal entry, "Hosanna to the Son of David" (Matt. 21:9). But the genealogical records, which they undoubtedly carefully checked, provided irrefutable proof of Jesus' Davidic descent.

The remainder of this chapter will focus on four highlights from this passage: the start of Jesus' ministry, the supposition of His ancestry, the similarity of two of His ancestors, and the significance of four names from His genealogy.

THE START OF JESUS' MINISTRY

When He began His ministry, Jesus Himself was about thirty years of age, (3:23*a*)

Except for the incident at the temple when He was twelve (2:41–51), Jesus had spent His life up to this point in obscurity. He grew up in the small village of Nazareth, living in subjection to His parents and working with His father (cf. Matt. 13:55 with Mark 6:3). Jesus **began His** public **ministry** at His baptism (cf. Acts 1:21–22; 10:37–38), at which point He **was about thirty years of age.** That was a customary age for men of God to begin their ministries. Ezekiel began his prophetic ministry at age thirty (Ezek. 1:1). Joseph was also thirty years old when he became the prime minister of Egypt (Gen. 41:46), and David was thirty when he ascended to Israel's throne (2 Sam. 5:4). Thirty was also the age at which the priests began to serve (Num. 4:3, 35, 39, 43, 47; 1 Chron. 23:3). Jesus thus began His public ministry at an age that people would consider appropriate.

THE SUPPOSITION OF JESUS' ANCESTRY

being, as was supposed, the son of Joseph, (3:23*b*)

This brief phrase is of profound theological significance. It **was** commonly **supposed** that Jesus was **the son of Joseph,** understandably so since as far as most people knew, Jesus was just one of Joseph and Mary's children (cf. Matt. 13:54–56). But that supposition was incorrect, and He was physically only the son of Mary. That affirms the reality of His virgin conception and birth (see the exposition of 1:34–38 in chapter 5 of this volume). The Greek text makes it clear that Joseph is not part of Luke's genealogy. All the other names are preceded by the definite article *tou,* but **Joseph** is not, thus indicating that the mention of his name is parenthetical. The phrase could be more accurately rendered, "Jesus ... being (as was supposed the son of Joseph) the son of Eli"; that is, the grandson of Eli through Mary. This is another compelling reason for viewing Luke's genealogy as Mary's. How could this be Joseph's genealogy when Luke's grammar makes it clear that Joseph was not part of it? Further, as R. C. H. Lenski points out,

> How Luke could think of appending a genealogy of Joseph after saying that Jesus was only *supposed* to be a son of Joseph, i.e., a physical son, Luke himself having shown at length that this supposition was wrong, and that Jesus was a physical son only of Mary, has yet to be made clear by those who find the genealogy of Joseph here. (*The Interpretation of St. Luke's Gospel* [Minneapolis: Augsburg, 1946],

218–19. Italics in original.)

THE SIMILARITY OF TWO ANCESTORS

Zerubbabel . . . Shealtiel (3:27)

The names from **Eli** (v. 23) to **Rhesa** (v. 27) and from **Neri** (v. 27) to **Mattatha** (v. 31) do not appear anywhere else in Scripture. All that can be said of them is that they were common Jewish names of the time. The names of **Zerubbabel** and **Shealtiel** sandwiched in between are known; in fact, they are the only two names after David's time that are common to both the genealogies of Luke and Matthew. It is possible that the names refer to different individuals, and that there was a father named Shealtiel and a son named Zerubbabel in both genealogies. Or a levirate marriage may account for their presence in both genealogies. **Zerubbabel** himself may have been the child of a levirate marriage, since 1 Chronicles 3:19 lists Pedaiah as his father, while the Old Testament elsewhere calls him the son of Shealtiel (e.g., Ezra 3:2; Neh. 12:1; Hag. 1:1), the brother of Pedaiah (1 Chron. 3:17–18). Similarly, Luke refers to **Neri** as the father of Shealtiel, while 1 Chronicles 3:17 lists Jeconiah as his father. Again, this is either another case of levirate marriage, or adoption.

THE SIGNIFICANCE OF FOUR NAMES

Four names in the genealogy sum up the person of Jesus Christ. As a **son of God** (v. 38*b*) by creation, Adam bore His image unspoiled, unpolluted, and uncorrupted until he fell into sin. That sin marred the image of God, so that none of Adam's descendants were true sons of God in the same manner that he had been before he sinned. Jesus in His humanity, however, was a man as Adam had been before the fall; sinless, and perfectly bearing the image of God. Moreover, Jesus was the Son of God in His deity, being of the same essence as the Father (Phil. 2:6; Col. 2:9).

As **the son of Adam** (v. 38*b*), Jesus was fully human, and because of that "we do not have a high priest who cannot sympathize with our weaknesses, but One who has been tempted in all things as we are, yet without sin" (Heb. 4:15).

As **the son of Abraham** (v. 34), Jesus is the seed promised to the patriarch (Gal. 3:16), in whom the promised blessings of the Abrahamic covenant will be realized.

Finally, as the **son of David** (v. 31), Jesus "will reign forever and ever" (Rev. 11:15; cf. Luke 1:33).

His royal ancestry, confirmed by both of His parents' genealogies, is yet another proof of Jesus' messianic credentials.

The Temptation of the Messiah (Luke 4:1–13)

22

Jesus, full of the Holy Spirit, returned from the Jordan and was led around by the Spirit in the wilderness for forty days, being tempted by the devil. And He ate nothing during those days, and when they had ended, He became hungry. And the devil said to Him, "If You are the Son of God, tell this stone to become bread." And Jesus answered him, "It is written, 'Man shall not live on bread alone.'" And he led Him up and showed Him all the kingdoms of the world in a moment of time. And the devil said to Him, "I will give You all this domain and its glory; for it has been handed over to me, and I give it to whomever I wish. Therefore if You worship before me, it shall all be Yours." Jesus answered him, "It is written, 'You shall worship the Lord your God and serve Him only.'" And he led Him to Jerusalem and had Him stand on the pinnacle of the temple, and said to Him, "If You are the Son of God, throw Yourself down from here; for it is written, 'He will command His angels concerning you to guard you,' and, 'On their hands they will bear you up, so that you will not strike your foot against a stone.'" And Jesus answered and said to him, "It is said, 'You shall not put the Lord your God to the test.'" When the devil had finished every temptation, he left Him until an opportune time. (4:1–13)

There are many ways to verify the truthfulness of Scripture. There is secular ancient history and archaeology that corroborates the biblical record. The Bible also contains hundreds of prophecies that were fulfilled exactly as predicted. Despite being written before the age of modern scientific discoveries, the Bible is completely accurate when it discusses scientific matters. The book of Job, written during the patriarchal period, says that God "stretches out the north over empty space and hangs the earth on nothing" (Job 26:7). Commenting on the scientific implications of that statement, Henry M. Morris writes,

> Job was saying that the north-pointing axis of the earth extended indefinitely beyond the boundaries of earth's surface, pointing to the polar star and orienting both the geography of the earth and the corresponding starscape of the stellar heavens.... Furthermore, the earth was not resting on the shoulders of Atlas or on the back of a cosmic elephant.... Suspended in the formless void of space without support, the earth is rigidly maintained in its orbit by a mysterious force we call gravity, but which could just as rationally be called nothing—or perhaps better, the will of God. (*The Remarkable Record of Job* [Grand Rapids: Baker, 1988], 40)

But the most compelling proof of the Bible's truthfulness is the person of the Lord Jesus Christ. Every character devised by fallen, finite human minds is somehow flawed. It is utterly impossible that mankind could invent Jesus as He is portrayed on the pages of Scripture. He is absolutely, sinlessly perfect; His wisdom is unerringly profound; His understanding of human nature unparalleled; His response to every situation He faced perfectly consistent with the nature of God. It is also inconceivable that Satan and the demons could have invented the story of Jesus to deceive the human race. Absolute evil cannot create absolute good. And why would demons or humans invent a person who defeats and ultimately destroys them?

The perfection of the Lord Jesus Christ is nowhere more evident than in the story of His confrontation with the archenemy of God, Satan. The devil assaulted Him with wave after wave of temptations, seeking to lure Him into sin and derail the plan of redemption. But Jesus defeated him, demonstrating the power He had to "destroy the works of the devil" (1 John 3:8) through His death and resurrection. His victory over Satan in the wilderness laid the groundwork for His later triumphs at Gethsemane, Calvary, and the grave. Without His victory over the devil's temptations, Christ's messianic credentials would not have been complete. If He was not able to defeat Satan in a head to head confrontation, He would not be able to redeem sinners.

But Jesus was not only the divine Son of God, but also the fully human son of Adam (Luke 3:38). It was in His humanity that Jesus endured the onslaught of temptation, "for God cannot be tempted by evil" (James 1:13). The question arises as to whether or not Jesus was impeccable; that is, not able to sin. Obviously, Jesus did not sin; He "knew no sin" (2 Cor. 5:21), "committed no sin" (1 Peter 2:22), and "in Him there is no sin" (1 John 3:5; cf. Heb. 4:15; 7:26; John 8:46). Some theologians, however, believe that He could have sinned, even though He did not. But the union of Christ's divine and human natures precludes the possibility of Jesus having sinned, as Wayne Grudem notes:

> If Jesus as a person had sinned, involving both his human and divine natures in sin, then God Himself would have sinned, and he would have ceased to be God. Yet that is clearly impossible because of the infinite holiness of God's nature. Therefore if we are asking if it was *actually* possible for Jesus to have sinned, it seems that we must conclude that it was not possible. The union of his human and divine natures in one person prevented it. (*Systematic Theology* [Grand Rapids: Zondervan 1994], 538–39. Italics in original.)

But even though Jesus could not sin, that does not mean the temptations He faced were not genuine; their reality did not depend on His ability to respond. Actually, since He never yielded to them, He endured their full force. Temptation was, therefore, more real for Him than for those who yield to it. It could be so intense that it made His "sweat [become] like drops of blood, falling down upon the ground" (Luke 22:44).

Comparing Adam's temptation with that of Jesus reveals some obvious differences and makes Jesus' victory over His temptation all the more remarkable. Adam faced temptation in the best possible surroundings, the garden of Eden. Jesus faced temptation in the worst imaginable setting—the wasteland of the Judean desert. Adam lived in the sinless perfection of the pre-fall world. Jesus lived in a sinful, fallen world. No overwhelming buildup of temptation lured Adam into sin, because he yielded to the first temptation he faced. Jesus, on the other hand, faced repeated temptations over the first thirty years of His life (Heb. 4:15), and intense temptation during the forty days before the final three recorded here. Adam feasted on all the lush provisions the garden had to offer. Jesus was weakened by forty days of fasting. In the best of circumstances, Adam fell; in the worst imaginable circumstances, Jesus did not. The consequences of Adam's fall to temptation were lethal to the human race; the consequences of Jesus' triumph over temptation were life-giving.

Jesus' conflict with Satan unfolds in three scenes: the preparation for the battle, the pattern of the battle, and the postmortem on the battle.

THE PREPARATION FOR THE BATTLE

Jesus, full of the Holy Spirit, returned from the Jordan and was led around by the Spirit in the wilderness for forty days, being tempted by the devil. And He ate nothing during those days, and when they had ended, He became hungry. (Luke 4:1–2)

After His baptism **Jesus** left the vicinity of the **Jordan,** impelled (Mark 1:12) by the **Holy Spirit. Full** (*plērēs*) means, "to be saturated with" or "to be permeated thoroughly with." John 1:14 records that Jesus was also "full (*plērēs*) of grace and truth." Luke has already noted that John the Baptist (1:15), Elizabeth (1:41), and Zacharias (1:67) were filled with the Spirit. On the day of Pentecost the 120 believers gathered in the upper room "were all filled with the Holy Spirit" (Acts 2:4). As he gave his defense before the Sanhedrin, Peter was "filled with the Holy Spirit" (4:8). The believers who gathered to hear Peter and John after their release "were all filled with the Holy Spirit" (4:31). The seven men chosen to serve in the early church were men "full of the Spirit" (6:3). Among them was "Stephen, a man full of faith and of the Holy Spirit" (v. 5). Later, on trial before the Sanhedrin, Stephen, "being full of the Holy Spirit . . . gazed intently into heaven and saw the glory of God, and Jesus standing at the right hand of God" (7:55). Acts 11:24 characterized Barnabas as "a good man, and full of the Holy Spirit." After his conversion on the road to Damascus, Paul was "filled with the Holy Spirit" (9:17), as he was when he confronted a false prophet on the island of Cyprus (13:9).

Being filled with the Spirit is the constant goal and lifelong pursuit of all believers (Eph. 5:18). But Jesus lived His entire life totally filled with and controlled by the Holy Spirit. He was, in His humanity, fully yielded to the Spirit's control, having voluntarily set aside the use of His divine attributes (see the discussion of 3:22 in chapter 20 of this volume). Jesus' submission to the Holy Spirit caused Him to always do the Father's will. His temptation did not result from His making wrong choices that left Him in a vulnerable situation. It did not result from Him straying from God's will; on the contrary, it was the will of God that He face and defeat the devil. For that purpose Jesus was literally driven into the wilderness by the Spirit (Mark 1:12) and then **was led around by the Spirit in the wilderness for forty days.**

As noted in the exposition of 3:2–3 in chapter 17 of this volume, **the wilderness** of Judea, where Jesus was most likely **tempted,** was the most barren, desolate region in all of Israel. Scarred by precipitous cliffs, deep ravines, and tumbled boulders, it was a region so barren that animals could not be pastured in it. In this remote, largely uninhabited area, Jesus might be more alone than anywhere else in Israel.

Luke had already noted the presence of evil in the world. The angel Gabriel told Zacharias that John the Baptist would "turn many of the sons of Israel back to the Lord their God" (1:16), indicating they had wandered from Him into sin. In 1:79, Zacharias spoke of "those who sit in darkness and the shadow of death." The sordid tale of Herod's sinful marriage to Herodias and his imprisonment of John the Baptist (3:19–20) provided an example of human wickedness and depravity. But here for the first time in his gospel, Luke gave evil a face, by introducing the **devil.**

The **devil** (*diabolos;* "slanderer" or "accuser") is Satan ("adversary"). Originally a holy angel ("Lucifer" according to Isa. 14:12 [NKJV]), the highest of all created beings, "blameless in [his] ways from the day [he was] created until unrighteousness was found in [him]" (Ezek. 28:15), he became arrogant, and in his pride sought to "raise [his] throne above the stars of God" (Isa. 14:13) and thus "make [himself] like the Most High" (v. 14; cf. Ezek. 28:11–15). As a result of his sin, Satan was cast out of heaven, apparently along with one third of the angels, who chose to join him in his rebellion (Rev. 12:4). The Bible describes him as a liar and a murderer (John 8:44), a dragon (Rev. 12:3–17), a snake (Gen. 3:1; Rev. 12:9; 20:2), the accuser (Rev. 12:10), the evil one (John 17:15), the god of this world (cf. John 12:31) who blinds the minds of the unbelieving (2 Cor. 4:4), the prince of the power of the air (Eph. 2:2), a roaring lion (1 Peter 5:8), and the tempter (1 Thess. 3:5), who succeeded in luring Adam and Eve, and through them the entire human race, into sin. Satan attempted to destroy the second Adam, Jesus Christ, in hopes of thwarting God's plan of redemption.

As noted above, Satan had tempted Jesus throughout His life, and intensely during the previous **forty days.** Adding to the fervency of the onslaught was the fact that the Lord had eaten **nothing during those days.** Finally, **when they had ended,** it was obvious **He became hungry.** Sensing that in His physically weakened state Jesus might be especially vulnerable, Satan hit Him with three final and especially potent temptations.

THE PATTERN OF THE BATTLE

And the devil said to Him, "If You are the Son of God, tell this stone to become bread." And Jesus answered him, "It is written, 'Man shall not live on bread alone.'" And he led Him up and showed Him all the kingdoms of the world in a moment of time. And the devil said to Him, "I will give You all this domain and its glory; for it has been handed over to me, and I give it to whomever I wish. Therefore if You worship before me, it shall all be Yours." Jesus answered him, "It is written, 'You shall worship the Lord your God and serve Him only.'" And he led Him to Jeru-

salem and had Him stand on the pinnacle of the temple, and said to Him, "If You are the Son of God, throw Yourself down from here; for it is written, 'He will command His angels concerning you to guard you,' and, 'On their hands they will bear you up, so that you will not strike your foot against a stone.'" And Jesus answered and said to him, "It is said, 'You shall not put the Lord your God to the test.'" (4:3–12)

The specific temptations with which Satan assaulted Jesus were unique to Him. No believer today, for instance, could be tempted to turn rocks into bread, or to fly. Nevertheless, the temptations the Lord faced are representative of the broader categories of temptation faced by all believers. The satanic assault on the sinless Savior came in three waves.

SATAN TEMPTED CHRIST TO DOUBT GOD'S LOVE

And the devil said to Him, "If You are the Son of God, tell this stone to become bread." And Jesus answered him, "It is written, 'Man shall not live on bread alone.'" (4:3–4)

What **the devil said** to Jesus throughout these three climactic temptations contained an element of truth. Deception can only hope to succeed when combined with partial truth. **If** is better translated **since.** Satan's words to Eve, "Indeed, has God said" (Gen. 3:1) were intended to raise doubts in her mind. But knowing the futility of such an approach with Jesus, Satan began by acknowledging His true identity as **the Son of God.** (For a discussion of the significance of Jesus' being the Son of God, see the exposition of 2:49 in chapter 16 of this volume.)

Unlike liberal theologians, cultists, and other heretical groups, Satan and the demons never denied the deity of the Lord Jesus Christ. They had always known His true identity, and always affirmed it in their conversations with Him (e.g., 4:34, 41; 8:28; Matt. 8:29; Mark 1:34; 3:11). Satan's affirmation of that undeniable reality is the core of truth in this first solicitation to evil.

The devil's suggestion that Jesus command a **stone to become bread** was not a temptation to self-indulgence, for it is not a sin to eat food when one is hungry. Still less was it aimed at getting Jesus to pridefully show off His powers, since He and Satan were alone and there was no audience to perform for. Satan's point was far more insidious and subtle. He was aware that in the incarnation, Jesus had voluntarily set aside the independent use of His divine power. The devil was attempting (as he had with Eve) to get Him to distrust God's love and provision for Him. He insinuated that God was indifferent and disinterested in Jesus' plight. After all, had God not provided food for the stubbornly rebellious Israelites during their forty years of wandering in the wilderness? Had not David testified, "I have been young and now I am old, yet I have not seen the righteous forsaken or his descendants begging bread" (Ps. 37:25)? If the Father truly loved His Son, why had He failed to provide food for Him these past forty days? Satan hoped to entice Jesus to question the love of the Father and the care of the Holy Spirit. This was a serious assault not only on the deity and perfection of Jesus Christ, but also on the unity of the Trinity.

As He would with the other two temptations, the Lord replied to Satan's half-truths and lies with the absolute, undeniable truth of God's word. **Jesus answered** him, **"It is written** (in Deut. 8:3), **'Man shall not live on bread alone.'"** What sustains a person's life is not food, but obedience to "everything that proceeds out of the mouth of the Lord" (Deut. 8:3). Christ's point is graphically illustrated by the deaths of the disobedient Israelites, who eventually died in the wilderness because of God's judgment, despite His provision of food for them. Jesus would later tell His disciples, "My food is to do the will of Him who sent Me and to accomplish His work" (John 4:34). In the Sermon on the Mount, He said,

> Do not worry then, saying, "What will we eat?" or "What will we drink?" or "What will we wear for clothing?" For the Gentiles eagerly seek all these things; for your heavenly Father knows that you need all these things. But seek first His kingdom and His righteousness, and all these things will be added to you. (Matt. 6:31–33)

Paul expressed his unshakeable confidence in God's provision when he wrote, "My God will supply all your needs according to His riches in glory in Christ Jesus" (Phil. 4:19).

Jesus refused to act on His own initiative but, in complete trust of His faithful Father's love and the Spirit's care, chose to remain in submission to God's will. And in due time, the Father did provide for His physical needs, sending angels to provide food for Him (Matt. 4:11).

Like Jesus, believers are often tempted to doubt God's love for them. If He did love them, they reason, He would not have permitted whatever painful, disappointing circumstances they find themselves in. Sometimes their frustration is heightened by the realization that blatantly ungodly people seem to be prospering. They find themselves in agreement with the psalmist, who wrote,

> For I was envious of the arrogant as I saw the prosperity of the wicked. For there are no pains in their death, and their body is fat. They are not in trouble as other men, nor are they plagued like mankind. Therefore

pride is their necklace; the garment of violence covers them. Their eye bulges from fatness; the imaginations of their heart run riot. They mock and wickedly speak of oppression; they speak from on high. They have set their mouth against the heavens, and their tongue parades through the earth. Therefore his people return to this place, and waters of abundance are drunk by them. They say, "How does God know? And is there knowledge with the Most High?" Behold, these are the wicked; and always at ease, they have increased in wealth. Surely in vain I have kept my heart pure and washed my hands in innocence. (Ps. 73:3–13)

But like Jesus, Christians must refuse to act outside of God's will, but continually trust in His loving provision (cf. Ps. 37).

SATAN TEMPTED CHRIST TO DOUBT GOD'S PLAN

And he led Him up and showed Him all the kingdoms of the world in a moment of time. And the devil said to Him, "I will give You all this domain and its glory; for it has been handed over to me, and I give it to whomever I wish. Therefore if You worship before me, it shall all be Yours." Jesus answered him, "It is written, 'You shall worship the Lord your God and serve Him only.' " (4:5–8)

Having failed to persuade Jesus to doubt God's love for Him, Satan tried a different approach. After **he led Him up** onto a high mountain (Matt. 4:8), Satan **showed Him all the kingdoms of the world in a moment of time,** evidently by means of a perspective belonging only to supernatural beings or simply by looking as far as our Lord's eyes could see on the representative kingdoms in view. Then **the devil** made an astonishing proposal. **"I will give You all this domain and its glory,"** he said, **"for it has been handed over to me, and I give it to whomever I wish."** Satan's goal was to get Jesus to doubt God's plan for Him, and to bypass it. "Ask of Me, and I will surely give the nations as Your inheritance," the Father had promised, "and the very ends of the earth as Your possession" (Ps. 2:8; cf. Dan. 7:13–14). Yet Jesus was here in the middle of nowhere, with nothing more than the clothes on His back. And even worse humiliation was to follow: a life of poverty with "nowhere to lay His head" (Luke 9:58); rejection by His people (John 1:11); the agony in Gethsemane; an unjust, illegal trial; a brutal scourging followed by a painful death on the cross. Worst of all, He would be forsaken by the Father as He bore sin on the cross, which would cause Him to cry out, "My God, My God, why have You forsaken Me?" (Matt. 27:46).

Satan's proposal would have allowed Jesus to bypass all that suffering and enabled Him to take immediately what was rightfully His. Once again, the devil used a partial truth to bait the hook for his temptation. It is true that Scripture calls Satan the god or ruler of this world (John 12:31; 14:30; 16:11; 2 Cor. 4:4). That does not mean, however, that he literally possesses it, but rather that he is the ruler of the evil world system that dominates the nations of the world. It is God who determines the times of the nations' existence and their boundaries (Acts 17:26), and rules over them (1 Chron. 29:11; 2 Chron. 20:6; Pss. 22:28; 47:2, 7-8; Dan. 2:21; 4:17, 25; Rom. 13:1). Satan was a liar, pretending to offer what was not his to give. Nor would he have surrendered authority over the nations to Jesus even if he did have it; the devil's false promise was based on nothing but brash, astoundingly evil pride.

The condition Satan imposed on his offer uncovers his true motive. Brazenly, he said to Jesus, **"Therefore if You worship before me, it shall all be Yours."** It was his illicit lust for the worship that belongs to God alone that led to Satan's downfall and expulsion from heaven (cf. Isa. 14:13-14). He still desires to be worshiped, and proliferates false religions that ultimately are all some form of worship given to him (cf. 1 Cor. 10:20; Rev. 9:20). But the supreme coup would have been for Satan to persuade the Son of God to worship him. That would have achieved his original goal of elevating himself above God (Isa. 14:14).

Christians must beware of the temptation to lose faith in God's plan, particularly when they are enduring difficult circumstances. There are no shortcuts; God's way is always the best. His infinite wisdom guarantees that any plan of His is perfect and cannot be improved upon. Believers must, therefore, wait patiently for God to act on their behalf and refuse the temptation to take matters into their own hands (Pss. 37:1; 40:1; Heb. 6:12; James 5:7-8, 10).

Jesus emphatically rejected Satan's blasphemous suggestion, quoting again from Deuteronomy (6:13) as He had when faced with the devil's first temptation. **"It is written,"** He declared, **'You shall worship the Lord your God and serve Him only.'"** Jesus refused to step outside of God's plan. There would be no deal with the devil; no shortcut to glory. He would follow His Father's plan whatever the cost to Him.

SATAN TEMPTED CHRIST TO TRUST GOD PRESUMPTUOUSLY

And he led Him to Jerusalem and had Him stand on the pinnacle of the temple, and said to Him, "If You are the Son of God, throw Yourself down from here; for it is written, 'He will command His angels concerning you to guard you,' and, 'On their hands they

will bear you up, so that you will not strike your foot against a stone.'" And Jesus answered and said to him, "It is said, 'You shall not put the Lord your God to the test.'" (4:9–12)

His first two attempts to lure Jesus into sin had failed completely, but Satan made one final effort. (It should be noted that Matthew places this temptation second. As he often did with the material in his gospel, Luke arranged the temptations thematically rather than chronologically.) Taking Jesus **to Jerusalem,** Satan **had Him stand on the pinnacle of the temple.** That probably refers to the southeast corner of the temple complex, overlooking the Kidron Valley several hundred feet below. There the devil said to Jesus, **"If** (since) **You are the Son of God, throw Yourself down from here.**

Rebuffed twice by Jesus' quotes of Scripture, Satan now quoted Scripture himself. He even introduced his quotation with the very phrase Jesus had used: **"For it is written, 'He will command His angels concerning you to guard you,' and, 'On their hands they will bear you up, so that you will not strike your foot against a stone.'"** Since Jesus would not deviate from His obedience to the plan of God, Satan offered Him an opportunity to allow God to fulfill His word. The passage the devil quoted (Ps. 91:11–12) is from a messianic Psalm, where God pledges to protect the Messiah. The devil hoped that one of two things would happen if Jesus did jump. If He was killed by the fall, He would not die on the cross as a substitute for sin as the Old Testament predicted He would (Ps. 22; Isa. 53). Or by forcing God to miraculously deliver Him, Jesus would cease to be in submission to His plan and will. The essence of this final temptation was to presume on God, to back Him into a corner where He would be forced to act. But Jesus refused to act presumptuously. Instead, He countered Satan's twisting of the Scriptures by quoting Deuteronomy 6:16, which plainly commands, **"You shall not put the Lord your God to the test."**

This type of temptation is perhaps the most subtle and dangerous of the three, because it seemingly encourages people to exercise faith in God. In reality, it arrogantly, brazenly demands things from God, turning Him into a utilitarian genie who grants people's every whim. That false view of faith, promoted in its most extreme form by the so-called prosperity gospel (also known as the "name it and claim it" movement), in essence makes man sovereign. If the right formula is used, God has to respond. When He does not deliver the goods they have claimed by faith, however, many become disillusioned and abandon Him.

In contrast to that false, even blasphemous view of faith, true faith humbly submits to God's will. It prays, as Jesus taught, "Your will be done, on earth as it is in heaven" (Matt. 6:10; cf. Luke 22:42).

THE POSTMORTEM OF THE BATTLE

When the devil had finished every temptation, he left Him until an opportune time. (4:13)

Jesus' victory was complete over **every temptation** hurled at Him by **the devil** over the entire forty-day period. Defeated and dismissed by Jesus (Matt. 4:10), Satan **left Him until an opportune time.** Such times of temptation occurred throughout Jesus' earthly ministry. In Luke 22:28, Jesus said to the disciples, "You are those who have stood by Me in My trials." Satan would through Peter tempt Jesus once again to avoid the cross, resulting in the Lord's stern rebuke, "Get behind Me, Satan! You are a stumbling block to Me; for you are not setting your mind on God's interests, but man's" (Matt. 16:23). The devil would successfully tempt Judas to betray Christ (John 13:27).

Several lessons may be drawn from observing Satan's assault on Christ. First, he uses the same strategies to tempt believers that he used on Christ. He attempts to get them to distrust God's love, doubt His plan, and presume on Him, and will twist Scripture to do so. Second, Satan takes advantage of specific circumstances to launch his assaults. He tempted Jesus after the spiritual high point of His baptism, when the Spirit and the Father publicly affirmed Him. He also assaulted Jesus when He was physically weak after forty days without food and isolated from other people. Finally, along with watchfulness and prayer (Matt. 26:41), Scripture is the essential weapon believers must wield to defeat temptation. To do so effectively requires both knowledge of the Bible and a commitment to obey it.

To be successful in their struggle against temptation, believers must follow the pattern set by the Lord Jesus Christ. They must trust God's love, submit to His plan, and refuse to presume on His promises and grace. By doing so, they will successfully "resist the devil" and see him "flee from [them]" (James 4:7).

Jesus Returns to Nazareth
(Luke 4:14–30)

23

And Jesus returned to Galilee in the power of the Spirit, and news about Him spread through all the surrounding district. And He began teaching in their synagogues and was praised by all. And He came to Nazareth, where He had been brought up; and as was His custom, He entered the synagogue on the Sabbath, and stood up to read. And the book of the prophet Isaiah was handed to Him. And He opened the book and found the place where it was written, "The Spirit of the Lord is upon Me, because He anointed Me to preach the gospel to the poor. He has sent Me to proclaim release to the captives, and recovery of sight to the blind, to set free those who are oppressed, to proclaim the favorable year of the Lord." And He closed the book, gave it back to the attendant and sat down; and the eyes of all in the synagogue were fixed on Him. And He began to say to them, "Today this Scripture has been fulfilled in your hearing." And all were speaking well of Him, and wondering at the gracious words which were falling from His lips; and they were saying, "Is this not Joseph's son?" And He said to them, "No doubt you will quote this proverb to Me, 'Physician, heal yourself! Whatever we heard was done at Capernaum, do here in your hometown as well.'"

And He said, "Truly I say to you, no prophet is welcome in his hometown. But I say to you in truth, there were many widows in Israel in the days of Elijah, when the sky was shut up for three years and six months, when a great famine came over all the land; and yet Elijah was sent to none of them, but only to Zarephath, in the land of Sidon, to a woman who was a widow. And there were many lepers in Israel in the time of Elisha the prophet; and none of them was cleansed, but only Naaman the Syrian." And all the people in the synagogue were filled with rage as they heard these things; and they got up and drove Him out of the city, and led Him to the brow of the hill on which their city had been built, in order to throw Him down the cliff. But passing through their midst, He went His way. (4:14–30)

Through the first thirty years of His life, Jesus had lived in obscurity in Nazareth. The only recorded incident from those silent years is His visit to Jerusalem and dialogue with the teachers in the temple when He was twelve. Apart from that, nothing is known about His childhood years except for the general statement that He "kept increasing in wisdom and stature, and in favor with God and men" (2:52). The next recorded event in Jesus' life was His appearance at the Jordan River to be baptized by John the Baptist. After His baptism Jesus, at the direction of the Holy Spirit, spent forty days in the wilderness being tempted by Satan.

All that happened in His life up to this point in Luke's gospel—the testimony of Gabriel, the angels who appeared to the shepherds, Zacharias, Elizabeth, Mary, Joseph, Simeon, Anna, John the Baptist, Jesus' affirmation at age twelve that He was the Son of God, and His public attestation by the Father and the Holy Spirit at His baptism—had established His messianic credentials. The time had now come for Jesus to step onto the stage of His full public ministry.

This introductory scene in Luke's account of Jesus' public ministry takes place in His hometown of Nazareth. It may be divided into three sections: the setting, the message, and the reaction.

THE SETTING

And Jesus returned to Galilee in the power of the Spirit, and news about Him spread through all the surrounding district. And He began teaching in their synagogues and was praised by all. (4:14–15)

Like a small door that leads into a vast art gallery, verses 14 and 15 are the entrance to a new section of portraits of Jesus in Luke's gospel. They introduce Jesus' ministry in **Galilee,** the northern part of Israel, which the Lord would be engaged in for about a year and a half. During that time Jesus went **in the power of the Spirit** (cf. Acts 10:38 and the discussion of 3:22 in chapter 20 and 4:1 in chapter 22 of this volume) "from one city and village [there were 240 cities and villages in Galilee according to the first-century Jewish historian Josephus (*Life*, 45)] to another, proclaiming and preaching the kingdom of God" (8:1). Jesus' powerful preaching and the miracles He performed created a huge sensation, so that **news about Him spread through all the surrounding district** (cf. 5:15), and even south into Judea (7:17). At this early stage in His ministry Jesus **was praised by all.** Galilee was not a large region, and Jesus would have thoroughly blanketed it in the year and a half of His ministry there. Perhaps that is why, as some have speculated, the Lord's commission of the apostles in Acts 1:8 refers to Judea and Samaria, but not to Galilee. The Galilean ministry will be the focus of Luke's gospel from verse 14 through verse 50 of chapter 9 (cf. Matt. 4:13–18:35; Mark 1:14–9:50).

It might appear from reading Luke's account, as well as the parallel histories of Matthew (4:12) and Mark (1:14), that the Lord's ministry in Galilee began immediately after His baptism. That was not the case, however. There was an interval of about a year between Jesus' baptism and the beginning of His Galilean ministry. While the Synoptic Gospels are silent about that year, which Jesus spent ministering in Judea, the gospel of John describes it in detail (chapters 1–4).

In keeping with John's purpose in writing his gospel (John 20:31), his account of Jesus' Judean ministry focuses on revelations that Jesus is God. After His baptism and temptation, Jesus returned to the vicinity of the Jordan where John was continuing his baptizing ministry. When he saw Jesus, John exclaimed, "Behold, the Lamb of God who takes away the sin of the world!" (1:29). On the following day John pointed out Jesus to two of his disciples (Andrew and John) and repeated his declaration, "Behold, the Lamb of God!" (v. 36). "The two disciples heard him speak, and they followed Jesus" (v. 37). Later in that same section Philip introduced Nathanael to Jesus. Nathanael was startled by His greeting, "Behold, an Israelite indeed, in whom there is no deceit!" (v. 47). To Nathanael's question, "How do You know me?" Jesus gave an even more astonishing reply, one that revealed His omniscience: "Before Philip called you, when you were under the fig tree, I saw you" (v. 48). Overwhelmed by Jesus' supernatural knowledge of him, "Nathanael answered Him, 'Rabbi, You are the Son of God; You are the King of Israel'" (v. 49).

The Lord's reply to Nathanael displayed another attribute of God, transcendence:"'Because I said to you that I saw you under the fig tree, do you believe? You will see greater things than these.' And He said to him, 'Truly, truly, I say to you, you will see the heavens opened and the angels of God ascending and descending on the Son of Man'" (vv. 50–51). Jesus' divine transcendence provides access to heaven for those who believe in Him.

Before leaving for Judea, Jesus made a brief detour back into Galilee to attend a wedding (2:1–11). The site was the village of Cana, not far from His hometown of Nazareth. During the celebration the wine ran out, an egregious breach of etiquette that could have stigmatized the couple for the rest of their lives. After His mother came and asked Him to help, Jesus miraculously created wine, thus displaying another attribute of deity, omnipotence.

After a brief stay in Capernaum (2:12), Jesus went to Jerusalem to celebrate Passover (2:13). This marked the start of His ministry in Judea. The first recorded event of that ministry, the cleansing of the temple (2:14–17), introduced yet another of Christ's divine attributes, His holiness. His supernatural insight into those who expressed a shallow, false, nonsaving faith in Him once again revealed Jesus' omniscience (2:23–25).

John's account of the Judean ministry also focused on the message Jesus proclaimed. That message had two essential elements. First, He taught the necessity of regeneration, or the new birth. In His conversation with the prominent Jewish teacher Nicodemus, Jesus declared, "Truly, truly, I say to you, unless one is born again he cannot see the kingdom of God" (3:3). Then in verses 11–21, Jesus taught that regeneration is appropriated through believing in Him. The familiar words of verses 16–18 summarize that truth:

> For God so loved the world, that He gave His only begotten Son, that whoever believes in Him shall not perish, but have eternal life. For God did not send the Son into the world to judge the world, but that the world might be saved through Him. He who believes in Him is not judged; he who does not believe has been judged already, because he has not believed in the name of the only begotten Son of God. (3:16–18)

Finally, John reveals Christ's mission. His encounter with a Samaritan woman showed that Jesus came to be "the Savior of the world" (4:42; cf. 1 John 4:14), not merely of the Jews. After staying "two days [in the Samaritan village Jesus] went forth from there into Galilee" (v. 43).

Because of His extended ministry in Judea, "when He came to Galilee, the Galileans received Him, having seen all the things that He did in Jerusalem at the feast; for they themselves also went to the feast" (v. 45).

They had been exposed to Jesus' teaching and the miraculous signs He performed when they went to Jerusalem for Passover. They were ready for more.

Luke's note that **He began teaching in their synagogues** introduces the pattern and the priority of the Lord's ministry. The priority for Jesus was **teaching** God's Word (cf. Mark 1:38), and throughout Luke's gospel He is constantly portrayed as a teacher of God's truth (cf. 4:31; 5:3, 17; 6:6; 11:1; 13:10, 22; 19:47; 20:1; 21:37; 23:5). He is also frequently referred to as the Teacher (7:40; 8:49; 9:38; 10:25; 11:45; 12:13; 18:18; 19:39; 20:21, 28, 39; 21:7; 22:11).

The numerous **synagogues** that existed in Galilee provided the perfect venue for Jesus' teaching. Since the minimum number of Jewish men required to form a synagogue was ten, most, if not all, of the 240 cities and villages in Galilee would have had at least one. Some of the larger cities may have had dozens of them (according to the Jerusalem Talmud there were 480 in Jerusalem, though that number is disputed). Synagogues were usually built out of stone, and typically faced Jerusalem. They existed primarily for instruction in the Scriptures. In a synagogue Sabbath service, a passage from the Old Testament would be read, followed by a teacher explaining its meaning to the congregation.

The synagogues were by no means considered a replacement for the Jerusalem temple, which was the heart and soul of Judaism. Only at the temple could the sacrifices prescribed in the law of Moses be offered and the feasts and ceremonies celebrated, not in the synagogues (there are no Old Testament references to synagogues). But after the Babylonians destroyed the temple when they sacked Jerusalem in 586 B.C., the Jewish exiles began gathering in small groups to hear the teaching of God's Word (cf. Ezek. 8:1; 14:1; 20:1; 33:31). Those informal gatherings eventually developed into the synagogues of Jesus' time. The Jews of the Diaspora (those who lived outside of Palestine) lacked ready access to the rebuilt Jerusalem temple. Thus they too built synagogues, as the book of Acts indicates (9:2, 20; 13:5, 14; 14:1; 17:1, 10, 17; 18:4, 19). The apostle Paul, like Jesus, frequently preached the gospel in those synagogues (Acts 17:17; 18:4, 19; 19:8).

The synagogues had no full-time pastors or teachers; the policy known as the "freedom of the synagogue" allowed for anyone approved by the ruler of the synagogue to teach. Thus, if a noted teacher was available, he would likely be invited to preach, as was Paul (cf. Acts 13:14–15). In the absence of a guest teacher, any of the men in attendance who were approved to do so might teach. The synagogues were ruled by elders (cf. Mark 5:22), the chief of which was the *archisunagōgos*, or ruler of the synagogue (Luke 13:14; Acts 18:8). It was his responsibility to conduct the worship service and approve the teachers. There was another officer besides the ruler of the synagogue and the elders, the *chazzan*. He was the keeper of the scrolls on which the Scriptures were written (cf. v. 20) and was responsible for getting the proper scrolls out for each day's reading and returning them to the chest where they were stored. In addition to serving as places of worship, the synagogues also provided instruction for children, much like today's elementary schools, and served as local courts (cf. 12:11; Matt. 10:17).

The order of worship in a typical synagogue of Jesus' day may be reconstructed as follows:

1. Thanksgivings or "blessings" spoken in connection with (before and after), the *Shema*: "Hear, O Israel, the Lord our God, the Lord is One, and you shall love the Lord your God with all your heart, and with all your soul, and with all your might."

2. Prayer, with response of "Amen" by the congregation

3. Reading of a passage from the Pentateuch (in Hebrew, followed by translation into Aramaic)

4. Reading of a passage from the Prophets (similarly translated)

5. Sermon or word of exhortation

6. The Benediction pronounced by a priest, to which the congregation responded with "Amen." When no priest was present a Closing Prayer was substituted for the Benediction. (William Hendriksen, *New Testament Commentary: The Gospel of Mark* [Grand Rapids: Baker, 1975], 75–76)

Luke's account of Jesus' visit to the synagogue in Nazareth began with Him reading a passage from the prophets (in this case from Isaiah), and then giving the exposition.

THE MESSAGE

And He came to Nazareth, where He had been brought up; and as was His custom, He entered the synagogue on the Sabbath, and stood up to read. And the book of the prophet Isaiah was handed to Him. And He opened the book and found the place where it was written, "The Spirit of the Lord is upon Me, because He anointed Me to preach the gospel to the poor. He has sent Me to proclaim release to the captives, and recovery of sight to the

blind, to set free those who are oppressed, to proclaim the favorable year of the Lord." And He closed the book, gave it back to the attendant and sat down; and the eyes of all in the synagogue were fixed on Him. And He began to say to them, "Today this Scripture has been fulfilled in your hearing." (4:16–21)

Of the many events that Luke could have chosen to begin his account of Christ's ministry, he picked His visit to **Nazareth.** He did so because what Jesus said on this occasion identifies Him as the Messiah and perfectly defines His ministry. This first of two recorded visits by Jesus to the city where He grew up took place near the beginning of His Galilean ministry; the other visit, recorded by Matthew (13:54–58) and Mark (6:1–6), took place near its end.

Nazareth was located in a hollow in the Galilean hills, just north of the plain of Esdraelon, about half way between the Sea of Galilee and the Mediterranean Sea. It was an insignificant village in Jesus' day (it was not mentioned in the Old Testament, the Talmud, or by Josephus), overshadowed by the larger city of Sepphoris just to the north. It was in this insignificant, off the beaten path village that Jesus **had been brought up** (cf. the exposition of 1:26 in chapter 4 of this volume). Although He was born in Bethlehem and later made Capernaum His hometown (Matt. 4:13), Jesus remained associated with Nazareth throughout His ministry (4:34; 18:37; Matt. 21:11; 26:71; Mark 1:24; John 1:45; Acts 10:38; 26:9), being scornfully called, "Jesus of Nazareth."

As was His custom, Jesus **entered the synagogue on the Sabbath.** Wherever He was during His ministry, the Lord attended a synagogue on the Sabbath (cf. 6:6; 13:10; Mark 1:21; 3:1–2; 6:2). On this Sabbath, He was chosen **to read** from the Old Testament Scriptures. Out of respect for the Scriptures Jesus, as was customary, **stood** up to read. Alfred Edersheim captures the drama of the moment:

> As the lengthening shadows of Friday's sun closed around the quiet valley, He would hear the well-remembered double blast of the trumpet from the roof of the Synagogue-minister's house, proclaiming the advent of the holy day. Once more it sounded through the still summer air, to tell all, that work must be laid aside. Yet a third time it was heard, ere the "minister" put it aside close by where he stood, not to profane the Sabbath by carrying it; for now the Sabbath had really commenced, and the festive Sabbath-lamp was lit.
>
> Sabbath morn dawned, and early He repaired to the Synagogue where, as a Child, a Youth, a Man, He had so often worshipped in the humble retirement of His rank, sitting, not up there among the elders and the honoured, but far back. The old well-known faces were around Him, the

old well-remembered words and services fell on His ear. How different they had always been to Him than to them, with whom He had thus mingled in common worship! And now He was again among them, truly a stranger among His own countrymen; this time to be looked at, listened to, tested, tried, used or cast aside, as the case might be. It was the first time, as far as we know, that He taught in a Synagogue, and this Synagogue that of His own Nazareth. (*The Life and Times of Jesus the Messiah* [Grand Rapids: Eerdmans, 1974], 1:430–31)

As stood up to read, **the book** (scroll) **of the prophet Isaiah was handed to Him** by the *chazzan*. It evidently was not unrolled to any text, so Jesus **opened the book and found the place where it was written, "The Spirit of the Lord is upon Me, because He anointed Me to preach the gospel to the poor. He has sent Me to proclaim release to the captives, and recovery of sight to the blind, to set free those who are oppressed, to proclaim the favorable year of the Lord."** He read from two passages in Isaiah, 61:1–2 and 58:6. What Jesus read was, as His hearers were well aware, messianic prophecy. The phrase **the Spirit of the Lord is upon Me** reflects the reality again that Messiah would be empowered by the Holy Spirit (cf. the expositions of 3:22; 4:1, 14 earlier in this volume). He would be **anointed** by the Spirit, set apart, and empowered for special service, as Isaiah 11:2 reveals: "The Spirit of the Lord will rest on Him [Messiah; cf. v. 1], the spirit of wisdom and understanding, the spirit of counsel and strength, the spirit of knowledge and the fear of the Lord" (cf. 48:16).

Verse 18 succinctly summarizes the Messiah's ministry. Four metaphors depict the desperate condition of needy sinners whom God seeks to rescue from hell. Though the religious in this world may imagine themselves to be rich, free, healthy, and unhindered, until receiving the salvation that Christ brings, they are in reality poor, prisoners, blind, and oppressed. Those metaphors graphically depict their utter lack of any spiritual resources to extricate themselves from their deadly dilemma. Only through the Messiah's work of salvation can they be rescued from eternal punishment in hell.

First, Messiah would **preach the gospel to the poor.** The good news of the gospel is that the spiritually impoverished can find salvation. *Ptōchos* (**poor**) derives from a verb that means, "to cringe," "to shrink back," or "to cower." It conveys the idea of a beggar cringing in the shadows, cowering in shame. In contrast to another Greek word, *penēs*, which describes the working poor, *ptōchos* describes those in extreme deprivation who are reduced to begging, such as the beggar Lazarus (16:20). In spiritual terms, the **poor** are those who recognize that they have nothing by which to commend themselves to God (cf. 6:20; Matt. 5:3). They acknowledge their moral bankruptcy, that all their righteous deeds are nothing but a filthy garment (Isa. 64:6). Messiah can only bring salvation to those who acknowledge that they are spiritually destitute and that only God can supply their needs.

Spiritual poverty is not an act; it is not false piety or humility, but genuine. The spiritually poor are "humble and contrite of spirit" (Isa. 66:2); they are "brokenhearted" and "crushed in spirit" (Ps. 34:18). Possessing a "broken spirit" and a "broken and a contrite heart" (Ps. 51:17), they are like the repentant tax collector, who was "unwilling to lift up his eyes to heaven, but was beating his breast, saying, 'God, be merciful to me, the sinner!'" (Luke 18:13). It is such people, Jesus declared, whom God justifies (v. 14). In contrast the Lord rebuked the members of the Laodicean church for thinking that they were "rich, and [had] become wealthy, and [had] need of nothing," while in reality they were "wretched and miserable and poor and blind and naked" (Rev. 3:17).

While the economically poor are not in view here, such people are often fertile soil for the gospel (cf. 1 Cor. 1:26–29). Their desperate circumstances drive them to a level of despair that those who are well off do not always experience. For that reason Jesus declared that "it is easier for a camel to go through the eye of a needle than for a rich man to enter the kingdom of God" (Luke 18:25). James wrote, "Did not God choose the poor of this world to be rich in faith and heirs of the kingdom which He promised to those who love Him?" (James 2:5). Those whose circumstances in life offer them little hope are often more open to receiving the good news of the gospel.

Second, Messiah will **proclaim** spiritual **release to the captives.** Lost sinners imagine that they are free, and see Christianity as infringing on their right to be and do what they want to. But that is a tragic deception; sinners are not free. All sinners owe God an unpayable debt for violating His law (James 2:10; cf. Matt. 18:23–35), and are in bondage to "Him who is able to destroy both soul and body in hell" (Matt. 10:28). The lost are also in bondage to Satan (Eph. 2:1–2), "held captive by him to do his will" (2 Tim. 2:26). Satan uses their fear of death to enslave them (Heb. 2:14–15). They are also slaves of sin (Rom. 6:6, 16–20), since "everyone who commits sin is the slave of sin" (John 8:34).

The good news of the gospel is that God has sent His Son to free those who are in spiritual bondage. In Isaiah 42:5–7 God said to the Messiah,

> Thus says God the Lord, who created the heavens and stretched them out, who spread out the earth and its offspring, who gives breath to the people on it and spirit to those who walk in it, "I am the Lord, I have called you in righteousness, I will also hold you by the hand and watch over you, and I will appoint you as a covenant to the people, as a light to the nations, to open blind eyes, to bring out prisoners from the dungeon and those who dwell in darkness from the prison."

Aphesis (**release**) means "forgiveness" (it is so translated in 1:77; 3:3; 24:47; Matt. 26:28; Mark 1:4; Acts 2:38; 5:31; 10:43; 13:38; 26:18; Eph. 1:7; Col. 1:14; Heb. 9:22; 10:18). Messiah will set the prisoners free by paying the penalty for their violation of God's law. Through His sacrificial death God has "canceled out the certificate of debt consisting of decrees against us, which was hostile to us; and He has taken it out of the way, having nailed it to the cross" (Col. 2:14). As Charles Wesley expressed it in his magnificent hymn "O For a Thousand Tongues,"

> He breaks the power of cancelled sin,
> He sets the prisoner free.

Third, Messiah's mission was to provide **recovery of** spiritual **sight to the blind.** Spiritual blindness is the natural condition of fallen man. "They do not know nor do they understand; they walk about in darkness" (Ps. 82:5); they "have eyes but do not see" (Jer. 5:21). "This is the judgment," Jesus declared, "that the Light has come into the world, and men loved the darkness rather than the Light, for their deeds were evil. For everyone who does evil hates the Light, and does not come to the Light for fear that his deeds will be exposed" (John 3:19–20). In addition to their natural blindness, God judicially blinds the minds of unrepentant sinners. The apostle John wrote, "He has blinded their eyes and He hardened their heart, so that they would not see with their eyes and perceive with their heart, and be converted and I heal them" (John 12:40; cf. Rom. 11:8). Satan also "has blinded the minds of the unbelieving so that they might not see the light of the gospel of the glory of Christ, who is the image of God" (2 Cor. 4:4).

But the Messiah came "to open blind eyes" (Isa. 42:7). He is the "Sunrise from on high" (1:78) who will "shine upon those who sit in darkness and the shadow of death" (v. 79). Since He is "the light of the world (John 8:12; 9:5; cf. 3:19; 12:46) those who follow Him "will not walk in the darkness, but will have the Light of life" (John 8:12). Paul reminded the Corinthians that "God, who said, 'Light shall shine out of darkness,' is the One who has shone in our hearts to give the Light of the knowledge of the glory of God in the face of Christ" (2 Cor. 4:6). "You were formerly darkness," Ephesians 5:8 says, "but now you are light in the Lord" (cf. Col. 1:13). Paul was sent to the Gentiles "to open their eyes so that they may turn from darkness to light and from the dominion of Satan to God, that they may receive forgiveness of sins and an inheritance among those who have been sanctified by faith in [Jesus]" (Acts 26:18).

Finally, Messiah came **to set free those who are** spiritually **oppressed.** These are people overwhelmed by life's painful circumstances, especially the wearying burden of sin and the inability to keep

God's law (cf. 11:46; Matt. 23:4; Acts 15:10). Jesus promises such people, "Come to Me, all who are weary and heavy-laden, and I will give you rest. Take My yoke upon you and learn from Me, for I am gentle and humble in heart, and you will find rest for your souls. For My yoke is easy and My burden is light" (Matt. 11:28–30)."For this is the love of God," John wrote, "that we keep His commandments; and His commandments are not burdensome" (1 John 5:3).

Because Jesus had already been ministering for many months (as noted above in the discussion of His Judean ministry), these things were already happening. For the spiritually bankrupt, imprisoned by their sin and awaiting sentence by the Judge of all the earth (Gen.18:25), blind to the truth, and oppressed by the heavy burden of their sins, **the favorable year of the Lord** had come. The "day of salvation" (Isa. 49:8) and the "year of redemption" (Isa.63:4) had arrived.

Stopping His reading of Isaiah 61:2 in the middle of the verse, Jesus **closed the book, gave it back to the attendant and sat down.** It was a dramatic moment, and **the eyes of all in the synagogue were fixed on Him** wondering what His message would be. What He said was shocking, unexpected, and unprecedented: **He began to say to them, "Today this Scripture has been fulfilled in your hearing."** Other teachers had spoken of a future fulfillment of Isaiah's prophecy, but Jesus told them that they were witnessing its fulfillment before their eyes. Salvation had come; the messianic era had begun; the Messiah was present that day in the synagogue in the person of Jesus, a man from that very village.

The Reaction

And all were speaking well of Him, and wondering at the gracious words which were falling from His lips; and they were saying, "Is this not Joseph's son?" And He said to them, "No doubt you will quote this proverb to Me, 'Physician, heal yourself! Whatever we heard was done at Capernaum, do here in your hometown as well.'" And He said, "Truly I say to you, no prophet is welcome in his hometown. But I say to you in truth, there were many widows in Israel in the days of Elijah, when the sky was shut up for three years and six months, when a great famine came over all the land; and yet Elijah was sent to none of them, but only to Zarephath, in the land of Sidon, to a woman who was a widow. And there were many lepers in Israel in the time of Elisha the prophet; and none of them was cleansed, but only Naaman the Syrian." And all the people in the synagogue were filled

with rage as they heard these things; and they got up and drove Him out of the city, and led Him to the brow of the hill on which their city had been built, in order to throw Him down the cliff. But passing through their midst, He went His way. (4:28–30)

At first, the reaction of the people to Jesus' message was positive, as **all were speaking well of Him.** They were especially **wondering at the gracious words which were falling from His lips.** The audience was in awe of His unmatched speaking ability, as those who heard the Sermon on the Mount were (Matt. 7:28–29) and those sent to arrest Him (John 7:46) later would be.

Yet shockingly, that positive reaction would quickly be reversed, and the people would attempt to kill the familiar Jesus. No Sabbath had ever begun so wondrously, and no Sabbath ever ended so tragically. What went wrong? What changed their assessment of Jesus so radically?

Some, no doubt, were wondering why Jesus stopped His reading of Isaiah 61:1–2 in the middle of verse 2, omitting the reference to "the day of vengeance of our God." The Jewish people expected that when Messiah came, He would take vengeance on their enemies. John the Baptist had spoken of the unquenchable fire of Messiah's judgment (3:17), and even he became perplexed when Jesus showed no signs of executing vengeance on the wicked (7:19–20).

Others could not reconcile the stunning power of Jesus' oratory with the reality that this was **Joseph's son.** Familiarity breeds contempt, and all experts are from out of town. They resented His claim to be the Messiah, especially since according to popular belief Messiah would be unknown until He suddenly appeared to redeem Israel (John 7:27). How then could this man, whom they had known since He was a child, possibly be the Messiah?

But most of all, the people resented Jesus' assertion that salvation is available only to those who acknowledge themselves to be the poor, prisoners, blind, and oppressed. They were not about to accept such labels, since they viewed themselves as righteous. After all, they kept the law (at least outwardly); they honored the Sabbath, paid their tithes, observed the ceremonies, and performed the rituals. Besides, as the Jewish leaders proudly reminded Jesus, "We are Abraham's descendants and have never yet been enslaved to anyone" (John 8:33). Rather than acknowledge their spiritual poverty, sinful bondage, blindness, oppression, and need of a Savior, they questioned whether Jesus was really the Messiah. How could He be if He could not even distinguish the righteous from the wicked?

Reading their minds, Jesus said to them, **"No doubt you will quote this proverb to Me, 'Physician, heal yourself!'"** In other words, prove your claims to us. He knew they were thinking He should reveal His power, and were ready to challenge Him to verify His messiahship miraculously. They thought, **"Whatever we heard was done at Capernaum, do here in your hometown as well."** If He wanted them to accept His claim to be the Messiah, then let Him perform the same signs that had reportedly been done in nearby Capernaum.

The question, however, was not lack of evidence, but hardness of heart. There were never enough miracles to satisfy. No one in Israel, not even the leaders (John 11:47), ever questioned the reality of Jesus' miracles, but neither would they accept what they proved. Rather, they continually demanded more signs as a condition of their belief (Matt. 12:38; 16:1–4), or even attributed His miraculous power to Satan (Matt. 12:24). No amount of miracles would convince those whose minds were hardened. "But though He had performed so many signs before them," John wrote, "yet they were not believing in Him" (John 12:37).

Jesus understood that, humanly speaking, it was difficult for them to accept that someone they were so familiar with could really be the Messiah. Acknowledging that, He made the now proverbial truism, **Truly** (*amēn;* a word used to introduce important statements) **I say to you, no prophet is welcome in his hometown** (cf. Matt. 13:57; John 4:44).

Then Jesus made a brilliant transition. In effect He said to them, "Speaking of unwelcome prophets, what about Elijah and Elisha?" The phrase **I say to you in truth** reiterates the importance of what He was about to say. The Lord reminded them first that **there were many widows in Israel in the days of Elijah.** Elijah prophesied during the reign of Ahab, one of Israel's most wicked kings, who "did more to provoke the Lord God of Israel than all the kings of Israel who were before him" (1 Kings 16:33). Influenced by his pagan Gentile wife Jezebel, Ahab was a worshiper of the Canaanite deity Baal, and under his influence Baal worship flourished in Israel.

As God's judgment on the apostate nation, Elijah announced a drought, and **the sky was shut up for three years and six months** (cf. James 5:17), as a result of which **a great famine came over all the land.** The severe conditions were especially hard on widows, since the people who were responsible to care for them (cf. Ex. 22:22; Deut. 14:29; 16:11, 14; 24:17–21) were unable (or unwilling) to do so. **Yet** despite the proliferation of widows in Israel, **Elijah was sent to none of them, but only to Zarephath, in the land of Sidon, to a woman who was a widow.** This was not a story that the Jewish people liked to be reminded of. Jesus' hearers no doubt began to get uncomfortable, or even angry at Him for bringing it up. It was bad enough from their perspective that Elijah ministered to a Gentile widow instead of an Israelite. But **the land of**

Sidon was the homeland of the wicked queen Jezebel (1 Kings 16:31). This particular widow, however, was a believer in the God of Israel (1 Kings 17:12, 24). Jesus' point, which must have shocked and outraged the audience, was that God would save an outcast Gentile woman who admitted her poverty, bondage, blindness, and oppression (cf. 1 Kings 17:18), but not a Jew who would not. The implication was that if they refused to abandon their self-righteousness and admit their desperate spiritual need they could not be saved.

But Jesus was not through. To the rising anger of those gathered in the synagogue at such an indictment, He added another familiar and somewhat distasteful Old Testament story. This one involved Elijah's protégé and successor, Elisha. **There were many lepers in Israel in the time of Elisha the prophet,** Jesus reminded them, **and none of them was cleansed, but only Naaman the Syrian.** If anything, this was even more shocking than Elijah's ministry to a Gentile widow. **Naaman the Syrian** was not only a Gentile, but also a leper, and hence doubly an outcast (cf. Num. 5:2; 2 Kings 7:3–4). As if that was not enough, he was also an enemy military commander, the "captain of the army of the king of Aram" through whom "the Lord had given victory to Aram" (2 Kings 5:1). When Elisha told him he would be cured of his leprosy if he bathed in the Jordan River, Naaman was at first unwilling (vv. 10–12). Later, however, he humbled himself, obeyed the prophet's word, was cured, and acknowledged the God of Israel as the only true God (vv. 14–15).

Jesus' point was clear and unmistakable. God has brought salvation by His arrival—but, as always, it is only for those who know they are spiritually poor, prisoners, blind, and oppressed. Unless His hearers were willing to humble themselves like that outcast Gentile widow and that Syrian leper terrorist did and admit their spiritual need, they could not be saved. That was too much for their nationalistic pride and self-righteousness to bear, and consequently and suddenly **all the people in the synagogue were filled with rage as they heard these things; and they got up and drove Him out of the city, and led Him to the brow of the hill on which their city had been built, in order to throw Him down the cliff.** They were an out of control lynch mob, intent on killing the one whom they knew so well and who had taught them the truth of God's Word. But Jesus' time had not yet come (cf. John 7:30; 8:20), so **passing through their midst, He went His way.** At last, the mob got a miracle, if not the one they were looking for, as Jesus supernaturally escaped their attempt to murder Him (cf. John 7:30; 8:59; 10:39).

The proud people of Nazareth never did humble themselves, despite the Lord's miraculous escape from their grasp. When Jesus returned some time later, "He wondered at their unbelief" (Mark 6:6; cf. Matt. 13:58). Their refusal to admit their spiritual destitution, bondage, blindness, and oppression stands in stark contrast to the repentant Gentile widow and leper. It is a striking illustration of the truth that "God is opposed to the proud, but gives grace to the humble" (James 4:6).

By all considerations, our Lord's approach in the synagogue was not "seeker friendly," but bold, confrontive, denunciatory, and infuriating to the religious crowd—to the severest degree. They were so outraged they tried to kill Him. The truth about the sinner's condition is always least acceptable to the religious hypocrite.

Jesus' Authority over Demons (Luke 4:31–37)

24

And He came down to Capernaum, a city of Galilee, and He was teaching them on the Sabbath; and they were amazed at His teaching, for His message was with authority. In the synagogue there was a man possessed by the spirit of an unclean demon, and he cried out with a loud voice, "Let us alone! What business do we have with each other, Jesus of Nazareth? Have You come to destroy us? I know who You are—the Holy One of God!" But Jesus rebuked him, saying, "Be quiet and come out of him!" And when the demon had thrown him down in the midst of the people, he came out of him without doing him any harm. And amazement came upon them all, and they began talking with one another saying, "What is this message? For with authority and power He commands the unclean spirits and they come out." And the report about Him was spreading into every locality in the surrounding district. (4:31–37)

"There are two equal and opposite errors into which our race can fall about the devils," wrote C. S. Lewis. "One is to disbelieve in their existence. The other is to believe, and to feel an excessive and unhealthy interest in them. They themselves are equally pleased by both errors and hail a materialist or a magician with the same delight" (*The Screwtape Letters* [New York: MacMillian, 1977], 9). Our postmodern, post-Christian culture leans toward the latter error. A veritable flood of books and movies have introduced fantasy worlds of wizards, spirits, and alien beings. Ironically, research has documented that skeptics, irreligious people, and people in liberal churches are far more likely to believe in superstition, the paranormal, and pseudoscience than evangelical Christians. But even within Christianity reality and fantasy have merged to create a confusing and often unbiblical view of the demonic realm. Many believers, churches, and ministries are preoccupied with demons. They view virtually everything that goes wrong in a Christian's life as the direct result of demonic activity, the cure for which is to exorcise the demon or demons responsible. But believers cannot be possessed by demons, and need not be terrified by them (see the discussion of those points later in this chapter).

There is no confusion in the Bible regarding Satan and his demon hosts; it reveals clearly their origin, present activity, and destiny. Originally, they were holy angels, and Satan was the highest-ranking of all of them. They lived in heaven, where they served and worshiped God. But through pride Satan rebelled against God (Isa. 14:12–14; Ezek. 28:12–16), and one third (Rev. 12:3–4) of the holy angels joined him in the attempted coup. As a result of their pride and rebellion, they were cast out of heaven along with their leader (Luke 10:18), though they still are granted access to it (Job 1:6; 2:1). During the tribulation, after a climactic battle with Michael and the holy angels, Satan and the demons will be permanently cast out of heaven (Rev. 12:7–9).

In the present age, demons operate in the world to achieve the purposes of Satan and thwart the purposes of God. They are behind the evil world system that dominates the lives of all those who do not belong to God through faith in Jesus Christ. In John 8:44, Jesus declared that all unbelievers are children of Satan, while Ephesians 2:1–2 and 1 John 5:19 say that the whole unbelieving world is in Satan's power. Satan is the god or ruler of this world (John 12:31; 14:30; 16:11), who blinds unbelievers to spiritual truth (2 Cor. 4:4) and leads them to deception (2 Cor. 11:13–15).

Demons made their first and only appearance in the Old Testament in Genesis 6:1–4 (though they are alluded to in Lev. 17:7; Deut. 32:17; Ps. 106:37), where they possessed fallen men who cohabitated with women (cf. 2 Peter 2:4–5; Jude 6). In the New Testament, demonic activity is confined to the Synoptic Gospels and Acts (though Jesus was accused of being demon possessed in John 7:20; 8:48–52; 10:20–21; and demons are alluded to in 1 Cor. 10:20–21; 1 Tim. 4:1; James 2:19; 3:15; Rev. 9:20; 16:14; 18:2), as they made a supreme assault on Jesus and the apostles. They are real, personal, fallen spiritual beings who are wholly given to wickedness.

   This passage introduces a new theme in Luke's gospel. Up to this point, Luke has focused on the person of Christ, presenting His credentials as Messiah, Son of God, and Savior. Starting with verse 31 and running through chapter 5, Luke revealed Jesus' power in the spiritual and physical realms, over everyone and everything, including demons, religion and religious teachers, disease, nature, and even death. He began by discussing Jesus' power over demons for a very important reason. If Jesus is to free those held in bondage by Satan and his demon hosts, He has to be able to break their power over the souls of men to free them from the kingdom of Satan (cf. 2 Cor. 10:3–5; Col. 1:13; Heb. 2:14–15). It is precisely that power over the demonic realm that the Lord demonstrates in this passage.

   The evil spirits knew why Jesus had come. They also are well aware of the fate that God pronounced against them—everlasting torment in the "eternal fire which has been prepared for the devil and his angels" (Matt. 25:41). The incarnation of the Son of God, who came to save sinners (Matt. 1:21; Luke 19:10), intensified the age-long battle for the souls of men. In desperation, during His earthly ministry the evil spirits launched their most widespread and visible assault ever. Even so, whenever confronted by the incarnate Son of God, the demons reacted with sheer terror and often screamed out loud (v. 33; cf. Mark 1:23–25; 3:11; 5:1–7). They are compelled to believe the truth, and tremble in fear because of it (James 2:19).

   This passage reveals four things about Jesus that terrified the demons: His preaching, purpose, purity, and power.

His Preaching

And He came down to Capernaum, a city of Galilee, and He was teaching them on the Sabbath; and they were amazed at His teaching, for His message was with authority. In the synagogue there was a man possessed by the spirit of an unclean demon, and he cried out with a loud voice, "Let us alone! What business do we have with each other, Jesus of Nazareth? (4:31–34a)

   Jesus was above all a preacher. Matthew 4:17 records that at the outset of His Galilean ministry "Jesus began to preach and say, 'Repent, for the kingdom of heaven is at hand.'" Matthew 11:1 notes that "when Jesus had finished giving instructions to His twelve disciples, He departed from there to teach and preach in their cities." Shortly after the incident recorded in this passage Jesus declared, "I must preach the kingdom of God to the other cities also, for I was sent for this purpose" (Luke

4:43; cf. v. 18; Mark 1:38). Luke 8:1 finds Him "going around from one city and village to another, proclaiming and preaching the kingdom of God." Nearing the end of His earthly ministry Jesus was still "teaching the people in the temple and preaching the gospel" (Luke 20:1). Even after His resurrection Jesus preached a final sermon to His disciples (Luke 24:27). The Lord's example underscores the vital importance of expository preaching in the church.

Capernaum, Jesus' adopted hometown (Matt. 4:13), was **a city of Galilee,** located on the northwest shore of the Sea of Galilee. Its name means, "city of Nahum," but whether it was named for the Old Testament prophet Nahum is not known. Capernaum was a significant enough city to have had a Roman centurion and a detachment of soldiers stationed there (Matt. 8:5). That the centurion had been there long enough to have built a synagogue for the Jewish inhabitants (Luke 7:5) suggests that he was permanently assigned there. A royal official (most likely in the service of Herod Antipas) also lived in Capernaum (John 4:46). In Luke 10:15, Jesus rebuked its people for their exalted view of their city's importance: "And you, Capernaum, will not be exalted to heaven, will you? You will be brought down to Hades!" In fulfillment of the Lord's words, Capernaum was eventually destroyed so completely that its exact location is unknown. In addition to Jesus, several of the apostles were associated with Capernaum, including Peter and Andrew (Mark 1:21, 29), who moved there from Bethsaida (John 1:44), and Matthew, whose tax collector's booth was in or near the city (Matt. 9:1,9).

As was His custom (cf. the exposition of 4:15–16 in chapter 23 of this volume), Jesus **was teaching them on the Sabbath** in the synagogue. It may be that the Lord chose the same text in Isaiah 61:1–2 that He preached on earlier in Nazareth. Whatever His text was, the people who heard Him **were amazed at His teaching, for His message was with authority. Amazed** translates a form of the verb *ekplēssō,* which describes shock, amazement, or astonishment. The crowd in the synagogue was surprised by the power of Jesus' teaching and His absolute **authority.** Unlike the teachers they were used to hearing, Jesus did not quote other rabbis, but declared the Word of God. His teaching was powerful, true, delivered with great clarity, and produced tremendous conviction. But on this occasion, the convicting force of the Lord's preaching hit, strangely enough, a demon. **In the synagogue** that day **there was a man possessed by the spirit of an unclean demon. That demon,** as the Greek text indicates, literally indwelt him. That Luke describes the demon as **unclean** does not indicate he was an especially evil demon; all demons are unclean spirits (cf. 6:18; Matt. 10:1; 12:43; Mark 3:11,30; 5:2,8,13; 7:25; 9:25).

In the New Testament, the unique and bizarre behavior associated with demon possession was never confused with insanity. The demons were always rational when they spoke; they understood who Jesus was and that He was going to destroy them. Even when a demon addressed unbelievers he spoke rationally, saying to some would-be exorcists, "I recognize Jesus, and I know about Paul, but who are you?" (Acts 19:15).

Demon possession was a widespread phenomenon during the earthly ministry of the Lord Jesus Christ and, to a lesser extent, during the ministries of the apostles (cf. Acts 16:16–18). During the future time of tribulation, demonic activity will again increase dramatically. Some of the demons now bound in the bottomless pit will be released to join those already operating on earth and they will wreak havoc (Rev. 9:1ff.).

Four New Testament phrases describe demon possession. First, sixteen times such people are said to have a demon or evil spirit (v. 33; 7:33; 8:27; 13:11; Matt. 11:18; Mark 3:22; 30; 9:17; John 7:20; 8:48, 49, 52; 10:20; Acts 8:7; 16:16), indicating that a demon-possessed individual was indwelt, controlled, and tormented by the demon. The repeated phrases "entered him" (Luke 8:30), "cast out" (Matt. 8:16; 9:33; 12:24, 28; Mark 1:34), "came out" (Matt. 8:32), "come out" (Mark 5:8), and "coming out" (Mark 5:13) also indicate that demons indwell their victims. Demon possession is a supernatural phenomenon, not explicable in psychological or physical terms (though there can be physical symptoms associated with it; cf. Matt. 9:32; 12:22; 17:14–15; Mark 1:26; 5:5; Luke 8:27; 9:42). It should be noted too that on no occasion when Jesus delivered an individual from demon possession was there a reference to forgiveness of sins. Nor did all those delivered repent and believe. The demon-possessed individuals whom Jesus delivered were not necessarily any more wicked than other sinners. The emphasis is on Jesus' power over the demons, not on the individuals being delivered. But after Jesus and the apostles passed from the scene, the only way to be delivered from demons is through saving faith in the Lord Jesus Christ.

The second phrase translates the verb *daimonizomai,* which appears thirteen times in the New Testament (8:36; Matt. 4:24; 8:16, 28, 33; 9:32; 12:22; 15:22; Mark 1:32; 5:15, 16, 18; John 10:21), and is translated, "demon-possessed," or "demoniacs." Like the first phrase, it refers to someone indwelt and controlled by a demon or demons to the point that he cannot successfully resist, not to the general influence demons have in promoting false doctrine (1 Tim. 4:1), false worship (1 Cor. 10:20–21), immorality (1 Tim. 4:1–3), and attitudes of jealousy, divisiveness, and pride (James 3:13–16).

Third, the Bible speaks of those with an "unclean" spirit (Mark 1:23; 5:2) or having one (Mark 7:25). Those phrases also indicate that demons indwell their victims.

Finally, Acts 5:16 speaks of those "afflicted with unclean spirits," emphasizing the torment demon-possessed people suffer.

In Matthew 12:43–45, Jesus gave an illustration of demon possession. The demon-possessed person is likened to a house (v. 44), once
again showing that demons indwell their victims. For some unspecified
reason, this demon left his victim. It may be that he sought another more
suitable person to indwell, or that he was annoyed by the attempts of
exorcists (like the sons of Sceva in Acts 19:13–14) and decided to leave. It
may even be that he was cast out by Jesus from an individual who never
came to saving faith in Him. In any case, the demon left his victim, and
"passe[d] through waterless places seeking rest, and [did] not find it" (v.
43). But unable to find a better situation, the demon decided to return to
the "house from which [he] came" (v. 44). When he returned, the demon
found the house "unoccupied, swept, and put in order" (v. 44)—a reference to moral and religious reform apart from true salvation. That made
him an even more attractive host for the demon and his friends; demons
can more successfully disguise themselves as angels of light (2 Cor.
11:14–15) in outwardly religious people. The net effect was that "the last
state of that man becomes worse than the first" (v. 45). Ritual exorcisms
and efforts at self-reform apart from true salvation will not free anyone
from Satan's kingdom. Only those who have "faith in Christ Jesus ... [are]
rescued ... from the domain of darkness, and transferred ... to the kingdom of His beloved Son" (Col. 1:4, 13).

There are some who argue that true Christians can be demon
possessed; that is, actually indwelt by a demon as opposed to merely
being influenced. One proponent of that view writes, "A genuine Christian may become possessed at least to some degree, even to the point
where they speak with strange voices or in foreign languages" (C. Fred
Dickason, *Angels, Elect and Evil* [Chicago: Moody 1975], 191). Yet Dickason cites no biblical evidence to support that claim, but rather alleged
"evidence from mission fields and clinical counseling" (p. 190).

In my book *How to Meet the Enemy*, I summarized the biblical
evidence that Christians cannot be demon possessed:

> There is no clear example in the Bible where a demon ever inhabited
> or invaded a true believer. Never in the New Testament epistles are
> believers warned about the possibility of being inhabited by demons.
> Neither do we see anyone rebuking, binding, or casting demons out of
> a true believer. The epistles never instruct believers to cast out demons,
> whether from a believer or unbeliever. Christ and the apostles were the
> only ones who cast out demons, and in every instance the demon-
> possessed people were unbelievers.

> The collective teaching of Scripture is that demons can never spatially
> indwell a true believer. A clear implication of 2 Corinthians 6, for example,
> is that the indwelling Holy Spirit could never cohabit with demons:

> What harmony has Christ with Belial, or what has a believer in com-
> mon with an unbeliever? Or what agreement has the temple of God
> with idols? For we are the temple of the living God; just as God said,
> "I will dwell in them and walk among them; and I will be their God
> and they shall be My people" (vv. 15–16).
>
> In Colossians 1:13, Paul says God "delivered us from the domain of
> darkness, and transferred us to the kingdom of His beloved Son."
> Salvation brings true deliverance and protection from Satan. In
> Romans 8:37, Paul says we overwhelmingly conquer through Christ. In
> 1 Corinthians 15:57, he says God gives us the victory. In 2 Corinthians
> 2:14, he says God always leads us in triumph. In 1 John 2:13, John says
> we have overcome the evil one. And, in 4:4, he says the indwelling Holy
> Spirit is greater than Satan. How could anyone affirm those glorious
> truths, yet believe demons can indwell genuine believers? ([Wheaton,
> Ill.: Victor, 1992], 22–23)

The Lord Jesus Christ's powerful preaching unnerved this particular demon **and he cried out** (an exclamation meaning to scream in dis-
may, fear, or terror) **with a loud voice** in the middle of Christ's message.
The demon felt the power of the presence of his sovereign, the Son of
God, who had come to invade the kingdom of darkness and free many
held captive by the devil by bringing them to salvation. As Jesus preached
the good news that He had come to deliver the poor, prisoners, blind, and
oppressed (cf. the exposition of 4:14–30 in chapter 23 of this volume), the
dreaded reality of his ultimate doom hit the demon, and he panicked.
"Let us alone!" he screamed. **"What business do we have with each
other, Jesus of Nazareth?"** The phrase **what business do we have
with each other** (literally, "what is it to us and to You"; cf. the same phrase
used by another demon in 8:28) is an idiomatic expression. What the
demon was saying is, "Why are You attacking us?" He knew all too well that
Jesus of Nazareth was God the Son, the second person of the Trinity,
who had absolute power and authority over him. It should be noted that
in a religious environment like Israel's, demons would rather stay hidden
as they sit in religious services. That is their disguise as "angels of light," and
they prefer not to blow their cover. Every false religion, no matter how
moral, is demon controlled and there are surely demons present in the
leaders and the deceived people. But they stay silent by design. They
could not hold their terror in when the Son of God was present.

His Purpose

Have You come to destroy us? (4:34*b*)

The demon was terrified not only because he knew who Jesus was, but also because he knew what His purpose for him and his fellow demons was. First John 3:8 states that purpose succinctly: "The Son of God appeared for this purpose, to destroy the works of the devil." **Destroy** translates a form of the verb *appollumi,* which means, "ruin," "bring to nothing," "abolish," or "bring to an end." The demons have been sentenced to eternal torment in hell for their rebellion against God. This one was terrified that Jesus was going to carry out that sentence right then and there and send him to the bottomless pit (cf. 8:31; Matt. 8:29).

The book of Revelation unfolds God's ultimate plan for Satan and the demons. In chapter 20 verses 1 to 3 the apostle John wrote,

> Then I saw an angel coming down from heaven, holding the key of the abyss and a great chain in his hand. And he laid hold of the dragon, the serpent of old, who is the devil and Satan, and bound him for a thousand years; and he threw him into the abyss, and shut it and sealed it over him, so that he would not deceive the nations any longer, until the thousand years were completed; after these things he must be released for a short time.

After the tribulation, as Jesus prepares for His thousand-year earthly reign, He will imprison Satan (and by implication the demons) in the abyss. The abyss is currently the temporary place of imprisonment for some of the demons (those who sinned in Gen. 6; cf. 1 Peter 3:18–20; Jude 6). It is not their final place of punishment, which is the lake of fire (Matt. 25:41). The abyss will be the holding cell, so to speak, for Satan and all the demons during the millennium. After one last, desperate assault on God and His people (Rev. 20:7–9), Satan and the demons will be thrown into the lake of fire, where they will undergo eternal punishment (Rev. 20:10).

HIS PURITY

I know who You are—the Holy One of God! (4:34c)

Unlike atheists, liberal theologians, and cultists, the demons know exactly who Jesus is. In fact, in the first half of Mark's gospel they are the only ones who are sure He is the Son of God. Expressing the sheer terror of one who is absolutely wicked in the presence of the One who is absolutely holy, the demon screamed, **I know who You are—the Holy One of God!** Like the rest of his fellow demons, this one was forced to acknowledge that Jesus is the absolutely holy Son of God (cf. v. 41; 8:28; Mark 1:34; 3:11). If God's people are afraid in His holy presence (cf. Isa.

6:5; Ezek. 1:28; Matt. 17:6; Rev. 1:17), how much more so a vile, wicked demon? Jesus, however, did not want or need the testimony of hell. Therefore, He silenced the demons whenever they affirmed His true identity (vv. 35, 41; cf. Mark 1:25, 34; 3:12; Acts 16:16–18). Since Christ lives in believers (Gal. 2:20), demons fear them, because the One they supremely dread indwells them.

HIS POWER

But Jesus rebuked him, saying, "Be quiet and come out of him!" And when the demon had thrown him down in the midst of the people, he came out of him without doing him any harm. And amazement came upon them all, and they began talking with one another saying, "What is this message? For with authority and power He commands the unclean spirits and they come out." And the report about Him was spreading into every locality in the surrounding district. (4:35–37)

As noted above, Jesus wanted no publicity from a demon. He, therefore, **rebuked him, saying, "Be quiet and come out of him!"** Jesus did not recite any incantations or perform any rituals; there was no discussion, debate, or struggle. He spoke, and the demon had no choice but to instantly obey. So **when the demon had thrown** the man **down in the midst of the people** in a final, futile act of defiance, **he** reluctantly **came out of him without doing him any harm.** Jesus in His compassion prevented the demon from hurting the man.

The crowd gathered in the synagogue had been amazed at Jesus' authoritative teaching. They were even more amazed by this demonstration of His absolute authority over the supernatural demonic realm, **and they began talking with one another saying, "What is this message? For with authority and power He commands the unclean spirits and they come out."** What they had witnessed was unprecedented. On another occasion a crowd that saw Jesus cast out a demon exclaimed, "Nothing like this has ever been seen in Israel" (Matt. 9:33). The **report** of this remarkable, astonishing act on Jesus' part spread like wildfire beyond Capernaum **into every locality in the surrounding district.**

This demonstration of Jesus' power over Satan and the demons reveals His ability to deliver sinners from their grasp. Though the forces of hell made an all-out assault on Him during His earthly ministry, Christ effortlessly defeated them. And by His sacrificial death on the cross, He accomplished the redemption of His people, delivering them forever from the kingdom of darkness (Col. 1:13). Believers share in Christ's victory over Satan and the demons through their salvation and union with Him (cf. Gen. 3:15; Rom. 16:20). Martin Luther expressed that truth in his hymn, "A Mighty Fortress Is Our God":

> The Prince of Darkness grim,
> We tremble not for him;
> His rage we can endure,
> For lo, his doom is sure;
> One little word shall fell him.

Jesus: The Divine Deliverer (Luke 4:38–44)

25

Then He got up and left the synagogue, and entered Simon's home. Now Simon's mother-in-law was suffering from a high fever, and they asked Him to help her. And standing over her, He rebuked the fever, and it left her; and she immediately got up and waited on them. While the sun was setting, all those who had any who were sick with various diseases brought them to Him; and laying His hands on each one of them, He was healing them. Demons also were coming out of many, shouting, "You are the Son of God!" But rebuking them, He would not allow them to speak, because they knew Him to be the Christ. When day came, Jesus left and went to a secluded place; and the crowds were searching for Him, and came to Him and tried to keep Him from going away from them. But He said to them, "I must preach the kingdom of God to the other cities also, for I was sent for this purpose." So He kept on preaching in the synagogues of Judea. (4:38–44)

The historical records of the life and ministry of Jesus Christ in the Gospels contain all that God has revealed about Him. Each of the four gospel writers wrote from his own unique perspective and for a distinct audience. Matthew wrote primarily to a Jewish audience, presenting Jesus as Israel's Messiah and rightful king. Thus, while Luke recorded Mary's genealogy to show Jesus' physical descent, Matthew gave Joseph's genealogy, since the royal line came through him. Matthew frequently cited the fulfillment of Old Testament prophecy in Jesus' life and ministry. He also referred to Jesus by the Jewish messianic title "Son of David." Sensitive to his readers' reverence for and reluctance to use the name of God, Matthew alone of the gospel writers substitutes the phrase "kingdom of heaven" instead of "kingdom of God."

Mark addressed his gospel to Gentiles, particularly the Romans. Thus he was careful to translate Aramaic words (e.g., 3:17; 5:41; 7:11, 34; 14:36; 15:22, 34) for his readers, and to explain Jewish customs with which they would not have been familiar (7:3–4). His fast-paced account, marked by the frequent use of the term "immediately" (more than forty times), would appeal to the practical, action-oriented Romans. Mark presented Jesus as the Servant, who came "to give His life a ransom for many" (10:45).

Luke presented a carefully researched, historically accurate account of the life of Jesus Christ. He addressed a broader Gentile audience than Mark, and presented Jesus as the Son of Man (a phrase he used more than two dozen times), the answer to mankind's needs and hopes.

John was written much later than the Synoptic Gospels (Matthew, Mark, Luke) to supplement and complement them. Its supreme, overarching purpose, as stated by John himself, is to present Jesus Christ as God, and to encourage its readers to come to faith in Him: "These have been written so that you may believe that Jesus is the Christ, the Son of God; and that believing you may have life in His name" (20:31). The same purpose could be given for the other three Gospels.

Yet despite their different emphases, all the Gospels present the revelation of Jesus Christ as God in human flesh. They reveal Him to have been born of a virgin, lived a sinless life, died as a substitute for believing sinners, and to have risen from the dead three days later, forever conquering death for all the redeemed. Repentance from sin and faith in Christ and His work bring complete forgiveness of sin and eternal life. The divine truths, spiritual realities, singular accomplishments, and glorious promises they record as part of the life and ministry of the Lord Jesus demand that the Gospels be studied carefully.

Along with the claims Jesus Christ made, the gospel writers also present convincing evidence for the validity of His assertions. To that end, Luke marshals the historical evidence to make an extensive, irrefutable case that Jesus is the God-man, Messiah, and only Savior. Luke's concern (like the other gospel writers), then, is not primarily with the historical details of Jesus' life and ministry, but rather with what those accurately recorded details incontrovertibly prove about Him.

This closing section of chapter 4 might appear at first glance to be a series of brief, disconnected comments that sum up a certain period in Jesus' life. But they are in reality very carefully connected. The Jewish people wanted to see signs to prove that Jesus was the Messiah (cf. 11:16; Matt. 12:38; 16:1; 1 Cor. 1:22), and in this brief passage Luke provided some for them. He revealed Jesus' divine power over three realms: the natural realm, the supernatural realm, and the eternal realm.

Jesus' Power over the Natural Realm

Then He got up and left the synagogue, and entered Simon's home. Now Simon's mother-in-law was suffering from a high fever, and they asked Him to help her. And standing over her, He rebuked the fever, and it left her; and she immediately got up and waited on them. While the sun was setting, all those who had any who were sick with various diseases brought them to Him; and laying His hands on each one of them, He was healing them. (4:38–40)

The physical effects of the fall are universal and devastating. Birth is the first step toward death. Deformity, illness, weakness, injury, disease, and death form the universal biography of mankind. If He is to be the Savior of His people and take them to the perfections of eternal heaven, the Messiah must have the power to reverse all these natural effects of the fall. This passage provides both a specific illustration of and a general reference to Jesus' power over the natural realm.

After preaching in the Capernaum synagogue and casting a demon out of a man in the audience (vv. 31–37), Jesus **got up and left the synagogue, and entered Simon's home.** The Sabbath service in the synagogue usually ended around noon and was followed by the main meal of the day. This is the second Sabbath mentioned in Luke's gospel (cf. 4:16–30), and both of them featured hostility (either human or demonic) to Jesus (cf. 6:6–11; 13:10–17).

Simon Peter had not yet been officially called to be a disciple (cf. 5:1–10; Matthew 4:18–22 and Mark 1:16–20 refer to a preliminary, temporary call; Luke to the final, permanent call to follow the Lord) or an apostle (6:13–14). Luke did not need to introduce him to his readers, because by the time he wrote his gospel, Peter was known to all of them. At this point in the narrative, however, he was still a member of the synagogue at Capernaum. Peter had been introduced to Jesus by his brother

Andrew (John 1:35–42). On that occasion Jesus changed his name to "Peter" (Greek) or "Cephas" (Aramaic) to indicate his future role as part of the foundation of the church (Matt. 16:16–18). Peter was originally from nearby Bethsaida (John 1:44) and now operated a fishing business in Capernaum with his brother Andrew (Matt. 4:18) and their partners, James and John (Luke 5:10), also recently called to follow Jesus (Mark 1:16–20). Having been present in the synagogue to hear Jesus' unparalleled exposition of the Word of God and witness the amazing display of His power over the demonic realm, Peter invited Him to his house for the Sabbath meal, along with Peter's brother Andrew, James, and John (Mark 1:29).

But Peter had more in mind than a meal, since upon arrival Jesus was confronted by a family crisis. **Simon's mother-in-law** (1 Cor. 9:5 refers to Peter's wife) **was** seriously ill, **suffering from** an infection and **a** resulting **high fever.** (Only Luke the physician specifies that it was a high [Gk., *mega;* lit. "large" or "great"] fever; Matthew [8:14] and Mark [1:30] merely refer to it as a fever.) Fully aware of Jesus' power to heal (cf. 4:14, 23), **they asked Him to help her.** The Lord immediately responded and **standing over her,** He took her by the hand in a gesture of tender compassion (Matt. 8:15; Mark 1:31), **rebuked the fever, and it left her. Rebuked** translates a form of the verb *epitimaō,* which is used almost exclusively in the New Testament to speak of rebuking people or demons (the only other instances of it being used to rebuke an inanimate object are in the accounts of Jesus' calming the sea [Mark 4:39; Luke 8:24]). Its use here demonstrates that Jesus has authority and power over the forces that debilitate the natural body. At Christ's word, the fever instantaneously **left her.** There was no lingering weakness, no recovery period; all her symptoms disappeared at once. Completely healed and needing no recovery of strength lost in the battle with the infection, **she immediately got up and waited on them,** preparing and serving the Sabbath meal to the many family members and guests.

The Lord's healing ministry set the pattern for the true biblical gift of healing. Six features characterized His healing ministry and set it apart from those of the fake "faith healers," who have paraded themselves before the church with their deceptive and abusive false promises.

First, Jesus healed with a word, as He did in the case of the centurion's servant (Matt. 8:5–13) or, as here with Peter's mother-in-law, a touch (cf. Mark 3:10; 5:25–34).

Second, Jesus healed instantly. There were no progressive healings; the people He cured did not gradually get better. As noted above, Peter's mother-in-law's symptoms vanished at once, and she was fully restored to health. Similarly, the centurion's servant "was healed that very moment" (Matt. 8:13); the woman with the hemorrhage was healed "immediately" (Mark 5:29); the ten lepers were cleansed of their disease as soon as they left to show themselves to the priests (Luke 17:14); after Jesus "stretched out His hand and touched [another leper]...immediately the leprosy left him" (Luke 5:13); when Jesus commanded the crippled man at the pool of Bethesda, "'Get up, pick up your pallet and walk,' immediately the man became well, and picked up his pallet and began to walk" (John 5:8–9). Some offer the Lord's healing of the blind man in Bethsaida (Mark 8:22–25) as an example of a progressive healing. But the man's statement, "I see men, for I see them like trees, walking around" (v. 24) merely defined his preexisting condition of blindness. The actual healing was instantaneous (v. 25). Had Jesus' healings not been instantaneous, they would not have demonstrated His supernatural power over disease. His critics could have claimed that the people were better as a result of natural processes.

Third, Jesus healed totally. Peter's mother-in-law was cured of all her symptoms and went at once from being bedridden to serving a meal. When Jesus healed a man "covered with leprosy" (Luke 5:12), "the leprosy left him" (v. 13). It was the same with all of Jesus' healings; "the blind receive[d] sight and the lame walk[ed], the lepers [were] cleansed and the deaf hear[d]" (Matt. 11:5).

Fourth, as verse 40 notes, Jesus healed everyone. He did not leave behind long lines of disappointed, distraught people who were not healed, like modern faith healers do. Matthew 4:24 says that "the news about Him spread throughout all Syria; and they brought to Him all who were ill, those suffering with various diseases and pains, demoniacs, epileptics, paralytics; and He healed them." According to Matthew 12:15, "Many followed Him, and He healed them all," while Luke 6:19 notes that "all the people were trying to touch Him, for power was coming from Him and healing them all." So widespread was Jesus' healing that He, in effect, banished disease from Israel during the three years of His ministry.

Fifth, Jesus healed organic disease. He did not heal vague, ambiguous, invisible ailments such as lower back pain, heart palpitations, or headaches. On the contrary, He restored full mobility to paralyzed limbs, full sight to blind eyes, full hearing to deaf ears, and fully cleansed leprous skin. Jesus healed "every kind of disease and every kind of sickness among the people" (Matt. 4:23; cf. 9:35). All of Jesus' healings were undeniable, miraculous signs, as even His most bitter enemies admitted (John 11:47).

Finally, Jesus raised the dead—not those who were in a temporary coma, or whose vital signs fluctuated during surgery, but a young man in his casket on his way to the graveyard (Luke 7:11–15), a young girl whose death was apparent to all (Mark 5:22–24, 35–43), and a man who had been dead for four days (John 11:14–44).

Unlike modern faith healers, Jesus performed His healings in public before huge crowds in various locations—not in the carefully orchestrated and highly controlled surroundings of modern healing venues or television studios. Nor were His healings contingent on the faith of the one being healed; most of those He healed were unbelievers, and hence unable to make a "positive confession" and claim their healing. So unprecedented was Christ's healing ministry that people exclaimed, "We have never seen anything like this" (Mark 2:12; cf. John 9:32).

The apostles (Luke 9:1), the seventy (Luke 10:1–9), and a few close associates of the apostles (Barnabas [Acts 15:12], Philip [Acts 8:6–7], and Stephen [Acts 6:8]) were also granted the gift of healing to authenticate them as the preachers of God's truth. Their healing was characterized by the same features that marked Christ's healing.

The apostles healed with a word or a touch. Peter merely said to Aeneas, "Jesus Christ heals you" and he was immediately healed (Acts 9:34). On the island of Malta after being shipwrecked, "Paul went in to see [the father of Publius, who was gravely ill with dysentery] and after he had prayed, he laid his hands on him and healed him" (Acts 28:8).

The apostles healed instantly. As already noted, Aeneas was made well immediately. When Peter and John healed a man "who had been lame from his mother's womb" (Acts 3:2), "immediately his feet and his ankles were strengthened. With a leap he stood upright and began to walk; and he entered the temple with them, walking and leaping and praising God" (vv. 7–8).

The apostles healed totally. "Aeneas, who had been bedridden eight years, for he was paralyzed.... Immediately ... got up"; his paralysis was gone (Acts 9:33–34). Paul encountered a man at Lystra who "had no strength in his feet, [was] lame from his mother's womb, [and] had never walked" (Acts 14:8). But when Paul "said with a loud voice, 'Stand upright on your feet'" the man "leaped up and began to walk" (v. 10).

The apostles were able to heal anyone of anything. Acts 5:16 records that "the people from the cities in the vicinity of Jerusalem were coming together, bringing people who were sick or afflicted with unclean spirits, and they were all being healed." After Paul healed Publius's father, "the rest of the people on the island who had diseases were coming to him and getting cured" (Acts 28:9).

The apostles healed organic conditions, such as lameness (Acts 3:2–8), paralysis (Acts 9:33–34), and dysentery (Acts 28:8).

Finally, the apostles raised the dead. God used Peter to bring Dorcas back to life, and Paul to bring Eutychus back to life after he fell to his death from a third-story window (Acts 20:9–12. As a physician Luke, who was present [v. 8], was certainly qualified to determine whether a person was dead.).

The gift of healing in the New Testament was not given to keep believers healthy, but as a sign to unbelievers verifying the truthfulness of the gospel and the authenticity of its preachers. To claim that healing is the norm in the church undermines its unique role in authenticating Jesus and the apostles as revealers of divine truth. In keeping with that purpose, healings faded from the scene as the apostolic era drew to a close. Paul (Gal. 4:13–15), Epaphroditus (Phil. 2:25–27), Timothy (1 Tim. 5:23), and Trophimus (2 Tim. 4:20) were all recorded to have been sick. None of them were healed. Nor do the New Testament Epistles, which define the life and theology of the church, refer to a ministry of healing. There is no evidence that the kind of healings seen in the era of Jesus and the apostles was to continue beyond them (cf. 2 Cor. 12:12). Nor were such healings a regular part of the purpose of God before them. They are extremely rare in the Old Testament; for example, none are recorded for the 750 years from Isaiah to Jesus Christ. God may choose to heal through the prayers of His people, but not through miracle working men as in the case of our Lord and His associates. (For an explanation of James 5:14–16, see *James,* the MacArthur New Testament Commentary [Chicago: Moody, 1998], 276–81.)

While the sun was setting, signifying the end of the Sabbath and its restrictions on travel and work, **all** (Mark 1:33 notes that "the whole city had gathered at the door") **those who had any who were sick with various diseases brought them** to Jesus. Word travelled fast and when the Sabbath ended, people could do what they were not permitted to do during the Sabbath—bring their needy friends and family to the house in hope of healing. They were not disappointed. In keeping with His compassion and power to heal anyone of any disease or condition, He was **laying His hands on each one of them** and **was healing them.** No one was excluded. The display of healing on that one day may have exceeded all the recorded healings in the entire Old Testament, and Jesus did such things over the three years of His ministry.

JESUS' POWER OVER THE SUPERNATURAL REALM

Demons also were coming out of many, shouting, "You are the Son of God!" But rebuking them, He would not allow them to speak, because they knew Him to be the Christ. (4:41)

As noted in the previous chapter of this volume, if Jesus is to free those held captive in Satan's kingdom of darkness, He must have power over him and his demon hosts. As He did earlier in the synagogue (4:33–35), Jesus demonstrated that power so that **demons also were**

coming out of many. Like the demon Christ cast out in the synagogue, these were terrified of Him. They knew His true identity, that He was God the Son, the second person of the Trinity incarnate, with absolute authority to send them into eternal torment. Confronted with the second member of the Trinity, in terror they were **shouting** or screaming, **"You are the Son of God!"** as they left their victims.

But Jesus did not want their testimony, so **rebuking them, He would not allow them to speak, because they knew Him to be the Christ.** Jesus not only had the power to cast them out, but also to silence them. To have demons affirming His identity would only create confusion. "It was altogether inappropriate that Jesus' Messiahship should be proclaimed by representatives of the evil one. Had He allowed this by not silencing the demons, He would have given grounds for a charge brought against him later by the Pharisees, that of being Satan's ally (Matt. 12:24; Mark 3:22)" (Robert L. Thomas and Stanley N. Gundry, *A Harmony of the Gospels* [Chicago: Moody, 1978], 50). Paul similarly rejected demonic testimony from a possessed slave girl in Philippi (Acts 16:16–18).

Jesus' authority over the demons revealed His power to deliver sinners whose minds have been blinded by the god of this world (2 Cor. 4:4) and his demon hosts. Believers even now have renewed minds (Rom. 12:2; Eph. 4:23), and one day will have minds completely free from the effects of demonic deception. The Savior of souls, the one who will rescue sinners from Satan's power (Eph. 2:1–3) and the kingdom of darkness (Col. 1:13–16), must demonstrate that He has absolute power over the demon captors.

JESUS' POWER OVER THE ETERNAL REALM

When day came, Jesus left and went to a secluded place; and the crowds were searching for Him, and came to Him and tried to keep Him from going away from them. But He said to them, "I must preach the kingdom of God to the other cities also, for I was sent for this purpose." So He kept on preaching in the synagogues of Judea. (4:42–44)

When day came on Sunday after a Sabbath in which He demonstrated massive power over the natural and supernatural realms, **Jesus left** Peter's house just before daybreak while it was still dark (Mark 1:35) **and went to a secluded place.** Mark reveals that His purpose in doing so was to pray (v. 35). But before long **the crowds were searching for Him, and came to Him and tried to keep Him from going away from them.** Awed by His power to deliver them from disease and demons, they understandably did not want Jesus to leave them. The Lord did not rebuke their interest in the miraculous signs He had performed. But those signs were not an end in themselves, but rather a means to an end. Jesus was not primarily a miracle worker, but a preacher of the gospel. Therefore, **He said to them, "I must preach the kingdom of God to the other cities also, for I was sent for this purpose."** Jesus repeatedly affirmed that the Father had sent Him (Matt. 10:40; Mark 9:37; Luke 10:16; John 4:34; 5:24, 30, 36, 37; 6:38, 39, 44, 57; 7:16, 28, 29, 33; 8:16, 18, 26, 29, 42; 9:4; 11:42; 12:44, 45, 49; 13:20; 14:24; 15:21; 16:5; 17:8, 18, 21, 23, 25; 20:21). He came not merely to demonstrate His power over the effects of sin in the body by physical healing and the mind by overcoming demonic influence, but most importantly His power to overcome sin's eternal consequences. For that to happen required repentance and faith in the gospel preached (cf. Rom. 10:13–17). Only by faith in the truth preached could sinners be rescued from Satan's kingdom of darkness and enter into **the kingdom of God.** This is the first of thirty-two uses of this important theological term in Luke's gospel (he used it six more times in Acts). The **kingdom of God** is the sphere or realm of salvation that those who respond in repentant faith to the preaching of the gospel enter, so in keeping with His kingdom mission, Jesus **kept on preaching in the synagogues of Judea,** which here is a generic term for the entire nation of Israel including Galilee (Mark 1:39), not merely the southern part.

The power the Lord displayed over the natural, supernatural, and eternal realms authenticated Him as the Son of God, sent by the Father to preach the saving gospel of salvation to lost sinners.

Characteristics of Jesus' Divinity
(Luke 5:1–11)

26

Now it happened that while the crowd was pressing around Him and listening to the word of God, He was standing by the lake of Gennesaret; and He saw two boats lying at the edge of the lake; but the fishermen had gotten out of them and were washing their nets. And He got into one of the boats, which was Simon's, and asked him to put out a little way from the land. And He sat down and began teaching the people from the boat. When He had finished speaking, He said to Simon, "Put out into the deep water and let down your nets for a catch." Simon answered and said, "Master, we worked hard all night and caught nothing, but I will do as You say and let down the nets." When they had done this, they enclosed a great quantity of fish, and their nets began to break; so they signaled to their partners in the other boat for them to come and help them. And they came and filled both of the boats, so that they began to sink. But when Simon Peter saw that, he fell down at Jesus' feet, saying, "Go away from me Lord, for I am a sinful man, O Lord!" For amazement had seized him and all his companions because of the catch of fish which they had taken; and so also were James and John, sons of Zebedee, who were partners with Simon. And Jesus said to Simon, "Do not

fear, from now on you will be catching men." When they had brought their boats to land, they left everything and followed Him. (5:1–11)

The last few centuries have seen an enormous number of books written about the Lord Jesus Christ. The nineteenth century quest for the "historical Jesus" saw countless explanations written about Jesus. Most were generated from a rationalistic, naturalistic perspective, in a purported attempt to get behind the fantasy biblical "Christ of faith" to the nondivine, nonsupernatural real "Jesus of history." Their authors' antisupernatural presuppositions controlled their research, as I. Howard Marshall notes:

> Many of these investigators believed that the real Jesus must have been an ordinary person with nothing supernatural or divine about him. His life must have conformed to ordinary human patterns, and be explicable in purely human categories. For such people the phrase "the historical Jesus" clearly meant a non-supernatural Jesus. (*I Believe in the Historical Jesus* [Grand Rapids: Eerdmans, 1977], 110–11)

It should come as no surprise that those who began with an antisupernatural bias wound up with a nonsupernatural Jesus. Marshall goes on to note that

> in every case the picture of Jesus was of a Jesus clearly fashioned by a nineteenth-century artist. The process reached its climax in the so-called "Liberal Jesus," a somewhat inoffensive teacher proclaiming "the fatherhood of God and the brotherhood of man."…The most damning criticism [of the "Liberal Jesus"] came from the pen of William Temple, Archbishop of Canterbury, who said quite simply, "Why anyone should have troubled to crucify the Christ of Liberal Protestantism has always been a mystery." (*I Believe in the Historical Jesus,* 113)

Albert Schweitzer's famous book, *The Quest of the Historical Jesus,* written early in the twentieth century, chronicled the nineteenth-century quest for the "historical Jesus" and pronounced all such efforts futile. (Ironically, he then proceeded to set forth his own skeptical, non-biblical interpretation of Christ's life.) But the twentieth century would produce its own aberrant views of Jesus. The influential German New Testament critic Rudolf Bultmann was noted for his "demythologizing" approach to the New Testament. As a result, "for Bultmann nothing survived of the deeds of Jesus and very little of his teaching" (Marshall, *I Believe,* 126). The so-called "new quest for the historical Jesus" in the post-World War 2 era concluded, like the old nineteenth-century one, that little, if anything, could be known about the life of Christ. The closing decades of the twentieth century saw the rise of the Jesus Seminar, whose members also reinvented Jesus to fit their Scripture-rejecting, anti-supernatural bias. They even had the audacity to arrogate to themselves the right to vote on which sayings of His were authentic. (For a defense of the historical reliability of the Gospel accounts of Jesus' life and ministry, see Lee Strobel, *The Case for Christ* [Grand Rapids: Zondervan, 1998]; for a scholarly critique of critical approaches to the Gospels, see Robert L. Thomas and F. David Farnell, *The Jesus Crisis* (Grand Rapids: Kregel, 1998.)

But all such skeptical efforts to find the "real" Jesus are doomed to fail, because they do not look for Him in the only place where He can be found—the divinely inspired, inerrant historical record of His life and ministry in the New Testament Gospels. To deny the truthfulness of the Gospels and then attempt to construct a life of Jesus is both futile and absurdly hypocritical.

Luke is the lengthiest of the four Gospels, but the reader does not have to work through the entire book for the truth concerning the Lord Jesus Christ to become evident. The real Jesus is unmistakably revealed in every section of Luke, and no more so than in this passage. Its eleven verses portray Him as fully human; He acted and talked like a man, and was accepted as one by the people around Him. Yet these same verses reveal that He is more than a mere man. The profound incident in His life presented here reveals clearly His essential nature as God. As this story of a fishing incident on the Sea of Galilee unfolds, five of Jesus' divine attributes are manifested. He is the source of truth, omniscient, omnipotent, holy, and merciful.

JESUS IS THE SOURCE OF TRUTH

Now it happened that while the crowd was pressing around Him and listening to the word of God, He was standing by the lake of Gennesaret; and He saw two boats lying at the edge of the lake; but the fishermen had gotten out of them and were washing their nets. And He got into one of the boats, which was Simon's, and asked him to put out a little way from the land. And He sat down and began teaching the people from the boat. (5:1–3)

The phrase **now it happened** indicates that an indefinite amount of time had passed since the events recorded in 4:38–44. The Lord was still in Galilee, preaching (v. 44), healing, and casting out demons (vv. 40–41), which, understandably, resulted in large crowds following Him (v. 42; cf. v. 14; 5:15; 6:17; 7:11–12, 24; 8:4, 42, 45; 9:11, 37; 11:14, 29;

12:1, 54; 14:25. Writing later in the first century, the Jewish historian Jose-phus estimated the population of Galilee at about three million, which allows for the vast size of the crowds that followed Jesus.). In a day when no media existed, gifted communicators drew huge crowds, and Jesus was obviously unparalleled (John 7:46).

On this occasion, **the crowd was pressing around Him and listening to the word of God** as **He was standing by the lake of Gen-nesaret.** The **lake,** more commonly known as the Sea of Galilee (the Old Testament refers to it as the Sea of Chinnereth [Num. 34:11; Josh. 13:27] or Chinneroth [Josh. 12:3], and the apostle John calls it the Sea of Tiberias [John 6:1; 21:1], the name by which it was known when he wrote), is a large (approximately thirteen miles wide by seven miles long) freshwater lake (nearly 700 feet below sea level) that is the dominant geographical feature of the entire region of Galilee. The name **Gennesaret** derives from the fertile plain of that name to the northwest of the lake. The primary source of water for the Sea of Galilee is the Jordan River, which arises from several sources near Mount Hermon (9,200 feet above sea level) and flows into the lake from the north. The enlarged Jordan River exits the southern end of the lake, and flows south into the Dead Sea.

On this as on other occasions (Mark 3:9; 4:1), the eager crowds surged around Jesus, pushing Him toward the water's edge. What cap-tured their attention was Jesus' preaching of **the word of God** (and surely the anticipation of miracles). That term is not here a synonym for the Bible as it commonly is in Christian circles today. The phrase **of God** is a subjective genitive in the Greek, indicating source; the people were **listening to** Jesus speak **the word** that came directly from **God.** When Jesus spoke, they literally heard God speaking. The subject was the good news of salvation; the truth about entering the kingdom of God. It was the glorious truth that the spiritually poor could be made rich; the spiritual prisoners set free; the spiritually blind given sight; and the spiritually oppressed delivered from their bondage (cf. the exposition of 4:18 in chapter 23 of this volume). It was the good news of forgiveness, salvation, and eternal life. "Truly, truly, I say to you," Jesus declared, "he who hears My word, and believes Him who sent Me, has eternal life, and does not come into judgment, but has passed out of death into life" (John 5:24).

Jesus' teaching and preaching was strikingly different than that of the rabbis, whose authority was connected to quoting other rabbis. But Jesus, being God, spoke the long-awaited divine revelation of the kingdom, which could be entered through faith in Him. Jesus did not speak as an Old Testament scholar or as a theologian. What He spoke was not philosophical speculation or rabbinic tradition; it was the voice of God. Jesus was the Son of God; God in human flesh (see the exposition of 2:49 in chapter 16 of this volume), and when He spoke He spoke with personal divine authority (Matt. 7:29; Mark 1:27).

Jesus is truth incarnate, since God is true (Ps. 31:5; Isa. 65:16). His word is an expression of His truth (Ps. 138:2). In John 14:6, Jesus declared, "I am the way, and the truth, and the life." Earlier in his gospel the apostle John wrote of Him, "And the Word became flesh, and dwelt among us, and we saw His glory, glory as of the only begotten from the Father, full of grace and truth.... For the Law was given through Moses; grace and truth were realized through Jesus Christ" (1:14, 17).

Jesus repeatedly taught that He had been sent by God and thus spoke the truth. In John 7:16, He "answered [the Jewish religious leaders] and said, 'My teaching is not Mine, but His who sent Me.'" Later "Jesus was saying to those Jews who had believed Him, 'If you continue in My word, then you are truly disciples of Mine; and you will know the truth, and the truth will make you free'" (John 8:31–32). "Because I speak the truth," He told the Jewish leaders, "you do not believe Me. Which one of you convicts Me of sin? If I speak truth, why do you not believe Me?" (John 8:45–46). In John 12:49–50, Jesus again affirmed that He spoke exactly as the Father commanded Him: "For I did not speak on My own initiative, but the Father Himself who sent Me has given Me a commandment as to what to say and what to speak. I know that His commandment is eternal life; therefore the things I speak, I speak just as the Father has told Me."

Being pressed against the water on that crowded shore, Jesus **saw two boats lying at the edge of the lake.** These were fishing boats, not small rowboats. They were large enough to hold Jesus and the twelve disciples (Matt. 8:23–24; 14:22–33; Mark 6:31–32; 8:10; cf. John 21:2–3 where seven of the disciples were in a boat). These particular boats were beached or anchored to the shore, and **the fishermen had gotten out of them and were washing their nets** in preparation for the next night's fishing. Fishing on the Sea of Galilee was generally done at night, and the fishermen washed and repaired their nets and worked on their boats and equipment during the day.

To create some space between Himself and the crowd that was shoving and jostling for position around Him, Jesus **got into one of the boats, which was Simon's** (the other may have belonged to James and John; cf. v. 10). The Lord's decision to enter that particular boat was not a random one; Jesus did nothing without a purpose. The time had come for Him to move not only into Peter's boat, but more intensely into his life, along with the other two who would become His inner circle, James and John, to lift them to the highest level of commitment.

Since the Lord had first encountered Peter (John 1:41–42) when his brother Andrew brought Peter to Him they, along with John (the unnamed second disciple of John the Baptist referred to in v. 35), began their initial voluntary interest in following Jesus as the Messiah. The

Lord's first actual calling of Peter, along with Andrew, James, and John (Matt. 4:18–22; Mark 1:16–20), drew them in as men chosen by the Lord to be followers of Him. In this passage, Luke alone records their final call, when they abandoned their fishing business and became permanent, full-time disciples of Jesus. The Lord targeted Peter in particular, since he would be the recognized leader of the Twelve (his name is first on all four New Testament lists of the apostles) and have a great influence on the rest (cf. John 21:3).

After entering Peter's boat, Jesus **asked him to put out a little way from the land.** Being on the water freed Jesus from being jostled by the crowd, allowed the people to see Him better, and may have provided better acoustics, since the flat, calm surface of the lake would to some extent amplify the sound of His voice. After the boat was moved a short distance from the shore and anchored in place, Jesus **sat down** (as rabbis traditionally did when teaching; cf. 4:20; Matt. 5:1; 13:1; John 8:2) **and began teaching the people from the boat** (cf. Matt. 13:2). No matter what the exigencies or difficulties, Jesus would not be deterred from preaching the Word of God, which the Father had sent Him to do (4:43; Mark 1:38).

JESUS IS OMNISCIENT

When He had finished speaking, He said to Simon, "Put out into the deep water and let down your nets for a catch." Simon answered and said, "Master, we worked hard all night and caught nothing, but I will do as You say and let down the nets." When they had done this, they enclosed a great quantity of fish, (5:4–6a)

The challenge always facing fishermen is finding the fish. Even experienced fishermen, using the latest fish-finding sonar, often come up empty. The Lord Jesus Christ, however, knew exactly where the fish were. As the One who created everything (John 1:3; Col. 1:16; Heb. 1:2), He has an exhaustive knowledge of all creatures—even to the point of knowing when a sparrow falls to the ground (Matt. 10:29)—since "there is no creature hidden from His sight" (Heb. 4:13). As the story unfolds, Jesus' omniscience becomes evident.

When He had finished speaking to the crowd, Jesus **said to Simon** (the verb is a second person singular), **"Put out into the deep water and** then said to the entire crew **let down** (this verb is a second personal plural) **your nets for a catch." The nets** were not the small ones used by individuals fishing from the shore or in shallow water (cf. Matt. 4:18) but large nets similar to modern seines, and used for fishing in the deeper water of the lake.

Perhaps surprised that a carpenter would presume to tell experienced fisherman how to fish, **Simon answered** the Lord **and said, "Master** (*epistatēs;* "chief," "commander"; a respectful title for one in authority, but not an affirmation of deity), **we worked hard all night** (when, as noted above, fishing was usually done) **and caught nothing."** Why then should He expect them to catch fish in the middle of the day? Besides, letting down the large nets and hauling them in was hard work. But then again, this was no ordinary carpenter, but one who had healed his mother-in-law, so Peter added, **"but I will do as You say and let down the nets."**

If Jesus' command surprised them, the result utterly dumbfounded them. **When they had** let down the nets, much to their amazement **they enclosed a great quantity of fish.** Nothing in their experience could have prepared them for such an unheard of catch in the middle of the day. But the omniscient Savior knew exactly where the fish were. Later He would tell Peter where to find one specific fish with a specific coin in its mouth (Matt. 17:27). And after His resurrection, the Lord would once again tell Peter and his companions where to let down their nets for a huge catch of fish (John 21:1–6).

Knowing where the fish in the Sea of Galilee were is merely one demonstration of Jesus' omniscience. He described exactly the man who would lead Peter and John to the upper room where they would celebrate the Last Supper (Luke 22:8–12). His supernatural knowledge of Nathanael's whereabouts (John 1:47–48) led Nathanael to exclaim, "Rabbi, You are the Son of God; You are the King of Israel" (v. 49). He was not deceived by the shallow, superficial, nonsaving professions of faith on the part of some, because "He Himself knew what was in man" (John 2:25). He "knew from the beginning who they were who did not believe, and who it was that would betray Him" (John 6:64). Christ's omniscience was convincing proof of His deity, and caused the disciples to say, "Now we know that You know all things, and have no need for anyone to question You; by this we believe that You came from God" (John 16:30; cf. 21:17). Those times when Jesus voluntarily restricted His omniscience (e.g., Matt. 24:36; Mark 11:13; Luke 8:45–46) are consistent with His submission to the Father during His incarnation (cf. the discussion of 3:22 in chapter 20 of this volume).

JESUS IS OMNIPOTENT

and their nets began to break; so they signaled to their partners in the other boat for them to come and help them. And they came and filled both of the boats, so that they began to sink. (5:6b–7)

That He knew the location of the fish demonstrated Jesus' omniscience, but the staggering, unprecedented size of the catch revealed His omnipotence. Peter and the others were shocked and amazed at the enormous number of fish, knowing that there was no possible human explanation for it. Nothing like this had ever happened before; no catch had been anywhere near this size. They were witnessing a display of divine power as the Lord gathered together in one location the vast number of fish that were now causing **their nets . . . to break.** Frantically, Peter and his crew **signaled to their partners in the other boat** (v. 7) **for them to come and help them.** Hurrying to their partners' assistance, the other boat **came** alongside Peter's **and** working frantically, the crews **filled both of the boats.** But so enormous was the catch that both boats began to sink under the staggering weight of the fish.

As they knew from the Old Testament, God not only created the world, but also controls it. Nehemiah prayed, "You alone are the Lord. You have made the heavens, the heaven of heavens with all their host, the earth and all that is on it, the seas and all that is in them. You give life to all of them and the heavenly host bows down before You. You are the Lord God" (Neh. 9:6–7). Extolling the Lord's sovereign control over His creation the psalmist wrote,

> O Lord, how many are Your works! In wisdom You have made them all; the earth is full of Your possessions. There is the sea, great and broad, in which are swarms without number, animals both small and great. There the ships move along, and Leviathan, which You have formed to sport in it. They all wait for You to give them their food in due season. You give to them, they gather it up; You open Your hand, they are satisfied with good. You hide Your face, they are dismayed; You take away their spirit, they expire and return to their dust. You send forth Your Spirit, they are created; and You renew the face of the ground. (Ps. 104:24–30)

In Isaiah 50:2*b*, God declared, "Behold, I dry up the sea with My rebuke, I make the rivers a wilderness; their fish stink for lack of water and die of thirst." Even the pagan king Nebuchadnezzar acknowledged God's sovereign control over all of His creation: "All the inhabitants of the earth are accounted as nothing, but He does according to His will in the host of heaven and among the inhabitants of earth; and no one can ward off His hand or say to Him, 'What have You done?'" (Dan. 4:35).

Those shocked, amazed, and frightened (see the exposition of v. 8 below) fishermen knew that they were witnessing confirmation of the truth that "power belongs to God" (Ps. 62:11).

JESUS IS HOLY

But when Simon Peter saw that, he fell down at Jesus' feet, saying, "Go away from me Lord, for I am a sinful man, O Lord!" For amazement had seized him and all his companions because of the catch of fish which they had taken; and so also were James and John, sons of Zebedee, who were partners with Simon. (5:8–10*a*)

The Lord Jesus Christ had just revealed Himself to be the omniscient, omnipotent God of the universe. **When Simon Peter saw** the evidence of **that** in the miraculous catch of fish, he was overwhelmed with the realization that he was face-to-face with Holy God. Peter, fully aware that if he saw deity, deity saw him too, and realizing that the One who could see the depths of the lake could see the depths of his heart, felt exposed. He immediately **fell down at Jesus' feet** (lit. His knees), saying, **"Go away from me Lord, for I am a sinful man, O Lord!"** No longer did Peter use the respectful term *epistatēs* as in v. 5, but *kurios*, by which he means, "God." As a devout Jew, Peter knew that God alone was to be worshiped (4:8; Deut. 6:13), yet he fell down before Jesus in the posture of a worshiper. The Lord's masterful teaching in the synagogue, His power to cast out a demon, and heal his mother-in-law, and above all the stunning catch of fish for which there was no human explanation, had brought Peter to the place where Jesus wanted him—to the recognition of his sinfulness. Whatever he may have thought about Jesus before this incident, Peter had no doubt now that He was God, and he recognized his unworthiness to be in the Lord's presence. Peter's attitude was like that of the repentant tax collector who, overwhelmed by his sinfulness, "was even unwilling to lift up his eyes to heaven, but was beating his breast, saying, 'God, be merciful to me, the sinner!'" (Luke 18:13).

Peter's response of fear and penitence is typical of those in the presence of God. Abraham described himself as "dust and ashes" (Gen. 18:27); Job humbly said, "I have heard of You by the hearing of the ear; but now my eye sees You; therefore I retract, and I repent in dust and ashes" (Job 42:5–6); after encountering the angel of the Lord (the preincarnate Christ) Samson's father "Manoah said to his wife, 'We will surely die, for we have seen God'" (Judg. 13:22); when the Israelites "perceived the thunder and the lightning flashes and the sound of the trumpet and the mountain [Mount Sinai] smoking ... they trembled and stood at a distance. Then they said to Moses, 'Speak to us yourself and we will listen; but let not God speak to us, or we will die'" (Ex. 20:18–19); after seeing a vision of God in His heavenly temple, Isaiah cried out in terror, "Woe is me, for I am ruined! Because I am a man of unclean lips, and I live among a people of unclean lips; for my eyes have seen the King, the Lord of hosts" (Isa. 6:5); after he saw a vision of God, Ezekiel fell on his face

(Ezek. 1:28); when the apostle John saw the glorified Christ, he "fell at His feet like a dead man" (Rev. 1:17).

The **amazement** that **had seized** Peter was shared by **all his companions,** who were equally overwhelmed by **the catch of fish which they had taken.** Luke specifically names **James and John,** the **sons of Zebedee, who were partners with Simon.** Along with Peter, they would form the inner core group of the apostles. Later, all three would see an even more awe-inspiring revelation of Christ's divine glory at the transfiguration (Matt. 17:1–6). That incident also traumatized them, and "they fell face down to the ground and were terrified" (v. 6).

JESUS IS MERCIFUL

And Jesus said to Simon, "Do not fear, from now on you will be catching men." When they had brought their boats to land, they left everything and followed Him. (5:10b–11)

In the terror of the recognition of his sinfulness, Peter wanted to send the Lord away, but Jesus wanted to draw Peter closer. The very point at which the sinner feels the most alienation is the point at which the Savior seeks reconciliation. In Psalm 51:17 David wrote, "The sacrifices of God are a broken spirit; a broken and a contrite heart, O God, You will not despise." Through the prophet Isaiah God declared, "For thus says the high and exalted One Who lives forever, whose name is Holy, 'I dwell on a high and holy place, and also with the contrite and lowly of spirit in order to revive the spirit of the lowly and to revive the heart of the contrite'" (Isa. 57:15; cf. 66:2). At their moment of deepest alienation when, overwhelmed by their sinfulness, Peter, James, and John sought to flee, Jesus reached out to pull them to Himself. This is the glorious moment of their repentance. He did the same with Isaiah who, in the presence of God, cursed his own sinfulness and deemed himself unworthy to be in the presence of the Holy One. But the Lord sought to cleanse him and use him as His instrument (Isa. 6:5–9).

Seeking to calm and reassure him, **Jesus said to Simon, "Do not fear."** There was no need for him and his companions to be terrified. There is a proper, healthy fear of God, expressed for instance in Deuteronomy 13:4: "You shall follow the Lord your God and fear Him; and you shall keep His commandments, listen to His voice, serve Him, and cling to Him." That reverential fear is different from the terror of the demons or the sinner, who fears the judgment of God and seeks to flee from His presence (cf. Rev. 6:15–17); it is the fear of love, awe, and adoration that causes the believer to cling to the "Father of mercies" (2 Cor. 1:3) and serve and obey Him (cf. Deut. 10:12–13; 1 Sam. 12:24). The proper fear of the Lord results in wisdom (Ps. 111:10; Prov. 9:10) and worship (Ps. 2:11).

Mercy would take them from cowering in fear to **catching men** (*zōgreō*), which literally means, "to capture alive." They had spent their lives catching fish for the purpose of killing them; now they would spend the rest of their lives catching men to give them life. Isaiah feared he would be destroyed, but instead was called to preach (Isa. 6:8–11). John feared that he would be destroyed, but instead was called to write (Rev. 1:19). Divine grace and mercy moved Peter, James, and John from cringing fear of judgment to evangelizing the lost, laying the groundwork for the great commission.

This was Jesus' formal and permanent call of these three men to full-time discipleship, so **when they had brought their boats to land, they left everything and followed Him** (cf. vv. 27, 28; 9:23, 49, 57, 59, 61; 18:22, 28, 43). At the very pinnacle of their earthly careers, having just made the greatest catch of fish ever seen on that lake, they abandoned their boats, turned their backs on their fishing business, left everything, and followed Jesus (cf. Luke 9:23–25).

Those who recognize their sinful unworthiness and embrace Jesus as the truthful, omniscient, omnipotent, holy, and merciful God are the ones He reconciles to Himself. He forgives their sin, takes away their fear of judgment that sin causes, and commissions them to the great task of evangelization, of catching men alive for the kingdom of God.

The Healing, Forgiving Savior
(Luke 5:12–26)

27

While He was in one of the cities, behold, there was a man covered with leprosy; and when he saw Jesus, he fell on his face and implored Him, saying, "Lord, if You are willing, You can make me clean." And He stretched out His hand and touched him, saying, "I am willing; be cleansed." And immediately the leprosy left him. And He ordered him to tell no one, "But go and show yourself to the priest and make an offering for your cleansing, just as Moses commanded, as a testimony to them." But the news about Him was spreading even farther, and large crowds were gathering to hear Him and to be healed of their sicknesses. But Jesus Himself would often slip away to the wilderness and pray. One day He was teaching; and there were some Pharisees and teachers of the law sitting there, who had come from every village of Galilee and Judea and from Jerusalem; and the power of the Lord was present for Him to perform healing. And some men were carrying on a bed a man who was paralyzed; and they were trying to bring him in and to set him down in front of Him. But not finding any way to bring him in because of the crowd, they went up on the roof and let him down through the tiles with his stretcher, into the middle of the crowd, in front of Jesus. Seeing

their faith, He said, "Friend, your sins are forgiven you." The scribes and the Pharisees began to reason, saying, "Who is this man who speaks blasphemies? Who can forgive sins, but God alone?" But Jesus, aware of their reasonings, answered and said to them, "Why are you reasoning in your hearts? Which is easier, to say, 'Your sins have been forgiven you,' or to say, 'Get up and walk'? But, so that you may know that the Son of Man has authority on earth to forgive sins,"— He said to the paralytic—"I say to you, get up, and pick up your stretcher and go home." Immediately he got up before them, and picked up what he had been lying on, and went home glorifying God. They were all struck with astonishment and began glorifying God; and they were filled with fear, saying, "We have seen remarkable things today." (5:12–26)

As we have seen, this section of Luke's gospel reveals Jesus Christ's absolute and total power over everyone and everything. In 4:1–13, He defeated every temptation hurled at Him by the devil, and further demonstrated His power over Satan's realm by casting out demons (4:33–35, 41). His healing of Peter's mother-in-law and many others (4:38–40) displayed Christ's power over disease, while the miraculous catch of fish (5:1–11) demonstrated His power over the realm of nature. The miracles He performed are critical testimony in the biblical record of Jesus' life, since they offer proof of His divine nature.

This passage records two more examples of Jesus' supernatural power over disease. He healed two conditions, leprosy and paralysis, whose cure was far beyond the limited medical knowledge of that day. But these healings do more than reveal Jesus' divine power and compassion. The story of His healing the leper provides an analogy of the penitent sinner's approach to Him, and the account of His healing the paralyzed man contains the revelation of His authority to forgive sin.

JESUS HEALS A LEPER:
THE PENITENT SINNER'S APPROACH TO HIM

While He was in one of the cities, behold, there was a man covered with leprosy; and when he saw Jesus, he fell on his face and implored Him, saying, "Lord, if You are willing, You can make me clean." And He stretched out His hand and touched him, saying, "I am willing; be cleansed." And immediately the leprosy left him. And He ordered him to tell no one, "But go and show yourself to the priest and make an offering for your cleansing, just as

Moses commanded, as a testimony to them." But the news about Him was spreading even farther, and large crowds were gathering to hear Him and to be healed of their sicknesses. But Jesus Himself would often slip away to the wilderness and pray. (5:12–16)

The exact time and location of the Lord's encounter with this leper is not known. It occurred during His Galilean ministry **in one of the cities** or villages near the Sea of Galilee. The encounter may be discussed under three headings: the dreaded disease, the desperate victim, and the divine compassion.

THE DREADED DISEASE

behold, there was a man covered with leprosy; (5:12*b*)

Like its Old Testament counterpart *lepras* (**leprosy**) is a general term for a number of skin conditions. The most severe of those was Hansen's disease, which is leprosy as it is known today. Luke's description of the man as being **covered with leprosy** suggests that he in fact had leprosy in the most extreme sense of the term. His desire for cleansing connects it to the familiar disease because it reflects the designation of the leper as unclean in Leviticus 13:45–46.

Leprosy, or Hansen's disease, is known from ancient writings (c. 600 B.C.) from China, India, and Egypt, and from mummified remains from Egypt. It was common enough in Israel to warrant extensive regulation in the Mosaic law of those suffering from it and related skin diseases (Lev. 13–14). The disease is caused by the bacterium *Mycobacterium leprae*, discovered by the Norwegian scientist G. H. A. Hansen in 1873 (it was the first bacterium to be identified as the cause of a human disease). The bacterium was communicable through touch and breath.

Leprosy attacks the skin, peripheral nerves (especially near the wrists, elbows, and knees), and mucus membrane. It forms lesions on the skin, and can disfigure the face by collapsing the nose and causing folding of the skin (leading some to call it "lion's disease" due to the resulting lionlike appearance of the face). Contrary to popular belief, leprosy does not eat away the flesh. Due to the loss of feeling (especially in the hands and feet), people with the disease wear away their extremities and faces unknowingly. The horrible disfigurement caused by leprosy made it greatly feared, and caused lepers to be outcasts, cut off from all healthy society, for protection.

And God had cursed people by giving them leprosy, such as

Gehazi (2 Kings 5:25–27) and Uzziah (2 Chron. 26:16–23). Thus, people with this disease were viewed as cursed by God—a familiar notion in ancient concepts of sin (cf. Job 4:7–9; John 9:1–3). The man likely saw his own disease in this way. (For further details about leprosy, see *Matthew 8–15*, The MacArthur New Testament Commentary [Chicago: Moody, 1987], 5–11.)

THE DESPERATE VICTIM

and when he saw Jesus, he fell on his face and implored Him, saying, "Lord, if You are willing, You can make me clean." (5:12c)

This poor, tragic outcast had no hope, humanly speaking. His disease was incurable, socially stigmatizing, and viewed as God's punishment for his sins. Having heard about Jesus, he came looking for Him (cf. Matt. 8:2), and **when he saw Jesus,** he approached Him. That was inappropriate behavior on his part, since lepers were strictly forbidden to come near other people (cf. Luke 17:12), or to interact with anyone except other lepers. So great was the fear of contagion that lepers were barred from Jerusalem or any other walled city (cf. 2 Kings 7:3). They were forbidden to come within six feet of a healthy person (one hundred and fifty feet if the wind was blowing from the direction of the leper) and were restricted to a special compartment in the synagogue. One rabbi refused to eat an egg bought on a street where there was a leper. Another advocated throwing stones at lepers to force them to keep their distance. (cf. Alfred Edersheim, *The Life and Times of Jesus the Messiah* [Grand Rapids: Eerdmans, 1974], 1:492–95).

It is now known that leprosy (Hansen's disease) is not highly contagious, since 90 to 95 percent of the human race is immune to it. Exactly how the disease is transmitted is not known for certain, but people living in close contact with those with untreated leprosy had a higher risk of becoming infected. But lepers in biblical times were isolated not only due to fear of infection, but also because they were ceremonially unclean (Lev. 13:45–46). In rabbinic teaching, leprosy was second only to contact with a dead body in terms of defilement. "Not merely actual contact with the leper, but even his entrance defiled a habitation, and everything in it, to the beams of the roof.... If he even put his head into a place, it became unclean." (Edersheim, *Life and Times*, 1:494,95).

That the leper approached Jesus in violation of rabbinic law reveals his desperation. He was past fear, past shame, and heedless of the danger to himself or others; he literally had nothing left to lose.

Coming to Jesus, the leper **fell on his face** in a posture of reverent worship. Matthew 8:2 says he "bowed down" (*proskuneō;* better translated "worshiped." This term is usually used in the New Testament of worshiping God.) Whatever his understanding of Jesus was, he was convinced that He was sent by God and called Him **Lord.**

That he **implored** or begged Jesus for help reveals the leper's sense of urgency. He was a sinful outcast, wretched and miserable, with nowhere else to turn.

The leper also approached the Lord in complete humility. He made no demands, knowing that he had no claim on Him. He did not doubt Jesus' ability to heal him, but acutely aware of his own unworthiness, he wondered if He was **willing** to do so, thus acknowledging the Lord's prerogative.

Finally, he approached Jesus in faith, affirming his confidence that Jesus had clearly displayed many times the power to heal him and **make** him **clean.**

The leper's approach to Jesus graphically illustrates penitent sinners' approach to Him. They come in desperation, casting aside their self-righteous efforts to save themselves as the filthy garments that they are (Isa. 64:6). They come in reverence, affirming Jesus as Lord (Rom. 10:9), God (John 8:24), and the only Savior (Acts 4:12). They come with a sense of urgency, knowing that "now is the acceptable time … now is the day of salvation" (2 Cor. 6:2). They come in humility, poor in spirit (Matt. 5:3), deserving nothing from the sovereign and knowing they have nothing to commend themselves. Finally, they come in faith, because "to the one who does not work, but believes in Him who justifies the ungodly, his faith is credited as righteousness" (Rom. 4:5).

THE DIVINE COMPASSION

And He stretched out His hand and touched him, saying, "I am willing; be cleansed." And immediately the leprosy left him. And He ordered him to tell no one, "But go and show yourself to the priest and make an offering for your cleansing, just as Moses commanded, as a testimony to them." But the news about Him was spreading even farther, and large crowds were gathering to hear Him and to be healed of their sicknesses. But Jesus Himself would often slip away to the wilderness and pray. (5:13–16)

Moved with compassion (Mark 1:41) for this helpless man and his desperate plight, Jesus, disregarding the prescription of Leviticus 5:3, **stretched out His hand and touched him.** The Lord frequently healed with a touch (cf. 4:40; 7:14 ; 13:13; 22:51; Mark 6:5), but to touch a leper was shocking and unprecedented. No one in Israel—least of all a rabbi—would have defiled himself by touching a leper. But sovereign love responded with sovereign power. Jesus said, **"I am willing; be cleansed," and immediately the leprosy left him.** As was the case with all of Jesus' healings, the leper was healed instantly, and completely (see the discussion of Jesus' healing in chapter 25 of this volume). There was no lingering recovery period while the leprosy gradually got better. Modern medical treatment can cure leprosy, but cannot completely reverse the disfigurement and damage the disease causes to the human body. But the disfigurement caused by this man's leprosy was also healed by Jesus' creative power, leaving no trace of the disease or its effects on his body. He was healed, restored, and physically fit to take immediately a long journey from Galilee to Jerusalem.

After healing the man, Jesus **ordered him to tell no one,** for the moment. There was something the now cleansed leper needed to do at once, so the Lord commanded him, **"Go and show yourself to the priest and make an offering for your cleansing, just as Moses commanded."** The process by which a cleansed leper was readmitted to society involved going to the temple for an examination by a priest, shaving, bathing, washing his clothes, offering multiple animal sacrifices, along with an offering of grain and oil (Lev. 14:1–20). The entire procedure lasted for eight days (Lev. 14:10). If he obeyed and went to recount to the priests how Jesus had healed him, it would be a powerful **testimony to them** that Jesus was indeed the Messiah and Son of God. This **testimony** would be either convincing to the priests so that they would acknowledge the claims of Christ, or if they rejected Him self-indicting, since they had personally examined the miraculously healed leper. Further, it would buy time for Jesus, since a miracle of that magnitude would surely swell the already large crowds that followed Him—crowds so huge that they had forced Him off the shore of the Sea of Galilee and into Peter's boat.

But selfishly overjoyed at his remarkable, miraculous healing, the man ignored Jesus' command and instead "went out and began to proclaim it freely and to spread the news around" (Mark 1:45), forfeiting the opportunity for such a powerful testimony. As a result, **the news about Him was spreading even farther, and large crowds were gathering to hear Him and to be healed of their sicknesses.** So vast were the crowds that Jesus "could no longer publicly enter a city, but stayed out in unpopulated areas; and they were coming to Him from everywhere" (Mark 1:45). The disobedience of the cleansed leper had put limitations on Jesus' ministry and forced Him into the countryside away from the populated towns. The ones who could find Him in the wilderness did so, but surely many of the most disabled in the towns were not able to experience His healing word and touch. To maintain His focus on preaching the word and sustain the power of His ministry Jesus, in His humanity, needed communion with the Father. Therefore, even in the unpopulated areas He **would often slip away** deeper into **the wilderness and pray** (cf. Luke 4:42). Prayer was an integral and essential aspect of Jesus' life and ministry (see the discussion of 3:21 in chapter 20 of this volume).

JESUS HEALS A PARALYZED MAN: HIS AUTHORITY TO FORGIVE SIN

One day He was teaching; and there were some Pharisees and teachers of the law sitting there, who had come from every village of Galilee and Judea and from Jerusalem; and the power of the Lord was present for Him to perform healing. And some men were carrying on a bed a man who was paralyzed; and they were trying to bring him in and to set him down in front of Him. But not finding any way to bring him in because of the crowd, they went up on the roof and let him down through the tiles with his stretcher, into the middle of the crowd, in front of Jesus. Seeing their faith, He said, "Friend, your sins are forgiven you." The scribes and the Pharisees began to reason, saying, "Who is this man who speaks blasphemies? Who can forgive sins, but God alone?" But Jesus, aware of their reasonings, answered and said to them, "Why are you reasoning in your hearts? Which is easier, to say, 'Your sins have been forgiven you,' or to say, 'Get up and walk'? But, so that you may know that the Son of Man has authority on earth to forgive sins,"— He said to the paralytic—"I say to you, get up, and pick up your stretcher and go home." Immediately he got up before them, and picked up what he had been lying on, and went home glorifying God. They were all struck with astonishment and began glorifying God; and they were filled with fear, saying, "We have seen remarkable things today." (5:17–26)

As was the case with the account of Christ's healing of the leper, the time of this event is not known. Luke merely notes that it happened **one day** when **He was teaching.** It most likely took place after one of the Lord's journeys around the lake area (Mark 1:39) when He was able to return to Capernaum (Matt. 9:1). The Lord's healing of the paralyzed man once again demonstrated His supernatural power over disease. But even more significantly, it revealed His authority to forgive sin—which is the prerogative of God alone, and the greatest need of man, so as to escape eternal judgment. Luke's account of this event explains the context, the claim, the confrontation, and the consequences.

One day He was teaching; and there were some Pharisees and teachers of the law sitting there, who had come from every village of Galilee and Judea and from Jerusalem; and the power of the Lord was present for Him to perform healing. And some men were carrying on a bed a man who was paralyzed; and they were trying to bring him in and to set him down in front of Him. But not finding any way to bring him in because of the crowd, they went up on the roof and let him down through the tiles with his stretcher, into the middle of the crowd, in front of Jesus. (5:17–19)

In keeping with the constant pattern of His ministry, the opening of this section finds Jesus **teaching.** He was not in a synagogue, but in a house, undoubtedly a big one since it accommodated the large crowd that had gathered (cf. Mark 2:2).

Luke focused his attention in particular on the **Pharisees and teachers of the law** who were **sitting there** in the crowd. This is the first reference in Luke's gospel to the **Pharisees,** one of the four main Jewish sects along with their archrivals the Sadducees (the wealthy, elite priests), the Zealots (political revolutionaries who sought independence from Rome), and the Essenes (ascetic monastics). Their name likely derives from a Hebrew verb meaning "to separate." The Pharisees were the "separated ones" in terms of their zeal for the Mosaic law (and their own traditions, which they added to it [cf. Matt. 15:2–6; Mark 7:8–13]).

The Pharisees originated during the intertestamental period, likely as an offshoot of the Hasidim (the "pious ones," who opposed the Hellenizing of Jewish culture under the notoriously evil Seleucid king Antiochus Epiphanes). Unlike the Sadducees, who tended to be wealthy priests or Levites, the Pharisees generally came from the middle class. Therefore, although few in number (there were about 6,000 at the time of Herod the Great, according to the first-century Jewish historian Josephus), their theology and tradition had great influence with the common people (who, ironically, the Pharisees often viewed with proud, self-righteous contempt [cf. John 7:49]). Despite being the minority party in the Sanhedrin, their popularity with the people gave them significant influence (cf. Acts 5:34–40).

With the disappearance of the Sadducees after the destruction of the temple in A.D. 70 and the Zealots after the Bar Kochba revolt (A.D. 132–35) was crushed, the Pharisees became the dominant force in Judaism. With the completion of the Mishnah (the written compilation of the oral law, rituals, and traditions) in about A.D. 200, and the Talmud (the combination of the Mishnah and the Gemara [three centuries of the rabbis' commentary on the Mishnah]) in about A.D. 500, the Pharisees' teaching became virtually synonymous with Judaism.

The Pharisees' theology was in many respects faithful to the teaching of Scripture. They believed in the resurrection (Acts 23:6–8), angels (Acts 23:8), demons, predestination, and human responsibility. They looked for Messiah to come and establish an earthly kingdom, and were devoted to protecting and teaching the law of God. Ironically, it was their zeal for the law that caused the Pharisees to become focused on rituals and externally keeping the law. They abandoned true religion of the heart for mere outward behavior modification and ritual (cf. Matt. 15:3–6), leading Jesus to scathingly denounce their pseudospirituality: "Woe to you, scribes and Pharisees, hypocrites! For you tithe mint and dill and cummin, and have neglected the weightier provisions of the law: justice and mercy and faithfulness; but these are the things you should have done without neglecting the others" (Matt. 23:23; cf. 6:1–5; 9:14; 12:2; Luke 11:38–39). Even worse, the wide gap between their teaching and their practice led to gross hypocrisy, which both Jesus (e.g., Matt. 23:2–3) and, surprisingly, the Talmud (which lists seven classes of Pharisees, six of which are hypocritical) denounced. Despite their zeal for God's law, they were "blind guides of the blind" (Matt. 15:14), who made their proselytes doubly worthy of the hell to which they themselves were headed (Matt. 23:15). The complex set of man-made rules and regulations was a crushing, unbearable burden (Matt. 23:4; Acts 15:10). In any case, keeping the law could never save anyone, "because by the works of the Law no flesh will be justified" (Rom. 3:20; cf. 3:28; Gal. 2:16; 3:11, 24; 5:4)—a truth that the zealous Pharisee Saul of Tarsus eventually realized (Phil. 3:4–11).

Luke also notes the presence of **teachers of the law.** Also called lawyers (7:30; 10:25; 11:45, 46, 52; 14:3; Matt. 22:35) and most commonly scribes (sixty-three times in the New Testament), they were professional scholars specializing in the interpretation and application of the law. They were commonly, but not exclusively, Pharisees (though distinguished from them by being mentioned separately; 5:21, 30; 6:7; 11:53; 15:2; Matt. 5:20; 12:38; 15:1; 23:2, 13, 14, 15, 23, 25, 27, 29; Mark 7:1, 5; John 8:3; Mark 2:16 refers to "the scribes of the Pharisees," and Acts 23:9 to "the scribes of the Pharisaic party"). Such scribes were also honored by being called rabbis ("great ones"), though others who taught the Word of God might also receive that title (cf. John 1:38, 49; 3:2; 6:25, where it is given to Jesus).

That the scribes and Pharisees there that day **had come from every village of Galilee and Judea and from Jerusalem** testifies to the level of concern the Jewish authorities had about Jesus. His first act in His Judean ministry had been to disrupt the Sadducees' temple business operations by driving out the money changers and merchants (John 2:14–16). They, along with the Pharisees, had watched in growing alarm (and jealousy; cf. Matt. 27:18) as His ministry of teaching and healing had drawn huge crowds, both in Judea and in Galilee (cf. 5:15). Now they dogged His steps, looking for something for which they could indict Him. The incident that was about to unfold would provide these hostile visitors with an unforgettable, undeniable (cf. John 11:47) experience— and a formidable challenge to their aberrant theology.

Luke's note that **the power of the Lord was present for** Jesus **to perform healing** reminds his readers of a truth that he had mentioned earlier. In His incarnation, when He "emptied Himself, taking the form of a bond-servant" (Phil. 2:7), Jesus set aside the independent use of His divine power. He ministered in submission to the Father, and in the power of the Holy Spirit (see the discussion of 3:22 in chapter 20 and 4:1 in chapter 22 of this volume.)

While the Lord was teaching, **some men** arrived (Mark 2:3 notes that there were four of them), **carrying on a bed a man who was paralyzed.** He was one of countless others with physical problems who sought out Jesus wherever He went. Unable to come to Jesus on his own, he was fortunate enough to have loyal and determined friends available to help him. How he became **paralyzed,** whether through a birth defect, spinal cord or brain injury, or a degenerative disease, is not stated. Unlike lepers, the paralyzed were not ostracized from society. They were stigmatized by their condition, however, since many would see all such disabilities as God's punishment for their sin (cf. John 9:2).

Having arrived at the house where Jesus was "speaking the word" (Mark 2:2), the paralyzed man's friends **were trying to bring him in and to set him down in front of Him. But** they could not find **any way to bring him in because of the** overflow **crowd** (cf. Mark 2:2). No one would move aside to allow the men to carry him in; the crowd formed a barrier both with their bodies and their hearts. Fortunately for the paralyzed man, his friends were both determined and resourceful. Unable to gain access to the house, **they went up on the roof.** Most houses in Israel were single story houses. The beams spanning the walls and supporting the roof were set below the tops of the walls to form an enclosed patio, which was accessible by a stairway. The larger houses had tiles between the beams, as this one did. After moving aside some of the **tiles** and digging through the underlying roof (Mark 2:4), the four men lowered their paralyzed friend **with his stretcher into the middle of the crowd, in front of Jesus.**

THE CLAIM

Seeing their faith, He said, "Friend, your sins are forgiven you." (5:20)

One can only imagine what went through the minds of the people in that crowded house as the four men began tearing up the roof above Jesus. They must have wondered what the scraping noise was, and noticed the pieces of the roof falling. Finally, the men broke through; the daylight streamed in and, to the crowd's amazement, an immobile man lying on a stretcher was slowly lowered to the ground in front of Jesus. It was a dramatic moment, with all eyes on Him to see how He would react.

There is no record that either the paralyzed man or his friends said anything; his need of physical healing was self-evident. On the other hand, what Jesus said was unexpected and shocking. **Seeing** the **faith** of all five men, **He said** to the paralyzed man, **"Friend, your sins are forgiven you"** (cf. 7:48). The Lord addressed first the more significant issue of the man's need of salvation. Shaken with grief and fear because of his sins, he wanted healing, but more important, Jesus knew he wanted forgiveness.

Forgiveness is both mankind's greatest need, and God's most important gift—and the only means for blessing in this life and eternal life in heaven. Jesus Christ came into the world to "save His people from their sins" (Matt. 1:21; cf. 26:28), and "through His name everyone who believes in Him receives forgiveness of sins" (Acts 10:43; cf. 5:31; 26:18; Eph. 1:7; 4:32; Col. 1:14; 2:13–14; 3:13; 1 John 1:9; 2:12; Rev. 1:5). Forgiveness is the distinctive message of the Christian proclamation (Luke 24:47; Acts 2:38; 13:38).

But forgiveness has always been the offer of redemption, so it is also the message of the Old Testament. After Adam and Eve sinned, "the Lord God made garments of skin for Adam and his wife, and clothed them" (Gen. 3:21). Killing animals to provide those garments pictured the ultimate sacrifice of Messiah, whose death would cover the shame and guilt of sin. The Lord described Himself to Moses as "the Lord, the Lord God, compassionate and gracious, slow to anger, and abounding in lovingkindness and truth; who keeps lovingkindness for thousands, who forgives iniquity, transgression and sin" (Ex. 34:6–7; cf. Num. 14:18). Nehemiah 9:17 calls Him a "God of forgiveness." In Psalm 65:3 David wrote, "Iniquities prevail against me; as for our transgressions, You forgive them," while in 86:5, he declared, "For You, Lord, are good, and ready to forgive, and abundant in lovingkindness to all who call upon You." In Psalm 103:12, David depicted the extensiveness of God's forgiveness when he noted that "as far as the east is from the west, so far has He removed our transgressions from us." In 130:3–4, the psalmist expressed his confidence in God's forgiveness: "If You, Lord, should mark iniquities, O Lord, who could stand? But there is forgiveness with You, that You may be feared." Speaking of the promised forgiveness in the New covenant, God declared, "I will forgive their iniquity, and their sin I will remember no more" (Jer. 31:34). Micah joyously exclaimed, "Who is a God like You, who pardons iniquity and passes over the rebellious act of the remnant of His possession?" (Mic. 7:18; cf. Isa. 55:7). The Old Testament likens God's forgiveness to His casting sins behind His back (Isa. 38:17), wiping them out (Isa. 43:25; cf. 1:18; 44:22), trampling them under His feet (Mic. 7:19), and burying them in the depths of the sea (Mic. 7:19).

Aware that the paralyzed man had genuine, penitent faith, Jesus, on His own divine authority, extended full and permanent forgiveness to him. He did not necessarily understand the truth that Jesus was God; people were forgiven in the Old Testament by acknowledging that they were sinners, deserving of God's judgment and unable to save themselves, confessing and repenting of their sin, and throwing themselves on God's mercy. The penitent tax collector is an example of how people were saved before the cross: "But the tax collector, standing some distance away, was even unwilling to lift up his eyes to heaven, but was beating his breast, saying, 'God, be merciful to me, the sinner!'" (Luke 18:13). His humble repentance and faith in God's grace and forgiveness resulted in his justification (v. 14). After the cross and resurrection, there is no salvation apart from believing in the only object of saving faith—the Lord Jesus Christ (John 14:6; Acts 4:12; 17:30–31; 1 Tim. 2:5). As Paul wrote in Romans 10:9, "If you confess with your mouth Jesus as Lord, and believe in your heart that God raised Him from the dead, you will be saved." It is because of Christ's sacrificial death on the cross that God can be "just and the justifier of the one who has faith in Jesus" (Rom. 3:26).

THE CONFRONTATION

The scribes and the Pharisees began to reason, saying, "Who is this man who speaks blasphemies? Who can forgive sins, but God alone?" But Jesus, aware of their reasonings, answered and said to them, "Why are you reasoning in your hearts? Which is easier, to say, 'Your sins have been forgiven you,' or to say, 'Get up and walk'? But, so that you may know that the Son of Man has authority

on earth to forgive sins,"—He said to the paralytic—"I say to you, get up, and pick up your stretcher and go home." (5:21–24)

Appalled and outraged that Jesus presumed to forgive the paralytic's sins, **the scribes and the Pharisees began to reason, saying, "Who is this man who speaks blasphemies? Who can forgive sins, but God alone?"** They were absolutely correct in their assertion that no one **can forgive sins,** in the fullest sense so that the sinner is cleansed, righteous, and never again guilty or condemned, **but God alone.** Only He as lawgiver and judge can forgive sin in that eternal way, since all sin is ultimately against Him (Ps. 51:4). But their characterization of Jesus as **this man who speaks blasphemies** (cf. Matt. 26:65; John 10:33) wrongly assumed that He was merely a man and not God incarnate. By claiming the authority to forgive sins, Jesus was either God, or a blasphemer. There is no middle ground; Jesus could not have been merely a good man, a true prophet, or a teacher of morality and ethics, if He were a blasphemer of God.

Blasphemy was the most heinous crime in Jewish thought, since it was a direct affront to the person of God. They defined three levels of blasphemy. First, one blasphemed God by speaking evil of His law, as Stephen (Acts 6:13) and Paul (Acts 21:27–28) were falsely accused of doing. A more serious form of blasphemy was to slander, speak evil of, or curse God Himself (Lev. 24:10–16; cf. Ex. 20:7). But the ultimate form of blasphemy was to assume the rights and prerogatives of God; to usurp the role of God and act as if one were God. It was this third and most severe type of blasphemy that the scribes and Pharisees accused Jesus of (cf. John 5:18; 8:58–59; 10:33; 19:7).

That **Jesus** was **aware** in His spirit (Mark 2:8) **of their reasonings** offers further proof of His deity, since only God knows the heart (1 Sam. 16:7; 1 Kings 8:39; 1 Chron. 28:9; Jer. 17:10; Ezek. 11:5). Yet Jesus "did not need anyone to testify concerning man, for He Himself knew what was in man" (John 2:25). Significantly, Jesus did not protest that they had misunderstood Him, that He was just a teacher or a prophet who was merely offering God's forgiveness to the paralytic, instead of claiming the right to forgive sins. If that was all He was claiming, His failure to correct their misunderstanding is inexplicable.

Unmasking their unspoken thoughts and escalating the confrontation, Jesus challenged them with the question, **"Which is easier, to say, 'Your sins have been forgiven you,' or to say, 'Get up and walk'?"** Obviously, both are impossible for a mere man to do, but that was not the question. Jesus asked **which is easier to say** as a convincing reality? They all knew that only God can forgive sin, which is the root cause of sickness. The end result of salvation will not be judgment, but will be glorification, when believers will be freed from all sin's consequences and effects both in the inner and outer man forever. They will have perfect souls, free from sin, and glorified bodies, free from disease and death. Since this would require forgiveness of all sins, truly the Messiah, God incarnate, had to demonstrate power to remove sin's consequences in the physical world. That would be proof He could overpower the effects of sin, implying forgiveness. He was about to do both.

The answer to the Lord's question is that it would have been easier to say to the paralytic that his sins were forgiven, because there was no way to empirically confirm or deny it. On the other hand, it would be obvious to all whether or not he actually got up and walked. Jesus chose to do the obvious miracle of physical healing **so that** they might **know that the Son of Man** (the Lord's favorite designation of Himself [used by Him more than eighty times] in the Gospels) had **authority on earth to forgive sins.** Turning to the man lying on his stretcher, **He said to the paralytic, "I say to you, get up, and pick up your stretcher and go home."** That was the acid test as to whether Jesus could negate the power, presence, and penalty of sin. There was no time to doubt, because the response came instantly.

THE CONSEQUENCES

Immediately he got up before them, and picked up what he had been lying on, and went home glorifying God. They were all struck with astonishment and began glorifying God; and they were filled with fear, saying, "We have seen remarkable things today." (5:25–26)

As was true of all of Christ's healings, the paralyzed man was healed completely and instantaneously. There were no lingering effects of his disability; no gradual healing, with a long period of rehabilitation before he was "healed." Instead, **immediately he got up before them, and picked up what he had been lying on, and went home.** Unlike the leper, the paralytic did not have a contagious disease, and hence was not required to go first and show himself to the priests. As was often the case when someone was healed, the paralytic went on his way **glorifying God** (cf. 13:13; 17:15; 18:43). He rejoiced not merely because he was physically healed, but even more so because his sins had been forgiven. Jesus connected His power over the effects of sin with His authority over sin's guilt. The One who healed necessarily could forgive.

Between the religious leaders, who remained implacably hostile despite this and other displays of Christ's divine power and authority (cf.

6:11; 11:15, 53; 13:17; 15:1–2; 19:47), on the one hand and the healed paralytic on the other was the crowd. **Struck with astonishment** at the amazing, unprecedented (cf. Mark 2:12) miracle they had just witnessed, they also **began glorifying God** (cf. 7:16; Matt. 15:31). Further, **they were filled with fear.** *Phobos* (**fear**) can refer to panic induced by frightening circumstances or events. It can also describe general, long-term apprehension or anxiety (it is the source of the English word "phobia"). Third, and most significantly, it is the fear that results from an understanding of God's holiness, power, and presence, which is how it is always used in the Synoptic Gospels and Acts (1:12, 65; 2:9; 7:16; 8:37; 21:26; Matt. 14:26; 28:4, 8; Mark 4:41; Acts 2:43; 5:5, 11; 9:31; 19:17). In that sense, it is a healthy fear. It can produce reverence for God, and help believers avoid sin (cf. 2 Cor. 7:1, 11) and lead godly lives (Phil. 2:12). Godly fear also motivates believers to mutually submit to each other and serve each other (Eph. 5:21). It also prompted Paul's desire to persuade others of his personal integrity (2 Cor. 5:11).

The crowd acknowledged that they had **seen remarkable things,** but not all of them were convinced of Christ's deity. Some concluded that He was merely a man to whom God had given authority (Matt. 9:8). Despite the unprecedented display of His divine, miraculous power, many refused to believe. "But though He had performed so many signs before them," John wrote, "yet they were not believing in Him" (John 12:37; cf. 1 Cor. 1:22). Paul explains the spiritual pathology of such senseless rejection:

> And you were dead in your trespasses and sins, in which you formerly walked according to the course of this world, according to the prince of the power of the air, of the spirit that is now working in the sons of disobedience. Among them we too all formerly lived in the lusts of our flesh, indulging the desires of the flesh and of the mind, and were by nature children of wrath, even as the rest. (Eph. 2:1–3)

> And even if our gospel is veiled, it is veiled to those who are perishing, in whose case the god of this world has blinded the minds of the unbelieving so that they might not see the light of the gospel of the glory of Christ, who is the image of God. (2 Cor. 4:3–4)

Calling a Wretched Sinner; Confronting Self-righteous Hypocrites
(Luke 5:27–32)

28

After that He went out and noticed a tax collector named Levi sitting in the tax booth, and He said to him, "Follow Me." And he left everything behind, and got up and began to follow Him. And Levi gave a big reception for Him in his house; and there was a great crowd of tax collectors and other people who were reclining at the table with them. The Pharisees and their scribes began grumbling at His disciples, saying, "Why do you eat and drink with the tax collectors and sinners?" And Jesus answered and said to them, "It is not those who are well who need a physician, but those who are sick. I have not come to call the righteous but sinners to repentance." (5:27–32)

Human beings are inherently religious. The image of God in man, though corrupted by the fall, still compels people to worship. As a result, there are thousands of religions, philosophies, and worldviews, ranging from primitive animistic religions all the way to sophisticated religious systems. But those religions, though differing widely from one another in the details, nevertheless fall into two categories. On the one hand, there is the religion of human achievement; on the other hand the religion of divine accomplishment. In every religion other than biblical

Christianity, man achieves salvation by his own efforts. Buddhists seek nirvana by following the Eightfold Path; Muslims hope to enter Paradise by following the Five Pillars of Islam; Mormons seek godhood through baptism, membership in the Mormon church, accepting Joseph Smith and his successors as prophets of God, and going through the temple ceremonies; Jehovah's Witnesses seek to earn everlasting life on earth by their morality and door-to-door proselytizing; Roman Catholics seek salvation by means of the Mass, sacraments, prayers, and good works that cooperate with grace to enable them to earn heaven (even if they have to be aided by the works of others to escape purgatory).

But all such self-righteous efforts to achieve salvation are utterly futile and serve only to damn the eternal souls of those who vainly trust in them. There is only one way to receive right standing before God, the religion of divine accomplishment—belief in the saving gospel of the Lord Jesus Christ. That gospel, the "glorious gospel of the blessed God" (1 Tim. 1:11), the "gospel of the grace of God" (Acts 20:24), "is the power of God for salvation to everyone who believes" (Rom. 1:16). The heart of the gospel is that "Christ died for our sins according to the Scriptures" (1 Cor. 15:3; cf. Matt. 26:28; 2 Cor. 5:21; Gal. 1:4; Eph. 1:7; 5:2; 1 Peter 2:24; 3:18; 1 John 2:2; Rev. 1:5), "so that whoever believes will in Him have eternal life" (John 3:15; cf. vv. 16, 18, 36; 1:12; 6:40, 47; 11:25–26; 20:31; Acts 16:31; Rom. 10:9). Salvation is entirely "by grace ... through faith; and that not of yourselves, it is the gift of God; not as a result of works, so that no one may boast" (Eph. 2:8–9). Grace completely excludes works as a means of salvation (Rom. 11:6). God justifies the "ungodly," not the godly (Rom. 4:5). The redeemed are those "to whom God credits righteousness apart from works" (v. 6) and "has saved ... and called ... with a holy calling, not according to [their] works, but according to His own purpose and grace which was granted [them] in Christ Jesus from all eternity" (2 Tim. 1:9).

By the time of Christ, the religion of Israel had degenerated into a system of works-righteousness, of external ritual instead of internal reality. As the apostle Paul lamented concerning his fellow Jews, "Israel, pursuing a law of righteousness, did not arrive at that law. Why? Because they did not pursue it by faith, but as though it were by works" (Rom. 9:31–32). Secure in their self-righteousness many, like those in the synagogue at Nazareth (4:14–30), refused to acknowledge that they were spiritually impoverished, imprisoned, blind, and oppressed (4:18).

It was against that backdrop of self-righteousness based on outward conformity to the law of God (cf. Mark 10:20) that Jesus made one of His most clarifying and definitive statements. In verse 32, He declared, "I have not come to call the righteous but sinners to repentance." That statement expressed the essential uniqueness of Christianity and concisely summarizes His mission. It sums up the whole glorious scheme of salvation: the Lord Jesus Christ came to save repentant sinners (19:10). Christ's statement also defines the church's mission. The heart of all gospel ministry is calling sinners to repentance. Salvation is not for those who think they are righteous, like those in the synagogue at Nazareth and the scribes and Pharisees, but for those who know they are not, like the tax collector in Luke 18:13–14. Thus Jesus centered His ministry on people who understood their lost condition. Often, these were the outcasts of society, which earned Him a reputation as "a friend of tax collectors and sinners" (Luke 7:34). Because such people were willing to come to grips with their true condition as hopeless sinners, the Lord was able to minister to them (cf. 1 Cor. 1:26–31).

This dramatic incident answers the question of whose sins Jesus would forgive. It reveals how deep into the dregs of society He would delve to rescue lost sinners. In this account Jesus saved someone at the very bottom—a hated, despised tax collector. The story of His call of Levi (Matthew) and its aftermath falls into two contrasting parts: His call of a wretched sinner, and His confrontation of self-righteous hypocrites.

CALLING A WRETCHED SINNER

After that He went out and noticed a tax collector named Levi sitting in the tax booth, and He said to him, "Follow Me." And he left everything behind, and got up and began to follow Him. And Levi gave a big reception for Him in his house; and there was a great crowd of tax collectors and other people who were reclining at the table with them. (5:27–29)

After healing the paralytic (5:17–26), Jesus **went out** of the house where He had been teaching. The Lord was followed by a huge crowd that dogged His steps in fascination and wonder, and He continued to teach them as He walked along a road near the shore of the Sea of Galilee (Mark 2:13). But Jesus had a divine appointment to keep, and He **noticed** (lit., "gazed intently at") **a tax collector named Levi sitting in the tax booth. Levi** is better known as Matthew, the author of the Gospel that bears his name. Since Capernaum was the largest city on the lake and a crossroads for east-west and north-south trade, he likely had a flourishing enterprise.

His occupation as **a tax collector** made Matthew one of the most hated and despised men in Israel. Tax collectors were the dregs of Jewish society; they were the lowest of the low on the social scale, and symbolized the worst sinners (cf. v. 30; 7:34; 18:11; Matt. 18:17; 21:31). That Jesus would save a tax collector, and then make him an apostle, was utterly inconceivable to the scribes and Pharisees.

The Roman occupation of Israel involved more than just a military presence; the nation was also subject to Roman taxation. The taxes in Galilee, for example, were forwarded by tax collectors to Herod Antipas, and by him to Rome. Antipas sold tax franchises to the highest bidder, and such franchises were a lucrative business. Tax collectors had a certain amount that they were required to collect, and whatever they collected beyond that they were permitted to keep (cf. Luke 3:12–13). In addition to the poll tax (on everyone, including slaves), income tax (about 1 percent), and land tax (one tenth of all grain, and one fifth of all wine and fruit), there were taxes on the transport of goods, letters, produce, using roads, crossing bridges, and almost anything else the rapacious, greedy minds of the tax collectors could think of. All of that left plenty of room for larceny, extortion, exploitation, and even loan sharking, as tax collectors loaned money at exorbitant interest to those who were unable to pay their taxes. Tax collectors also employed thugs to physically intimidate people into paying, and to beat up those who refused.

All of that was anathema to the Jewish people, who believed God was the only one to whom they should pay taxes. Tax collectors were viewed as traitors to their people, were classified as unclean, and were barred from the synagogues. They were also forbidden to give testimony in a Jewish court, because they were considered to be liars. Repentance was deemed especially difficult for tax collectors.

The Talmud listed two types of tax collectors, the *gabbai*, who collected the more general taxes such as the land, poll, and income taxes, and the *mokhes*, who collected the more specific taxes mentioned above (Alfred Edersheim, *The Life and Times of Jesus the Messiah* [Grand Rapids: Eerdmans, 1974], 1:515–18). There were two kinds of *mokhes,* the great *mokhes,* and the little *mokhes.* The great *mokhes* did not himself collect taxes but employed others as substitutes. The little *mokhes* would be employed by a great *mokhes* to actually sit in a tax booth and collect taxes. Because they were the ones in contact with the people, they were the most despised of all tax collectors. Since Jesus found him **sitting in the tax booth,** Matthew would have been a little *mokhes*—one of the most hated men in Capernaum. That his booth was located near the shore (Mark 2:13–14) suggests that he collected taxes from the fishermen, which would have made him even more despised by them than the average little *mokhes.*

Undeterred by Matthew's status as a social outcast, Jesus stopped at his tax booth and **said to him, "Follow Me."** The Lord knew his heart. He saw that Matthew was wretched and miserable; that he was distressed and burdened by his sin and hungering and thirsting for righteousness.

Matthew undoubtedly knew of Jesus, since the Lord had made Capernaum His home base (Matt. 4:13) and the word of His powerful preaching and the miracles He performed had spread far and wide (Luke 4:37). Although he may not have understood at this point that Jesus was God, Matthew certainly recognized Him as a great prophet and preacher of God's Word. Like the Old Testament saints, Matthew knew that he was a sinner, and that his only hope for forgiveness lay in God's mercy (see the discussion of 5:20 in chapter 27 of this volume). In time Matthew, like the rest of the Twelve, would come to understand and fully believe the truth that Jesus is God. Jesus forgave him based on his repentant heart and called him to be a disciple, and later to be an apostle (6:15).

Matthew's immediate response revealed the genuineness of his desire for righteousness and salvation: **he left everything behind, and got up and began to follow** Jesus. The change in his life was miraculous. The tough, hard-nosed little *mokhes* became a humble man; in fact, there is no record in the Gospels of him speaking. In his gospel, Matthew refers to himself only in his account of his calling (Matt. 9:9) and in the list of the twelve apostles (Matt. 10:3). That Matthew's own account of this incident (Matt. 9:9) omits any reference to leaving everything behind further indicates his humility. His willingness to forsake everything and follow Jesus is in stark contrast to the rich young ruler. When the Lord said to him, "Go and sell all you possess and give to the poor, and you will have treasure in heaven; and come, follow Me" (Mark 10:21), he "was saddened, and he went away grieving, for he was one who owned much property" (v. 22).

Matthew's decision was final; he was abandoning his career. The great *mokhes* for whom he worked would have someone else manning his tax booth almost at once. He, therefore, made a far more drastic break with his past than his fellow apostles who were fishermen. They could always have returned to fishing as a living (and tried to, at least temporarily [John 21:1–3]).

The aorist tense of the verb *anistēmi* (**got up**) coupled with the imperfect tense of the verb *akoloutheō* (**began to follow**) illustrates Matthew's response. There was a decisive decision to break with his past, then a continual pattern of following Christ. He began to experience new longings, new aspirations, new affections, a new mind, and a new will; in short, he became a new creature (2 Cor. 5:17). The traitor, extortioner, robber, and outcast sinner became the apostle and evangelist of Jesus Christ. Matthew lost a temporal career, but gained an eternal destiny; he forfeited material possessions, but gained "an inheritance which is imperishable and undefiled and will not fade away, reserved in heaven" (1 Peter 1:4); he lost sinful companions, but gained the fellowship of the Son of God.

A significant indication of the reality of Matthew's transformed life is that he **gave a big reception for** Jesus **in his house.** That it was able to accommodate a **great crowd** suggests that Matthew's house was a large one, and is a further indication of the lucrative position he was walking away from. Having experienced the joyous, liberating experience of having his sins forgiven and his heart transformed, he wanted to expose everyone he knew to the Savior. Matthew did not invite the proud, elite, religious leaders (who would never have accepted an invitation from a tax collector), but his companions—the outcasts of society with whom he worked and lived daily. There were, of course, many of Matthew's fellow **tax collectors,** along with some whom Luke tactfully referred to as **other people** (Matthew called them "sinners" [Matt. 9:10]). This group undoubtedly included thieves, thugs, enforcers, drunks, prostitutes—the very people whom the Son of Man came to seek and save (Luke 19:10). They had probably all heard of Jesus, and perhaps some had receptive hearts like Matthew's.

Luke's note that they **were reclining at the table** indicates that this was a lengthy meal, with lots of time for extended conversation among friends. No self-respecting Jew would eat a meal with the likes of this crowd. Meals were important social statements of acceptance in Israel, and Luke describes several in his inspired record of Jesus' ministry (cf. 7:36; 10:38–40; 11:37; 14:1; 22:14; 24:30). This one not only celebrated the end of Matthew's old life and the beginning of his new one, but was also an evangelistic outreach, with the Savior as guest of honor. It is an amazing picture of Jesus receiving lost sinners.

REJECTING THE RIGHTEOUS

The Pharisees and their scribes began grumbling at His disciples, saying, "Why do you eat and drink with the tax collectors and sinners?" And Jesus answered and said to them, "It is not those who are well who need a physician, but those who are sick. I have not come to call the righteous but sinners to repentance." (5:30–32)

Their haughty disdain for the riffraff inside prevented them from attending Matthew's banquet, but that did not mean that the **Pharisees and their scribes** (see the exposition of 5:17 in chapter 27 of this volume for background information on the scribes and Pharisees) weren't aware of what was going on inside. They expressed their disapproval by **grumbling** (*gogguzō;* an onomatopoetic word) **at** Jesus' **disciples.** They would not deign to speak to any of the tax collectors and sinners attending the banquet. But they evidently expected the Lord and His disciples to follow the prescriptions of the rabbinic law, hence their anger and resentment toward them.

Their question, **"Why do you eat and drink with the tax collectors and sinners?"** reflects the scribes' and Pharisees' outrage that Jesus and His disciples would associate with those unclean outcasts. Their question was a rhetorical one, intended as a stinging rebuke for what they viewed as outrageous behavior on the part of the Lord and His disciples. The question exposes the scribes and Pharisees as proud, focused on externals, and hypocritical. Imagining themselves to be the religious elite, they were in reality void of grace and strangers to salvation. Jesus turned His back on the outwardly moral, and focused on transforming repentant sinners into a holy people.

Overhearing the scribes and Pharisees, **Jesus answered** their challenge. His reply consisted of three parts. The Lord first gave an analogy, pointing out the self-evident fact that **it is not those who are well who need a physician, but those who are sick.** The scribes and Pharisees could not dispute that the tax collectors and sinners were spiritually sick; they were the sickest of the sick. How could they argue that the Great Physician should not minister to them? The Lord's reply was a powerful indictment of their cold hearts, wickedness, and hatred of the very downtrodden sinners they should have sought to help. They saw no sin in themselves and no good or value in others.

Second, Jesus answered them from Scripture. Matthew 9:13 records that He also told the scribes and Pharisees to "go and learn [an expression used by the rabbis to rebuke unwarranted ignorance] what this means: 'I desire compassion, and not sacrifice.'" The quote is from Hosea 6:6, and declares that God does not want external sacrifices but a heart that shows mercy (cf. Prov. 21:3; Isa. 1:11–17; Amos 5:21–24; Mic. 6:8). Those who show mercy to others as the Lord commanded (Luke 6:36) will themselves receive mercy from God (Matt. 5:7), but "judgment will be merciless to one who has shown no mercy" (James 2:13). The scribes and Pharisees, who prided themselves on their rigid adherence to the law, had no excuse for failing to show mercy to those who so desperately needed it.

Finally, Jesus answered them from His own personal authority as God incarnate, declaring, **"I have not come to call the righteous but sinners to repentance."** It is a statement full of irony, even sarcasm (cf. Paul's sarcastic deflation of the conceited Corinthians in 1 Cor. 4:8). Accepting on the surface the scribes' and Pharisees' evaluation of themselves as righteous and hence not in need of a Savior, Jesus judicially left them to their self-righteous folly (cf. Matt. 15:14). Later He would again make this point when He told His hearers that "there will be more joy in heaven over one sinner who repents than over ninety-nine righteous persons who need no repentance" (Luke 15:7). God seeks the truly repentant heart, not the hardened, self-righteous one. It was the humble, repentant tax collector, not the self-exalting, self-righteous Pharisee who Jesus said was justified (18:14). It was His classifying of them as sinners in need of repentance that inflamed the Pharisees' hatred of Jesus.

The truth is that God cannot save those who refuse to see themselves as sinners, who ignore, gloss over, or trivialize their sin. Only those who understand by the grace of God and the convicting work of the Holy Spirit that they are the poor, prisoners, blind, and oppressed, headed for a Christless, Godless eternity in hell, and trust in Christ's work on the cross as payment in full for their sins (Col. 2:13–14) can be saved. As James wrote, "God is opposed to the proud, but gives grace to the humble" (James 4:6).

The scribes and Pharisees had badly misunderstood God's purpose in giving the law. He did not give the law as a means of achieving self-righteousness, but to provoke self-condemnation, awareness of sin, conviction, repentance, and pleading to God for mercy. The law is "our tutor to lead us to Christ, so that we may be justified by faith" (Gal. 3:24). As Paul wrote in 1 Timothy 1:9–10,

> [God's] law is not made for a righteous person, but for those who are lawless and rebellious, for the ungodly and sinners, for the unholy and profane, for those who kill their fathers or mothers, for murderers and immoral men and homosexuals and kidnappers and liars and perjurers, and whatever else is contrary to sound teaching.

Only those who recognize themselves to be in the latter group can embrace the glorious gospel of forgiveness. Such a one was Paul, the self-proclaimed foremost of all sinners (1 Tim. 1:15), who nevertheless found that "the grace of our Lord was more than abundant" to save even him (v. 14).

The Uniqueness of the Gospel (Luke 5:33–39)

29

And they said to Him, "The disciples of John often fast and offer prayers, the disciples of the Pharisees also do the same, but Yours eat and drink." And Jesus said to them, "You cannot make the attendants of the bridegroom fast while the bridegroom is with them, can you? But the days will come; and when the bridegroom is taken away from them, then they will fast in those days." And He was also telling them a parable: "No one tears a piece of cloth from a new garment and puts it on an old garment; otherwise he will both tear the new, and the piece from the new will not match the old. And no one puts new wine into old wineskins; otherwise the new wine will burst the skins and it will be spilled out, and the skins will be ruined. But new wine must be put into fresh wineskins. And no one, after drinking old wine wishes for new; for he says, 'The old is good enough.'" (5:33–39)

In an age of religious pluralism and postmodernist relativism, the Christian gospel is unique. It stands alone, and is incompatible with any and all other religions. Any form of syncretism is unacceptable; the Christian gospel, the "gospel of God" (Mark 1:14; Rom. 1:1; 15:16; 2 Cor. 11:7; 1 Thess. 2:2,8,9; 1 Peter 4:17), cannot be mixed with any man-made religion or humanistic philosophy. That is the clear teaching both of the Lord Jesus Christ and the apostles. Jesus said, "I am the way, and the truth, and the life; no one comes to the Father but through Me" (John 14:6; cf. 1:17). On trial before Israel's supreme court, the Sanhedrin, Peter and John fearlessly testified that "there is salvation in no one else [other than Jesus Christ]; for there is no other name under heaven that has been given among men by which we must be saved" (Acts 4:12). When it comes to salvation, "no man can lay a foundation other than the one which is laid, which is Jesus Christ" (1 Cor. 3:11). There are not many paths to the top of the mountain, as those who maintain the essential unity of all religions falsely imagine; on the contrary, there is "one mediator also between God and men, the man Christ Jesus" (1 Tim. 2:5).

Unfortunately, many who claim to be evangelicals seem to have forgotten those foundational, nonnegotiable truths. Embracing the radical skepticism about the possibility of absolute truth that marks post-modernism, many in the emerging church movement apply that skepti-cism to biblical truth. The idea that there could be certainty regarding what Scripture teaches makes them uncomfortable; they, to accommo-date their sinful indulgence, view the Bible's meaning as vague, indis-tinct, uncertain, and probably ultimately unknowable. Further, under the guise of religious tolerance, they are scornfully intolerant of those who hold to biblical absolutes. Such uncertainty leads to apathy. Since truth either does not exist or cannot be discovered, why bother about it? They prefer instead to focus on fulfilled living and social causes. But without a commitment to the clear truth of Scripture, there can be no standard by which to fulfill God's priorities.

Such agnosticism regarding biblical truth is the antithesis of true faith. It is nothing more than love of self and sin in religious garb, mas-querading as humility. Scripture teaches that absolute truth exists and that every person is accountable to it. As Paul wrote in 2 Thessalonians 2:10, failing to love the truth is the mark of unbelievers, who are damned by their unbelief. On the other hand, believers are those who know the truth and have been set free by it (John 8:32). In the prologue to his gospel Luke declared that he had done careful research (1:3) so that his readers "may know the exact truth about the things" of which he wrote (v. 4). Jesus taught that acceptable worship of God must be consistent with the truth (John 4:23–24), that the Holy Spirit is the Spirit of truth (John 14:17; 15:26; 16:13), that God's Word is truth (John 17:17, 19), and that He came into the world to testify to the truth (John 18:37). Paul taught that those who refuse to obey the truth will face God's wrath (Rom. 2:8), that the gospel is "the message of truth" (Eph. 1:13), that the "truth is in Jesus" (Eph. 4:21), that sal-vation comes through "faith in the truth" (2 Thess. 2:13; cf. 1 Tim. 2:4), that the church is "the pillar and support of the truth" (1 Tim. 3:15), that unbelievers are "deprived of the truth" (1 Tim. 6:5), "have gone astray from the truth" (2 Tim. 2:18), are "always learning and never able to come to the knowledge of the truth (2 Tim. 3:7), "oppose the truth" (2 Tim. 3:8), and "turn away their ears from the truth" (2 Tim. 4:4; cf. Titus 1:14).

The scandal of the gospel is, as Francis Schaeffer said years ago, that Christians preach an exclusive Christ in an inclusive age. But now, as noted above, the world's inclusivism and pluralism has infiltrated the church. Shockingly, some voices within the church are even suggesting that adherents of other religions can follow Jesus Christ without leaving their religions or identifying with Christianity. In fact, some argue that those in non-Christian religions may actually be aided in coming to God by those false religions. Clark Pinnock writes,

> When we approach the man of a faith other than our own, it will be in a spirit of expectancy to find how God has been speaking to him and what new understanding of the grace and love of God we may ourselves discover in this encounter. Our first task in approaching another people, another culture, another religion is to take off the shoes, for the place we are approaching is holy.... we may forget that God was here before our arrival. (Cited in Erwin Lutzer, *Christ Among Other gods* [Chicago: Moody, 1994], 185.)

Then, shockingly, he adds,

> God ... has more going on by way of redemption than what happened in first-century Palestine. (Lutzer, 185)

The theme of this closing section of chapter 5 is an appropriate one in this age where diversity of belief, openness to other religious views, and inclusivism are seen as the primary religious virtues. In His confrontation with the Jewish religious leaders over the question of fasting, the Lord Jesus Christ set forth clearly the uniqueness and exclusivity of the gospel. He did not come as merely another rabbi within the framework of contemporary Judaism. Nor did He come to make a few minor tweaks to the existing religious system of His day. Jesus came to preach the gospel, which fulfilled the Old Testament and was incompatible with the Jewish religion of His day. Judaism was concerned with self-righteousness (Luke 16:15; 18:11–12) the gospel with heart righteousness; Judaism was concerned with what men thought (Matt. 6:2, 5, 16; 23:5), the gospel with what God thinks; Judaism was concerned with external behavior (Matt. 23:25–28), the gospel with internal attitudes.

It was Jesus' uncompromising insistence on the gospel's exclusivity that lay at the heart of His ongoing conflict with the Jewish religious leaders. That hostility, already evident in two earlier incidents in chapter 5, the healing of the paralytic (vv. 17–26) and the confrontation at Matthew's banquet (vv. 30–32), escalates in this passage. All three Synoptic Gospels place this incident immediately after the banquet given by Matthew, suggesting that it happened shortly afterward. The text contains three simple elements: the inquisition, the interpretation, and the illustrations.

THE INQUISITION

And they said to Him, "The disciples of John often fast and offer prayers, the disciples of the Pharisees also do the same, but Yours eat and drink." (5:33)

Luke's failure to specify the antecedent of **they** further links this passage to the previous one. If this incident took place at a different time, Luke would have needed to identify the people who were speaking. According to Matthew's account, the disciples of John the Baptist were the ones asking the question (Matt. 9:14). There is no contradiction between Matthew and Luke, however, since Mark 2:18 records that both the Pharisees and John's disciples approached Jesus. No doubt individuals from both groups fired the same question at the Lord.

That the **disciples of John** appeared with the scribes and Pharisees is surprising. After all, John was Jesus' forerunner, who pointed Him out as "the Lamb of God who takes away the sin of the world!" (John 1:29; cf. v. 36) and pointed his own disciples to Jesus (John 1:37; cf. 3:28–30). Why would his disciples be associated with Jesus' bitter enemies?

It must be remembered that not all of those who followed John were present when Jesus was baptized, or when John pointed Him out as the Lamb of God. Nor were they all convinced that Jesus was the Messiah; even John had his moment of doubt (Luke 7:19), and years later Paul encountered some disciples of John who did not even then know that Jesus was the Messiah (Acts 19:1–7). Since John was by this time in prison (Luke 3:20), he was not available to confirm to his disciples that Jesus was the One he heralded. Many of John's followers who did not believe Jesus was the Messiah had nonetheless made a serious spiritual confession when they were baptized. They had acknowledged their sin and sought forgiveness, in an effort to prepare themselves for Messiah's coming kingdom. It was natural for such committed people to associate with the religious elite, the Pharisees and scribes.

John's disciples and the Pharisees reproached Jesus' disciples for violating Jewish religious custom by failing to **fast and offer** ritual

prayers. Fasting was one of the three major practical expressions of Jewish piety, along with prayer and giving alms. All three were done publicly and ostentatiously by the religious elite to showcase their supposed godliness before men. In the Sermon on the Mount Jesus warned against such hypocrisy:

> So when you give to the poor, do not sound a trumpet before you, as the hypocrites do in the synagogues and in the streets, so that they may be honored by men. Truly I say to you, they have their reward in full. But when you give to the poor, do not let your left hand know what your right hand is doing, so that your giving will be in secret; and your Father who sees what is done in secret will reward you. When you pray, you are not to be like the hypocrites; for they love to stand and pray in the synagogues and on the street corners so that they may be seen by men. Truly I say to you, they have their reward in full. But you, when you pray, go into your inner room, close your door and pray to your Father who is in secret, and your Father who sees what is done in secret will reward you. . . . Whenever you fast, do not put on a gloomy face as the hypocrites do, for they neglect their appearance so that they will be noticed by men when they are fasting. Truly I say to you, they have their reward in full. But you, when you fast, anoint your head and wash your face so that your fasting will not be noticed by men, but by your Father who is in secret; and your Father who sees what is done in secret will reward you. (Matt. 6:2–6, 16–18)

Though the Pharisees fasted twice a week (Luke 18:12) on Monday and Thursday, there is only one fast mandated in the Old Testament. On the Day of Atonement, the Lord commanded the people of Israel to humble or afflict their souls (Lev. 16:29, 31), which is a reference to fasting (cf. *The Zondervan Pictorial Encyclopedia of the Bible*, s.v. "Fasting"). The rabbinical writings forbade eating—even as much as a single date—or drinking on the Day of Atonement. On a day set aside for mourning over and repenting from sin, eating was deemed inappropriate. There are nonrequired fasts mentioned in the Old Testament (e.g., Judg. 20:26; 1 Sam. 7:6; 31:13; 2 Sam. 1:12; 12:16; 1 Kings 21:27; 2 Chron. 20:3; Ezra 8:21, 23; Neh. 1:4; 9:1; Est. 4:1–3; Ps. 69:10; Dan. 9:3; Joel 1:13–14; 2:12, 15), but they were spontaneous, associated with grief, mourning, and humbly seeking God.

What outraged the scribes, Pharisees, and disciples of John was that the disciples of Jesus ignored the traditional ritual fasts and continued to **eat and drink.** Accosting Jesus, they demanded an explanation for that egregious breach of Jewish custom.

THE INTERPRETATION

And Jesus said to them, "You cannot make the attendants of the bridegroom fast while the bridegroom is with them, can you? But the days will come; and when the bridegroom is taken away from them, then they will fast in those days." (5:34–35)

Jesus defended His disciples' failure to fast, interpreting their behavior in its true light. Using a familiar experience, He reminded them that the **attendants,** the close friends **of the bridegroom** involved in a wedding, could hardly be expected to **fast while the bridegroom** was **with them.** After all, no one fasts at a wedding; that would be completely inappropriate. A wedding is a time for joyous feasting, not mournful (cf. Matt. 9:15) fasting. It is a time to laugh, not to weep; a time to dance, not to mourn (Eccl. 3:4). The Old Testament never refers to Messiah as a **bridegroom** (though it refers to Israel as the bride of the Lord; e.g., Isa. 62:4–5; Jer. 2:2; Hos. 2:16–20); that is a New Testament concept introduced here by Jesus (cf. Matt. 9:15; Mark 2:19–20 and John the Baptist's use of a similar analogy in John 3:29). Later in Revelation, the church is depicted as the bride of Christ (19:7; 21:2, 9; 22:17).

So it was equally ridiculous to expect Jesus' disciples to fast and mourn while He was present with them. But the bridegroom would not always be with them. **The days will come,** Jesus said, **when the bridegroom is taken away from them, then they will fast in those days.** The time of joy would end when the bridegroom was suddenly **taken away** in the midst of the celebration. In the future, the Lord pointed out, He would be executed, and the disciples would lose Him. (This is the first time in Luke's gospel that Jesus referred to His death.) When that happened they would be overcome with fear and grief; the prophecy of Zechariah 13:7, "strike the Shepherd that the sheep may be scattered" would be fulfilled (cf. Matt. 26:31; Mark 14:50). The disciples did not understand Jesus' repeated predictions of His death (cf. Mark 9:31–32), since it did not fit into their preconceived notion that the Messiah would conquer Israel's enemies and set up His kingdom. Even their leader, Peter, missed the point. When

> Jesus began to show His disciples that He must go to Jerusalem, and suffer many things from the elders and chief priests and scribes, and be killed, and be raised up on the third day. Peter took Him aside and began to rebuke Him, saying, 'God forbid it, Lord! This shall never happen to You'" (Matt. 16:21–22).

But what Isaiah had predicted centuries earlier concerning the Messiah, "By oppression and judgment He was taken away" (53:8), would come to pass. After Jesus was taken from them, His disciples did fast (cf. Matt. 6:16–18; Acts 13:2–3; 14:23).

THE ILLUSTRATIONS

And He was also telling them a parable: "No one tears a piece of cloth from a new garment and puts it on an old garment; otherwise he will both tear the new, and the piece from the new will not match the old. And no one puts new wine into old wineskins; otherwise the new wine will burst the skins and it will be spilled out, and the skins will be ruined. But new wine must be put into fresh wineskins. And no one, after drinking old wine wishes for new; for he says, 'The old is good enough.' " (5:36–39)

To illustrate the uniqueness of the gospel, Jesus told **a parable** (*parabolē;* a figurative example, metaphor, analogy, or story), or more specifically, a series of three parables. First, He pointed out that **no one tears a piece of cloth from a new garment and puts it on an old garment.** To do so would be foolish for a couple of reasons. In the first place, tearing **a piece of cloth from a new garment** obviously would ruin that garment. Nor would the new patch work if sewn in the old garment, since **the piece from the new will not match** the faded color or the pattern of **the old.** Even worse, after the patched garment is washed, "the patch [from the new, unshrunk garment] pulls away from the [old, patched] garment, and a worse tear results" (Matt. 9:16). The end result is two ruined garments.

The Lord's point is that the gospel cannot be patched into Judaism (or any other system of salvation by works). His teaching was completely at odds with that of the Jewish leaders. They viewed themselves as righteous (Luke 16:15); He preached the necessity of repentance (Luke 5:32; cf. Matt. 4:17). They were proud of their supposedly exalted religious status (Luke 20:46–47); He proclaimed the need for humility (Matt. 5:3). They focused on external ceremony, ritual, and outward observance of the law; He focused on the heart (Matt. 15:7–9; Luke 11:39–52). They loved the approval of men; He offered the approval of God (Matt. 23:5–7; John 12:43).

The old garment in the Lord's illustration is not the Old Testament. It is not God's eternal law, which is holy, righteous, and good (Rom. 7:12), and which Jesus came to fulfill, not to replace (Matt. 5:17–19). Rather, it is the ritualistic, legalistic religion based on rabbinic tradition, with its man-made regulations (Matt. 15:3–6) that obscured the Law of God. Jesus did not come to patch that system, but to replace it with the garment of salvation (Isa. 61:10)— the good news of salvation by faith in Him. No works-righteousness system can be patched into the gospel of grace and faith.

It would be just as foolish and futile to put **new wine into old wineskins;** because **the new wine will burst the skins and it will be spilled out, and the skins will be ruined.** Wine was typically stored in containers made of animal skins. As the new, fresh wine fermented, gas would be released and the skins would expand. If anyone was foolish enough to put **new wine into old,** stretched-out wineskins, **the new wine** would **burst the skins,** the wine would **be spilled out** and lost, **and the skins** would **be ruined.** New wine had to be stored in **fresh wineskins,** which were still supple enough to expand during the fermentation process.

Like the first illustration, this one also highlights the futility and impossibility of mixing the gospel of grace with any system of works-righteousness. Grace is antithetical to and not compatible with any such system (Rom. 11:6; Gal. 5:4).

The Lord's final illustration describes the tragedy of those who reject the gospel of grace and cling to their false system of works-righteousness. Jesus likened such people to those who are content with the old wine they have been drinking, and have no desire to taste the new. **No one,** Jesus said, **after drinking old wine wishes for new; for he says, "The old is good enough."** False religion deadens the spiritual senses. Far enough into the drinking experience, the drinker does not care about the taste of the wine. It is one of the chief ways that the "god of this world [blinds] the minds of the unbelieving so that they might not see the light of the gospel of the glory of Christ, who is the image of God" (2 Cor. 4:4). Like wine drinkers sloshing their familiar drink, people stubbornly cling to their comfortable religious traditions, and have little or no interest in the new, fresh saving truth of the gospel.

For those unwilling to leave their false religions and embrace the gospel, there is no hope of salvation (John 14:6; Acts 4:12). The church's goal is not to make unbelievers comfortable in their false religious systems or to help them assimilate Jesus into those systems. The commission the Lord gave to the church is to "go therefore and make disciples of all the nations, baptizing them in the name of the Father and the Son and the Holy Spirit, teaching them to observe all that I commanded you; and lo, I am with you always, even to the end of the age" (Matt. 28:19–20).

Bibliography

Bock, Darrell L. *Luke 1:1–9:50*. Baker Exegetical Commentary on the New Testament. Grand Rapids: Baker, 1994.

Bruce, Alexander B. "The Synoptic Gospels," in W. Robertson Nicoll, ed. *The Expositor's Greek Testament*. Vol. 1. Reprint. Peabody, Mass.: Hendrickson, 2002.

Carson, D. A., Douglas J. Moo, and Leon Morris. *An Introduction to the New Testament*. Grand Rapids: Zondervan, 1992.

Ellis, E. Earle. *The Gospel of Luke*, The New Century Bible Commentary. Grand Rapids: Eerdmans, 1974.

Gooding, David. *According to Luke*. Grand Rapids: Eerdmans, 1987.

Guthrie, Donald. *New Testament Introduction*. Revised edition. Downers Grove, Ill.: InterVarsity, 1990.

Hendriksen, William. *Exposition of the Gospel According to Luke*, New Testament Commentary. Grand Rapids: Baker, 1978.

Hiebert, D. Edmond. *An Introduction to the New Testament*. Vol. 1, *The Gospels and Acts*. Chicago: Moody, 1975.

Lenski, R. C. H. *The Interpretation of St. Luke's Gospel*. Minneapolis: Augsburg, 1961.

Liefeld, Walter L. and David W. Pao. "Luke," in Tremper Longman III and David E. Garland, eds. *The Expositor's Bible Commentary*. Vol. 10. Revised edition. Grand Rapids: Zondervan, 2007.

Marshall, I. Howard. *The Gospel of Luke,* The New International Greek Testament Commentary. Grand Rapids: Eerdmans, 1978.

Morris, Leon. *The Gospel According to St. Luke,* The Tyndale New Testament Commentaries. Grand Rapids: Eerdmans, 1975.

Plummer, Alfred. *The Gospel According to St. Luke,* The International Critical Commentary. Edinburgh: T. & T. Clark, 1969.

Stein, Robert H. *Luke,* The New American Commentary. Nashville: Broadman & Holman, 1992.

Indexes

Index of Greek Words and Phrases

agalliaō, 79
agoradzō, 96
akoloutheō, 331
anatolē, 122
anistēmi, 331
antilegō, 184
apeithēs, 40
aphesis, 272
apokathistanō, 132
appollumi, 286
archisunagōgos, 267

daimonizomai, 283
diabolos, 255
dialegomai, 193
diatarassomai, 47
didaskalos, 193
doulē, 60, 80

doulos, 159

ekplēssō, 282
eleos, 120
episkiazō, 57
epistatēs, 305, 307
epitimaō, 292
eulabēs, 176
euangelizō, 29, 157

hiatros, 12
hieron, 180
hupsistos, 49

kataluma, 149
kōphos, 90
koinē, 11
kurios, 159, 307

lepras, 313
logos, 205
lutrōsis, 96

mega, 292
megalunō, 79
megas, 48
mē genoito, 111
mokhes, 330,331
monogenēs, 149,196

naos, 180

pandocheion, 149
parthenos, 44,56
penēs, 270
peplērophorēmenōn, 13
phobos, 325
phronēsis, 40

pinakidion, 90
plērēs, 254
prokoptō, 197
prophēteuō, 96
proskuneō, 315
prōtotokos, 149, 196
ptōchos, 270

rhema, 205

splagchna, 120
sungenis, 58

thaumazō, 163
tithēmi, 132
tou, 248

zōgreō, 309

Index of Scripture

Genesis

1:2	57	12:2–3	106, 127	17:5	108
2:17	27	12:3	106	17:5, 23	89
3:1	255, 256	12:4–5	106	17:7	109, 128
3:1–5	217	12:7	106, 174	17:9–14	89, 167
3:6–13	58	13	107	17:13	109
3:15	42, 55, 174, 288	13–15	217	17:15–19	174
3:21	321	14:14	176	17:15–21	109
4:5	244	14:18–20	49	17:19	90, 109
5:24	35	15	106, 107	18:1–15	59
6	286	15:6	21, 24, 176	18:9–15	106
6:5–7	27	15:7	107	18:10, 14	174
9:9–17	95	15:8	107	18:25	273
9:26	96	15:9–17	108	18:27	307
10	244	15:14–15	127	19:24	27
11	244	15:17	127	21:1–2	174
11:30	106	15:18	107	21:1–3	109
11:31	105, 106	15:18–21	108	21:1–8	106
12	106, 107	16:3	108	21:6	88
12:1	106, 127	16:11	108	21:12	196
12:1–3	83, 106	17	107, 108	21:33	71
12:2	106	17:2	108	21:34	109
		17:4	108	22	107, 109

22:1–18	76	22:22	275	**Numbers**	
22:2	109	23:17	192	1:23	176
22:11–12	109	23:20, 23	29	3:3	24
22:12	157	24:4–8	115	3:12–13	170
22:18	174	24:16–17	156	3:41, 44, 45	170
25:21–23	69	24:17	156	4:3, 35, 39, 43, 47	248
25:26	89	29:8–9, 44	23	4:5–6	75
26	107	29:9	24	5:2	276
26:24	157	30:7–8	26	5:14–15	24
27:28, 37	36	31:2–3	180	6:23–27	29
28	107	32	115	10:9	154
29:33	176	32:7–8	74	11:17	239
30:1–2, 23	25	33:22–34:5	156	11:23	91
30:2	71	34:6	153	11:25	180
30:22–23	59	34:6–7	321	14:18	206, 321
33:5	25	34:7	206	18:7	23, 24
34:25	176	34:22–23	192	18:15–16	170
35	107	34:29, 35	156	20:14–21	22
35:19	147	40:13–15	24	23:19	87
38:8	247	40:34–35	156	25:10–13	95
40:20	140			25:13	113
41:46	248	**Leviticus**		26:53–55	244
42:18	157	5:3	315	26:59	59
43:33	149	10:1–7	29	34:11	302
49:10	42	12:1–5	169	35:25	203
		12:3	89, 167		
Exodus		12:6	171	**Deuteronomy**	
3:1	155	12:8	171	3:24	59
3:11	64	13–14	313	4:13	95
3:14–15	159	13:45–46	313, 314	4:14–18	74
4:1	64	14:1–20	316	5:24	156
4:22	196	14:10	316	6:13	259, 307
4:25	89	15:19	169	6:16	260
5:2	82	16:12–13	26	7:7–8	128
12:1–51	191	16:29, 31	339	7:9	174
12:26–27	192	17:7	280	7:13	36, 71
13:1–2	169, 170	18:21	153	8:3	257
13:11–15	170	19:18	220	9:4	21
15:1, 21	94	20:2–5	153	10:12–13	309
15:1–21	82, 94	20:10	60	10:16	167
15:6	91	20:21	231	13:4	308
15:20	185	21:7, 14	24	14:29	275
18:21	157	21:17–23	24	16:11, 14	275
20:3	79	24:10–16	323	16:16	192
20:3, 23	74	25:10	146	17:6	165
20:7	323	25:25	244	18:15–18	42, 175
20:18–19	307	26:42	83	19:15	165
21:22–25	37			20:4	153

21:15–17	149	16:17	37	22:14	49
22:13–21	60	20:26	339	23:5	99
23:14	154				
24:17–21	275	**Ruth**		**1 Kings**	
25:5–7	247	4:1–6	244	2:4	174
27:11–26	116	4:10	247	8:10–11	156
28:1–14	115	4:14	96	8:24–25	174
28:15–68	116	4:17	89	8:39	323
29:1	118			8:46	179
29:29	47	**1 Samuel**		8:56	28, 87, 174
30:1–3	118	1:1–2:10	60	8:66	98
30:6	119, 167	1:2, 5	54	9:5	174
30:8–10	25	1:4–11	25	15:12	74
32:4	174	1:6	59	16:31	276
32:8	49	1:7, 10–16	185	16:33	275
32:17	280	1:11	77	17:1	39
33:29	154, 167	1:19–2:10	31	17:18	276
		2:1–10	77, 94	18:12	239
Joshua		2:10	97	18:17–18	38
1:8	25, 76	5:6, 9	92	18:26	152
4:23–24	92	7:6	339	18:27	152
10:23–26	82	10:8	75	18:28	152
12:3	302	12:24	309	18:29	152
13:27	302	13:12	75	21:17–29	39
21:45	87, 174	15	147	21:27	339
23:14	28	16:7	323		
24:2	105	16:11–13	155	**2 Kings**	
24:15	116	17:12	147	2:16	239
24:16	116	20:6	147	5:1	276
24:20	116	31:13	339	5:25–27	314
24:21, 24	116			7:3	314
		2 Samuel		7:3–4	276
Judges		1:12	339	14:7	22
2:7	116	3:18	98, 154	17:6–12	74
2:10–15	116	5:4	248	17:39	154
2:18	154	5:7–9	147	20:2–3	65
4:4	185	6:3	75	22:14	185
5:1–31	94	6:3–4, 6–7	30	23:10	153
5:3	94	7	128		
5:24	71	7:1–17	35	**1 Chronicles**	
6:12	47	7:12	45, 128	1–9	244
6:16–23	64	7:12–13	128, 174	3:17–18	249
6:22–23	27	7:12–14	100	3:19	249
6:23	157	7:13, 16	100	5:1	149
6:34	239	7:16	174	11:7	147
6:36–40	65	12:16	185, 339	16:35	167
8:34	154	22:1, 4	154	23:3	248
13:22	307	22:3	77, 153	24:4–19	24

28:9	323	9:4	59	36:5	174
29:11	259	15:14	58, 179	37	258
29:12	26	25:4	46	37:25	257
		26:7	252	40:7–8	43
2 Chronicles		28:28	157	40:8	167, 171
5:12–14	94	33:4	57	40:10	174
7:1–3	156	34:24	82	50:23	77
7:14	219	37:23	91	51:4	323
15:1	239	42:5–6	307	51:5	58, 169
20:3	339			51:9	207
20:6	259	**Psalms**		51:17	271, 308
21:3	149	1:1–2	171	62:11	91, 306
26:16–21	30	1:2	76	63:6	76
26:16–23	314	1:4	223	65:3	207, 321
29:11	26	2:2	98	66:16	157
30:6	185	2:6	211	69:10	339
30:11	185	2:6–9	42, 175	73:3–13	258
		2:7	175, 240	78:65	36
Ezra		2:8	258	82:5	122, 272
2:36–38	24	2:9	50	86:5	207, 322
2:61–62	244	2:11	309	86:11	76
3:2	249	4:4	76	86:15	120
7:21–26	146	7:10	167	89	99, 128
7:27	96	7:17	49, 93	89:3–4	174
7:28	92	16:8	79	89:8	174
8:21, 23	339	17:7	153	89:13	60
8:23	185	19:7	86	91:4	174
8:31	154	19:7–8	24	91:11–12	260
		22	131, 136, 260	92:1	93
Nehemiah		22:26	164	98:3	83
1:4	185, 339	22:28	259	99:3	77
6:14	185	23:1	155	100:4	164
7:2	157	24:3–4	77	100:5	174
8:10	93	25:5	153	103:1	76
9:1	339	29:10	61	103:8	153
9:6–7	306	30:4	93, 164	103:12	207, 322
9:17	153, 206, 321	31:5	303	103:17	82
12:1	249	31:23	79	104:1–2	156
		32	206	104:24–30	306
Esther		32:1–2	25	104.30	57
4:1–3	339	32:1–2, 5	207	105:2	93
		33:1	164	106:10	100, 154
Job		33:4	174	106:21	153, 167
1:1	25	34:1	164	106:37	280
1:6	280	34:2	77	107:10, 14	122
1:9	157	34:10	82	110	99
2:1	280	34:18	271	110:1	175
4:7–9	314	35:13	185	110:4	175

111:10	157,309	6:1–5	157	43:13	79
113:9	25	6:1–10	49	43:25	207,322
119:15,23,48,78,	76	6:5	157,308	44:2	157
97,99,148		6:5–9	308	44:22	207,322
119:70,77,92,174	171	6:8–11	309	45:1–4	146
119:90	174	7:14	43,48,55,174	45:15	153
119:105	37	8:3	185	45:15,17	168
119:142,160	77	8:13–15	183	45:21	153,168
127:3	25,71	9:1	44	45:22	168
130:3–4	24,207,322	9:1–2	182	45:25	181
132	99,128	9:2	20,122,158	46:13	181
132:17	98	9:6	175	48:1	78,217
136:23	77	9:7	100,174	49:6	182
137:7	22	10:5–7	146	49:6–9	158
138:2	303	11:9	211	49:8	273
139:23–24	76	13:6	216	49:8–13	178
145:8	120	13:18	71	49:14–16	211
		14:12	255	49:26	153,168
Proverbs		14:12–14	280	50:2b	306
1:7	157	14:13	255	50:6	175
2:13	122	14:14	49,259	51:1–3,12	211
3:34	47	19:16	92	51:3,12	178
4:19	122	26:3	62	51:4	158
9:10	157,309	29:13	21,78,217	51:4–5	182
15:33	157	29:18	175	52:9	178,211
16:5	79	30:18	88	52:10	182
20:1	36	34:8	216	53	104,131,136,
20:9	179	38:17	207,322		153,260
21:1	146	40	210,211	53:4–6	153,175
21:3	333	40–66	166	53:4–6,8,10–12	122
31:6	37	40:1	178	53:6	58
		40:3	21,175	53:8	153,341
Ecclesiastes		40:3–4	245	53:9	167
2:3	36	40:3–5	210	53:10	168
2:14	122	40:6–11,28–31	211	53:10–12	154
3:4	340	40:10	178	54:4–8	211
5:7	157	40:11	155	54:10	123
7:20	58,179	41:8–10,13	211	54:11	178
8:12	157	42:5–7	271	55:6–7	177,207
12:13	62,157	42:6	158,182	55:7	322
		42:6–7	122	55:8–9	82
Isaiah		42:7	272	57:15	80,308
1:4–5	219	42:8	49,79	57:18	178,211
1:11–17	333	43:1,5	157	58:6	270
1:11–20	75	43:3	168	59:1	168
1:18	207,322	43:3,11	153	59:2	209
2:2	211	43:11	77,153,	59:9–10	122
2:12	216		168,229	59:16	122

59:20	122	31:33–34	129	36:26	119, 222
59:21	122	31:34	120, 206, 322	36:26–27	180
60:1–3	158, 182	31:35	129	36:27	120, 223
60:1–5	122	32:17, 27	59	36:32	130
60:16	153, 168	32:35	153	36:37, 38	130
60:19–20	123	33:8	206	37:14	223
61:1	155	33:15	211	37:26	200
61:1–2	178, 270,	33:21–22	98	38:22	223
	274, 282	33:26	121	39:25	83, 121
61:2	211, 216	44:16–19	61	43:2	156
61:10	25, 35, 342	46:27–28	157	44:22	24
62:4–5	340	50:20	206		
63:1, 8	168			**Daniel**	
63:4	216, 273	**Lamentations**		1:8–16	35
63:8–9	153	3:23	174	2:19–20	96
63:9	121, 154	3:35, 38	49	2:21	259
64:6	21, 315	3:57	157	2:44–45	211
65:16	303			4:17, 25	259
65:17–19	49	**Ezekiel**		4:35	306
66:2	271, 308	1:1	238, 248	4:37	61
66:10–13	179	1:3	205	5:20	82
66:12–13	211	1:27–28	156	7:13–14	258
		1:28	157, 287, 308	7:14, 27	50
Jeremiah		3:23	157	7:15–16	27
1:1–2	205	8:1	267	8:15–18	157
1:4–5	38	9:3	156	9:3	185, 339
2:2	340	10:4, 18, 19	156	9:9	24, 207
4:4	167	11:5	323	9:25–26	43, 159
5:21	272	11:19	222	10:7–9, 16–17	157
7:16–20	61	11:22–23	156	10:12, 19	27, 157
12:2	21, 78, 217	13:5	216	10:13, 21	29
13:23	179	14:22–23	179		
14:8	153, 168	16:1–5	160	**Hosea**	
17:9	114, 179	16:60–63	206	1:1	205
17:10	323	18:4	27	1:4, 6, 9	90
20:13	94	18:30–32	207	2:16–20	340
22:24–30	247	25:12–14	22	3:5	211
23:5	43, 97, 174	28:11–15	255	4:11	36
29:10	96	28:12–16	280	6:6	333
31	129	28:15	255	11:12	174
31:13	179	30:3	216	13:4	153, 168
31:20	83	33:19	207, 219		
31:31	129	33:31	78, 267	**Joel**	
31:31–34	119, 177,	33:31–32	217	1:1	205
	200	34:23–24	211	1:13–14	339
31:32	119	35:15	22	1:15	216
31:32–33	129	36:24–27	130	2:1	216
31:33	119	36:25	120	2:1, 11	216

2:12,15	339	1:18	223	1:22–23	174	
2:13	40,153	3:8	220	1:23	48,49,55,	
3:1–2	220	3:11–13	49		56,234	
3:12–14	220			1:24	148	
3:14	216	**Haggai**		1:24–25	148	
		1:1	205,249	1:25	56,149	
Amos				2:1	175	
1:11–12	22	**Zechariah**		2:1–3	145	
5:18	216	1:9	27	2:1–12	189	
5:21–24	79,333	1:17	179	2:1–19	230	
5:21–27	75	2:3	27	2:1–22	22	
		4:1	27	2:2	23	
Obadiah		7:12	180	2:11	171	
1–14	216	9:9	43	2:13,14,19–21	246	
1–21	22	12–14	131	2:13–15	189	
15	216	12:10	101,110,120,	2:16–18	23,189	
15–21	216		131,136	2:19–23	189	
		13:1	131	3:1	86,204	
Jonah		13:1,8	211	3:1–3	175	
1:1	205	13:7	340	3:1–6	39	
3:10	219	14:1	216	3:2	117	
4:2	153	14:4	101	3:3	117	
		14:9	131	3:4	34	
Micah		14:16–21	49	3:5	205,214	
1:1	205			3:5–6	205	
3:8	180,239	**Malachi**		3:6	205,209	
4:13	97	2:7	24	3:7	217	
5:2	142,147,	3:1	21,38,117,160,	3:7–10	87,117	
	148,174		175,200,245	3:7–11	38	
6:8	333	4:2	20,122,200	3:7–12	205,210	
6:9	157	4:5	117,216	3:13–17	57	
7:18	322			3:14	236	
7:18–19	24,177	**Matthew**		3:15	167,197,237	
7:19	207,322	1:1	50	4:8	258	
		1:1–16	149	4:10	74,261	
Nahum		1:5	246	4:11	257	
1:3	91	1:11	247	4:12	39,228	
		1:16,18,19,20,24	246	4:12–16	182	
Habakkuk		1:18–2:12	42	4:13	282,331	
1:13	240	1:18–25	67	4:13–18:35	265	
2:4	24	1:19	68,148,166	4:17	281,341	
3:3–4	156	1:19–25	60	4:18	292,304	
		1:20–21	147	4:18–22	291,304	
Zephaniah		1:20–21,24–25	68	4:23	293	
1:1	205	1:20–23	163	4:24	283,293	
1:7	216	1:21	13,48,81,90,	5–7	217	
1:7,14	216		120,154,159,167,	5:1	304	
1:7–14	216		171,181,281,321	5:1–12	206	

5:3	270, 315, 341	11:1	281	15:3–6	319, 342
5:7	333	11:2–6	66	15:7–9	78, 341
5:17–19	341	11:5	175, 293	15:14	319, 333
5:20	206, 319	11:8	205	15:31	325
5:21–47	206	11:11	25, 54, 66,	16:15	234, 291
5:48	206		214, 222, 228	16:16–18	292
6:1–5	319	11:13–14	39	16:21–22	340
6:1–18	206	11:18	283	16:23	261
6:2, 5, 16	24, 337	11:19	156	17:1–2	157
6:2–6, 16–18	339	11:25	61	17:1–5	240
6:10	261	11:27	229	17:1–6	308
6:16–18	341	11:28–30	163, 273	17:1–8	49
6:31–33	257	12:12	319	17:5	57, 235
7:13	206	12:15	293	17:5–6	157
7:13–14	210	12:24	275, 296	17:7	157
7:19	219, 223	12:31–32	240	17:10–13	39
7:23	214	12:34	78, 217	17:24–27	237
7:26–27	206	12:38	291, 319	17:27	305
7:28–29	225, 274	12:42–45	284	18:4	47
7:29	303	12:43	282	18:16	165
8:2	314, 315	12:46–47	149	18:17	329
8:5–13	292	12:46–50	80	18:23–35	271
8:12	216	12:48–50	184	19:26	59
8:13	292	13:1	304	20:16	40
8:15	292	13:2	304	20:28	150
8:16	283	13:38	196	21:9	247
8:23–24	303	13:42, 50	216	21:11	269
8:29	195, 256, 286	13:49	176	21:12–13	204
9:1	317	13:54–56	248	21:31	329
9:8	325	13:54–57	80	21:31–32	220
9:9	331	13:55	248	21:42–44	183
9:10	332	13:55–56	149, 183	22:16	23
9:10–13	156	13:58	276	22:17–21	220
9:12	12	14:1–10	39	22:35	319
9:13	333	14:2	232	22:37–38	220
9:14	319, 338	14:3–4	34	23:1	166
9:15	340	14:5	231	23:1–3	204
9:16	341	14:6	140	23:1–33	200
9:33	287	14:6–10	87	23:2, 13, 14, 15,	319
9:34	50	14:7	232	23, 25, 27, 29	
9:35	293	14:9	231	23:2–3	319
10:1	282	14:10	232	23:4	206, 319
10:3	331	14:22–33	303	23:5	337
10:17	268	14:26	325	23:5–7	21, 341
10:28	157, 271	14:27	157	23:15	195, 319
10:29	304	14:33	195	23:23	319
10:32–33	206, 236	15:1	319	23:25–28	337
10:40	297	15:2–6	318	23:27–28	21

23:33	217	2:2	318,320	8:22–25	293
23:39	101	2:3	320	9:7	57
24:30	10,157	2:4	320	9:25	90,282
24:36	305	2:8	323	9:31–32	340
25:1–13	45	2:12	294,325	9:37	297
25:31	184	2:13	329	9:48	216
25:41	219,281,286	2:13–14	330	10:20	328
25:41,46	216	2:16	319	10:21	331
26:28	154,272,	2:17	12	10:22	331
	321,328	2:18	338	10:45	40
26:31	340	2:19–20	340	11:13	305
26:41	261	3:1–2	269	12:13	23
26:63–66	195	3:9	302	12:28–31	115
26:65	323	3:10	292	13:31	79
27:18	320	3:11	256,281,286	13:36	160
27:40,43	195	3:11,30	282	14:36	290
27:46	238,259	3:12	287	14:50	340
27:51	171	3:17	195	14:65	175
27:54	195	3:22	283,296	15:22,34	290
27:55	13	4:1	302	15:40–41	13
28:2–4	157	4:12	39		
28:4,8	325	4:39	292	**Luke**	
28:5,10	157	4:41	157,325	1:1–3a	11
28:19–20	31,158,	5:1–7	281	1:1–4	9
	182,342	5:2	283	1:2–3	3
		5:2,8,13	282	1:3	336
Mark		5:8	283	1:3b–4	15
1:1	195	5:22	267	1:4	4,336
1:5	205	5:22–24,35–43	293	1:5	59,142,175,230
1:12	254	5:25–34	292	1:5–14,18–25	19
1:14	228,335	5:26	12	1:5a	22
1:14–9:50	265	5:29	293	1:5b–7	23
1:16–20	291,292,304	5:33	157	1:6	172,176
1:21	269	6:2	269	1:7	204
1:23	283	6:3	50,248	1:7,24	54
1:23–25	281	6:5	315	1:8–10	26
1:24	234	6:6	276	1:9,21,22	180
1:25,34	287	6:14,22	231	1:11–14	27
1:27	303	6:14–29	34	1:12,26–30	157
1:29	292	6:19	231	1:12,30,65	5
1:31	292	6:31–32	303	1:12,65	325
1:33	295	6:45–8:26	13	1:13–17,76	227
1:34	256,283,286	7:1	319	1:14,44,47,58	4
1:35	238,296	7:6–7	21,75	1:15	35,180
1:38	282,304	7:8–13	318	1:15,35,41,67	5
1:39	297,317	7:25	282,283	1:15–17	33
1:41	315	7:32,37	90	1:16	28
1:45	316	8:10	303	1:16,17b	39

1:17	105, 175, 245	1:67–71	93, 105	2:21	48, 166
1:17*a*	38	1:67–75	117	2:21–24	149, 165
1:18–25	28	1:67–79	4, 94,	2:21–38	166
1:19	157		181, 186	2:22, 23, 24, 27, 39	166
1:21, 63	163	1:68	158	2:22–24	168, 180, 189
1:26	43	1:68–69	189	2:22–38	191
1:26–2:20	42	1:68–69, 77	153	2:23	171
1:26–33	41	1:69	181	2:25	155, 175
1:26–38	163	1:69*b*	97	2:25, 38	200
1:27	44	1:70	98	2:25–27	5
1:27, 30–56	246	1:71	100	2:25–32	5
1:28–30	45	1:72	121	2:25–35	176
1:30	27	1:72–75	103	2:25–38	173, 174, 189
1:31–33	48	1:72*a*	105	2:25*a*	176
1:31–35	141	1:72*b*–73	106	2:25*b*	177
1:32–33	159, 174	1:74–75	109	2:25*c*–27	179
1:33	250	1:76	200	2:26, 29	176
1:34	56	1:76–77	207	2:28–33	181
1:34–35	175	1:76–80	113	2:30	153
1:34–38	53	1:77	118	2:30–32	158
1:35	57, 189, 194, 239	1:78–79	189	2:33	163
1:36	58	1:78*a*	120	2:34	51
1:37	59	1:78*b*–79	121	2:34–35	164, 183
1:38	47, 60	1:80	141, 200, 236	2:35	197
1:39–40	67	2:1	201	2:36	94, 245
1:39–45	63	2:1–3	142	2:36–38	184
1:41	180	2:1–7	139	2:38	96, 105,
1:41–45	4, 94,	2:1–11	266		155, 175
	181, 186	2:4	158	2:38–39	189
1:41*a*, 44	68	2:4–5	146	2:39	171
1:41*b*–43, 45	69, 70	2:5, 16, 19, 34	246	2:39–52	187, 188
1:46–48*a*	78	2:6–7	148	2:40	190
1:46–55	4, 73,	2:7	160	2:41–51	183, 191, 199
	181, 186	2:8–10*a*	155	2:44	192
1:46*b*, 47*b*	81	2:8–20	151, 152, 175	2:49	184, 191
1:47	153, 166, 168	2:9	160, 325	2:51	200
1:48*b*–55	81	2:9–10	5	2:52	197
1:50	121	2:10	4, 27	3	123
1:52	155	2:10–11, 27–32,	189	3:1	22, 143
1:54	121	34, 38		3:1–2*a*	201
1:56–58	87	2:10*b*	158	3:1–6	199
1:56–66	85	2:11	152, 153, 181	3:2*b*–3*a*	204
1:59	167	2:11–12	158	3:3	4, 117
1:59–63	88	2:13–14	5, 94, 160, 186	3:3*b*	205
1:63	95	2:13–14, 38	181	3:4–5	215
1:64	164	2:15–21	162	3:4–6	210
1:64–66	91	2:18, 33	193	3:7–17	210, 213, 214
1:67	131, 180	2:19, 51	92	3:7*a*	215

3:7b	217	4:31–34a	281	5:30–32	332, 338
3:8a, 9–14	218	4:31–37	279	5:31	12
3:8b	221	4:33–35, 41	312	5:32	155, 341
3:12	193	4:34b	285	5:33	185, 338
3:12–13	330	4:34c	286	5:33–39	335
3:15	92	4:35–37	287	5:34–35	340
3:15–17	222	4:37	331	5:36–39	341
3:15–20	15	4:38–40	291, 312	5:42	301
3:16, 22	5	4:38–44	289, 301	5:44	301
3:18	157, 228	4:39	91	6:7	319
3:18–20	225	4:40	315	6:11	325
3:19	230	4:41	195, 295	6:12	5
3:20	202, 338	4:42	317	6:15	331
3:21	5, 238, 317	4:42–44	296	6:16	226
3:21–22	233, 236	4:43	281–82, 304	6:19	293
3:22	190, 305, 320	5:1	205	6:23	4
3:22a	238	5:1–3	301	6:36	120, 333
3:22b	240	5:1–11	299–300, 312	6:37	4
3:23	197, 201	5:4–6a	304	6:45	114
3:23–38	243	5:6b–7	305	7–17	228
3:23a	248	5:7	306	7:1–10	15
3:23b	248	5:8	71, 157	7:5	282
3:27	249	5:8–10a	307	7:9	163
3:30	176	5:9	194	7:11–15	293
4:1	320	5:10	157, 292	7:12	149
4:1, 14, 18	5	5:10, 26	5	7:14	315
4:1–2	254	5:10b–11	308	7:16	5, 158, 164, 325
4:1–13	251, 312	5:12	293	7:19	338
4:3, 9	195	5:12–16	312–13	7:19–20	223
4:3–4	256	5:12–26	311–12	7:22	157
4:3–12	255–56	5:12b	313	7:30	319
4:5–8	258	5:12c	314	7:34	329
4:8	307	5:13	293	7:36	332
4:9–12	259–60	5:13-16	315	7:36–50	16
4:13	261	5:15	320	7:37–38	156
4:14–15	264	5:16	5, 238	7:41–50	4
4:14–30	263–64, 285, 328	5:17	332	7:48	321
		5:17–19	318	8:1	157
4:16–21	268–69	5:17–26	317, 329, 338	8:1–3	13
4:18	328	5:20	321, 331	8:19–21	197
4:18, 43	157	5:20–25	4	8:24	292
4:20	304	5:21, 30	319	8:25	163
4:21	155	5:21–24	323	8:25, 37, 50	5
4:22	163, 194	5:25–26	164, 324	8:25, 56	194
4:22, 32, 36	194	5:27–28	309	8:27	283
4:23	12	5:27–29	329	8:28	285, 286
4:28–30	184, 273–274	5:27–32	327	8:30	283
4:31	267	5:30	329	8:42	149

8:43	12	13:2–5	193	19:1–10	16, 220
8:44	91	13:10, 22	267	19:8	220
8:45–46	305	13:13	164, 315, 324	19:10	4, 13, 15, 48, 81,
9:6	157	13:14	267		154, 159, 281, 332
9:6–7	43	13:17	4, 325	19:47	158, 184, 325
9:9	202	13:24–28	221	20:1	157, 282
9:18	238, 294	13:28	216	20:6	222
9:18, 28-29	5	13:31–35	184	20:14–20	184
9:22–23	15	13:35	110	20:26	163, 194
9:23, 49, 57, 59, 61	309	14:1	332	20:36	196
9:23–25	309	14:3	319	20:41–44	193
9:28–32	156	14:11	47, 80	20:46–47	341
9:34	5, 57	14:15–23	15	21:23	158
9:38	149	14:25	302	22:8–12	305
9:42	283	15:1–2	156, 325	22:11	149
9:43	163, 194	15:1–32	4	22:14	332
9:44–45	196	15:2	319	22:20	117
9:54	223	15:5–10, 22–32	4	22:28	261
9:58	150, 258	15:7	334	22:32, 40–46	5
10:1–9	294	15:7, 10, 20–27	88	22:42	261
10:18	280	15:10	161	22:44	2, 253
10:21	5	15:11–32	16, 168	22:51	315
10:21–22	194	16:8	196	22:53	122
10:25	319	16:15	21, 337, 341	22:66	158
10:32	245	16:16	157	23:5	267
10:34	149	16:24–26	221	23:5, 14	158
10:38–40	332	17:3–4	4	23:7–12	202, 232
11:1	5	17:12	314	23:13–24	50
11:4	4	17:14	293	23:46	2, 236
11:13	5	17:15	164, 324	23:47	164
11:14	194	17:25	15	23:49, 55	13
11:14, 38	163	18:8	50	24:12, 41	163
11:15, 53	325	18:11	329	24:21	96
11:19–20	193	18:11–12	337	24:25	133
11:27	71	18:11–13	143	24:25, 26, 44	15
11:27–28	197	18:12	339	24:25-27	43
11:28	62	18:13	271, 307, 322	24:25–27, 44–47	175
11:31	100	18:13–14	4, 156, 329	24:27	282
11:37	332	18:14	16, 322, 334	24:30	332
11:38–39	319	18:19	46	24:41	194
11:39–52	341	18:22, 28, 43	309	24:44	10, 233
11:45, 46, 52	319	18:24	155	24:44–53	17
11:53	319	18:25	271	24:45–48	14
12:10	4	18:31	133	24:47	4, 182, 321
12:10, 12	5	18:31–34	15	24:50–51	238
12:32	157	18:32–33	133	24:52	4
12:51	183	18:34	196	24:52–53	164
13:1	202	18:43	91, 164, 324		

John					
1:1	54	2:25	305, 323	6:64	305
1:3	304	3:2	319	7:3, 5, 10	149
1:5	184	3:8	286	7:16	303
1:6	38	3:13	194	7:20	280, 283
1:6–8	222	3:15	328	7:27	274
1:7	234	3:16	159, 168	7:30	276
1:9	21, 122	3:16, 18	196	7:37	163
1:9–13	183	3:19	122, 184,	7:46	225, 274, 302
1:10	150		208, 272	7:48	155
1:11	50, 258	3:19–20	272	7:49	318
1:12	241	3:22–36	228	8:2	304
1:14	54, 58, 140,	3:23, 26	205	8:3	319
	190, 254	3:26	234	8:12	122, 204, 272
1:14, 17	28, 303	3:28–30	338	8:16, 18, 26,	297
1:14, 18	196	3:29	69, 340	29, 42	
1:15	38, 70	3:36	10, 40, 166, 183	8:18–19, 28–29,	194
1:17	336	4:22	107, 158	38, 49	
1:19–20	222	4:23–24	76	8:20	276
1:19–27	34	4:24	78	8:24	10, 51, 160,
1:21	39	4:25–26	71		183, 315
1:27	223	4:26	233	8:31–32	303
1:28	205	4:34	194, 257, 297	8:32	336
1:29	13, 87, 120,	4:42	154	8:33	221, 274
	154, 192, 215	4:44	275	8:34	96, 271
1:29, 36	338	4:53	40	8:37–40	209
1:31	236	5:7	27	8:39	221
1:32–33	238	5:8-9	293	8:41	56
1:32–34	57	5:17	195	8:44	196, 255
1:34	195	5:18	195, 323	8:45–46	303
1:35	303	5:24	302	8:46	58, 167, 253
1:35–42	292	5:24, 30, 36, 37	297	8:48, 49, 52	283
1:37	338	5:30	194	8:58–59	323
1:38, 49	319	5:33	234	8:59	276
1:41–42	303	5:35	175	9:1–3	25, 314
1:44	282, 292	5:36	233	9:2	320
1:45	269	5:39	10, 175, 233	9:5	122, 272
1:46	80	5:40	163	9:32	294
1:47–48	305	6:1	302	10:6	196
1:49	58, 195, 305	6:14–15	118	10:11, 14	155
2:1–11	45, 183	6:25	319	10:21	283
2:4	80, 184	6:37	120	10:30	49
2:11	36	6:37, 44	163	10:33	323
2:12	149	6:38	194	10:36	195
2:13–16	204	6:38, 39, 44, 57	297	10:39	276
2:14	203	6:38, 42	194	10:40	205
2:14–16	320	6:39–40	194	11:14–44	293
2:20	201	6:40, 47	328	11:27	195
		6:44	120	11:41–42	238

11:47	275, 293, 320
11:49–50	203
11:51–52	203
12:16	196
12:28	238
12:31	259, 280
12:36	196
12:37	275, 325
12:40	272
12:41	49
12:43	341
12:44, 45, 49	297
12:46	122, 272
12:49–50	303
13:27	261
14:6	120, 183, 303, 322, 336, 342
14:15, 21, 23	166
14:17	179, 336
14:27	123
14:30	280
15:6	223
15:10, 14	166
15:16	38
15:26	234, 336
16:8	208
16:11	280
16:13	336
16:13–14	234
16:15	71
16:21	169
16:30	305
17	238
17:8, 18, 21, 23, 25	297
17:12	195
17:15	255
17:17	77, 87
17:17, 19	336
18:37	336
18:38	202
19:7	195, 323
19:12–16	50
19:25	184
19:25–27	80, 164
19:35	234
20:28	71
20:29	63
20:30–31	14
20:31	195, 265, 290
21:1	302
21:1–3	331
21:1–6	305
21:2–3	303
21:3	304
21:17	305
21:24–25	14

Acts

1	131
1:1	1, 3, 16
1:1–2	131
1:3	131
1:6	132, 181
1:7	132
1:8	234
1:14	80, 149
1:18	120
1:19	2
1:21–22	14, 248
1:61	100
2:2	160
2:4	254
2:5	177
2:7	163
2:22–24	15
2:32–36	175
2:38	272, 321
2:42	14
2:43	325
2:47	77
3	133
3:2	294
3:2–8	294
3:12	163
3:13–15	133
3:18	133
3:19–21	133
3:20–22	175
3:22	42
3:25	174
3:25–27	133
3:26	208
4:6	203
4:8–12	70
4:12	10, 51, 120, 154, 181, 183,

	214, 229, 315, 322, 336, 342
4:13	163
4:19	35
4:31	70
4:33	234
4:36	245
5:16	283, 294
5:31	153, 208, 214, 321
5:31–32	234
5:32	76, 166
5:34–40	318
5:37	145
5:42	157
6:7	166
6:8	294
6:13	323
7:2	105
7:3	106
7:31	163
7:48	49
7:55	238
7:58–60	226
8:2	177
8:4, 12, 25, 35, 40	157
8:6–7	294
8:7	283
8:13, 18–23	214
9:2, 20	267
9:3	160
9:4	157
9:20	195
9:33–34	294
9:34	294
10:22	176
10:28	143, 181
10:34–48	15
10:36	157, 161
10:37–38	248
10:38	265, 269
10:42–43	120
10:43	86, 321
11:3	143, 181
11:18	208, 218
11:20	157
11:24	254
12:1–2	225, 230

12:12–16	28	20:5–21:18	3	3:25	10
13:1	176	20:9–12	294	3:26	10, 322
13:2–3	341	20:21	234	3:28	63, 114, 319
13:3	185	20:24	328	4:3, 9, 21–22	21
13:14–15	267	21:9	185	4:5	315, 328
13:22–23	35, 174	21:27–28	323	4:6	328
13:23	153	21:38	166	4:11–12	105, 110
13:27–28	50	22:12	177	4:19	54
13:32	157	23:6-8	319	4:25	10
13:38	321	23:8	166, 319	5:1	123, 161
13:41	163	23:9	319	5:6	168
14:7, 15, 21	157	23:26	16	5:10	161
14:8	294	24:3	16	5:12	58
14:23	185, 341	24:27	13	5:19	58
14:24–27	15	26:9	269	6:6, 16–20	271
15	134	26:18	272, 321	6:14	88
15:10	206, 273, 319	26:20	218	7:8–11	115
15:12	294	26:23	181	7:12	24, 121, 341
15:12–19	15	26:25	16	7:23, 25	115
15:13–18	134	27:1–28:16	3	8:1–2	120
15:14	176	28:8	294	8:5–9	76
15:35	158	28:9	294	8:9	180
16:7	239			8:15	157
16:10	158	**Romans**		8:24	10
16:10–17	3	1:1	335	8:25	64
16:16–18	283, 287,	1:3	45, 106, 174	8:29	196
	296	1:4	58, 195	8:32	168
16:25	164	1:5	166	8:33–34	25
16:31	328	1:9	76	8:37	285
17:2	193	1:16	158, 328	9:3	177
17:6	144	1:17	176	9:4	106
17:7	143	1:18–23	74	9:4–5	96
17:17	267	2:4	154	9:5	106
17:18	158	2:5, 8	215	9:6	126
17:24	61	2:6	218	9:6–7	221
17:26	259	2:8	336	9:6–8	134
17:30–31	322	2:28–29	177, 206, 221	9:7	109, 196
18:4, 19	267	3:1–3	100	9:9	174
18:8	267	3:1–4	134	9:13, 15	134
18:26	16	3:2	106	9:16, 18	135
19:1–5	16	3:3	174	9:27	70, 154
19:1–7	338	3:10, 23	159	9:31–32	328
19:8	267	3:10–12	179	9:32–33	183
19:10	14	3:10–18	114	10:2–3	21
19:13–14	284	3:17	123	10:9	160, 315,
19:15	283	3:20	21, 114, 319		322, 328
19:17	325	3:23	10, 114, 179	10:13–17	297
19:27	144	3:24	40, 46, 47, 96	10:14	162

11:1	245	9:5	292	**Galatians**	
11:1–2	111	10:13	174	1:8–9	54
11:1–32	211	10:20	259	1:14	218
11:5	154	10:20–21	280, 283	1:15–16	35, 38
11:6	328, 342	11:25	117	2:16	63, 114, 319
11:8	272	12:3	159	2:20	63, 195, 287
11:11	111	12:13	180	3:6	21
11:17	111	15:3	328	3:6–7	105, 110
11:23	111	15:6	13	3:7, 29	221
11:25	111	15:17, 19	54	3:9	109, 110
11:25–26	119	15:22	58	3:11	114, 176, 319
11:25–27	107	15:24–28	50	3:11, 24	319
11:26	110, 111, 120	15:47	229	3:13	154
11:26–27	135	15:57	285	3:16	174, 249
11:26*a*	135			3:22	58
11:29	111, 135	**2 Corinthians**		3:24	115, 334
12:2	296	1:3	309	3:28	181
13:1	259	1:18	174	4:3	96
13:7	220	1:19	195	4:4	158, 167, 174
13:8–10	220	1:20	28, 79, 87, 174	4:6	239
13:12	122	2:14	285	4:6–7	157
13:13	37	4:3–4	325	4:13–15	295
14:6	10	4:4	255, 259, 272,	4:28	109
14:17	123		280, 296, 342	5:4	114, 319, 342
15:9–12	44	4:6	272	5:14	220
15:12	50, 98	4:18	64	5:22	93, 123
15:16	335	5:7	64	6:16	126
15:18	166	5:11	325		
16:20	288	5:17	119, 218, 331	**Ephesians**	
16:26	71, 166	5:18–19	161	1:4	36
		5:19–20	40	1:6	88
1 Corinthians		5:21	58, 154, 167,	1:7	46, 88, 272, 321
1:4	47		168, 197, 237	1:13	336
1:9	174	6:2	315	1:21	49
1:22	291, 325	6:12	120	1:22	229
1:24	44	6:14	122	2:1	179, 208
1:26	155	6:15–16	284–285	2:1–2	271, 280
1:26–29	205, 271	7:1, 11	325	2:1–3	325
1:26–31	329	7:9–11	208	2:2	196, 255
1:30	25	7:15	120	2:4	121
2:8	71, 152	10:3–5	281	2:6–8	183
2:12–13	15	11:2	56	2:7	88
3:5–9	14	11:3	217	2:8	47
3:11	183, 336	11:7	335	2:8–9	179, 328
4:8	333	11:13–15	280	2:9	161
6:11	25	11:14–15	284	2:10	219
7:22	80	12:12	295	2:12	142
7:23	96	13:1	165	2:14	181

2:16	161	
4:10	229	
4:13	195	
4:18	122	
4:21	336	
4:23	296	
4:32	321	
5:2	154	
5:6	215	
5:8	272	
5:8,11	122	
5:18	37,254	
5:19	93	
5:21	325	
6:6	80	
6:12	122	

Philippians

1:8	120
1:17	232
1:19	239
1:20	79
2:1	120
2:6–7	150,239,249
2:7	152,160,197,239,320
2:8	197
2:9–11	229
2:12	325
2:25–27	295
3:3	164
3:4–8	218
3:4–11	319
3:5	245
3:9	198,206,237
3:10	164
3:20	153
4:7	123
4:19	257

Colossians

1:4,13	284
1:13	50,122,272,281,285,288
1:13–16	296
1:14	272,321
1:15,18	196
1:16	196,304

1:16–17	57
1:18	196
1:20–22	161
2:9	49,229,240,249
2:13–14	321,334
2:14	272
3:1	236
3:6	215
3:12	120
3:13	321
3:16	93
4:10,11	11
4:10–14	2
4:12–17	11
4:14	1,4,10,11,12

1 Thessalonians

1:4	36
1:9	208
2:2,8,9	335
2:14–16	50
3:5	255
5:3	160
5:18	79
5:24	174

2 Thessalonians

1:7	223
1:8	166
1:9	216
2:3	195
2:10	336
2:13	336
3:3	174

1 Timothy

1:1	153
1:9–10	334
1:11	328
1:13	121
1:14	334
1:15	48,334
1:16	121
2:2	75
2:3	35,153
2:3–4	168
2:4	336

2:5	47,159,322,336
2:5–6	120,183
2:14,15	169
3:15	336
4:1	56,280,283
4:1–3	283
4:10	153,154,168
5:19	165
5:23	295
6:5	337

2 Timothy

1:8–9	168
1:9	46,88,328
1:10	153
2:9	227
2:18	337
2:25	208,218
3:5	214
3:7	337
3:8	337
3:16	15
4:3	232
4:4	337
4:11	1,10
4:20	295

Titus

1:2	28
1:3	153,168
1:4	153
1:14	337
1:16	214
2:10	153,168
2:13	153
2:14	83,96
3:4	153
3:4–5	168
3:5	40,121
3:6	153
3:7	46

Philemon

7,12,20	120
24	1,4,10,13

Hebrews

1:1–2	159
1:2	304

1:3	49, 91, 175, 236	13:20	117, 155	4:19	174
1:5	175			5:4	155
1:6	196	**James**		5:5	79
2:14–15	96, 271, 281	1:13	253	5:8	50, 255
3:1	159	1:25	62	5:10	88
4:13	304	2:5	271		
4:14	195	2:8	220	**2 Peter**	
4:15	167, 190, 197,	2:10	271	1:2, 11	153
	249, 253	2:13	333	1:19	122
4:16	88	2:19	280	1:20–21	15
5:5–6	175	2:26	166	1:21	70
5:8	190	3:13–16	283	2:4–5	280
5:9	79, 166	3:15	280	2:20	153
6:2	209	4:6	47, 79, 80,	3:7–12	91
6:6	195		88, 277, 334	3:9	214
6:13–14	134	4:7	261	3:18	153
6:16–17	134	5:7–8, 10	259		
7:3	195	5:11	120	**1 John**	
7:14	170	5:14–16	295	1:1–3	14
7:22	114	5:17	275	1:5	122
7:25	159	5:19–20	39	1:6–7	20
7:26	58, 71, 253			1:9	174, 321
8:1	236	**1 Peter**		2:1	236
8:6	114, 117	1:1–2	166	2:1–2	154
8:7–13	114	1:2	37	2:2	10
9:1–5	26	1:3	96, 121	2:12	321
9:12	47	1:4	331	2:12–14	164
9:14	239	1:6, 8	79	2:13	285
9:15	117	1:8	63, 158	3:2	196
9:22	272	1:11	239	3:5	58, 167, 253
9:28	154	1:18–19	96, 198	3:8	252
10:10–12	175	1:19	58	3:17	120
10:18	272	2:5	74	4:2	54
10:22	77	2:7–8	183	4:4	285
10:23	28, 87, 174	2:8	40	4:9	196
10:24–25	74	2:9	31	4:10	168
10:27	223	2:10	121	4:14	153, 154, 157,
10:28	165	2:17	157		168, 266
10:29	195	2:22	167, 253	4:15	195
11:1	64	2:24	150, 154,	5:3	273
11:5	35		175, 328	5:5, 10, 12, 13, 20	195
11:9	174	2:25	155	5:6–8	235
11:17	196	3:6	159	5:9*b*–11	235
11:19	109	3:15	31	5:10	229
12:2	236	3:18	154, 197, 328	5:11–12	183
12:23	176	3:18–20	286	5:19	280
12:24	117	3:22	229	5:20	58
13:15	76, 164	4:17	335		

2 John		5:5	42	17:14	159
7	54	5:9	82,94	18:2	280
		5:11	160	19:7	340
Jude		5:11–12	160	19:10	10,27,174,233
3	82	5:11–14	162	19:10–20:6	39
6	280,286	6:15–17	309	19:11	238
6–7	219	6:16–17	215	19:11–21	101
7	223	7:4–8	107	19:15	50
9	29	7:11–12	160	19:15–16	175
25	153,168	9:20	259,280	19:16	159
		11	39	20:1–3	50,286
Revelation		11:15	50,250	20:2	217,255
1:1	80	12:3–4	280	20:4–6	211
1:1–2,9	234	12:3–17	255	20:7–9	286
1:5	48,83,196,	12:4	255	20:10	216,286
	321,328	12:5	50	21:2,9	340
1:10	180	12:7	29	21:10	180
1:13–16	156	12:7–9	280	21:10–11,23	157
1:17	157,287,308	12:9	217,255	21:33	156
1:19	309	12:10	255	22:8–9	27
2:13	226	12:13–17	107	22:16	50,122
2:18	194	13:8	36	22:17	340
3:17	271	14:10–11	216,223		
4:2	180	16:14	280		
4:11	91	17:3	180		

Index of Subjects

Aaron,24,30,74,170
Abihu,30,74
Abijah (priest),23–24
Abraham,54,59,127,196,221–22,249
Abrahamic covenant,95,105–11,
    119–20,127–28,131
Abyss,286
Actium (Battle of),144
Adam,42,246,249,253,255
Aeneas,294
Agrippa I,22,225,231
Agrippa II,22
Ahab,231,275
Altars,135
Amillennialism,50,126,127,131–34
Ancestry,244
    See also Genealogies
Andrew,225,282,303–4

Angels,27–30,56,156,160–63
Angels of light,284,285
Anna,184–86
Anna,111
Annas,201,203–4
Antiochus Epiphanes,107,318
Antipas (Herod the Tetrarch),22,34,
    202,204,228,230–32,282,330
Antipas (pastor at Smyrna),226
Antony,22,143,144
Apostasy,116,119,126,130
Arabs,69,108
Archelaus,22,202
Aretas,230
Aristarchus,11
Ark of the covenant,75
Artaxerxes,146
Asher,185,245

Augustus Caesar (Octavian), 142–44, 145, 146, 201

Baal, 275
Babylon, 107
Bainton, Roland H., 141
Baptism, 205, 209, 210, 222, 228–29, 236–38
Bar Kochba revolt, 319
Bar Mitzvah, 192
Barak, 94
Barnabas, 195, 245, 294
Bartholomew (Nathanael), 226, 265, 305
Believers, 180, 284, 285
Benedictus. *See* Zacharias's Song of Salvation (Benedictus)
Benjamin (tribe), 245
Bethesda, 293
Bethlehem, 142, 146–48, 156, 158, 162, 171
Bible, 252
Birthdays, 140
Births, 53–54
Blaiklock, E. M., 44
Blasphemy, 323
Blessing, 71, 72, 107
Blindness, 272
Boaz, 246
Bock, Darrell L., 1, 144, 145, 203, 240
Brown, Louise, 54
Brutus, 143
Buddhism, 328
Bultmann, Rudolf, 300

Caesar Augustus. *See* Augustus Caesar (Octavian)
Caesaria, 23
Caesarion, 144
Caiaphas, 201, 203–4
Caligula, 230, 231
Calvin, John, 25, 177
Calvinism, 125–26
Cana, 266
Capernaum, 269, 275, 282, 291, 317, 330–331
Caravans, 192, 193
Cardiac, Jean Louis, 188

Cassius, 143
Catholic Church. *See* Roman Catholicism
Censuses, 144–46, 244
Centurion's servant, 293
Ceremonial uncleanness, 169, 171
Charnock, Stephen, 76
Child prodigies, 188–89
Christian life, 164
Christmas, 41–42, 140–41
Church
    Calvinism and, 125–26
    mission of, 328
    as new Israel, 110, 132, 135
    replacement theology and, 135–36
    second coming and, 137
Circumcision, 89, 167, 169
Clement of Alexandria, 2, 144–45
Cleopatra, 143, 144
Consolation/comfort, 177–79
Constantinople, 226
Council of Constance, 227
Covenants, 95–101, 103–11
Cyrus, 146

Daniel, 43
Darkness. *See* Spiritual darkness
David (King), 20, 45, 49, 58, 75, 98, 147, 155, 247, 250
Davidic covenant, 95, 97–101, 119–20, 128, 131
Day of Atonement, 26, 339
Day of the Lord, 216
Dead Sea, 204
Deborah, 94
Demon possession, 283–85
Demons, 252, 280–88, 295–96
Devil, 255, 257
    See also Satan
Dickason, C. Fred, 284
Dies Natalis Solis Invicti, 140
Dio Chrysostom, 12
Dionne sisters, 53
Diprose, Ronald, 135–36
Disease, 292–95, 312
Dispensationalism, 131, 135
Division of Abijah, 14
Dorcas, 294

Drunkenness, 36, 37

Edersheim, Alfred, 203, 269–70, 314
Edomites, 22
Edwards, Jonathan, 135
Egypt, 146, 154, 189
Election, 127, 128, 132, 136
Eli (Jesus's grandfather), 246, 247, 248
Elijah, 38–39, 86, 87, 275
Elisha, 276
Elizabeth, 4, 24, 27, 30–31, 37, 58–59,
    66–72, 90, 94, 204
Elwell, Walter A., 55
Emmaus, 43
Engagement, 44–45, 148
Epaphroditus, 295
Esau, 69
Eschatology, 126, 131, 136–37
Essenes, 166, 318
Eudoxia, 226
Eutychus, 294
Eve, 42, 255
Evil, 184, 255, 256
    See also Sin
Exclusivism, 337–38
Exorcism, 284

Faith, 63–64, 109, 110
Faith healers, 292, 294
Farnell, F. David, 301
Fasting, 185, 338–41
Fathers (of Israel), 105
Fear, 27, 157, 308, 309, 324–25
Feast of Tabernacles, 191
Feasts, 191
Fire metaphor, 223
First Triumvirate, 143
Firstborn, 168, 170, 196
Fishermen, 331
Fishing, 303–9
Forgiveness, 114, 206–9, 321–24, 322
Frame, John M., 54

Gabriel, 21–22, 28–29, 35, 39, 43–44, 51,
    59, 68, 77
Gaebelein, Frank E., 201
Galen, 12
Galilee, 147, 265–67, 268, 282, 302, 320

Garden of Eden, 253
Gehazi, 313–14
Genealogies, 45, 158, 244–50
Gennesaret, 302
Gentiles
    Jews and, 142, 209, 276–77
    Luke as, 1–2, 11, 15–16
    Mark's gospel addressing, 290
    salvation and, 134, 180–82
Gideon, 64–65
Gift giving, 140
Glory, 49, 156–57, 160–61
Gnosticism, 237
God
    confirms His promises, 64–72
    faithfulness and, 174
    glory of, 156–57
    grace of, 46–47, 55, 88–90
    power of, 91–92
    provision of, 257, 258
    sovereignty of, 59–60
    will of, 257, 260–61
Good news, 29, 157–64
Gospel, the, 328
Grace, 46, 47, 55, 88–90, 190
Greatness, 33, 35, 40, 48–49
Grudem, Wayne, 253
Gundry, Stanley N., 3, 247, 296

Hagar, 108
Hannah, 25, 54, 60, 77, 94, 185
Hansen, G.H.A., 313
Hansen's disease (leprosy), 313
Harris, R. Laird, 55
Hasidim, 318
Healing of paralytic, 320–25
Healings, 291–95, 320–25
Heinecken, Christian Friedrich, 188
Hell, 10, 215–16, 223, 334
Hendriksen, William, 90, 268
Herod Agrippa I, 22
Herod Agrippa II, 22
Herod Antipas, 22, 34, 201, 202, 204, 228,
    230–32, 282, 330
Herod Archelaus, 202
Herod I (the Great), 22–23, 142, 145,
    146, 201–2, 230, 318
Herod Philip, 22, 202

Herodian rulers, 22
Herodians, 23
Herodias, 230–32
Herodotus, 11
Hezekiah, 65, 185
High priests, 26, 203
Historical events, most significant 103, 104
"Historical Jesus," 300
Hoehner, Harold, 145
Holidays, 41–42
Holocaust, 107
Holy Spirit
    anointing of Jesus and, 238–40
    being filled with, 37, 69, 70, 254
    Jesus and, 57, 229
    as witness to Jesus, 234–35
    in worship, 76
Horace, 144
Huldah, 185
Humility, 79, 80, 81
Huss, Jan, 226–27
Hypocrisy, 319

Idolatry, 74, 75, 143, 205
Ignatius, 55, 226
Incense, 26, 29
Inclusivism, 337
Inspiration/inerrancy, 14–15
Irenaeus, 2
Isaac, 54, 59, 109, 196
Isaiah, 42, 43, 185, 210–11, 270
Ishmael, 108
Ishtar (Ashtoreth), 61
Israel
    believing remnant in, 175
    covenants and, 96, 106–8, 120
    law and, 115
    leprosy and, 313
    modern, 119
    prophecy and, 69, 96
    replacement theology and, 126
    during Roman Empire, 97, 171, 200
    true believers and, 129, 134
    See also Jewish people

Jacob, 42, 69
Jacob (Jesus's grandfather), 247

James (brother of John), 195, 303, 304, 308–9
James (son of Alphaeus), 226
Jeconiah, 247, 248
Jehovah Witnesses, 328
Jeremiah, 37–38
Jerusalem
    passover in, 266
    Roman destruction of, 107, 219, 244
    temple and, 219, 244, 267
Jesse, 98
Jesus Christ
    authority of, 229, 281, 282, 287, 296
    demons and, 280–88
    genealogies of, 45, 244–50
    historical impact of, 104
    kingdom of, 49–50
    as Lord, 159–60
    naming of, 48, 166–68
    powers of, 291–97
    preaching of, 281–85, 297, 304
    as Savior, 152–54, 159–60, 168
    as Son of God, 189, 194–96
    as Son of Man, 290
    temptation of, 252–61
    testimony to, 233–35, 240–41
    virgin birth of, 54–56, 58
Jesus Justus, 11
Jewish feasts, 191
Jewish people
    Abraham and, 221–22
    circumcision of, 89
    Gentiles and, 209
    kingdom theology and, 136
    salvation and, 96, 106–7
    See also Israel
Jews of the Diaspora, 267
Jezebel, 231, 275, 276
John (apostle), 70, 195, 225, 294, 303
John Chrysostom, 226
John the Baptist
    disciples of, 338–39
    as forerunner, 21–22, 25, 38, 66, 71, 92, 117
    Herod Antipas and, 202, 231–32
    message of, 205–10
    naming of, 89–91
    personal character of, 35–38

preaching of, 39–40, 86–87, 214, 228–30, 232
Jordan River, 204–5, 265, 276, 302
Joseph, 45, 49, 142, 146–48, 162–63, 166, 171, 183, 189, 192, 246–48
Josephus, 11, 201, 231, 265, 318
Joshua, 116, 246
Joy, 158
Judah, 42, 58, 66, 67, 119
Judaism, 319, 341
Judas Iscariot, 195, 261
Judea, 265, 266, 297, 320
Judean desert, 253, 254
Judgment, 216–17
Julius Caesar, 143
Justin Martyr, 2, 110–11

Kee, Howard C., 11–12
Kim Ung-Yong, 188–89
Kingdom
    Christ's earthly, 100–101
    of God, 290, 297, 302
    of heaven, 290
    of Jesus Christ, 49–50
    messianic, 100–101, 136
    millennial, 99, 110–11, 129, 137, 211

Latimer, Hugh, 227
Law, 206, 319
    See also Mosaic law
Legalistic religion, 200, 205–6, 217–18, 341–42
Lenski, R.C.H., 248–49
Leo XIII, 46
Lepers, 277, 278, 293, 314–16
Lepidus, 143
Leprosy, 312–14
Levi, 245
Levi (Matthew), 226, 282, 329–32
Levites, 170–71
Lewis, C.S., 279–80
Liberalism (theological), 300–301
Light, 122–23, 156, 272
Linnemann, Eta, 3
Livy, 144
Lollards, 227
Lucian, 12
Luke, 1–2, 10–11, 145

Luke (gospel of)
    authorship of, 2–3
    date of writing, 3, 4,
    eyewitness testimony in, 14
    inspiration/inerrancy of, 14–15
    as logical/systematic, 15, 16
    outline of, 5–8
    purpose/themes of, 4–5
    salvation/redemption emphasis in, 13, 15–16
Luther, Martin, 141, 288
Lysanias, 202–3

MacArthur, John, 55, 91, 99–100
Magnificat, 73–83, 77, 79, 94
Malachi, 20–21, 200
Malta (island of), 294
Malthace, 230
Manger scene, 141
Mangers, 149
Manoah's wife, 54
Marcion, 2
Mariamne, 22
Mariolatry, 46–47
Mark Antony, 22, 143–44
Mark (apostle), 11
Mark (gospel of), 3
Marriage, 44–45, 148
Marshall, Howard, 142, 147, 161
Marshall, I. Howard, 300
Martyrs, 225–27
Mary (mother of Jesus), 246
    Elizabeth and, 37, 67–72, 87
    escape to Egypt and, 189
    genealogy and, 45, 98
    Jesus in the temple and, 191–96
    Jesus' conception and, 37, 43, 56–62
    Magnificat and, 4, 73–83, 94
    in Roman Catholicism, 46–47, 60–63, 71–72, 149, 167, 171
    sacrifice for sin of, 171
    shepherds and, 162–63
    suffering of, 182–84, 197
Mary Tudor ("Bloody Mary"), 227
Masada, 23
Matthew (Levi), 226, 282, 329–32
Meals, 332
Mediterranean Sea, 269

Mercy,105,120–21,308–9,333
Mesopotamia,105
Messenger (forerunner of Messiah),21
Messiah,214,222–23
Micah,147
Michael,29
Midianites,64,65
Mill,John Stuart,188
Millennial kingdom,50,99,110–11,
        128,129,137,211
Miracles
    birth of John the Baptist as,21,30
    of healing,291–95,320–25
    Jesus's divine power and,291–97
    reality of,275,291–93,296–97
    See also specific miracles by name
Miraculous conception,68
Miriam,185
Mishnah,319
Mistletoe,140–41
Mithraism,140
Modalism,235
Mormonism,328
Morris,Henry M.,252
Morris,Leon,147–48,156,203,246
Mosaic covenant,95,113–14,118,119,
        121
Mosaic law,166,167,231,313,318
Moses,30,42,64–65,68,74,89,94,
        115–16,155
Mount Gerizim,202
Mount Hermon,302
Mount of Transfiguration,49,156–57
Mozart,Wolfgang Amadeus,188
Muhammed Ali,33
Muslim religion,328
Mycobacterium leprae, 313

Naaman,276
Nadab,30,74,147
Naming (of children),89–91,166–68
Nathan (prophet),98
Nathan (David's son),246,247
Nathanael (Bartholomew),226,265,
        305
Nazareth,44,142,146,189,200,264,269,
        276
Nazirites,37

Nebuchadnezzar,82
Nero,3
New Covenant,95,97,117–23,129–30
New Testament,1,280,284
Nicholas (Saint),141
Noadiah,185
Noahic covenant,95,113
Northern kingdom,119

Obedience,60,62,115,116,128,135,
        166
Octavia,143
Octavian (Caesar Augustus),22,
        142–44,146,201
Old Testament,174–75
    amillenialism and,127
    on demons,280
    Mary (Jesus's mother) and,73,77
    nation of Israel and,146–47
Omnipotence,305–6
Omniscience,304–5
Origen,2,140
Ott,Ludwig,46
Outline,5–8
Ovid,144
Owen,John,114

Paralytic.*See* Healing of paralytic
Parthian invasion,22
Passover,191–93,237,266
Paul,1,13,37,226,294,295
Peace,123,160–61
Pentecost,70,179–80,191
Pentecost (feast of),191
Persecution,225–27
Peter
    amillennialism and,133
    fishing on Sea of Galilee,304–6
    healing miracle of,294
    Jesus's purpose for,303–9
    martyrdom of,225
    mother-in-law of healed,291
Pharisees,166,318–19,332–34,339
Philip (Antipas's half-brother),230,231
Philip (apostle),225–26,265,294
Philip (daughters of),185
Philip (Herodian ruler),22,202
Phinehas,113

Physicians,12–13
Pilate,201–2,204
Pinnock,Clark,337
Pius IX,45
Pius X,46,47
Plutarch,12
Polybius,11
Polycarp,226
Pompey,22
Pontius Pilate,201–2,204
Poor,the,270–71,274
Pope,227
Postmillennialism,50
Postmodernism,335–36
Praise,93–95,164
Prayer,185,237–38,317
Preaching
    of Jesus,281–85,297,304
    of John the Baptist,39–40,86–87,
        214,228–29,230,232
Predictions.*See* Prophecy
Pride,79,80
Priestly covenant,95,113
Priests,23–24,26
Promises,174
Prophecy
    about John the Baptist,210–11
    of coming Messiah,42–43
    confirmation of,66–72
    filling of the Spirit and,69
    of future Davidic kingdom,99,100
    Old Testament and,174–75
    of Zacharias,96
Prophetesses,185
Prophets,25,31,39,40
Prosperity gospel,260
Publius's father,294
Purification,169

"Queen of heaven,"61,62
Quirinius,145
Qumran,204–5

Rachel,25
Raising the dead,293,294
Ramsay,William,144,145
Rebekah,69

Redemption,51,96,97
    See also salvation
Redemption price,170–71
Reformed theology,125,126
Reformers,227
Regeneration,266
Religion
    absolute truth and,335–37
    of Jewish people,200
    ritualistic/legalistic,205–6,217–18,
        341–42
    variations of,327–28
Repentance
    believers' preaching of,40
    ethnic heritage and,221–22
    good works and,218–19
    Pharisees/Sadducees and,117–18
    salvation and,208–10
    self-righteousness and,333–334
    true/genuine,214–15,222–23
Replacement theology,126,132,135
Ridley,Nicolas,227
Righteousness,47,166,167,176–77,
        206,237
Ritual,135–36,217–18,341–42
Robertson,A.T.,145
Roman Catholicism
    immaculate conception and,171
    Mary and,46–47,60–62,71–72,167
    reformers and,227
    replacement theology in,135–36
    salvation and,328
Roman Empire,142–46,200
Rome,4,22,226
Rosenkowitz sextuplets,53

Sabbath,155,268–69
Sabellianism,235
Sacrifices,104,107–8,171
Sadducees,166,318–19
Safford,Truman Henry,188
Salome,231–32
Salvation
    doctrine of,16
    for Gentiles,180–82
    as God's redemptive plan,13,153
    light of,122

New covenant and, 120, 129–30
repentance and, 208–10
spiritual, 154
Samaria, 265
Samaritan woman, 266
Samaritans, 202
Samson, 54
Samuel, 75
Sanctification, 177
Sanhedrin, 318
Santa Claus, 141
Sarah, 54, 59, 106, 108–9
Satan
demonic forces and, 280–81
millennium and, 50, 286
origin/destiny of, 280
as serpent, 217
temptation of Jesus, 252–61
worship and, 74
Saul, 75
Savior, 152–54, 158–59, 168, 229
Scarborough, John, 12
Sceva, 284
Schaeffer, Francis, 337
Schurer, Emile, 131
Schweitzer, Albert, 300
Scientific discoveries, 103–4
Scribes, 319–20
Scrolls, 268, 270
Sea of Chinnereth, 302
Sea of Galilee, 269, 302, 316
Sea of Tiberias, 302
Second coming, 136, 157
See also Millennial kingdom
Second Triumvirate, 143
Self-righteousness, 217–18, 276, 328,
334, 337
Sepphoris, 269
Sermon on the Mount, 206, 217, 339
Sextus Julius Africanus, 140
Shealtiel, 249
Shepherds, 155–58, 160–63
Sickness, 295
See also Disease
Sidis, William James, 188
Signs, 64–66
Simeon
Anna and, 186

character of, 176–77
Holy Spirit and, 179–80
prediction of, 182–84
proclamation of, 158, 180–82
testimony of, 175
theology of, 111, 177–79
Simon Peter. *See* Peter
Simon the Zealot, 226
Simon's mother-in-law, 291
Sin
Jesus as Savior and, 159
law of, 115
New covenant and, 120
recognition of, 307, 308
repentance from, 215
self-righteousness and, 333–34
sinlessness of Jesus and, 58, 253
spiritual bondage and, 271–72
temptation and, 252–53
Singing, 93–94, 141
Sinterklaas, 141
Skepticism, 336
Smyrna, 226
Soldiers, 220–21
Solomon, 20, 98, 100, 247
Son of God, 189, 194–96, 290, 302
Son of Man, 290
Southern kingdom, 119
Spiritual darkness, 20–21, 122, 272
Stein, Robert H., 2
Stephen, 226, 294
Stories, 9
Strobel, Lee, 44, 301
Supersessionism, 126, 132
Synagogues, 267–69, 273, 277, 314
Syria, 145

Talmud, 319
Tatian, 2
Tax collectors, 220–21, 282, 307, 329–33
Taxation, 143, 144, 237, 244, 330
Teachers (Jewish), 193, 267
Temperance, 35, 37
Temple, 180, 203–4, 244, 259–60, 267
Temple, William, 300
Ten Commandments, 74, 115
Tertullian, 2

Thaddeus (Judas the Son of James), 226
Theocracy, 171
Theophilus, 1, 164
Thomas, 226
Thomas, Robert L., 3, 247, 296, 301
Thucydides, 11
Tiberias, 230
Tiberius, 144, 201, 202
Tiglath-pileser, 146
Timothy, 37, 295
Titus, 3
Tozer, A. W., 121
Transcendence, 265–66
Transfiguration, 49, 57, 308
Tribulation, 107, 280, 286
Trinity, 234–35
Trophimus, 295
Truth
    absolute, 335–37
    of God's promises, 87–88
    Jesus as source of, 301–3
    worship and, 76–77
Turkey, 226

Unbelievers, 280, 294, 295
"Unclean spirits," 283
Uncleanness, 169, 171
United Pentecostal Church, 235
Ur of the Chaldeans, 106, 107
Uzzah, 75
Uzziah, 313–14

Valerius Gratus, 203
Vengeance, 274
Virgil, 144
Virgin birth, 54–58
Virgins, 44, 45, 48

Water into wine miracle, 36–37

Weddings, 266, 340
Wesley, Charles, 272
Widows, 275, 276, 277
Wilderness, 204–5, 207, 253, 254
Wine, 36–37, 266
Wisdom, 190
Wise men, 171
Witnesses, 165, 166
Women, 169, 192
Wonder-workers, 12
Works-righteousness, 328, 342
    See also Self-righteousness
Worship
    attitude of, 78–81
    components of, 76–77
    Holy Spirit and, 76
    idolatry and, 74, 75
    motive of, 81–83
    objects of, 81, 164, 259, 307
Wycliffe, John, 226–27

Young, Edward J., 55–56

Zacharias
    divine punishment of, 28–29, 86
    naming of John the Baptist, 90
    prophecy of, 39–40
    response of to angel, 27–29
    righteousness of, 23–25, 31
    temple service of, 26
Zacharias's Song of Salvation (Benedictus)
    Abrahamic covenant and, 105–11
    Davidic covenant and, 97–101
    New covenant and, 117–23, 131
    See also Covenants
Zealots, 166, 318–19
Zechariah (prophet), 27
Zerubbabel, 249
Zipporah, 89

MOODY
Publishers™

From the Word to Life

Lift your study to new heights with the *complete* MacArthur New Testament Commentary series.

Respected Bible scholar and author John MacArthur opens up the wonder of the New Testament, offering verse-by-verse analysis, theological insights, and points of application. These works are sure to enrich your study of the Bible, and indeed your faith.

The MacArthur New Testament Commentary series includes:

Matthew 1–7
Matthew 8–15
Matthew 16–23
Matthew 24–28
Mark 1–8
Mark 9–16
Luke 1–5
Luke 6–10
Luke 11–17
Luke 18–24
John 1–11
John 12–21
Acts 1–12
Acts 13–28
Romans 1–8
Romans 9–16
First Corinthians
Second Corinthians
Galatians
Ephesians
Philippians
Colossians & Philemon
First & Second Thessalonians
First Timothy
Second Timothy
Titus
Hebrews
James
First Peter
Second Peter & Jude
First–Third John
Revelation 1–11
Revelation 12–22

www.MoodyPublishers.com | 1-800-678-6928